THE POWER OF THE INTERNATIONAL COURT TO DETERMINE ITS OWN JURISDICTION

AF859903

THE POWER OF THE INTERNATIONAL COURT TO DETERMINE ITS OWN JURISDICTION

COMPÉTENCE DE LA COMPÉTENCE

by

IBRAHIM F. I. SHIHATA
S.J.D. (Harvard)

WITH A PREFACE BY
LOUIS B. SOHN

Springer-Science+Business Media, B.V.

ISBN 978-94-017-5644-0 ISBN 978-94-017-5908-3 (eBook)
DOI 10.1007/978-94-017-5908-3

Copyright 1965 by Springer Science+Business Media Dordrecht
Originally published by Martinus Nijhoff, The Hague, Netherlans in 1965.
Softcover reprint of the hardcover 1st edition 1965

All rights reserved, including the right to translate or to reproduce this book or parts thereof in any form

To the memory of my brother
Ahmad Husni
1941–1964

PREFACE

In the interdependent world of today brought together by science and rent asunder by ideological and economic differences, it has become necessary to study deeply and to solve constructively the twin problems of disarmament and peacekeeping. Peacekeeping in turn is divided into two main areas: The maintenance of international peace through an international force, and the settlement of international conflicts which endanger peace. These conflicts usually involve legal questions; even when they are predominantly political, the clarification of related legal questions may facilitate the settlement of the whole controversy.

When a legal question is submitted to an international court for decision, it happens rather frequently that the defendant State claims that the court has no jurisdiction. Consequently, international courts have had to determine in a large number of cases whether they have jurisdiction over the questions submitted to them.

Mr. Shihata approaches this complicated subject in a positive manner. He emphasises the inherent importance of the power of an international court to determine its own jurisdiction. He condemns severely all the attempts to curtail that power, and defends strongly the various methods used by international tribunals to overcome such attempts. Mr. Shihata analyses carefully not only all the relevant decisions of the tribunals themselves, but also all the principal arguments presented by the parties to the proceedings.

This exhaustive work should for a long time serve as an example to be followed by young scholars investigating similar topics. Both in thoroughness of his research and in depth of his analysis, Mr. Shihata has set a new standard for doctoral dissertations. His book is at the same time a practical one; it should prove useful to international lawyers faced with a jurisdictional question before an international tribunal.

Louis B. Sohn

Bemis Professor of International Law
Harvard Law School

TABLE OF CONTENTS

TABLE OF CASES

I. ARBITRAL CASES

II. CASES BEFORE THE PERMANENT COURT OF INTERNATIONAL JUSTICE

III. CASES BEFORE THE INTERNATIONAL COURT OF JUSTICE

ABBREVIATIONS

A.B.A.J.	American Bar Association Journal
Am. J. Int'l L.	American Journal of International Law
Annuaire	Annuaire de l'Institut de Droit International
Brit. Yb. Int'l L.	British Yearbook of International Law
Cmd.	British Command Papers
For. Rel.	Foreign Relations of the United States
Geo. L.J.	Georgetown Law Journal
Harv. L. Rev.	Harvard Law Review
I.C.J. Rep.	International Court of Justice: Reports of Judgments, Advisory Opinions and Orders
I.C.J.Y.B.	International Court of Justice Yearbook
I.L.C. Yearbook	Yearbook of the International Law Commission
I.L.Q.	International Law Quarterly
Ill. L. Rev.	Illinois Law Review
Int'l & Comp. L.Q.	International and Comparative Law Quarterly
Int'l Org.	International Organization
The International Court	Both the Permanent Court of International Justice (Permanent Court) *and* the International Court of Justice (present Court).
L.N.T.S.	League of Nations Treaty Series
Lapradelle et Politis, Recueil	Lapradelle et Politis, Recueil des Arbitrages Internationaux, vols. I, II, 1905, 1924
Malloy, Treaties	Malloy, Treaties, Conventions, International Acts, Protocols and Agreements between the United States of America and Other Powers 1776–1909. 2 vols. 1910
Martens, N.R.G.	Martens, Nouveau Recueil Général de Traités
Martens, N.R.T.	Martens, Nouveau Recueil de Traités. 20 vols. (1817–1842) (1ère sér. 1843–1875; 2me sér. 1876–1908; 3me sér. 1909–1943)

Minn. L. Rev.	Minnesota Law Review
Moore, Arbitrations	Moore, History and Digest of International Arbitrations to which the United States Has Been a Party. 6 vols. 1898
Moore, Digest	Moore, Digest of International Law. 8 vols. 1906
P.C.I.J.	Permanent Court of International Justice
P.C.I.J. Ann. Rep.	Permanent Court of International Justice Annual Report
Proc. Am. Soc. Int'l L.	Proceedings of the American Society of International Law
Recueil des Cours	Recueil des Cours de l'Academie de Droit International de La Haye
Rec. des déc. des trib. arb. mixtes	Recueil des décisions des tribunaux arbitraux mixtes
Rev. Egyptienne	Revue Egyptienne de Droit International
Rev. Gén. Dr. Int'l Pub.	Revue Générale de Droit International Public
Rev. Hellénique	Revue Hellénique de Droit International
Rev. Dr. Int'l (Genève)	Revue de Droit International (Genève)
Rev. Dr. Int'l (Paris)	Revue de Droit International (Paris)
Rev. Dr. Int'l & Lég. Comp.	Revue de Droit International et de Législation Comparée
Rosenne, The Time Factor	Rosenne, The Time Factor in the Jurisdiction of the International Court of Justice 1960
Stat. Int'l Ct. Just.	Statute of the International Court of Justice
Stat. P. Ct. Int'l Just.	Statute of the Permanent Court of International Justice
Systematic Survey	[United Nations Secretariat] Systematic Survey of Treaties for the Pacific Settlement of International Disputes 1928–1948 (U.N. Pub. Sales No. 1949, v. 3)
Transact. Grot. Soc'y	Transactions of the Grotius Society
U.N. Conf. Int'l Org.	United Nations Conference on International Organizations. San Francisco 1945. Documents
U.N. Gen. Ass. Off. Rec.	United Nations General Assembly Official Records
U.N. Rep. Int'l Arb. Awards	[United Nations] Reports of International Arbitral Awards. 12 vols. 1948–1963
U.N.T.S.	United Nations Treaty Series

ACKNOWLEDGMENTS

This work was first completed as a doctoral dissertation submitted to Harvard Law School in May, 1964. At that stage it was the product of two years of research in the treasure-like Harvard Law Library with the advice and encouragement of Professor Louis B. Sohn, Bemis Professor of International Law at Harvard. The first draft of the manuscript was read by Miss Maureen Ahern who, although she is not a lawyer, took the pain of trying to understand it all and helped in putting it in a more readable form. The second draft was read in full by Professor Sohn who gave me many a valuable suggestion. The work was then read by Professors Milton Katz, R. R. Baxter and Roger Fisher of Harvard Law School, by Mr. Georges Abi Saab of the Geneva *Institut des Hautes Etudes Internationales*, and by Dr. El Kosheri of Ain Shams University in Cairo. I had the privilege of discussing it with all those scholars and was fortunate enough to review it after that in the surroundings of the Peace Palace at the Hague where the International Court is seated. Consequently a few changes were introduced to the original manuscript, though the work remains as a whole what it was in May, 1964.

On the suggestion of Professor Sohn, Nijhoff Publishers were kind enough to undertake the publication of this book. And it was through the efforts of Mr. Priem, Director of their Publishing Department, and his able assistant, Miss Knopper, and through the skill of their printers that the manuscript was made a book in a matter of three months.

I am only grateful to all those individuals who have spaced their time and effort to make his work worth reading. It is to them that any value it may have must be imparted.

IBRAHIM F. I. SHIHATA

Cairo, December, 1964.

"Jurisdictio est potestas de publico introducta, cum necessitate juris dicendi."

INTRODUCTION

One need not profess adherence to that school of legal thought which conceives of law as "the prophecies of what the courts will do in fact," in order to recognize the prominance of the part played by courts in the development of law. Montesquieu's assertion that judges are nothing but "*la bouche qui prononce les paroles de la loi*" [1] has long been abandoned. Instead, it is now realized that judicial organs have possibly preceded legislative organs in different domestic legal systems.[2] This, at any rate, is obviously so in relation to international law. In this system the centralization of the "law-applying" function has partly been accomplished, whereas centralized universal "law-making" and "law-enforcing" organs are yet lacking. "Natural legal evolution – wrote Kelsen – tends first toward an international judiciary, and not toward international government or legislation." [3]

This international judiciary, developing from individual arbitrators to fully developed judicial institutions, is still far from completing its evolution. Resort to international tribunals, is to this moment, an exceptional and, at any rate, an optional means of solving disputes. It results, it is true, in providing the parties to a dispute with a "decisional procedure" that greatly depoliticizes their conflict.[4] It also extends to the parties the equal protection of law which is otherwise difficult to attain. Yet, it is a limited procedure. In principle, the parties exclusively decide whether or not to resort to the international judge. When they do, the power of the latter to hear the dispute, his legal aptitude to render a decision, will all be circumscribed by their

[1] Montesquieu, *L'Esprit des Lois*, Liv. XI, ch. VI at 181 (Edit. de Leyde 1749).

[2] See Kelsen, "Compulsory Adjudication of International Disputes," 37 *Am. J. Int'l L.* 397, 400 (1943); Politis, *La Justice Internationale*, 252–53 (1924). Compare, Lauterpacht, *The Function of Law in the International Community*, 423–25 (1933).

[3] Kelsen, *supra*, note 2 at 400.

[4] See L. Gross, "Some Observations on the International Court of Justice," 56 *Am. J. Int'l L.* 33, 41 (1962); Delbez, *Les Principes Généraux du Contentieux International*, 15 (1962).

agreement. *Qui peut le plus, peut le moins*. This feature of international adjudication, i.e., its consensual basis that results in the limited jurisdiction of its organs,[1] presents the important problem which invites this study.

Why is it that jurisdictional problems occupy the greatest place in the work of the international judiciary, particularly in the work of the International Court? [2]

A study of the development of legal systems in general instructs us that the ascendency of the law of actions is as great in the infancy of all courts of justice.[3] As Sir Henry Maine once noticed "substantive law has at first the look of being generally secreted in the interstices of procedure." [4] This, it will be shown, could be concluded from a simple reading of the literature relating to the International Court, despite the little concern this Court has given to the concept of "form."

International jurisdiction is also a limited one. As such it is necessarily problematic. A tribunal, or for that matter any organ, of limited capacities, encounters far more jurisdictional problems than one endowed with general powers to hear and decide. In fact, the problems of jurisdiction and admissibility grow in importance proportionately with the amount of curbs and limitations involved in the judicial function.

On the other hand, international tribunals deal primarily with states. "Only States may be parties in cases before the [International] Court." [5] In this domain, the ease with which individuals accepted

[1] The consensual basis of jurisdiction is not altogether alien to domestic courts. It is generally the rule in cases brought against Governments before such courts that jurisdiction could in principle be exercised only after the Government involved has waived its judicial immunity either on *ad hoc* basis or by a general enactment. Even in private suits, the consent of the parties has been the test of jurisdiction in exceptional cases. This latter phenomenon was known in Roman law under the name of *jurisdictio in consentientes*. Known now as "prorogated jurisdiction," it still has modern applications. See e.g., I Erskine, *An Institute of the Law of Scotland*, 42 (new ed. Macallan 1838); Tunc, *Cours de Procédure Civile*, 235–8 (1961).

[2] It is pendantic to affirm the importance of jurisdictional issues in the jurisprudence of the International Court. More has been written in the work of the present Court on jurisdiction than on the merits. Out of the 28 judgments rendered by this Court 15 judgments related exclusively to jurisdiction and admissibility. [See Appendix I]. In fact only 9 out of these 28 judgments did not deal with issues related to the Court's jurisdiction [Appendix II-B]. As to the Permanent Court, 8 judgments out of a total of 31 related only to jurisdiction (besides the first interlocutory judgment accepting Poland's intervention in the *S.S. Wimbledon* (1923)) [Appendix I]. Jurisdictional questions were discussed in 15 other judgments, leaving only 7 judgments where no jurisdictional issue was mentioned [Appendix II-A]. The importance of the question of jurisdiction is not less apparent in the advisory function of the Court as will later be shown.

[3] See Maine, *On Early Law and Custom*, 389 (1890).

[4] *Ibid.*

[5] *Stat. Int'l Ct. Just.*, art. 34, para. 1.

domestic adjudication as a principle of social order is missing. International tribunals had to practice meticulous care in exercising their jurisdiction. They trace their powers, at pains,[1] from the will of states that are generally reluctant to accept judicial intervention. Thus "[t]he question whether and to what extent the Court has jurisdiction is frequently of no less, if not of more, political importance than the decision on the merits." [2] Jurisdictional issues presented before international tribunals are far from being mere technicalities. They have their ramifications which influence not only the future of the case but also that of the tribunal itself.

In practice, the importance of the jurisdictional limits has had a two-fold manifestation: one legal, the other political. Legally, objections to jurisdiction are raised whenever there is a possibility, however faint, to escape the judicial action. In almost every case where a defendant state was brought before the International Court by unilateral application, it pleaded against the Court's jurisdiction. Politically, the lack of a preestablished jurisdiction generally discourages the parties to submit their disputes to a judicial settlement. On the other hand, objections to jurisdiction have resulted in depriving tribunals from continuing the adjudication,[3] and, at times, in blocking the execution of a decision already delivered.[4] In all such aspects,

[1] *Cf.*, Lauterpacht, *The Development of International Law by the International Court*, 201 (1958). And see Ch. de Visscher, *Theory and Reality in Public International Law*, 345 (Trans. by Corbett, 1957).

[2] Rosenne, *The International Court of Justice*, 338 (1957).

[3] Arbitrators were withdrawn from abrital tribunals after unfavorable decisions affirming the tribunals' jurisdiction. A noted example of this is the recall of the Rumanian arbitrator from the Hungarian-Roumanian Mixed Arbitral Tribunal after its decision in the *Hungarian Optants case* (*Kulin* v. *Etat Roumain, 7 Rec. des déc. des trib. arb. mixtes*, 138 (1927)). See Deák, *The Hungarian-Rumanian Land Dispute*, 74 (1928). Withdrawal of national arbitrators resulted also in suspending or ending the arbitral procedure before the first French-Mexican claims commission, see its Decision No. 23, in 5 *U.N. Rep. Int'l Arb. Awards*, 559 (1929), and in the German-United States Mixed Claims Commission in the case of *Lehigh Valley Railroad Company* where a decision was eventually given in the absence of the German Commissioners. See 8 *id.* at 225 (1939).

Before international *courts*, where their institutionalized nature makes such a withdrawal unlikely, some Governments responded to unfavorable decisions on jurisdiction by absenting themselves from further proceedings. See the telegram of the Albanian Government dated 15.11.1949 in 2 *Corfu Channel Case*, Pleadings, Oral Arguments, and Documents 288 (*I.C.J.*, 1949), and the last judgment in this case in [1949] *I.C.J. Rep.*, 244, 248.

[4] For a list of arbitral awards refused execution on the basis of an alleged excessive excercise of jurisdiction (*excès de pouvoir*) on the part of the tribunal, see Carlston, *The Process of International Arbitration*, 88-155 (1946); Hambro, *L'Exécution des Sentences Internationales*, 11–29 (1936).

It will be shown that the same basis was invoked in the only instances where a decision or an order of the Court were not complied with.

jurisdictional considerations proved to be *"le point faible"* of international justice.[1]

If the jurisdiction of international courts has this great significance, being in fact thought of as the counterpart of the states' freedom of action (their sovereignty),[2] it will then be of the utmost importance to designate the authority that will have to decide whether or not such a jurisdiction exists. The Statute of the International Court has, from the outset, entrusted this power, in the event of a dispute, to the Court itself.[3] This did not, however, put the question beyond controversy. The scope of this power has been challenged.[4] Its exercise in the different cases manifested conflicts that have been "more conspicuous and more interesting to observe" than in any other sphere of the Court's activity.[5] Different judges have had different attitudes in defining the very nature of the Court's jurisdiction. The Court itself has been waivering between varying and conflicting principles of acknowledged validity that led it in some cases to contradict what seemed to be an established precedent. At times, it felt so entangled with considerations of law and propriety that it tended to avoid the problem rather than to solve it. A good many writers have thus become content to advise that the judicial choice the Court has to undertake on the matter of its jurisdiction does not lend itself to easy prediction, and is decided on the merits of each case. The principle, nevertheless, remains that the power to decide the limits of the Court's jurisdiction is the Court's own business. As this jurisdiction finds its sole foundation in the consent of the parties, the power to decide jurisdiction relates mainly to the finding of the Court on whether this assent was given. It is then a research in the will of the parties (their intention) as revealed in the relevant facts and instruments. Such a research, dealing with so difficult a matter as the real intention of Governments, can be conducted in ways that differ from one extreme to another. It does not help much to say that its nature will be determined in each case independently and according to the absolute

[1] Bos, *Les Conditions du Procès en Droit International Public* [19 *Bibliotheca Visseriana*], 103 (1957). And see Hudson, *International Tribunals*, 130–1 (1944).

[2] See Lauterpacht, *The Development of International Law by the Permanent Court of International Justice*, 105 (1934): "Once a State has accepted the jurisdiction of the Court in a given case or generally, the metaphysical majesty of sovereignty has largely departed from it . . . ." But *cf.*, 2 Oppenheim, *International Law*, 64–65 (7th ed. Lauterpacht 1952).

[3] *Stat. P. Ct. Int'l Just.*, art. 36, para. 4; *Stat. Int'l Ct. Just.*, art. 36, para. 6.

[4] See the Letter From the Minister of Foreign Affairs of Guatemala dated September 9, 1952 addressed to the President of the Court, in, 1 *Nottebohm Case*, Pleadings, Oral Arguments and Documents 162, 166 (*I.C.J.* 1955).

[5] Lauterpacht, *supra*, p. 3, note 1 at 95–96.

discretion of the Court. This has led in other jurisdictions to the growth of a "procedural jungle." [1] The behavior of the Court, in conducting this research, should be examined with the purpose of discovering the standards, or the tendencies, that govern the exercise of its jurisdiction. The degree of the inevitable flexibility of such standards should also be measured. It should not be forgotten, on doing this, that it is the Court's attitude that is of the first importance here. If the consent of the parties lays foundation to the Court's jurisdiction, it is in fact this consent *as found and determined by the Court* that really matters. As a result, the finding of the Court as to its jurisdiction, that is the consensus of its simple majority on what the intention of the parties was, provides the core of this study. How, and why, does the Court find in one case that it has jurisdiction, in another that it does not? What are the techniques it uses to reach such a decision one way or the other? What are the criteria which can allow us to predict, with the greatest possible precision, what the Court's decision on its proper jurisdiction might be?

In an attempt to answer such questions, municipal analogies will be of little value. True, the draftsmen of the first Statute tried to benefit cautiously from the domestic judicial experience,[2] but the international legal and judicial processes have their independent evolution. Transplanting to them the fine distinctions that have developed through centuries of legal experience in domestic systems may prove to be valueless, if not misleading. "Even the words posses different meaning" in each field.[3] Accordingly, this study will follow the tradition of the International Court of having little or no regard to "the various codes of procedure and the various legal terminologies in use in different countries." [4] Reference will, however, be made

[1] See a reference to the dangers involved in letting English courts determine the limits of their jurisdiction before the Great Law Reform, in Fitzmaurice, "The Law and Procedure of the International Court of Justice, 1951–1954: Questions of Jurisdiction, Competence and Procedure," 34 *Brit. Yb. Int'l L.* 1, 26 n. 5 (1958).

[2] See the Report of Leon Bourgeois on the Draft of the Advisory Committee of Jurists for the Establishment of a Permanent Court of International Justice, presented to the Council of the League of Nations on August 3, 1920. Société des Nations, *Cour Permanente de Justice Internationale* 23 (1920).

[3] Rosenne, *supra*, p. 3, note 2 at 249. And see a detailed distinction between internal and international adjudication in Balasko, *Causes de Nullité de la Sentence Arbitrale en Droit International Public*, 1–5 (1938). See also *infra*, Chapter II at 68 for the application of the concept of *excès de pouvoir* to international decisions, and Chapter III at 107 for the distinction between jurisdiction and admissibility.

[4] *Case Concerning Certain German Interests in Polish Upper Silesia*, *P.C.I.J.*, ser. A, No. 6 at 19 (1925).

to some domestic jurisdictional conceptions whenever the analogy should be deemed useful.[1]

The wealth of experience gained through the history of international arbitration is, on the other hand, of great relevance to this study. Differences in nature and effect between the arbitral and judical procedures are well appreciated. Nevertheless, the former provides the latter with the most pertinent source of rule-making. The present Court has unequivocally recognized this relationship on the very point of the Court's power to determine its jurisdiction.[2] For this reason the study proposed here, though primarily concerned with the International Court (both the Permanent Court and the present one), will cover the relevant jurisdictional problems which confronted arbitral tribunals. The rich source material of international arbitration is apt to provide at least guidance in understanding the attitude of the Court itself.

But the subject-matter of this study is, first and foremost, the power of the *International Court* to define the limits of its own jurisdiction, its *compétence de la compétence* (*Kompetenz-Kompetenz*). The exercise of such a power has brought into existence and developed the "law of jurisdiction" of this Court. Such law enables the Court to "do justice" between the litigating states.[3] Its rules are, more than any rule of substantive law, mainly of the Court's own making; for judicial legislation has indeed found its widest scope in the domain of pleas relating to the Court's jurisdiction, despite, and in part because of, all the limitations surrounding this jurisdiction.[4] A sound study of

[1] In the *Mavrommatis Palestine Concessions Case* (1924), M. Politis (Counsel of the Greek Government) suggested that the very invocation of objections to the jurisdiction of the Permanent Court was "l'imitation d'une habitude courante dans les moeurs judiciaires des pays anglo-saxons ..." *P.C.I.J.*, ser. C, No. 5-I at 43 (1924). This remark was refuted in the dissenting opinion of Judge Moore who found that the Court's ascertaining of its jurisdiction was an "elementary conception common to all systems." *P.C.I.J.*, ser. A, No. 2 at 57–8 (1924).

It should be particularly noticed in this respect that in the domestic field objections to jurisdiction present themselves mainly as questions of forum (which of two or more possible forums is the correct one), whereas in the international field the question is usually whether the parties have agreed that any tribunal at all has jurisdiction. See Fitzmaurice, *supra*, p. 5, note 1 at 11; Rosenne, *supra*, p. 3, note 2 at 249. And see *The Anglo-Iranian Oil Co. Case* (Interim Measures), [1951] *I.C.J. Rep.*, 89, 96 (Joint Diss. Op. of Judges Winiarski and Badawi).

[2] See *Nottebohm Case*, [1953] *I.C.J.*, 111, 119. And see details in Chapter I, *infra*.

[3] See this term as used in the *Nottebohm Case*, *id.* at 121 and in the case concerning the *Effect of Awards of Compensation made by the United Nations Administrative Tribunal*, [1954] *I.C.J. Rep.*, 47, 58–9 (Adv. Op.).

[4] See Lauterpacht, *supra*, p. 3, note 1 at 201, 202, 205. Even the framers of the present Statute "confidently anticipated that the jurisdiction of this tribunal [the International Court of Justice] will be extended as time goes on ..." Report of Mr. Al-Farsy, the Rapporteur of Committee IV/1 to Commission IV of the San Francisco Conference, Doc. 913, IV/1/74(1), 13 *U.N. Conf. Int'l Org. Docs.* 381, 393 (1945).

the topic should, therefore, concentrate on the work of the Court itself. Pleadings and arguments made before the Court, its orders, judgments, and opinions provide the first source material.

This study could not be complete without covering the power of the Court as exercised in advisory as well as in contentious cases. Although the term "jurisdiction" was generally avoided in dealing with the former cases,[1] they raise jurisdictional questions that are of no less importance than those involved in the contentious procedure. In fact, issues of politics and propriety assume a greater role in the advisory function of the Court. Judicial caution and judicial techniques have sometimes been, in this context, more interesting to examine and more telling of the Court's outlook towards its jurisdiction in general. This is particularly true as the Court insisted from the beginning that it must exercise its advisory function judicially and to apply to it, as far as practicable, the rules of the contentious procedure. Furthermore, the preliminary objection procedure has become applicable, at least since 1936, both to contentious and advisory cases.[2] Article 36(6) of the Statute of the present Court was itself specifically invoked in an advisory case.[3] This was perhaps "the nearest approach [in practice] to a formal invocation of the preliminary objection procedure," [4] and leaves no doubt as to the pertinence to this study of defining the scope that the Court has envisaged for its advisory function.

Finally, no doubt should be left as to the proper limits of this work. It does not deal with the substantive law of the International Court. It does not deal, except when relevant, with the details of the substantive jurisdiction of the Court. It deals with a phase of the judicial action which comes even prior to that preliminary phase (substantive jurisdiction); that is, the power, or the jurisdiction, to decide whether that substantive jurisdiction exists. This power is obviously incidental and pre-preliminary. It comes next only to the seisin of the Court and

[1] Instead, the Court has preferred to use in this context terms such as "competence" and "power." See examples of this practice and an explanation of its wisdom in Rosenne, "The Advisory Competence of the International Court of Justice," 30 *Revue de Droit International* (The Int'l L. Rev.) 10, 12–3 (Geneva, 1952).

[2] See an extract from the minutes of the discussions that took place between the members of the Permanent Court on the occasion of the last revision of its Rules of procedure, in *P.C.I.J.*, ser. D, No. 2 (4th Add.) at 248–9 (1936).

[3] See Letter of the Czechoslovak Government dated 16 January 1950 addressed to the Registrar of the Court, *Interpretation of Peace Treaties with Bulgaria, Hungary and Rumania*, Pleadings, Oral Arguments, and Documents 204 (*I.C.J.* 1950).

[4] Rosenne, *supra*, note 1 at 32.

is exercised, necessarily, even in the absence of any substantive jurisdiction.

The first "Part" of this study is a descriptive analysis of the principle that endows the Court with the power to determine its own jurisdiction. It traces, in the first Chapter, the evolution of such a power, and examines, in the second Chapter, its nature and principal characteristics. It is a study of the power in itself.

The second "Part" is concerned with the subject matter of this power, or its merits,[1] i.e., the Court's substantive jurisdiction. It introduces in Chapter Three the concepts developed in this study concerning the sources of the Court's jurisdiction with particular emphasis on the procedural aspects and the proper use of terms which are generally in confusion. Then it deals, in Chapter Four, with the operation of the power as applied to the different patterns of the Court's jurisdiction.

The third and last "Part" of the study analyzes the attitude of the Court in exercising the power at issue. It first deals in Chapter Five with the techniques that have been used, or are likely to be used, in defining the Court's jurisdiction. This being done, Chapter Six treats the question in its climax – the problem of the challenge to the Court's power to determine its jurisdiction. This Chapter will cover the possible attitudes which the self-judging Court may adopt when it confronts anew a party that claims for itself on jurisdictional issues the same right of deciding whether or not the Court's jurisdiction extends over the dispute.

The whole work is, therefore, a search for judicial standards through an investigation of the practice of the international judicial institutions and of the states that submit, or fear to submit, their disputes to them.

[1] "Were one jurisdictional issue leads to another, and the first jurisdictional issue is whether the tribunal has jurisdiction to determine the second, then the second issue might, in relation to the first, be said to constitute the 'merits' of the case. Fitzmaurice, *supra*, p. 5, note 1, at 23.

PART ONE

THE POWER IN ITSELF – A DESCRIPTIVE ANALYSIS

CHAPTER I

THE EMERGENCE AND DEVELOPMENT OF THE POWER OF INTERNATIONAL COURTS TO DETERMINE THEIR JURISDICTION

Presenting the first "Draft Convention on Arbitral Procedure" to the General Assembly of the United Nations in 1952, the International Law Commission stated that Article 11 of that draft "lays down a general principle [and] calls for no comment." [1] This Article provided that: "The Tribunal, as the judge [Fr. *maître*] of its own competence, possesses the widest powers to interpret the *compromis*." Following developments proved, however, this short remark of the Commission to be mistaken. Commentators in the Sixth Committee of the General Assembly contended that this Article, in its French wording, included a "serious innovation," [2] and claimed that it diverged from the actual practice.[3] Later on, when the Commission replaced its Draft Convention by a Model Draft, it substituted Article 9 for the objectionable Article 11 after a modification that removed from its French version the phrase "*maître de sa compétence*" (making it only "*juge de sa compétence*"), and excluded the word "widest" as a description of the tribunal's powers to interpret the *compromis*.[4]

This modern example illustrates the still controversial limits of

[1] See Report of the International Law Commission Covering the Work of its Fourth Session, *U.N. Gen. Ass. Off. Rec.*, 7th Sess., Supp. No. 9 at 7 (Doc. No. A/2163) (1952).

[2] See the presentation of Amado [Brazil] in *U.N. Gen. Ass. Off. Rec.*, 8th Sess. at 120 (Doc. No. A/C6.383) (1953) (French text).

[3] See *e.g.*, presentations of Adamiyat [Iran], *id.* (Doc. No. A/C6.384) at 123; Loutfi [Egypt], *id.* (Doc. No. A/C6.385) at 129; Povetyer [Byelorussia], *id.* at 130; Morozov [U.S.S.R.], *id.* (Doc. No. A/C6.388) at 145–6.

[4] See Report of the International Law Commission Covering the Work of its Tenth Session, *U.N. Gen. Ass. Off. Rec.*, 13th Sess., Supp. No. 9 at 7 (Doc. No. A/3859); (A/CN.4/117) (1958). And see the discussions in the Commission which preceded these amendments in *I.L.C. Yearbook*, 43–46 (1958–I): Amado argued that the Article was being drafted "in a grandiloquent form." *Id.* at 43. Liang objected to the words "widest powers." *Id.* at 43–44. Yokota suggested that it was doubtful that an arbitral tribunal was always the judge of its own competence. *Id.* at 45. And Tunkin asserted that an arbitral tribunal "could only interpret the instruments by virtue of which it had been set up," and that provisions like that in the first draft "would seem to place the arbitral tribunal above the States which had set it up." *Ibid.*

the rule at issue. It comes at the end of a long history through which the evolution of the power of international tribunals to determine their jurisdiction culminated in a general recognition of this power as a right, and a duty, of every international tribunal. Such a power has not become, however, an arbitrary or absolute judicial privilege.[1] To trace the details of its development will help also to define its nature and to allow a proper description of its characteristics.

A. THE ARBITRAL EXPERIENCE

1. Before the Alabama – The Earlier Precedents

Despite the fact the *Alabama Arbitration* (1872) is often cited as the starting point of the rule that gives arbitral tribunals the power to determine their jurisdiction, earlier, and in fact more significant, precedents are on the record. First among these, in the modern period of arbitration,[3] are perhaps the controversies that arose before the two commissions established under Articles VI and VII of the treaty between the United States and Great Britain signed on 19 November 1794 (the Jay Treaty).[4] In the commission established under Article VI, a disagreement between the commissioners on jurisdictional issues led to the withdrawal of the American commissioners.[5] This was a clear denial, on their part, of the right of the commission to determine by a majority vote its own jurisdiction. The reverse took place before the commission established under Article VII. The British commissioners were in the minority and, believing that the commission had no jurisdiction to deal with a specific issue in the *Betsey case* (1797), they asserted the right to withdraw.[6] Fortunately, this did not bring the issue to a halt. The two American commissioners filed separate opinions

[1] In a recent discussion in the "Institut de Droit International" the present Court was said to have "le droit absolu ... de déterminer sa propre compétence." See Fernandes de Visscher's proposal in his comment on Jenks' Report, 48 *Annuaire* 59, 156 (1959, II). On adopting the wording of this proposal in its final resolution the "Institut" dropped the word "*absolu*". *Id.* at 359–60.

[2] The term "precedent" as used above simply refers to the judicial practice of international tribunals as a depository of legal experience – a source and an evidence of the applicable rules.

[3] For international arbitration in earlier periods, see generally, 5 Moore, *Arbitrations*, 4821–51 (1898).

[4] Treaty of Amity, Commerce and Navigation, signed on 19 Nov. 1794, (entry into force 29 Feb. 1796), 1 Malloy, *Treaties*, 590, 594–7; 2 Miller, *Treaties and Other International Acts of the United States of America*, 245, 249–53.

[5] 3 Moore, *Arbitrations*, 2277.

[6] 1 *id.* at 324. The issue involved was whether the commission could review the validity of the decrees of the English High Court of Appeals in Prize cases.

defending the right of the majority of the board to determine the board's own jurisdiction.[1] These two opinions present the earliest known judicial defense of this power on the scene of international adjudication. They found such a power to be "self-evident" and "absolutely necessary" to decide on the justice (merits) of the claim.[2] Its exercise was deemed "incident" to the powers conferred upon the commission, and the lack of it, it was said, would make the treaty a "disgraceful mockery," "perfectly lifeless and intrinsically a nullity." [3] The major arguments behind this thesis were the following:

(a) The parties did not entertain the idea of a future reference to themselves to determine the cases which should be submitted to the board. If such reference were contemplated, it was hardly possible to conceive that the parties should have neglected to mention it.[4]

(b) If the board could not decide itself on its jurisdiction and was not asked to refer the question to the parties, it should either take for granted that the case was within its jurisdiction, or refer it to some other tribunal to determine this issue. "The former could not be that diligent and careful examination directed, and might work great injustice; for the latter there is no permission, much less authority, in the treaty, neither is there any tribunal or person authorized to make this determination." [5]

(c) The power to decide whether the claim was a case described in the arbitration treaty was implied in, if not explicitly understood from, the very power to decide on the justice of the claim. Any denial of this would involve a contradiction "too glaring to be persisted in." [6]

(d) The Commission did previously dismiss several claims upon the sole ground of want of jurisdiction after the King's Agents questioned its competency. Such a dismissal, taken by the agreement of the commissioners, was a proper use of an established right for the board to determine its jurisdiction.[7]

(e) Had such an established power been subject to exceptions, it would be proper for those who hold so "to show where those exceptions are to be found or whence they infer them." [8]

[1] See Opinion of Commissioner Gore in 3 *id.* at 2278–91, and Opinion of Commissioner Pinkney in *id.* at 2291–303. The two opinions are exposed conjointly in the text above.

[2] See *id.* at 2282, 2293, 2298.

[3] *Id.* at 2298, 2303.

[4] *Id.* at 2279.

[5] *Id.* at 2282.

[6] *Id.* at 2289.

[7] *Id.* at 2298, 2303.

[8] *Id.* at 2299.

(f) The analogy with municipal experience shows that courts of justice "must decide jurisdiction whensoever the point occurs." [1]

(g) Finally, if there was a danger in allowing the commission this power, the answer is obvious: "it is that of the Law of Nations, of the Common Law of England and of common sense – a party is not bound by the decision of arbitrators in a case not within the submission – such decision would be a dead letter – it would be no decision." [2]

Notwithstanding these arguments, the question was referred to the respective Governments and according to the diplomatic negotiations which consequently took place, the opinion of Lord Chancellor Loughborough was sought. He was then reported to have said "that the doubt respecting the authority of the Commissioners to settle their own jurisdiction was absurd; and that they *must necessarily* decide upon cases being within or without their competency." [3] As a result, the British Government declined to sustain its commissioners and left it to the board to determine its jurisdiction in respect of that case.

The significance of the *Betsey* case lies, then, in the fact that it brought the parties to accept explicitly, for the first time, the principle that disputes over the limits of the commission's jurisdiction would be solved by the commission itself. It was not the commission, however, that enunciated the principle. Rather, it came as a result of the insistence of the American commissioners, the opinion given by the British Lord Chancellor after diplomatic intervention, and the acquiescence of the British Government. The role of the parties in admitting the principle was clear. They did not, however, commit themselves to its applicability in each future case. When four years later a jurisdictional problem arose in the *Sally* case (1798)[4] before the same commission, the British commissioners proposed a reference for an arrangement by the parties.[5] The American Commissioners objected again and filed two separate opinions to the effect that the board had the power to determine the issue by a majority vote.[6] This time, however, the question was disposed of by an arrangement that was reached diplomatically and not judicially. The *Sally* case thus proved

[1] *Id.* at 2297.

[2] *Id.* at 2290.

[3] 1 *id.* at 327 (Emphasis added).

[4] See *id.* at 333–6; 3 *id.* at 2304. The issue involved was whether the commission could take cognizance of a case still pending in the British admiralty courts on the basis that the claimant could not obtain adequate compensation in the ordinary course of judicial proceedings.

[5] 3 *id.* at 2305.

[6] See Gore's opinion in *id.* at 2305–6, and Pinkney's at 2306–12.

that the principle reached in the *Betsey* case was not to apply automatically and was far from being settled.

Further developments before the *Alabama Arbitration* added to the controversial nature of the emerging principle. The United States and Mexican Claims Commission created by the Convention of April 11, 1839,[1] provided several occasions in which the principle was affirmed. Yet, the affirmation came, not from the commission itself, but from one of the parties to the convention.[2] On more than one occasion, Mr. Webster, the United States Secretary of State at the time, affirmed that the commission was "essentially a judicial tribunal with independent attributes and powers in regard to its peculiar functions." "Its rights and duties – he wrote to the Mexican commissioners – ... like those of other judicial bodies, are to determine upon the nature and extent of its own jurisdiction ..." [3] This position, consistently maintained, should however be viewed with caution. The commission was dealing with *individual* claims in each of which the State Department could have little interest and would normally prefer to leave them completely to the commission to deal with.

Almost at the same time, an arbitral tribunal created in 1839 to arbitrate a dispute between two German principalities took liberty to decide a challenge to its jurisdiction and to the characterization of the claims presented to it.[4] This, however, was a quasi-domestic tribunal established by a resolution of the German *Diet* to deal with parties neither of which had a full international personality. In 1855, the United States and British Commission, organized by the Convention of February 8, 1853, faced a challenge to its jurisdiction regarding which the commissioners disagreed.[5] The question was consequently referred to the umpire, Bates, who, agreeing with the American commissioners, found that for the purposes of that commission the

[1] See 2 *id.* at 1231.

[2] The commission, however, found occasions to emphasize its "power to ascertain the amount and validity of the claims." *Louis S. Hargons* (*U.S.A.*) v. *Mexico* (1839), *id.* at 1267.

[3] See the letter of Mr. Webster to the Mexican members of the commission in *id.* at 1241. And see his answer to the request of the claimant Santangelo in *id.* at 1242. The attitude of Mr. Webster was also followed some forty years later by Secretary Evarts with relation to the Spanish-American Commission of 1871. See 3 *id.* at 2599. The same attitude became a tradition when a third Secretary of State, Mr. Olney, adopted it in 1895 in regard to the United States-Chilean arbitration. See his letter of June 28, 1985, in 7 Moore, *Digest*, 34–5 (1906).

[4] *Affaire des Baillages de Shieder, Blomberg et Lipperode* (Lippe-Detmold c. Schaumbourg-Lippe) (1839), 1 Lapradelle et Politis, *Recueil*, 401, 407–9, 418–9.

[5] The issue involved related to the admissibility of certain claims presented by applicants whom the United States considered "for the purpose of the commission" to be Mexican citizens and not British subjects. See *The Messrs. Laurent's case* (1855), 3 Moore, *Arbitrations*, 2671.

claimants were not British subjects and that "the commissioners do not form a tribunal competent to entertain their claims." [1] The power of the umpire to reach this decision was apparently within the provisions of the convention and was not disputed thereafter. Later in 1860, the commission created by the Convention between the United States and Paraguay of February 4, 1859, rendered its decision in the case relating to the *Claim of the United States and the Paraguay Navigation Co.*[2] Here the claimants asserted that the commission had only the power to assess the amount of damage as "a simple question of how much." Instead, the commission proceeded to a "full and unrestricted examination" of the merits of the claim and a discussion of the very issue of liability, on the basis of which it held in favor of Paraguay.[3] This was a clear case in which the question of the limits of the tribunal's powers was not referred, when it was raised, to the parties but was decided, broadly, by the tribunal itself. The principle was further emphasized, though indirectly, two years later in the *Isaac Harrington* case (1862) before the United States and Costa Rican Commission established by the treaty of July 2, 1860. In this case the umpire, citing Vattel, made it clear that interpreting the arbitration treaty was not to be left to the discretion of either of the parties but was a matter for the arbitrator himself to decide.[4]

The weight the principle seemed to be gaining was not, however, impressive. Up to that time there was not one judicial decision that enunciated clearly the principle that arbitral tribunals have the power to determine their jurisdiction. Moreover, the decision of the umpire in the *Colombian Bond* cases (1866) [5] showed, indeed, that the direction could easily be reversed. For these were cases in which the jurisdiction of the United States and Colombian Commission was challenged, the commissioners were unable to agree ,and the umpire was expected to exercise his power to define the limits of the Commission's jurisdiction; instead, he declared that:

[I]n all cases in which reasonable doubt exists as to its competence, and especially in those now under consideration which interest directly the credit

[1] *Id.* at 2690–1. Art. 3 of the *compromis* provided explicitly that: "It shall be competent for the Commissioners conjointly, or for the arbitrator or the umpire, if they differ, to decide in each case whether any claim has or has not been duly made, preferred, and laid before them, either wholly or to any and what extent, according to the true intent and meaning of this Convention." 16 Martens, *N.R.G.*, 491, 494–5.

[2] 2 Moore, *Arbitrations*, 1485, 1504.

[3] See *id.* at 1506–28.

[4] See *id.* at 1551, 1564–5.

[5] 4 *id.* at 3614.

and the good faith of one of the contracting parties, the commission is bound to decline to entertain them, and to construe its powers in a limited and not in an extensive sense.[1]

He also justified this conservative attitude by the fear of "the charge of assuming powers, the exercise of which is always jealously reserved by governments to themselves." By this he was referring to the argument that the jurisdiction of an international tribunal being derived from the will of the parties cannot be determined contrary to their expressed views. He might have also had in mind the other argument raised against the power at issue that a tribunal determining its own jurisdiction would be *judex in re sua,* contrary to the general principles of justice.

It was, at any rate, at this stage of opposed pronouncements and conflicting arguments that the question arose again in one phase of the important *Alabama Arbitration.*

2. *The Alabama Arbitration – The Value of a Precedent*

In the famed *Alabama Arbitration* (1872),[2] a controversy arose as to whether the arbitration convention covered only the direct losses inflicted on the United States Government in consequence of the destruction of vessels and their cargoes by the insurgent cruisers and the national expenditures in the pursuit of those cruisers, or whether the convention also covered other indirect claims.[3] After lengthy negotiations, both sides allowed the arbitrators to decide the issue on the understanding that "any expression on the subject *would not be binding upon either of the two Governments unless assented to by both.*" [4] Consequently, the tribunal met and unanimously agreed in principle upon the disposition to be made of the indirect claims. However, instead of drafting itself its declaration to that effect, it handed a draft proposed by the United States to the British arbitrator

[1] *Ibid.* Award by Sir Frederick Bruce. (Emphasis added). And *cf.* the argument of the Venezuelan Commissioner, Mendez, in the British-Venezuelan Commission established under the Convention of Sept. 21, 1868, in the case of *Blondel, Hartman, Dumaine and Others* (1869), Report of the Mixed Commission on the Claims of British Subjects Against the Government of Venezuela 6–9, 13–17, 26 (1871); 2 Lapradelle and Politis, *Recueil,* 531, 534.

[2] The *Alabama Claims* (United States v. Great Britain), 1 Moore, *Arbitrations,* 495–682. The case was arbitrated on the basis of the Treaty between the United States and Great Britain signed on May 8, 1871, at Washington, Article 14 of which contained a provision identical with that mentioned on p. 16, note 1 *supra.* See text in 20 Martens, *N.R.G.,* 698, 707.

[3] See *id.* at 624–46.

[4] *Id.* at 644. This was presented as part of a suggestion of the British Agent and was later accepted by both sides as "all that need stand" of that suggestion.

to be communicated to the British agent with a desire "to have the declaration made in a form acceptable to both parties. A counter draft was received from the British side and an agreement was soon reached. This was announced on behalf of all the arbitrators as *their* declaration. They reached in it the conclusion that the indirect claims:

> ... do not constitute upon the principles of international law applicable to such cases good foundation for an award of compensation or computation of damages between nations, and should upon such principles be wholly excluded from the consideration of the tribunal in making its award, *even if there were no disagreement between the two governments as to the competency of the tribunal to decide them.*[1]

The parties acquiesced in this declaration, therefore allowing the continuation of the proceedings. It has since been cited as the undoubted authority behind the power of arbitrators to determine their jurisdiction.[2] It will be a mistake, however, to exaggerate its value in this respect. In fact, it was the parties, not the arbitrators, who decided that the jurisdiction of the tribunal should be determined by its decision, as a device to save the procedure from a stalemate. Furthermore, the parties agreed that such a decision was not to be binding unless assented to. The declaration was also the product of the parties' draftsmanship and was meant to be acceptable to them. This could hardly be a proper "judicial" decision in the technical sense. It was not, at any rate, a decision on jurisdiction. The "indirect claims" were excluded on grounds related to the substantive law, and regardless of the question of jurisdiction.[3] The wording of the declaration leaves no doubt as to this latter point.

The *Alabama Arbitration* did not, therefore, create a clear-cut rule as to the *compétence de la compétence.* It emphasized, however, an important fact – the *compétence de la compétence* is a useful device which insures that adjudication will continue even when the parties disagree in the course of the proceedings. This simple recognition could

[1] Declaration of June 19, 1872, *id.* at 646. (Emphasis added).

[2] See *e.g.*, 2 Cavaré, *Le Droit International Public Positif*, 230 (2d ed. 1962); Fitzmaurice, "The Law and Procedure of the International Court of Justice, 1951–4, Questions of Jurisdiction, Competence and Procedure," 34 *Brit. Yb. Int'l L.* 1, 26 (1958); Berlia, "La Jurisprudence des Tribunaux Internationaux en ce qui concerne Leur Compétence," 88 *Recueil des Cours*, 109, 119, 122 (1955); Ch. Rousseau, *Droit International Public*, 496 (1953).

In these writings the *Alabama* precedent is held as the "*arret de principe*" that "definitely resolved the issue." See also, *Nottebohm Case*, [1953] *I.C.J. Rep.* 111, 119.

[3] In fact, the American commissioners had prior to that declaration expressed the view that the indirect claims, "though incapable from their nature of computation, and from their magnitude incapable of compensation, were to be submitted to the tribunal of arbitration ..." See the answers given by the American commissioners to Mr. Fish in 1 Moore, *Arbitrations*, 628.

be surmized from the case only with caution. The assent of the parties was needed to allow the tribunal the power to determine the issue and was necessary to give its declaration a binding character.

3. The Aftermath of the Alabama – The Principle Codified and Implemented

Two years after the *Alabama Arbitration*, the *Institut de Droit International* took up the task of preparing a draft of rules of procedure of arbitral tribunals. Goldschmidt presented the first *Projet* of which Article 18 left no doubt as to the right of the tribunal to determine its jurisdiction.[1] The final *Projet* adopted by the Institut in 1875 reiterated the principle in detail. After stipulating that: "arbitrators were obliged to decide upon objections to the jurisdiction of the arbitral tribunal," Article 14 of this draft added:

> If the doubt concerning the jurisdiction depends on the interpretation of a clause in the *compromis*, the parties are presumed to have given the arbitrators power to settle the question, unless otherwise stipulated. [Fr. *sauf clause contraire*][2]

Whether this Article was adopted *qua lex lata* could of course be questioned. Yet, it is an early presentation of the clear but cautious attitude of the publicists at that time; tribunals must have *compétence de la compétence* in case a dispute arises as to their jurisdiction, and provided that the doubt concerning jurisdiction depends on the interpretation of the *compromis* and that the parties did not stipulate otherwise. This clear presentation helped the tribunals established in later periods to face more boldly the problems of their proper jurisdiction. The article was also used as a basis of similar provisions in subsequent treaties. And by mentioning that the power is presumed unless excluded, it prompted, on the other hand, a practice of "*clauses contraires*" inserted in arbitration treaties to reserve for the parties the power to decide themselves some or all jurisdictional problems. A review of the subsequent practice will affirm these points.

1 "Le Tribunal arbitral est juge de sa compétence ..." Goldschmidt, "Projet de Règlement pour Tribunaux Arbitraux Internationaux," Art. 18, 6 *Rev. Dr. Int'l & Leg. Comp.*, 421, 440 (1874).

An earlier doctrinal statement of the principle is found in a provision introduced in the second edition of Bluntschli, *Le Droit International Codifié*, Art. 492 bis., at 288 (2e éd. trad. par Lardy 1874). The author cited the *Alabama Arbitration* which has obviously caused this addition.

2 "Projet de Règlement pour la Procédure Arbitrale Internationale," Art. 14, 1 *Annuaire*, 126, 129–30 (1877).

The United States-French Claims Commission, established by the convention of January 15, 1880, dismissed the claim of *Le More* (1884), for want of jurisdiction after a controversy in which the United States sought a solution through negotiations but France insisted that the decision on jurisdiction should be left to the commission.[1]

In 1892, the Chile-United States claims commission exercised in the *Didier* case its *compétence de la compétence*,[2] to have it reaffirmed three years later by Mr. Olney, then United States Secretary of State.[3]

The principle was again affirmed in the Proposed Treaty of Permanent Arbitration between the United States and the United Kingdom, which was signed on January 11, 1897, but was never ratified.[4] Article 7 of this proposed treaty envisaged that the tribunal would decide on whether the claim "involves the decision of a disputed question of principle of grave general importance affecting the national rights of [a] party as distinguished from the private rights where of it is merely the international representative ..." Providing arbitral tribunals with such a power, i.e., to determine the nature of the controversy and its relevance to the vital interests of the States in dispute, would have been a very progressive step in 1897. As will be shown, this aspect of the *compétence de la compétence* was the most controversial and is still not universally accepted.

The question as a whole became the subject of discussion in the first Peace Conference at the Hague (1899), which was the first intergovernmental conference to codify the rules of international arbitration. The Russian delegation to that Conference presented a draft giving the arbitral tribunal, alone, the authority to determine its competence.[5] This provision, though lacking in other drafts presented, appeared with a slight modification in wording, in Convention No 1. for the Pacific Settlement of International Disputes (Article 48).[6] It

[1] See 2 Moore, *Arbitrations*, 1133, 1143–4.

[2] See 4 *id.* at 4329, 4331.

[3] See 7 Moore ,*Digest*, 34–5.

[4] 1 Moore, *Arbitrations*, 983, 986.

[5] See Russian Draft of Arbitral Code ,Art. 18, [Scott] *The Proceedings of the Hague Peace Conferences. The Conference of 1899. Translation of the Official Texts* 801, 803 (1920).

The Russian delegation presented also a copy of the Rules of Procedure of the arbitration between Great Britain and Venezuela (1897) Article 14 of which contained a similar provision. See *id.* at 183, 185.

[6] "The Tribunal is authorized to declare its competence in interpreting the compromis as well as the other treaties which may be invoked in the case, and in applying the principles of international law." *Id.* at 243. (Original French text in [Ministère des Affaires Etrangères] *Conférence Internationale de la Paix* 231 (1899)). In the same year (1899) a conference of the International Law Association held in Buffalo (U.S.A.) accepted a draft of "Rules Relating to a Permanent Tribunal of International Arbitration" in which Art. 21 provided for the jurisdiction of the Tribunal "to decide on the regulating of its constitution and on the valadity

was the first time the principle appeared in a multilateral convention which meant to declare it as a general pre-existing rule. The *compétence de la compétence* was thus admitted formally in the law of international arbitration. "Not to accept this view – commented Descamps, the Rapporteur of the Third Commission of the Conference – would be to place the tribunal in the condition of a court incapable of acting, and obliged to divest itself of jurisdiction of the controversy every time that it might please one of the parties to maintain, even against evidence, that the tribunal could not take cognizance of such a question." [1] On signing the convention some states made sure, however, to declare that they, and not the tribunal, would still be the judges of arbitrability of some types of cases,[2] thus suggesting that the *compétence de la compétence* of such tribunals would apply to them only within limits.

The principle was again affirmed in the arbitration treaty between the Argentine Republic, Bolivia and other nations signed on January 21, 1902.[3] It was also upheld by the United States-Venezuelan Commission in the *Flutie* cases (1903).[4] Here, the commission cited the attitude of the United States Secretary of State in relation to the United States and Spanish Commission (1871),[5] to conclude that the commission, "as the sole judge of its jurisdiction" ought to determine for itself the question of citizenship of the claimant (as a condition of the admissibility of the claim). The power was then exercised by tribunals of the Permanent Court of Arbitration particularly in the *Pious Fund* case (1902),[6] and in the cases of the *Preferential Treatment of Claims of Blockading Powers against Venezuela* (1904).[7] In the latter cases the tribunal found itself incompetent to review the actions of prior arbitral commissions set between the parties, or to decide on the nature of the military operations undertaken against the re-

and interpretation of the reference to itself." See text in Darby, *International Tribunals* 592, 600 (4th ed. 1904).

[1] [Chevalier Descamps] Report of the Third Committee to the Conference, Annex to the Minutes of the Seventh Meeting, July 25, 1899, in [Scott] *id.* at 106, 147. In the Third Commission itself the Article (then No. 47) was adopted without discussion. *Id.* at 614–5.

[2] See the declarations of the United States and of the Ottoman Empire in *id.* at 155.

[3] See text in 1 *Am. J. Int'l L.* (Supp.), 299, 300 (1907); Darby, at 726.

[4] *Flutie* cases (United States v. Venezuela), 9 *U.N. Rep. Int'l Arb. Awards*, 148, 151 (1903).

[5] *Supra*, p. 13, note 2.

[6] 9 *U.N. Rep. Int'l Arb. Awards* 1, 12–3; Scott, *Hague Court Reports*, 5 (Perm. Ct. Arb. 1902).

[7] 9 *U.N. Rep. Int'l Arb. Awards*, 99, 108; Scott, *Hague Court Reports*, 58–9 (Perm. Ct. Arb. 1904). Another tribunal of the same Court also exercised the power by setting aside a preliminary request as to the admissibility of the claim in the *Interests on Indemnities* case Russia *v.* Turkey). Scott, *id.* at 297, 300–2. (Perm. Ct. Arb. 1912).

spondent. Yet this decision was reached after the tribunal had verified the limits of its jurisdiction and was not an automatic response to a plea advanced by one of the parties. The year 1904 witnessed also a treaty of commerce between Italy and Switzerland in which it was agreed that disputes related to interpretation, including the preliminary question of whether the dispute was so related, would be decided by an arbitral tribunal on the request of either party.[1] Such a provision was then conferring on the tribunal both the jurisdiction to interpret the treaty *and* the power to decide whether that jurisdiction existed.[2]

The second occasion for a formal codification of the rule in a multilateral convention was provided by the Second Peace Conference at the Hague (1907). Article 48 of the 1899 Convention No. I was retained as Article 73 of the new convention on the Pacific settlement of International Disputes with minor changes in the wording.[3]

With such a continually maintained trend it was perhaps justifiable for the arbitrator in the *Walfish Bay Boundary* case to declare in 1911 that:

> [I]t is *a constant doctrine of public international law* that the arbitrator has power to settle questions as to his own competence by interpreting the range of the agreement submitting to his decision the question in dispute.[4]

In fact, the principle was by that time based on comfortable grounds. Up to the date of the first World War, one could trace a good number of arbitration treaties which accepted not only the general power of arbitrators to interpret the *compromis* (even on matters of their jurisdiction), but also their power to settle the nature of the contro-

[1] Traité de Commerce entre L'Italie et La Suisse, Art. 18, signed in Rome on July 13, 1904, 33 Martens, *N.R.G.*, (2e Sér.) 539; 11 *U.N. Rep. Int'l Arb. Awards* 259. And see other treaties concluded by Italy with other powers in the period between 1907 and 1911 providing for the arbitration of questions related to the classification of disputes, as referred to in Hudson, *The Permanent Court of International Justice* 464 n. 67 (2d ed. 1943).

[2] See the case that arose under the Article cited above: "Affaire Relative à l'Interprétation du Traité de Commerce Conclu Entre L'Italie et La Suisse le 13 Juillet 1904," 11 *U.N. Rep. Int'l Arb. Awards*, 257 (1911).

[3] The changes introduced in the old article (p. 20, note 6, *supra*) involved the omission of the word "international" and the substitution of the words "papers and documents" for the word "treaties." See text of Art. 73 in 1 [Scott] *The Proceedings of the Hague Peace Conferences. The Conference of 1907. Translation of the Official Texts* 611 (1920). The purpose of such changes was to widen the limits of the power provided for in the text, "in accord with the thought of the authors" of the 1899 Convention. See *id.* at 433.

[4] Award of Prida, arbitrator in the matter of *the Southernmost Boundary of the Territory of Walfish Bay* (Germany *v.* Great Britain), 9 *U.N. Rep. Int'l Arb. Awards*, 263, 294 (19)11 (Emphasis added).

versy where this was disputed between the parties.[1] Yet, whereas the trend of entitling arbitrators the *compétence de la compétence* through the interpretation of the *compromis* continued in practice, almost undisputed and firmly sanctioned by agreements,[2] and by arbitral awards,[3] the problem of the right to determine the nature of the controversy had an independent development. This distinction, hardly noticed in current writings, will shortly be expounded. However,

[1] See R. R. Wilson, "Reservation Clauses in Agreements for Obligatory Arbitration," 23 *Am. J. Int'l L.*, 68, 83 (1929). And see details in Wilson, *International Agreements for Obligatory Arbitration* (Doctoral Thesis – Harvard), 71–122, particularly at 120 (1927) (Limited Publication).

[2] See *e.g.*, *Compromis d'Arbitrage* between France and Peru, Art. 3 signed on 2.2.1914 (reference to the Hague Convention of 1907), 1 *U.N. Rep. Int'l Arb. Awards*, 216, 217; Convention between Great Britain and Costa Rica for the Submission to Arbitration of Certain Claims Against the Government of Costa Rica, Art. 1, signed on 12.1.1922, *id.* at 371, 372; Rules of the Belgo-German, Belgo-Austrian and Belgo-Bulgarian Mixed Arbitral Tribunals, Art. 3 (in each), 1 *Rec. des déc. des trib. arb. mixtes*, 33, 171, 231 (1921); Rules of the French-German, French-Bulgarian and French-Austrian Mixed Arbitral Tribunals, Art. 87 (in each), *id*, at 56, 121, 252 (1921); Rules of Greco-German Mixed Arbitral Tribunal, Art. 84, *id.* at 72 (1920); Agreement between Spain and the United Kingdom related to the British Properties in Spanish Morocco, Art. 2, signed on 29.5.1923, 2 *U.N. Rep. Int'l Arb. Awards* 620–1; *Compromis* between the United States and the Netherlands, Art. 5, signed on 23.1.1925 (tribunal given power to determine "any question of procedure"), *id.* at 831, 833, *Compromis* between Germany and the *Commissaire aux Revenues Gagés*, signed on 26.4.1926 (reference to the Hague Convention of 1907), *id.* at 757, 759; *Compromis* between Germany, Belgium and Other Powers, Art. 15(8) signed on 20.1.1930 (parties given also the right to refer the question of jurisdiction to the P.C.I.J.), 3 *id.* at 1373; *Compromis* between the United Kingdom and Portugal related to the *Campbell case*, Art. 13, signed on 1.9.1930, 2 *id.* at 1147, 1150; *Compromis* between France and the United Kingdom concerning the *Chevreux case*, Art. 6, signed on 4.3.1930 (reference to the Hague Convention of 1907), *id.* at 1115, 1116; *Compromis* between Finland and Great Britain related to the *Finish Shipowners Case*, Art. 8, 3 *id.* at 1481, 1483; *Compromis* between Belgium and France concerning the Tardieu Accord, Art. 2, signed on 5.5.1936 (reference to the Hague Convention of 1907), *id.* at 1703, 1704; *Compromis* between France and Spain concerning the Interpretation of the Treaty of Bayonne related to the Utilization of the Waters of *Lac Lanaux*, Art. 6, signed on 9.11.1956 (reference to the Hague Convention), 62 *Rev. Gén. Dr. Int'l Pub.* 80, 81 (1958).

[3] See *e.g.*, *Cession of Vessels and Tugs for Navigation on the Danube*, 1 *U.N. Rep. Int'l Arb. Awards* 97, 103 (1921); *The Rio Grande Irrigation and Land Company*, 4 *id.* 135–6 (1923); *Administrative Decision No. I* of the Tripartite Claims Commission constituted by the United States, Austria and Hungary, 6 *id.* at 203, 208 (1927); *Affaire de la Dette Publique Ottomane*, 1 *id.* at 529 (1925); *Illinois Central Railroad Company*, 4 *id.* 21, 22 (1926); *Archiduc Frédéric de Habsbourg-Lorraine c. Etat roumain*, 7 *Rec. des déc. des trib. arb. mixtes* 128, 136 (1927); *Kulin* v. *Etat hongrois* (*Hungarian Optants case*), *id.* at 138, 146 (1927); *Affaire de la Compagnie d'Electricité de Varsovie* (*Compétence*), 3 *U.N. Rep. Int'l Arb. Awards* 1669, 1673–4 (1929); *Affaire Chevreau*, 2 *id.* at 1113, 1137 (1931); *Salem Case*, *id.* at 1161 (1932); *Honduras Borders Case*, *id.* at 1307, 1317–21 (1933); *Zeltweg-Wolfsberg and Unterauburg-Woellan Railways* (Prel. Obj.), 3 *id.* at 1795, 1803 (1934); *Compagnie Radio-Orient*, *id.* at 1871, 1878; 37 *Am. J. Int'l L.* 341, 346 (1943).

Compare, *Herman and Elsa Ventense c. Etat serbe-croate-slovène*, 7 *Rec. des déc. des trib. arb. mixtes* 72, 75–7 (1922); *Losinger Company v. Yugoslavia*, in, *P.C.I.J.*, ser. C., No. 78 at 105–118 (Arbitral Award of 30.10.1935), *Walwal Case*, *Société des Nations*, *Journal Officiel*, 16th Sess. 973 (Sep. Op. of the Italian Commissioners) (1935).

In these latter instances arbitrators declared themselves ' without jurisdiction" to decide jurisdictional issues, which should be distinguished from a negative decision on substantive jurisdiction as a result of the exercise of the *compétence de la compétence*.

it may be appropriate at this stage to review first the attitude of the "publicists," whose teachings constitute a subsidiary source of international law (Art 38(d) of the Statute of the International Court) and provide an evidence of its contents, toward this power that arbitrators have accustomed us through practice to identify with their judicial task. Has the rule undergone in the scholar's writings the same development it achieved in the decisions of international tribunals? If so, what are the theoretical grounds that the former provided to complement the task of the latter?

B. THE THEORETICAL BACKGROUND

1. The Argument In Theory

It was only natural for the early writers on international law to envisage arbitration as a limited means of solving international disputes. When resorted to, the arbitrator was often qualified as a "mandatory" who would violate his strict "mandate" if he arrogates to himself the right to interpret the *compromis* or to adjudicate on his own competence.[1] This characterization was not, however, accepted by all. As the incidents in which international tribunals exercised their *compétence de la compétence* became more frequent, writers started to mention the controversy about that power and generally agreed that its exercise was both proper and necessary.[2] Despite this general consensus, that incidentally became beyond doubt at the time

[1] See Heffter, *Le Droit International de l'Europe* 238 n. 5 (Trad. par Bergson, 1883); Holtzendorf, *Eléments de Droit International Public* 523 (Trad. par Zographos, 1891); Bonfils, *Manuel de Droit International Public* 523 (1st ed. 1894) (Same position maintained in following editions till the 5th ed. (1908) at 569 where the author denied that the arbitrator is a mandatory; new position maintained through 7th ed. (1914) at 654–5).

See also, for the characterization of the *compromis* as a mandate in relatively recent writings, Borel, "Les Voies de Recours Contre les Sentences Arbitrales," 52 *Recueil des Cours* 5, 72 (1935–II). And *cf.*, the opinions of writers defending the Rumanian argument in the *Hungarian Optants Case*, in 1 *La Réforme Agraire en Roumanie et les Optants Hongrois de Transylvanie devant la Société des Nations* 56 (Appleton), 201 (Le Fur), 294–5 (Prudhomme) (1927). But see, *id.* at 45 (Alvarez), and at 437–9 (Strupp).

[2] See, *supra*, p. 19 notes 1 and 2. And see, Rolin-Jaequemyns, "Quelques Mots sur la Phase Nouvelle du Différend Anglo-Américain", 4 *Rev. Dr. Int'l & Lég. Comp.* 127, 137, 139 (1872); 2 Fiore, *Trattato di Diritto Internazionale Pubblico* 574–5 (3rd ed. 1888); 3 Martens, *Traité de Droit International* 153 (Trad. par Leo, 1887); 2 Piedelièvre, *Précis de Droit International Public* 68 (1895); Merignhac, *Traité Théorique et Pratique de L'Arbitrage International* 245–5 (1895); 3 Calvo, *Droit International* 481 (5th ed. 1896); 2 Oppenheim, *International Law* 25 (1st ed. 1906); 7 Moore, *Digest* 33–5 (1906) (See also his comment in 2 Moore, *Arbitrations* 1241 (1898)). Politis was therefore stating an almost undisputed fact when, referring to the *compétence de la compétence,* he wrote in 1924: "Cette règle est aujourd'hui hors de doute." Politis, *La Justice Internationale* 79 (1924).

of the drafting of the Statute of the Permanent Court, publicists, nevertheless, differed in the theoretical justification of the power.[1] Some relied on one or another exclusive ground, some mentioned different bases, but, on the whole, they were repeating the arguments which the two American arbitrators, Gore and Pinkney, first wrote in the *Betsey* case.[2] On examining these arguments two major views may be discerned – one inferring the *compétence de la compétence* from the will of the parties (real or constructive), the other basing it on the nature of the arbitral tribunal as such. In the first view the parties are assumed to have agreed to confer on the tribunal the power to determine its jurisdiction.[3] It follows that such a power could not be exercised by the tribunal if the parties stipulated to reserve it to themselves or to another organ. The whole question is then reduced, in this view, to the interpretation of the silence of the parties in accordance with a rebuttable presumption that favors attributing the *compétence de la compétence* to the tribunal.[4] If the parties express their will one way or the other, there would be no silence and, hence, no presumption.

The other view, mostly upheld by more modern writers, deals with the *compétence de la compétence* as a power that is on the one hand inherent in every judicial organ, and on the other hand independent from the will of the parties.[5] Without this power, the tribunal is found

[1] See, for a detailed account, Iaccarino, "Della c.d. Competenza sulla Competenza dei Tribunali Internazionali", 14 *Diritto Internazionale* 357, 363–75 (1960), where the theories dealing with the problem are classified into three: one that restricts the powers of arbitrators to the limits mentioned in the parties' "mandate" (*teoria del mandato*), one that founds the *compétence de la compétence* on the authorization of the parties (*teoria volontaristica pura*), and one that contends the existence in modern international aw of an establishedc rule endowing international tribunals with that power (*teoria normativistica*).

[2] The debate concerning the *Hungarian Optants* case provided an excellent occasion for a reconsideration of the theoretical justification of the *compétence de la compétence*. In this respect, some new arguments were introduced reaching their maximum in George Scelle's contention that an international tribunal refusing to determine its jurisdiction will be committing a "denial of justice." See, Scelle, "La Litige Roumano-Hongrois devant le Conseil de la Société des Nations," in *La Réforme Agraire Roumanie en Transylvanie devant la Justice Internationale et le Conseil de la Société des Nations – Quelques Opinions* 301, 309 (1928).

[3] See, *e.g.*, the Project adopted by the *Institut du Droit International* in 1875, Art. 14, *supra*, p. 19, note 2, 6 Pradier-Fodéré, *Traité de Droit International Public* 424 (1894); Merignhac, *supra*, p. 24, note 2 at 257; Lapradelle, "L'Excès de Pouvoir de l'Arbitre", 2 *Revue de Droit International* 5, 32 (Paris, 1928); Bosco, *Rapporti e Conflitti fra Giurisdizioni Internazionali* 45 (1932).

[4] See, Berlia, "La Jurisprudence des Tribunaux Internationaux en ce qui concerne leur Compétence", 88 *Recueil des Cours* 109, 118 (1955).

[5] See, *e.g.*, 2 Cavaré, *Le Droit International Public Positif* 228 (2d ed. 1962); Iaccarino, *supra*, note 1 at 375, 399, 402; Carlston, *The Process of International Arbitration* 74–5, 76 (1946); Balasko, *Causes de Nullité de la Sentence Arbitrale* 182–3, 185, 186 (1938); Rousseau, "Le conflit Italo-Ethiopien," 44 *Rev. Gén. Dr. Int'l Pub.* 5, 22–5 (1937); Ralston,

to be "a judicial counter-sense" denied the right to act at all.[1] It follows that that power is, in this view, necessary for the mere functioning of the tribunal,[2] and could not therefore be reserved by one party or even by the agreement of both. Such a conclusion is based in turn on further arguments:

If the judge has the power to interpret the *compromis* for the purpose of reaching a decision on the merits, why should he be deprived of the same right when it comes to a decision on jurisdiction? *Juge d'action est juge d'exception.* This is a valid rule for municipal and also for international tribunals.[3] It has contributed to the characterization of such institutions as "courts of justice." If it is denied to international tribunals, who else could, for practical purposes, decide the issue – the parties who are not in agreement, or the non-existent higher court? In order, therefore, that the dispute on jurisdiction and consequently the one on the merits be solved at all, the tribunal must itself exercise this "inherent" power. Arbitration is not to be subjugated to the diplomatic action. And as the substantive jurisdiction of the tribunal is limited by the parties' own agreement, there is no danger in letting the tribunal exercise such a power. Should a danger present itself, it would, at any rate, be materially less burdensome and practically less probable than the dangers involved in leaving the issue for the defendant to solve.[4]

Such are then the two views involved. They differ in the characterization given to the tribunals' power to determine their jurisdiction and in the legal consequences derived therefrom, but they agree that such power prevails, in principle. The agreement is however confined, as in the case of international practice, to acknowledging the power as a matter of interpreting the *compromis* to reach a decision on jurisdiction. As to the question of determining the nature of the contro-

The Law and Procedure of International Tribunals 47–8 (rev. ed. 1926); 3 Calvo, *supra*, p. 24, note 2 at 381; Rolin-Jaequemyns, *supra*, p. 24, note 2 at 137.

Cf., Kelsen's comment on Jenk's Report to the *Institut du Droit International* on the Compulsory Jurisdiction of International Judicial and Arbitral Tribunals, in 48 *Annuaire* 68 (1959).

1 Ralston, *supra*, p. 25, note 5 at 47–48. *Accord*, Iaccarino, *supra*, p. 25, note 1 at 403; Carlston, *supra*, p. 25, note 5 at 74–5; Balasko, *supra*, p. 25, note 5 at 186. And see, Salvioli, "Sul Potere dell' Arbitro a Pronunciarsi sulla Competenza," 13 *Diritto Internazionale* 119, 121–2 (1959).

2 Iaccarino, *supra*, p. 25, note 1 at 399–403.

3 See Bos, *Les Conditions du Procès en Droit International Public* 271 (1957); Hudson, *International Tribunals* 111 (1944); Balasko, *supra*, p. 25, note 5 at 183; Wittenberg, *L'Organisation Judiciaire, la Procédure et la Sentence Internationales* 368, 409 (1937); Politis, *supra*, p. 24, note 2 at 79. And see *Ambatielos Case* (Prel. Obj.), [1952] *I.C.J. Rep.* 28, 55 (Individual Op. of Judge Spiropoulos).

4 2 Cavaré, *supra*, p. 26, note 5 at 228; Balasko, *supra*, p. 26, note 5 at 186.

versy (e.g., whether the controversy is justiciable or political, international or domestic, and all related questions), publicists, like tribunals, responded to the reluctance of states in this respect, allowing an important distinction to take place.

2. *Two Stages in the Exercise of the Compétence de la Compétence* – A distinction between: (a) the power to determine the nature of the controversy, and (b) the power to determine, through the interpretation of the jurisdictional instruments, whether jurisdiction was accepted by the parties

Granted that the exercise of the *compétence de la compétence* by an arbitral tribunal involves nothing but a simple investigation of the relevant instruments and facts in order to find out whether the parties have agreed to arbitrate "this" dispute before "this" tribunal, practice has, nonetheless, imposed a fine distinction not commonly observed in this process of investigation. Since the rise in the latter part of the nineteenth century of the claim that arbitration was suitable for the settlement of all disputes, and the emergence of the practice of making *general* arbitration treaties, resort to arbitration became subject in many cases to reservations by means of which certain areas of disputes relating to the vital interests of states were not to be adjudicated by any organ other than the state concerned.[1] As a result, in such cases a party to a dispute brought before an arbitral tribunal might first raise the question whether such a dispute belonged to the reserved area. To allow tribunals to determine this issue would in many ways frustrate the purpose of the reservation. Consequently, and in order to respect the will of the parties, the reservation was normally understood to

[1] Before that, the "vital interests" of states were safeguarded by the fact that resort to arbitration was made on *ad hoc* voluntary basis. The standard formula reserving questions of "national honor, vital interests and the interests of third states" could be traced at least to the time of the First Conference of American States in 1889–90. See [2 International American Conference] *Reports of Committees and Discussions Thereon*, Plan of Arbitration, Arts. 3 and 4 at 955 (1890); [Scott] *The International Conferences of American States 1889–1928* at 40, 41 (1931). After 1890 reservation clauses were commonly inserted in arbitration treaties concluded by American and European States. But see, a treaty concluded in 1898 between Colombia and Peru accepting the obligation to arbitrate "in general" all cases of future controversy, cited in Wilson, *supra*, p. 23, note 1 at 78. The vital interests clause began to fall in disuse after World War I, though incidents of its use could be found in later dates. *E.g.*, Convention between the United States and Sweden, Art. 1, signed at Washington on 24.6.1925, *U.S.T.S.* No. 708; Arbitration Convention between the United States and Liberia, Art. 1, signed at Monrovia, on 10.2.1926, *U.S.T.S.* No. 747; Treaty of Conciliation, Judicial Settlement and Arbitration between Switzerland and Turkey, Art. 1, signed at Ankara on 9.12.1928, 159 *L.N.T.S.* 219, 220. See generally, Cory, *Compulsory Arbitration of International Disputes* (1932).

mean that even the preliminary question of whether the dispute is within or without the reserved area, would be left to the parties.[1] Many arbitration treaties provided expressly for this conclusion.[2] The result of such an extension is that a tribunal will be allowed to proceed with the case only after the *defendant* decides, explicitly or tacitly that the dispute is not one related to the reserved domain. Such a decision does not, however, necessarily mean that the tribunal has jurisdiction over the dispute. Chances are still open for objections to jurisdiction based on other grounds. In case such objections arise the tribunal will exercise its *compétence de la compétence* to dispose of these objections. It will do so primarily by interpreting the jurisdictional instrument to reach a conclusion on whether the parties have consented to adjudicate before it the dispute at hand.

It is clear from this analysis that in the above situation the power to determine jurisdiction passes through two stages. In the first it is reserved to the parties; only they could decide whether the nature of the controversy is such as could be adjudicated. In the second stage, which would come to existence only if this primary question is answered in the affirmative, the tribunal becomes the judge of its own competence.

Failure to recognize this distinction has led some modern writers to deny, in the absence of a provision to the contrary, the power of arbitral tribunals to decide whether the dispute falls within their jurisdiction.[3] This denial is based on the fact that in many arbitral cases the question of the nature of the controversy was practically determined by the defendant. Yet this fact should not be misunderstood. It only occurs when the parties reserve certain areas of disputes to be decided by themselves, and it does not, as shown above, preclude the tribunal's exercise of its *compétence de la compétence* beyond this primary question.

[1] See Simpson and Fox, *International Arbitration* 15–6 (1959), Brierly, "Vital Interests and the Law", 21 *Brit. Yb. Int'l L.* 51 (1944); Kelsen, "Compulsory Adjudication of International Disputes", 37 *Am. J. Int'l L.* 397, 403 (1943); Wilson, *supra*, p. 23, note 1 at 74; Barclay, *The New Method of Adjusting International Disputes in the Future* 67 (1917).

See also, League of Nations, *Documents Concerning the Action Taken by the Assembly on the Statute of the Permanent Court* 206, 211 (1921) (Report by Hagerup (Norway) submitted to the Third Committee of the Assembly).

[2] See instances in *Systematic Survey* 27, 32, 39 (1949); Wilson, *supra*, p. 23, note 1 at 77; 2 Guggenheim, *Traité de Droit International Public* 107, n. 2, 147 n. 1 (1954). But see *Convention d'Arbitrage* between France and Denmark signed at Copenhagen on 19.8.1911; 5 Martens, *N.R.G.* (3 Sér.) 682, 683. After providing for the traditional exclusions in Article 1, the treaty enumerated in Article 2 categories of cases to be subject to arbitration "sans que les réserves mentionnées à l'article 1er puissent être invoquées."

[3] See *e.g.*, Delbez, *Les Principes Généraux du Contentieux International* 70 (1962).

It will soon be proved that the distinction expounded above was clearly recognized by those responsible for the drafting of the Statute of the Permanent Court. It was also apparent in the first draft convention on arbitral procedure presented by the International Law Commission in 1952. This draft included two articles related to the *compétence de la compétence:* Article 11 which made the tribunal the "judge of its own competence" and clothed it with "the widest powers to interpret the *compromis*," and Article 2 which, referring to the period prior to the constitution of the arbitral tribunal, provided that if the parties disagree as to "the existence of a dispute, or as to whether an existing dispute is within the scope of the obligation to have recourse to arbitration," such a question may, unless otherwise stipulated by the parties, be "brought before the International Court of Justice." [1] Obviously this latter Article deals with the determination of the nature of the controversy and introduces a practical solution which the Commission described as ' an important innovation" though the provision was not without precedents.[2] Yet, it must be noticed that the proposed solution confines the resort to the International Court of Justice to the case wherein the question of arbitrability arises prior to the constitution of the arbitral tribunal, leaving the tribunal to decide the issue if it is raised after its establishment. It could, therefore, be maintained that the Commission's draft was motivated by practical considerations rather than by the traditional difference between the two stages in the exercise of the *compétance de la compétence*. This concept became even clearer in the final Article 1(3) of the model draft rules submitted by the Commission in 1958 which provided that: "If the arbitral tribunal has already been constituted, any dispute concerning arbitrability shall be referred to it." [3]

One could thus infer that the International Law Commission has presented a modern attempt to put an end to the distinction at issue by entitling the arbitral tribunal to exercise the *compétence de la compétence* in all its aspects whenever this is practically possible. This is

[1] See Report of the International Law Commission covering the Work of its Fourth Session, *U.N. Gen. Ass. Off. Rec.*, 7th Sess., Supp. No. 9 at 4, 7 (Doc. No. A/2163) (1952).

[2] See *id.* at 4. And see, the Resolution of the Institut de Droit International on the classification of justiciable conflicts, in 29 *Annuaire* 258–9 (1922). For practical examples see, *Systematic Survey*, 32–3, 34. And see, in particular, the General Act for the Pacific Settlement of International Disputes, signed at Geneva on 26.9.1928, Art. 41 (Entry into force 16.8.1929). *id.* at 435; 93 *L.N.T.S.* 343 (P.C.I.J. made competent in disputes concerning "the classification of disputes and the scope of reservations.")

[3] Report of the International Law Commission covering the Work of its Tenth Session, *U.N. Gen. Ass. Off. Rec.*, 13th Sess., Supp. 9 at 6 (Doc. No. A/3859); (A/CN.4/117) (1958).

only allowed, however, under the assumption that the parties do not stipulate otherwise.

3. The Principle Applied a Fortiori to the Judicial Procedure

International arbitral law in the present stage of its development entitles tribunals to interpret the *compromis* in order to ascertain the will of the parties and to examine whether the *conditions de procès* have been fulfilled. Through this examination the arbitral tribunal can reach a decision on the objections raised by the parties against its jurisdiction to deal with the case submitted to it. Nothwithstanding some theoretical objections, the parties may agree to keep for themselves the power to define the limits of the arbitrators' jurisdiction even after the case is submitted to the latter. As seen above it was not uncommon in practice for states to reserve certain areas of disputes out of arbitration, deciding themselves in each case whether the controversy belonged or not to the reserved area. The *compétence de la compétence* of arbitral tribunals, though universally recognized, is thus subject to some extent to the will of the parties. This is usually understood to be one consequence of the nature of international arbitration. The arbitral procedure is characterized by "the autonomy of the will of the parties both with regard to the choice of the arbitrators, the law to be applied and the procedure of the arbitral tribunal." [1] If despite this autonomy the tribunal can exercise the power to determine its jurisdiction, the same should apply *a fortiori* to the more institutionalized international courts where the role of the will of the parties is less prevalent.[2] This logical deduction is affirmed by the verification of practice. No international court with continued jurisdiction was established without this power being conferred on it.[3]

[1] Report of the International Law Commission covering the work of its Fifth Session, *U.N. Gen. Ass. Off. Rec.*, 8th Sess., Supp. 9 at 7 (Doc. No. A/2456) (1953). *Accord*, [Secretariat of the League of Nations] Memorandum on the Different Questions Arising in Connection with the Establishment of a Permanent Court of International Justice, in *P.C.I.J.*, *Documents Presented to the Committee Relating to Existing Plans for the Establishment of a Permanent Court of International Justice* 113 (1920). And see *Free Zones Case, P.C.I.J.*, ser. A, No. 24 at 33–8 (1930) (Observations of Judge Kellogg).

[2] The *a fortiori* argument invoked above is clear in the comparison between an *ad hoc* arbitral tribunal and a permanent court, but not necessarily in the comparison between a tribunal with voluntary jurisdiction and another with an obligatiory jurisdiction. See Berlia, *supra*, p. 25, note 4 at 154.

[3] Compare, Treaty Instituting the European Coal and Steel Community signed at Paris on 18.4. 1951 (Entry into force 23.7.1952), 261 *U.N.T.S.* 143, 165–173, which provided for the establishment of the "Court of Justice" of this Community. The jurisdiction of this court having been organized in the fashion of the French *Conseil d'Etat*, it seems that it was found otiose to provide for the court's power to determine its jurisdiction. However, the "Rules"

This could be traced in the constituent instruments of the Central American Court of Justice (1907),[1] the Permanent Court of International Justice (1920),[2] the International Court of Justice (1945),[3] the Administrative Tribunal of the International Labor Organization (1946),[4] the Administrative Tribunal of the United Nations (1949),[5] the European Court of Human Rights (1950),[6] and in the projects of other international and regional courts.[7]

of the court provide that "the Court is competent to decide all objections raised by the parties." Rules of 4.3.1953, Art. 69(1), *Journal Officiel de la Communauté Européenne du Charbon et de l'Acier* 302 (1954). This court was replaced in 1957 by a single court to serve also as the "Court of Justice of the European Economic Community" and the "Court of Justice of the European Atomic Energy Community." No reference is made in the constituent act of the new court to its *compétence de la compétence* except for allowing the court to give interlocutory judgments concerning, *inter alia*, "the interpretation of this treaty." Treaty Establishing the European Economic Community signed at Rome on 25.3.1957 (Entry into force 1.1.1958), Art. 177, 298 *U.N.T.S.* 11, 76. See also, the Statute of the Court of Justice of the E.E.C., in 5 *European Yearbook* 439 (1959).

It should be noticed that this particular court is of a unique jurisdiction; "it may not be compared with an international tribunal" as it "operates as an international court only in a few instances." Bebr, *Judicial Control of the European Communities* 21, 22 (1962).

[1] See the Convention Establishing the Central American Court of Justice, signed at Washington on 20.12.1907, Art. 22, 2 *For. Rel.* 692 (1907); 2 *Am. J. Int'l L.* (Supp.) 229, 240 (1908). The minutes of the conference which prepared the convention suggest that this article was based on Art. 48 of the Hague Convention No. 1 (1899) (*Supra*, p. 20, note 6). See *Minutes of the Central American Peace Conference at Washington 1907* at 65.

And see a similar provision in the Convention for the Establishment of an International Central American Tribunal (an arbitral tribunal in force between 1925–1934), Art. 8, signed at Washington on 7.2.1923, *Conference on Central American Affairs 1922–1923* at 296.

[2] See *Stat. Perm. Ct. Int'l J.*, Art. 36, para. 4: "In the event of a dispute as to whether the Court has jurisdiction the matter shall be settled by the decision of the Court."

[3] See *Stat. Int'l Ct. J.*, Art. 36, para. 6 (same wording as above).

[4] See Statute of the Administrative Tribunal of the International Labor Organization, Art. 2(7). League of Nations Documents T.A. 4; 1 Hudson, *International Legislation* 212. First created on 26.9.1927 as the Administrative Tribunal of the League of Nations, this tribunal was converted by the last Assembly of the League into the Tribunal of the I.L.O. The modified Statute was adopted by the General Conference of the I.L.O. on 9.10.1946 and was then amended on 29.6.1949, but Art. 2(7) remained the same.

[5] See Statute of the Administrative Tribunal of the United Nations, Art. 2(3), in *United Nations Administrative Tribunal, Statute and Rules* (AT/11/Rev. 2) (U.N. Pub. Sales No. 62.X.3).

[6] See Convention for the Protection of Human Rights and Fundamental Freedoms, signed at Rome on 4.11.1950, Art. 49, 213 *U.N.T.S.* 221; 45 *Am. J. Int'l L.* (Supp.) 24, 35 (1951). No similar provision is included in the Articles related to the "Commission" of Human Rights (as distinguished from the Court), but it is generally understood that the Commission has this power and, in fact, did exercise it. See Goldman, "Human Rights Tribunals", in [Union International des Avocats] *International Courts* 73, 93 (1958).

[7] See, *e.g.*, the Draft Statute of the Arab Court of Justice, Art. 20 (prepared by the Three-Man Commission appointed by the Council of the Arab League at its 12th Ordinary Session, April 13, 1950). English translation in Foda, *The Projected Arab Court of Justice* 230 (1957); 2 Khalil, *The Arab States and the Arab League – A Documentary Record* 72, 75 (1962).

C. THE POWER AND THE INTERNATIONAL COURT

1. The Principle in the Statute

The idea of empowering the International Court with the *compétence de la compétence* finds its origin in the earliest proposals for establishing an international court. As the issue arose in the Paris Peace Conference that followed the first World War, each of the submitted proposals for a permanent international court included one or more provisions on the power of the proposed court to determine its jurisdiction. Not surprisingly, most of these provisions attempted to clothe the court not only with the power to interpret its Statute but also with the right to determine whether the controversy submitted was of the type covered by its jurisdiction.[1] This trend, traced in the early proposals of 1919 proves the consciousness of the jurists of that time of the distinction prevailing in the arbitral practice and their attempt to avoid it in the new judicial institution. The same holds true as to the members of the Advisory Committee of Jurists charged in 1920 with the task of preparing the Statute of the new court. The President of this Committee, Baron Descamps, after suggesting that non-legal questions and legal questions involving "inalienable rights" should be considered in a separate category,[2] affirmed that "nothing is more natural or more just" than to confide the contest on the nature of the question to the international court itself.[3] He then proposed to follow the article dealing with the categories of cases subject to the jurisdiction of the Court by an article stipulating that: "When the legal nature of a case is disputed, the Permanent Court will decide the point as an interlocutory question." [4] This proposal was twice reworded before the Drafting Committee put it in the form submitted

[1] See, *e.g.*, Proposals of the German Government for the Establishment of a League of Nations, May 9, 1919, Art. 33(1), *P.C.I.J., Documents, supra*, p. 30, note 1 at 127; suggestions submitted by Professor Lammasch to the Paris Conference, June 23, 1919, Arts. 13(2), 14(2), *id.* at 131, 132; Statut Constitutionnel de la Ligue des Nations, Art. 39 presented by the Consultative Commission of the Swiss Federal Council, *id.* at 265. But see, Draft Scheme on a Convention Concerning an International Judicial Organization, Art. 8, drawn up by the Committees nominated by the Governments of Denmark, Norway and Sweden, *id.* at 171; Plan for the Establishment of a Permanent Court of International Justice, Art. 22(2), submitted by the "five neutral powers," *id.* at 301, 311.

[2] 1 *Procès-Verbaux of the Proceedings of the Advisory Committee of Jurists* 243 (1920).

[3] *Id.* at 244, 255.

[4] *Id.* at 272.

to the Council of the League.[1] In this form Article 29 of the text prepared by the Drafting Committee (which became Article 34 in the final Draft Scheme) provided first for the categories of disputes concerning which the Court had jurisdiction to hear and determine. Then the Article stipulated that:

In the event of a dispute as to whether a certain case comes within any of the categories above mentioned, the matter shall be settled by the decision of the Court.[2]

This was a categorical affirmation of the power of the proposed court to define the nature of the controversy as a step in determining its jurisdiction. Such an emphasis became even clearer when the Advisory Committee rejected a proposal by de Lapradelle to substitute the words "within its competence" for the words "within any of the categories above mentioned."[3] In fact such proposal, had it been accepted, would have turned the paragraph into a repetitive statement of another Article in the Draft Scheme, i.e., Article 30 which provided that:

Whenever a party refuses to recognize the jurisdiction of the Court it will be for the Court to decide whether the party has agreed to submit to its jurisdiction by virtue of some previous convention.[4]

The existence of the two texts in the draft is then ample proof that its framers wanted the proposed Court to exercise the *compétence de la compétence* in all its aspects, both by verifying the consent of the parties and by determining the nature of the controversy. However, the Advisory Committee which refused De Lapradelle's proposal to change the wording of Article 29 (2) was later persuaded to delete Article 30 after another proposal on his part. A good reason for this could be that whereas the provision of Article 30 was generally accepted as an established rule, the power of an international tribunal to determine the nature of the controversy was by no means settled. At any rate, the final Draft Scheme adopted by the Advisory Com-

[1] The Proposed Article was first amended by Ricci-Busatti to read: "If a question arises whether a certain dispute is or is not included in the categories enumerated in the first Article, the Permanent Court shall decide it as an interlocutory question." *Id.* at 275. Then, Lord Phillimore reworded it as follows: "In case of a dispute on the question whether a given case does or does not fall within the classification of the preceding article, the Permanent Court will render an interlocutory judgment." *Id.* at 277.

[2] *Id.* at 566.

[3] *Id.* at 583.

[4] *Id.* at 566.

mittee included again two texts related to the *compétence de la compétence:* Article 33 providing, *inter alia,* that "the Court shall first of all decide whether the preceding conditions have been complied with," and Article 34 including in its last paragraph the provision of the former Article 29 (2). Both Articles were, however, amended by the Council of the League of Nations in such a way as to cancel the proposed compulsory jurisdiction and to include no provision on the power of the Court to determine its jurisdiction.[1] A new solution was then reached in the Third Committee of the Assembly according to which the Optional Clause system was introduced in the Statute.[2] The last paragraph in Article 34 of the Advisory Committee's Draft was retained, as Article 36 (4), with an important change. It stated the general principle giving the Court the power to decide, in the event of a dispute, whether or not it has jurisdiction, without particular reference to the power to determine the nature of the controversy. Yet, it was understood that the general terms of the new provision will also cover the power provided for in the old text.[3] Remaining in the same wording as Article 36(6) of the Statute of the present Court, this provision was carried out in the practice of both of the two Courts in such a manner as to allow them, as will later be explained, the widest, though not necessarily the exclusive, power to define the limits of their jurisdiction.

2. *The Principle in the Work of the Court*

Although it could be generally said that the Court exercises its *compétence de la compétence* in every case it disposes of, and although

[1] See [League of Nations], *Documents Concerning the Action Taken by the Council of the League of Nations under Article 14 of the Covenant and the Adoption by the Assembly of the Statute of the Permanent Court* 44 (1921).

[2] First the Sub-committee of this Third Committee adopted, after a proposal of Mr. Fernandes (Brazil), an optional provision for obligatory jurisdiction. League of Nations Doc., *Records of First Assembly, Committees,* 1, at 566 (1920). The Third Committee then adopted the provision for an optional declaration for the acceptance of obligatory jurisdiction. *Id.* at 314, 317.

[3] See *id.* at 317, 571, 576. Yet, in introducing the final provision of the Article to the Assembly, the Third Committee pointed out that if a convention establishes obligatory jurisdiction subject to certain reservations (vital interests, independence, honor, etc.) "the question whether any of these are involved in the terms of the Treaty, *being for the parties themselves to decide,* the parties cannot have recourse to the international tribunal without a preliminary agreement (*compromis*)." League of Nations Doc., *Records of the First Assembly, Plenary Meetings* 462–3 (Emphasis added.) This conclusion may suggest that the jurisdiction provided for in Art. 36(4) of the Permanent Court's Statute covered the power to determine whether the controversy falls within the categories enumerated in that Article, but not whether it falls within the reserved area defined in the treaty. Whether such is an acceptable suggestion will be shown through the review of practice in the following chapters.

this power was consciously exercised whenever the Court's jurisdiction was disputed,[1] few are the cases where the Court had to announce openly that the exercise of this power is a part of its judicial task. Individual opinions were, nevertheless, more outspoken in this respect, as in respect of most other issues. Judge Moore, dissenting in the *Mavrommatis Palestine Concessions Case* (1924), pointed out that the Court verifying its jurisdiction and declining to hear and adjudge the merits if it lacks it, is an elementary conception common to all systems of jurisprudence.[2] To eastablish his point he cited municipal decisions in France and the United States thereby contributing to a practice which is seldom found in the work of the Court. The Permanent Court came, a few years later, to a clear recognition of the principle when it announced, rather broadly, in its Advisory Opinion No. 16 dealing with the competence of the Greco-Turkish Commission, that:

> As a general rule, any body possessing jurisdictional powers has the right in the first place itself to determine the extent of its jurisdiction.[3]

This opinion was rendered in the same year in which the Court pronounced its famous decision in the *Minority Schools in Upper Silesia Case* (1928).[4] Here, the Court concluded that it was competent to deal with the merits from the simple fact that the respondent state had not objected at the proper time to its jurisdiction – a conclusion testifying for the conscious and liberal exercise of the *compétence de la compétence* with which the Permanent Court has honored Article 36(4) of its Statute.[5]

The principle now embodied in Article 36(6) of the Statute, received more attention in the work of the present Court. It was invoked in the Pleadings in the *Interpretation of the Peace Treaties with Bulgaria,*

[1] For a list of these cases, see Appendix II. Obviously, the power was not exercised in such cases where the preliminary objection was withdrawn, or the case was discontinued, before adjudicating on the jurisdictional issue.

[2] *Mavrommatis Palestine Concessions, P.C.I.J.*, ser. A., No. 2 at 57–8 (1924) (Diss. Op. of Judge Moore). See also, *Case concerning certain German Interests in Polish Upper Silesia*, ser. A, No. 6 at 30 (Diss. Op. of Judge Anzilotti); *The Electricity Company of Sofia and Bulgaria*, ser. A/B, No. 77 at 102–3 (Diss. Op. of Judge Urrutia); *id.* at 109 (Diss. Op. of Judge Van Eysinga); *id.* at 118 (Diss. Op. of Judge Hudson).

[3] *Interpretation of the Greco-Turkish Agreement of December 1st, 1920, P.C.I.J.*, ser. B, No. 16 at 20 (1928) (Adv. Op.).

[4] *P.C.I.J.*, ser. A, No. 15 (1928).

[5] Compare, Bruns, "La Cour Permanente de Justice Internationale, son Organisation et sa Compétence," 62 *Recueil des Cours* 551, 637 (1937–IV), where he reaches a conclusion as to the practice of the Permanent Court based particularly on the *Serbian Loans Case*, and the *Brazilian Loans Case*, Ser. A, No. 20/21 (1929), to the effect that that Court had practically modified its Statute so as to allow itself the power to determine its jurisdiction only according to the *compromis* or the arbitration treaty but not according to the Statute itself.

Hungary and Roumania Case (1950) both in relation to the Court and the Commissions to be established in accordance with these treaties,[1] and was found applicable to them all.[2] The generality of the rule was reaffirmed in two individual opinions in the first phase of the *Ambatielos Case* (1952).[3] The *Nottebohm Case* (Preliminary objection) (1953) was, however, undoubtedly the occasion on which the Court, unanimously, gave the principle its most extensive treatment. It stated in detail that:

> Paragraph 6 of Article 36 merely adopted, in respect of the Court, a rule consistently accepted by general international law in the matter of international arbitration. Since the *Alabama* case, it has been generally recognized following the earlier precedents, that, in the absence of any agreement to the contrary, an international tribunal has the right to decide as to its own jurisdiction and has the power to interpret for this purpose the instruments which govern that jurisdiction. This principle was expressly recognized in Article 48, 73 of the Hague Convention of July 29th, 1899, and October 18th, 1907, for the Pacific Settlement of International Disputes...
>
> This principle, which is accepted by general international law in the matter of arbitration, assumes particular force when the international tribunal is no longer an arbitral tribunal constituted by virtue of a special agreement between the parties for the purpose of adjudicating on a particular dispute, but is an institution which has been pre-established by an international instrument defining its jurisdiction and regulating its operation, and is, in the present case, the principal judicial organ of the United Nations."[4]

And:

> The Court "whose function is to decide in accordance with international law such disputes as are submitted to it" (Article 38, paragraph 1 of the Statute), should follow in this connection what is laid down by general international law. The judicial character of the Court and the rule of general international law referred to above are sufficient to establish that the court is competent to adjudicate on its own jurisdiction in the present case.[5]

In the year following the adoption of this unequivocal stand, the Court was faced with an unusual situation. After filing its application in the *Monetary Gold Case* (1954), Italy (the applicant itself) challenged the jurisdiction of the Court by presenting what it termed a "preliminary question." The Court, affirming its jurisdiction to adjudicate

[1] See *Interpretation of the Peace Treaties with Bulgaria, Hungary and Roumania Case*, Pleadings, Oral Arguments and Documents 204 (letter of the Czechoslovak Government), 277–8 (Statement of Mr. Benjamin Cohen on behalf of the U.S.A.) (*I.C.J.* 1950).

[2] See *Interpretation of Peace Treaties Case*, [1957] *I.C.J. Rep.* 65, 72.

[3] *Ambatielos Case* (Prel. Obj.), [1952] *I.C.J. Rep.* 28, 55 (Indiv. Op. of Judge Spiropoulos); *id.* at 83 (Diss. Op. of Judge Klaestad).

[4] *Nottebohm Case* (Prel. Obj.), [1953] *I.C.J. Rep.* 111, 119.

[5] *Id.* at 120. See origins of this statement in the Observations of Liechtenstein, 1 *Nottebohm Case*, Pleadings, Oral Arguments and Documents 170, 177–80 (*I.C.J.* 1955), and in the oral pleadings of M. Sauser-Hall, 2 *id.* at 27, both quoted in Chapter II, *infra* at 40–41.

upon the validity, withdrawal or cancellation of an application which has been submitted to it "found that the preliminary objection thus presented was 'not contrary to the Rules or to the Statute,"[1] and declared itself without jurisdiction both on considerations of law and of propriety, as later discussions will reveal in detail.

The *Effect of Awards Made by the United Nations Administrative Tribunal* (1954) provided another occasion where the principle embodied in Article 36(6) of the Statute was cited by the Court as one example of the general rules of judicial character which are "generally laid down in statutes or laws issued for courts of justice."[2] An even more certain description of the principle appeared in Judge Cordova's dissent in the *Judgments of the Administrative Tribunal of the I.L.O.* (1956) where he stated that "the first obligation of the Court – as of any other judicial body – is to ascertain its own competence and, in order to do that, it has first to determine what is the nature of the case which is brought before it."[3] This opinion is of particular interest here, in that it describes the *compétence de la compétence* as an "obligation" of the Court and it clearly includes "the power to determine the nature of the case" as the first step in performing that obligation. This latter point had the emphasis it deserves in the detailed opinions of Judge Lauterpacht in the *Norwegian Loans Case* (1957) and the *Interhandel Case* (1959) where the principle was asserted in order to justify the exercise by the Court of the power to discuss, even in the silence of the parties, the nature of the controversy and the validity of the jurisdictional instruments involved. This, Lauterpacht found, was inherent in the Court's function, Article 36(6) of the Statute being only "declaratory of one of the most firmly established principles of international arbitral and judicial practice,"[4] and "one of the most fundamental principles of international, and national jurisprudence..."[5]

Finally, the principle was upheld by the Court in the case of *Certain*

[1] *Case of the Monetary Gold Removed from Rome in 1943* (Prel. Question), [1954] *I.C.J. Rep.* 19, 28, 29.

[2] *Effect of Awards of Compensation Made by the United Nations Administrative Tribunal*, [1954] *I.C.J. Rep.* 47, 52 (Adv. Op.).

[3] *Judgment of the Administrative Tribunal of the I.L.O. Upon Complaints Made Against the UNESCO*, [1956] *I.C.J. Rep.* 77, 163 (Adv. Op.).

[4] *Interhandel Case* (Prel. Obj.), [1959] *I.C.J. Rep.* 6, 104 (Diss. Op. of Judge Lauterpacht). *Accord, id.* at 56 (Sep. Op. of Judge Spender) and at 92 (Diss. Op. of Judge Armand-Ugon).

[5] *Certain Norwegian Loans*, [1957] *I.C.J. Rep.* 9, 44 (Diss. Op. of Judge Lauterpacht). *Accord, id.* at 69 (Diss. Op. of Judge Guerrero).

Expenses of the United Nations (1962) to apply not only to the Court and similar judicial bodies but, "in the first place at least," to each organ of the United Nations.[1]

[1] *Certain Expenses of the United Nations,* [1962] *I.C.J. Rep.* 151, 168 (Adv. Op.). *Accord,* Report of the Rapporteur of Committee IV/2, As Approved by the Committee (as to the power to interpret the Charter), Doc. No. 933, IV/2/42(2), 13 *U.N. Conf. Int'l Org. Docs.* 703, 709; Wehberg, *Réponse* [au questionnaire de M. Rousseau, Rapporteur], 43 *Annuaire* 39, 41 (1950–I); Hambro, *Réponse,* 44 *id.* 165; Iaccarino, *supra* p. 25, note 1 at 360. And see, as to the power of the Security Council to determine its jurisdiction, Van Kleffens, "Sovereignty in International Law," 82 *Recueil des Cours* 1, 105 (1953–I), and as to the conferment of this power in *all* international organizations, P. Reuter, *International Institutions* 235 (Trans. by Chapman 1958).

The I.C.J. is, however, the only organ of the United Nations entitled by an *explicit* provision to determine its jurisdiction.

CHAPTER II

PRINCIPAL CHARACTERISTICS OF THE POWER OF THE INTERNATIONAL COURT TO DETERMINE ITS JURISDICTION

The foregoing survey emphasizes the fact that in its present wording Article 36(6) of the Statute of the International Court of Justice enunciates a rule of general applicability. As has been declared by the Court itself, the principle would apply even in the absence of that provision which is an evidence, but not the source, of the Court's *compétence de la compétence*.[1] The provision has, however, the value of clearly extending this incidental jurisdiction as a statutory power of the Court.[2] In practice, objections to jurisdiction may yet exceed the limit of disputing the Court's substantive jurisdiction to challenge, in the first place, the power of the Court to pronounce on this issue.[3] This will be a denial of what a simple objection to substantive jurisdiction normally implies – leaving jurisdictional issues for the Court to decide.[4] These two types of objection, one invoking the *compétence de la compétence*, the other opposing its exercise, have both enabled the Court to build through the cases the general characteristics of this power. In the light of these characteristics the process of shaping the Court's jurisdiction in each specific case is being undertaken; hence, the importance of their analysis at this stage of the study.

[1] See, *Nottebohm Case* (Prel. Obj.), [1953] *I.C.J. Rep.* 111, 120. Compare, Hudson, *The Permanent Court of International Justice* 408 (2d ed. 1943) where he states that Art. 36(4) of the Permanent Court's Statute "goes so far that some limits must be set upon the jurisdiction which it confers.

[2] See this power described as "*la juridiction institutionnelle*" in Briggs, "La Compétence Incidente de la Cour Internationale de Justice en tant que Compétence Obligatoire," 64 *Rev. Gén. de Dr. Int'l Pub.* 217, 228 (1960). And see, Rosenne, *The International Court of Justice* 326–7 (1957) where the power is said to have an "objective characteristic" because it rests "only indirectly upon the consent of the parties."

[3] See this distinction made between the "*simple contestation de compétence*" and the "*double contestation de compétence*" in Berlia, "La Jurisprudence des Tribunaux Internationaux en ce qui concerne leur Compétence," 88 *Recueil des Cours* 109, 110–1 (1955).

[4] *Cf.*, Salvioli, "Sul Potere dell'Arbitro a Pronunciarsi sulla Competenza," 13 *Diritto Internazionale* 119 (1959).

A. GENERALITY OF THE SCOPE OF THE POWER

The first characteristic of the Court's power to determine its jurisdiction is that it is general in scope. It covers the Court's competence both in contentious and advisory cases, and it applies to the former whether or not jurisdiction is related to Article 36(2) of the Statute, and regardless of its substantive or incidental character.

1. The contentious procedure

In the contentious procedure, the general scope of the power was never disputed before the Permanent Court. None of the declarations accepting the continued jurisdiction of that Court included any reservations as to the power contained in Article 36(4) of its Statute, either.[1] As to the present Court, the *Nottebohm Case* (1953) presents the only instance in which the Court's *compétence de la compétence* was alleged to be confined to questions as to whether a given dispute falls within the categories enumerated in paragraph 2 of Article 36 of the Statute.[2] This contention presented by the respondent Government (Guatemala) in its objection to the Court's jurisdiction was based only on a certain understanding of the history of the drafting of Article 36. It was sharply contested by the applicant (Liechtenstein) which argued first in its Observations that such a contention had no foundation in law as it ran counter to the general terms of the provision of Article 36(6), as well as to the "impressive body of precedent" in the practice of the Court.[3] Furthermore, it added that "even if Article 36(6) had been omitted from the Statute of the Court, the Court would nevertheless have possessed under customary international law and under general principles of law the power which the Government of Guatemala now seek to deny it."[4] This argument was further advocated in the oral pleading of Liechtenstein's Counsel, M. Sauser-Hall, who described Article 36(6) as a clear and categorical provision which codified a general rule of customary international law and a general principle of law recognized by civilized nations which the Court should apply in

[1] Compare the declaration of El Salvador. Appendix VI, No. 35. And see Chapter VI, *infra* at 271–72.

[2] See, Letter from the Minister of Foreign Affairs of Guatemala to the President of the Court, dated 9.9.1952, in, 1 *Nottebohm Case*, Pleadings, Oral Arguments and Documents 162, 166 (*I.C.J.* 1955).

[3] *Id.* at 170, 177–80.

[4] *Id.* at 179.

any event by virtue of Article 38 of its Statute.[1] As to the limitation suggested by Guatemala on the scope of Article 36(6), he stated that:

> ni le droit positif, ni la jurisprudence, ni la doctrine du droit des gens ne fournissent le moindre appui à une interprétation aussi restrictive...[2]

Such an argument was not met with any further comments on the part of Guatemala, and had its direct effect on the Court which refuted the Guatemalan contention on the same grounds.[3]

In conformity with this view, the Court has exercised the power to determine its jurisdiction in all types of contentious cases, regardless of the alleged basis of jurisdiction,[4] and under certain circumstances, when no such basis existed prior to the institution of proceedings.[5]

On the other hand, the Court's *compétence de la compétence* is not limited to verifying in each case whether the Court can deal with the merits. It extends to all incidental judicial powers as well. The Court has, therefore, discussed in many cases such questions as whether or not to allow intervention of a third party in a case pending before it,[6] the exigency and propriety of indicating interim measures of protection,[7] the admissibility of counter-claims,[8] along with the limits of

[1] 2 *id.* at 27.

[2] *Ibid.*

[3] *Nottebohm Case* (Prel. Obj.), [1953] *I.C.J. Rep.* 111, 119, 120, (text quoted in Chapter I, *supra*, at p. 34.) No writer has supported this contention of Guatemala, either. Lauterpatch listed it among "unsubstantial pleas to the jurisdiction." See, Lauterpacht, *The Development of International Law by the International Court* 349 (1958). Fitzmaurice added two subsidiary grounds for its unsubstantiality: [a] that any issue of jurisdiction being a question of international law would come under head (b) of Art. 36(2), and [b] that at the very least Art. 36(6) must relate to the whole Art. 36 including paragraph 1 under which a dispute as to whether the parties had referred the case to the Court would be covered. See, Fitzmaurice, "The Law and Procedure of the International Court of Justice," 34 *Brit. Yb. Int'l L.* 30 n. 2 (1958).

[4] See Appendices I and II.

[5] See, *e.g.*, *Corfu Channel Case*, [1947–1948] *I.C.J. Rep.* 15, 26. And see Chapter IV, *infra*, at 128–35.

[6] See, the *S.S. Wimbledon, P.C.I.J.*, ser. A, No. 1 at 11–3 (1923); *Haya de la Torre Case*, [1951] *I.C.J. Rep.* 71, 76. In the *Eastern Greenland Case* (1931) before the Permanent Court an application for intervention submitted by Iceland was later withdrawn. *P.C.I.J.*, ser. C, No. 67 at 4081–2, 4118–9.

[7] See, *Denunciation of the Treaty between China and Belgium Case, P.C.I.J.*, ser. A, No. 8 at 7–8 (1927); *Chorzow Factory Case*, ser. A, No. 12 (1927); *South Eastern Greenland Case*, ser. A/B, No. 48 (1932); *Administration of the Prince Von Pless Case*, ser. A/B, No. 54 (1933); *Polish Agrarian Reform Case*, ser. A/B, No. 58 (1933); *Electricity Company of Sofia and Bulgaria Case*, ser. A/B, No. 79 (1939); *The Anglo-Iranian Oil Company Case*, [1951] *I.C.J. Rep.* 93; *Interhandel Case*, [1957] *I.C.J. Rep.* 105. And see details of this question in Chapter IV, *infra*, at 170–80.

[8] See, *Chorzow Factory Case, P.C.I.J.*, ser. A, No. 17 at 37–8, 63–4 (1928); *Diversion of Water from the Meuse Case*, ser. A/B, No. 70 at 28, 32 (1937); *Panevezys-Saldutiskis Case*, ser. A/B, No. 76 at 7–9 (1939); *Asylum Case*, [1950] *I.C.J. Rep.* 280–1, 288. In other cases counter-claims were submitted but no jurisdictional issues were invoked. See Chapter V, *infra*, at 262–64.

the interpretation of its own judgments.[1] By extending the scope of the power in issue to all matters within the incidental jurisdiction of the Court,[2] the Court has established this power as the most pre-preliminary function the Court undertakes; its exercise being the first occupation of the Court after it is properly seized of a dispute.

2. *Advisory cases*

The Court also exercises its *compétence de la compétence* in advisory cases in order to decide whether or not to comply with requests for an advisory opinion, and to ascertain the proper limits of such an opinion when it is within its power to deliver. Article 65(1) of the Statute of the present Court expresses in a clearly permissive language that the Court "may give" an advisory opinion on "any legal question" when it is so requested by "whatever body... authorized by or in accordance with the Charter of the United Nations to make such a request." This Article, along with Article 68 which provides that the Court shall in the exercise of its advisory function be guided by the Statute's provisions which apply in contentious cases (including Article 36(6)) "to the extent to which *it* recognizes them to be applicable," leaves no doubt as to the power of the Court to determine, in every advisory case, whether an opinion could, or should, be given.

However, this point was not always as clearly established under the Permanent Court. The original Statute of that Court was, until its amendment went into effect in 1936, silent on the subject of advisory jurisdiction.[3] The only source of this jurisdiction was, thus, Article 14

[1] See, *Interpretation of Judgment No. 3 Case, P.C.I.J.*, ser. A. No. 4 (1925); *Interpretation of Judgments No. 7 and 8 Case*, ser. A, No. 13 (1927); *Asylum Case* (Interpretation), [1950] *I.C.J. Rep.* 395.

[2] Not to be confused with the above issue is the fact that the Court had from the start, following an earlier arbitral practice, extended its substantive jurisdiction over questions incidental to the decision on a point in regard to which it had jurisdiction. See the details of this sequence of the Court's exercise of its *compétence de la compétence* in Chapter V, *infra* at 194–98.

[3] The Advisory Committee of Jurists charged with drafting the Statute provided in Art. 32 of its first draft that: "The Court shall give [Fr. *donne*] an advisory opinion upon any question or dispute of an international nature referred to it by the Council or Assembly." See the text and the discussion based on it in 2 *Procès-Verbaux of the Advisory Committee of Jurists* 584–5, 649 (1920). In the Assembly of the League the Draft was referred to the Third Committee and in turn to a Sub-Committee, where two proposals for amending this Article [then Art. 36] were discussed and one of them was accepted. Some members of the Sub-Committee expressed their doubts as to the propriety of exercising the advisory function in actual disputes. See League of Nations, *Records of First Assembly, Committees*, I, at 386–7 (1920). Later, M. Fromageot, then a member of the Sub-Committee, stated that the Committee had been unanimous in thinking that the entire Article should be suppressed. 'In reality – he added – the Covenant in Article 14 contained a provision in accordance with

of the Covenant of the League of Nations, the wording of which was a major source of the confusion. The French version read that the Court "*donnera*" [English: "shall" or "will" give] advisory opinions, whereas the English version used the permissive "may give," to which a French equivalent should have been "*peut donner.*" Though the French version was the one mentioned in the discussions of the Committees responsible for drafting the Statute, the English text of the Covenant was equally authoritative and could hardly be ignored. The question, therefore, became so baffling in the writings of jurists, the solution depending in many cases on the version relied upon by each.[1] While a member of the Court, Judge Moore submitted a Memorandum that dealt extensively with the issue. There he found that the "obligation" to perform the advisory function "cannot be deduced from two contradictory texts, both of which are official."[2] Thus, he concluded that Article 14 of the Covenant could not be regarded as imposing on the Court an obligation to render such opinions unconditionally and on request.[3] Such an obligation, he found, would be "admittedly inconsistent with and potentially destructive of the judicial character with which the Court has undoubtedly been invested..."[4]

The question was again raised during the drafting of the Rules of the Court in 1922. A text was suggested to the effect that the Court "reserves the right to refrain from replying to questions put to it which require an opinion on a theoretical case."[5] No such provision was

which *the Court could not refuse to give advisory opinions*. It was therefore unnecessary to include a rule to the same effect in the constitution of the Court." This remark, though based only on the French version of Art. 14 of the Covenant passed unopposed by other members (except for M. Loder who thought that Art. 36 in the draft and Art. 14 in the Covenant did not cover the same ground), and Fromageot's proposal was unanimously accepted. Art. 36 in the draft was suppressed. See *id.* at 401. However, in the Revision Protocol of Sept. 14, 1929, (effective, Feb. 1, 1936) four articles related to the advisory function were added to the Statute (Arts. 65–68) among which Art. 68 was particularly meant to extend to the advisory function such provisions of the Statute as Art. 36(4) which dealt with the *compétence de la compétence*. See generally, on this latter point, Hammarskjöld, "Quelques Aspects de la Fonction Consultative de la Cour Permanente de Justice Internationale," in his *Juridiction Internationale* 283, 284–93 (1938).

1 Compare, *e.g.*, A. De Bustamante, *The World Court* 254 (Trans. by Read, 1925), with Magyary, *La Juridiction de la Cour Permanente de Justice Internationale* 93 (1931); Fachiri, *The Permanent Court of International Justice* 80 (2d ed. 1932).

In the first edition of his treatise on the Permanent Court (1934), Hudson maintained, at p. 444, that the Court 'should not go ... to determine that a request [for an advisory opinion] was invalidly adopted." In the second edition (1943) he adopted at p. 499, the view that the Court is bound to entertain the request but is not bound to give the opinion requested.

2 Memorandum Submitted by Judge J. B. Moore to the Permanent Court of International Justice, Feb. 18th, 1922, *P.C.I.J.*, ser. D, No. 2 at 383, 385.

3 *Id.* at 397.

4 *Id.* at 384–5.

5 *P.C.I.J.*, ser. D, No. 2 at 308 (1922).

adopted, however, and the brief discussion that took place on that occasion between some members of the Court was not revealing of what the Court's attitude would be in a specific case.[1] This attitude was soon to be tested in the *Eastern Carelia Case* (1923).[2] The Council of the League requested the Court to give an advisory opinion concerning the legal effect of certain articles in a treaty between Russia and Finland and an annexed declaration regarding the autonomy of Eastern Carelia. The Russian Government which was directly involved in the dispute and which had refused to participate in the Council's consideration of it, declined to take part in the examination of the question by the Court on the ground that the problem was a matter of Russian domestic jurisdiction and that neither the League nor the Court were impartial in that matter.[3] The Court thus faced for the first time with a challenge to the proper limits of its advisory function, exercised its *compétence de la compétence* and declined to give the opinion requested. Principal among the reasons given by the Court for this attitude was the fact that Russia, a party to the actual dispute on which the opinion was sought, was not then a member of the League and had not consented, as Article 17 of the Covenant required, to the solution of such disputes "according to the methods provided for in the Covenant." This amounts, in fact, to saying that the Court did not have competence to give the opinion because the Council was not competent to request it. In other words, the Court did not only exercise its power to determine its jurisdiction but had, in order to do so, to determine also whether the Council had jurisdiction in the first place to make the request. By reaching the conclusion that no such jurisdiction existed, the Court set a landmark in its jurisdiction that has not since been repeated. It also provided a clear instance of the distinction between the question of the *compétence de la compétence* and that of substantive jurisdiction. Whereas the first was broadly exercised in the case, the latter was not exercised at all. The *Eastern Carelia Case* (1923) testifies therefore that even when the Court tended to restrict its substantive jurisdiction, it was broadly exercising its pre-preliminary *compétence de la compétence.*

If the *Eastern Carelia Case* (1923) was the only instance in which

[1] Judge Altamira asked whether a clearer text allowing the Court to refuse to give advisory opinions should not be inserted in the Rules. Lord Finally preferred not to insert anything to this effect. And Judge Weiss thought that the proposed text was clear enough for this purpose. See *id.* at 161.

[2] *P.C.I.J.*, ser. B, No. 5 (1923).

[3] See the text of the telegram of the Russian People's Commissionary for Foreign Affairs to the Court dated June 11th, 1923, in, *id.* at 12–14.

the Court declined to give a requested advisory opinion, it is by no means the only one in which it considered whether or not to do so. As an affirmative decision on jurisdiction is equally a result of the exercise of the *compétence de la compétence*, this power is manifest in many cases where the opinion requested was eventually given.

Shortly after the *Eastern Carelia Case*, the Court gave its Opinion in the *German Settlers in Poland Case* (1923) where it examined its competence in detail and, in particular, indicated that it would be without jurisdiction if the question submitted was beyond the competence of the League Council.[1] Later, that Council brought to the Court the case of the *Frontier between Iraq and Turkey* (1925) in circumstances somewhat similar to those of the *Eastern Carelia Case*. A request was made for an advisory opinion on the interpretation of a treaty, this being in dispute between the parties. Turkey, a party to the dispute, claimed that the question was beyond the Court's powers and therefore refused to be represented before the Court. However, the Court assumed in this case, for reasons which will be subject to further analysis, that the Council had been duly seized of the dispute and that its request for an opinion on its own competence and procedure could be properly answered.[2]

In the later work of the Permanent Court emphasis was occasionally made, particularly by Judge Anzilotti, on the Court's independence in the exercise of its advisory function. Thus, in the *Free City of Danzig and the I.L.O. Case* (1930), Judge Anzilotti found it "inadmissible for the Court to comply with a request based on a hypothesis which is legally unsound."[3] The same judge, disagreeing with the majority in the *Customs Regime between Germany and Austria Case* (1931) where a part of the question was left unanswered in the Opinion, was also "unable to admit that the Court can answer a question other than that which has been put to it or confine itself to answering a part of that question" and insisted that the Court should either "refuse to give the opinion asked for" or "give it on the question as a whole."[4] Finally, he left no doubt as to the power of the Court to determine the limits of its advisory jurisdiction by writing in the case concerning the *Consistence of Certain Decrees with the Constitution of the Free City* (1935) that:

[1] See, *P.C.I.J.*, ser. B, No. 6 at 19 (1923).

[2] See, *P.C.I.J.*, ser. B, No. 12 (1925). And see an analysis of this attitude in Chapter IV, *infra*, at 121.

[3] *P.C.I.J.*, ser. B, No. 18 at 20 (1930).

[4] *P.C.I.J.*, ser. A/B, No. 41 at 69 (1931).

It is indeed difficult to see how the Court's independence of the political organs of the League of Nations could be safeguarded, if it were in the power of the Assembly or the Council to oblige the Court to answer any question which they might see fit to submit to it.[1]

The Permanent Court itself has never admitted any such obligation. On the contrary, by its practice and by the provisions added to its Statute in 1936, its advisory function was made subject to its judicial discretion. It was not therefore surprising that at the time of the last revision of this Court's Rules, the provision dealing with preliminary objections was intentionally reworded in broader terms to allow, *inter alia*, the invocation of such objections in relation to the advisory procedure.[2]

The present Court whose Statute allows it from the outset to give, or not to give, the opinion requested, had more instances in which its advisory competence was disputed. Among its thirteen advisory opinions six include explicit affirmations of the Court's jurisdiction over the case.[3] In one case a state objecting to the power of the Court to give the requested opinion (i.e., to its substantive jurisdiction) explicitly asked the Court to apply Article 36(6) of the Statute and to decide first on its competence.[4] This was the *Peace Treaties Case* (1950) in the first stage of which an opinion was given solely on the jurisdictional question much like the judgments on preliminary objections in contentious cases. In giving this Opinion and in its consideration of the later requests, the present Court has developed, however, an important presumption of jurisdiction in the exercise of the advisory function.[5] The details of this presumption will later be examined. The point of emphasis now is only that the Court, by its Statute and by its practice, extends its *compétence de la compétence* over its advisory jurisdiction. By so doing, it often reaches the position

[1] *P.C.I.J.*, ser. A/B, No. 65 at 61 (1935).

[2] See, *P.C.I.J.*, Ser. D, No. 2 (4th Add.) at 248–9 (1936).

[3] See, *Admission of a State to the United Nations*, [1948] *I.C.J. Rep.* 57, 61–2; *Competence of the General Assembly For the Admission of a State to the United Nations*, [1950] *I.C.J. Rep.* 4, 6; *Interpretation of Peace Treaties with Bulgaria, Hungary and Roumania*, [1950] *I.C.J. Rep.* 65, 71–6; *Reservations to the Convention on the Prevention and Punishment of the Crime of Genocide*, [1951] *I.C.J. Rep.* 15, 19–20; *Judgments of the Administrative Tribunal of the I.L.O. upon Complaints Made Against UNESCO*, [1956] *I.C.J. Rep.* 77, 84; *Certain Expenses of the United Nations*, [1962] *I.C.J. Rep.* 151, 155.

[4] See the Letter of the Government of Czechoslovakia to the Registrar of the Court in *Interpretation of Peace Treaties with Bulgaria, Hungary and Roumania*, Pleadings, Oral Arguments and Documents 204 (*I.C.J.* 1950).

[5] See *Interpretation of Peace Treaties*, [1950] *I.C.J. Rep.* 65, 71; *Reservations to the Genocide Convention*, [1951] I.C.J. Rep. 15, 19; *Judgments of the Administrative Tribunal of the I.L.O.*, [1956] *I.C.J. Rep.* 77, 86; *Certain Expenses of the United Nations*, [1962] *I.C.J. Rep.* 151, 155. And see Chapter IV, *infra* at 123–25.

of questioning the competence of the very organ submitting the request. This is not, however, to say that the Court can arrogate to itself the power to determine the jurisdiction of the requesting organ for any purpose other than defining its own jurisdiction. Both the Court and the requesting organ are independent entities. As Judge Bustamante put it in his dissent in the last Opinion delivered by the Court (though his remark was dealing with the merits of the case):

> [T]he General Assembly's power to determine the limits of the questions upon which it asks an opinion is not incompatible with the power of the Court as master of its own reasoning, to take into consideration all the elements of appraisement which it thinks useful or necessary in order to arrive at a definition of its standpoint on the question on which an opinion is asked.
> Any limitation whatever on this point would run counter to the principle of judicial independence.[1]

B. IS THE POWER INHERENT IN THE JUDICIAL FUNCTION? – EFFECT OF THE *CLAUSE CONTRAIRE*

Despite a few writings to the contrary,[2] it is generally accepted that the parties can deprive an *arbitral* tribunal of its power to determine its jurisdiction by reserving this power to themselves or by investing it in another organ.[3] It is only with this reservation that the present Court had stated the general principle in international arbitration,[4] and it is only with this being borne in mind that the *compétence de la compétence* could be termed "inherent" in the arbitral function.[5] Does the same reservation extend to the Court's power to determine its jurisdiction? Can the parties by a mutual agreement provide that in the event of a dispute as to whether the Court has jurisdiction, one

[1] *Certain Expenses of the United Nations, id.* at 288 (Diss. Op. of Judge Bustamante). *Cf.* Magyary, *supra*, p. 43, note 1 at 93.

[2] See authorities cited in Chapter I, *supra*, p. 26, note 1, and in particular Iaccarino, "Della c.d. Competenza sulla Competenza dei Tribunali Internazionali," 14 *Diritto Internazionale* 357, 375, 403–4 (1960). (Many of the references cited by that author do not, however, support his proposition).

[3] See Chapter I, *supra*, at 25–30. A suggestion made by Huber in the discussions of the "Institut de Droit International" in 1922 went to propose the establishment of a special arbitral tribunal "chargé de statuer sur les questions préjudicielles et fonctionnant comme une sorte de Tribunal des Conflits." 29 *Annuaire* 241 (1922). The "Institut" failed, however, to adopt a general rule to this effect, recommending instead the appeal to the Permanent Court for decisions on whether the dispute between the parties is justiciable. *Id.* at 259. And see the principle adopted in the draft code and the model draft prepared by the International Law Commission as discussed in Chapter I, *supra* at 29–30.

[4] See *Nottebohm Case* (Prel. Obj.), [1953] *I.C.J. Rep.* 111, 119.

[5] This power is, therefore, "inherent" in the sense that it prevails in principle and "can only be taken away by a provision framed for that express purpose." *Rio Grande Irrigation and Land Company Ld. (Great Britain) v. United States, 6 U.N. Rep. Int'l Arb. Awards* 131, 136 (1923).

or both of them, or a third party, or even another organ would decide the issue instead of the Court?

The question is not merely hypothetical. A treaty conferring jurisdiction on the Permanent Court had reserved a certain jurisdictional question to be answered only by the Council of the League.[1] Other treaties explicitly empowered the parties thereto to decide by the unilateral declaration of each whether the dispute related to the area excluded from the Court's jurisdiction.[2] This has been even clearer in some declarations of acceptance of the present Court's continued jurisdiction.[3] It was indeed in this latter domain that the Court had the only chances to pronounce on the issue, though it managed in all cases to avoid an explicit answer. This aspect of the problem is however examined in a later part of this study where the question is reconsidered in a wider perspective.[4] Our concern here is limited to the problem as presented in the jurisdiction conferred on the Court by an agreement between the parties, that is to say, to the type of jurisdiction which is closely analogous to that of arbitral tribunals. This type of jurisdiction is based on Article 36(1) of the Statute and is normally subject to the powers of the Court provided for in other provisions including Article 36(6). By stipulating for the deprivation of the Court of the power contained in this last provision, the parties are obviously departing from, or at least are not acting in conformity with, the Statute. Whether such non-conformity is necessarily incompatible with the Statute is not agreed upon. The arguments for and against the validity of the *clause contraire* are mainly centered around this controversial point.

1. Arguments Militating Against the Validity of the Clause Contraire

Major among the possible arguments against depriving the Court by the explicit agreement of the parties of the power provided for in

[1] See, Pact of Non-Aggression and Arbitration between the Hellenic Republic and the Kingdom of Roumania, Art. 5, signed at Geneva on March 21, 1928, 108 *L.N.T.S.* 187, 191.

[2] See, *e.g.*, Convention of Judicial Settlement, Arbitration and Conciliation between Czechoslovakia and Turkey, Art. 2, signed at Ankara, on March 17, 1931, 133 *L.N.T.S.* 151. And see Economic Cooperation agreements concluded with the United States where compromissory clauses limited the resort to the present Court "by the terms and conditions of such effective recognition as [each party] has heretofore given to the compulsory jurisdiction of International Court of Justice under Article 36 of the Statute of the Court" in [1948–1949] *I.C.J.Y.B.* 152–5. As a result of such clauses the self-judging reservation in the U.S. declaration [Appendix VI, no. 145] is inserted in these treaties.

[3] See Appendix VII, No. 6(B), No. 7.

[4] See Chapter VI, *infra*.

Article 36(6) of the Statute, are the following:

(a) The Court as an international court of justice, in fact the principal one, should be differentiated in this respect from arbitral tribunals. The principle of the *compétence de la compétence,* as said the Court itself, "assumes particular force when the international tribunal is no longer an arbitral tribunal constituted by a special agreement between the parties for the purpose of adjudicating on a particular dispute, but is an institution which has been pre-established by an international instrument defining its jurisdiction and regulating its operation and is... the principal judicial organ of the United Nations."[1] Assuming this stronger position in the structure of the Court, the principle becomes more independent from the will of the parties, and acquires an objective character as a "structural rule" necessary for the proper functioning of the Court.[2]

(b) As the *compétence de la compétence* is provided for in the Statute of the Court, it becomes all the more inadmissible for the parties to repeal it by their accord, the Statute being higher in this respect to any agreement between the parties. Both the present Court and its predecessor have indicated that they would not depart from the Statute on the proposal of the parties,[3] giving room to the proposition that special agreements "must be considered to have, as tacitly appended clauses thereto, all the pertinent articles of the Court's Statute."[4] This superiority of the Statute does not of course follow from the general rules of construction such as the rule of *lex specialis* and of *lex posterior,* both of which would lead here to the opposite conclusion, nor does it need to be based on a theoretical hierarchy of norms. By the provisions of its Statute (Article 1) and of the Charter of the United Nations (Article 92), the Court is supposed to function only in accordance with the Statute. Besides, the acceptance of the Statute, which is itself an integral part of the Charter (Article 92) creates "an obligation under the Charter" in the sense of Article 103 thereof, and thus prevails by virtue of this latter Article over any other conflicting agreement made between members of the United Nations.[5] This last argument could not, however, apply to states accepting the jurisdiction of the Court which are not members of the

[1] *Nottebohm Case* (Prel. Obj.), [1953] *I.C.J. Rep.* 111, 119.

[2] See Iaccarino, *supra,* p. 25 note 1 at 403; Berlia, *supra,* p. 25, note 4 at 116–8, 150.

[3] See Chapter III, *infra* at 104–6.

[4] See, Observations of Judge Kellogg in the *Free Zones Case, P.C.I.J.*, ser. A, No. 24 at 33 (1930).

[5] See this argument expounded in Gross, "Bulgaria Invokes the Connally Amendment", 56 *Am. J. Int'l L.* 357, 380 (1962).

United Nations, as these undertake to accept only the obligations under Article 94 of the Charter,[1] and are, consequently, not bound by Article 103.

(c) The Statute is, after all, a multilateral treaty, Article 36(6) of which is an important institutional provision conferring on the Court a serious power that contributes in distinguishing it as a judicial institution. Any reservation by one or more of the parties as to this provision could not therefore be permitted under the general rules applicable to reservations to multilateral conventions which may apply here by analogy.[2] According to these rules no such reservation becomes valid unless unanimously accepted by all other parties to the Convention;[3] or, if we apply the less rigid criterion adopted by the Court in the *Reservations to the Genocide Convention Case*, a reservation could not be valid if it is incompatible with the subject and purpose of the Convention.[4] If the first criterion is not likely to be applied here because other parties to the Statute would not normally express their views on stipulations in a bilateral agreement made *inter alios;* the second criterion is capable of invalidating any stipulation denying the Court an important power conferred on it by its Statute.

(d) Should the rules related to reservations to multilateral conventions prove not directly applicable in this respect, it is to be noticed that the Statute of the Court – like the General Act of Berlin in the words of Judge Van Eysinga – "does not create a number of contractual relations between a number of States, relations which may be replaced as regards some of these States by other contractual relations; it does not constitute a *jus dispositivum*, but provides... a regime, a statute, a constitution."[5] Such a "constitution" could be amended only in

[1] See Security Council Resolution of October 15th, 1946, Para. 1, in *U.N. Security Council Off. Rec.*, 1st Year, 2d Sess., No. 19 at 468 (1946); [1962–1963] *I.C.J.Y.B.* 21–2.

[2] A reservation under these general rules is usually a declaration submitted by a state *on signing, ratifying, accepting or acceding* to a treaty, as a condition of its willingness to become a party to the treaty.

See Harvard Research, Draft Convention on the Law of Treaties, Art. 13, 29 *Am. J. Int'l L.* (2 Supp.) 657, 659 (1935); Texts of Articles of the Code of the Law of Treaties Prepared by Sir Gerald Fitzmaurice, Special Rapporteur for the International Law Commission, [1956] *I.L.C. Yearbook* 104 at 115 (Arts, 37, 38); U.N. Doc. No. A/CN 4/101 (1956). And see generally for a differentiation between the above and reservations in instruments accepting the Court's jurisdiction, Maus, *Les Réserves dans les Déclarations d'Acceptation de la Juridiction Obligatoire de la Cour Internationale de Justice* 93–5 (1959); Hudson, *The Permanent Court of International Justice* 397 (1st ed. 1934).

[3] See this view as expressed in Report of the International Law Commission Coverning the Work of its Third Session, *U.N. Gen. Ass. Off. Rec.*, 6th sess., Supp. No. 9 at 2–8 (Doc. No. A/1858) (1951).

[4] [1951] *I.C.J. Rep.* 14, 24–8 (Adv. Op.).

[5] The *Oscar Chinn Case*, *P.C.I.J.*, ser. A/B, No. 63 at 133–4 (Indiv. Op. of Judge Van Eysinga).

accordance with its provisions (Articles 69 and 70) and not by a special agreement between some of the parties thereto. A departure from the rule embodied in Article 36(6) will thus constitute an unauthorized amendment of the Statute as far as the parties to the agreement are concerned.

(e) Finally, the clause accepting the submission of disputes to the Court while simultaneously reserving to the parties the right to determine unilaterally whether a specific question is covered or not by it, may be regarded as ' devoid of an element of effective legal obligation." Regardless of its validity as a legal instrument, such a clause cannot be invoked as a basis of jurisdiction against the will of the respondent. For this reason, it has no practical significance either. The consent of the respondent which is required to make the agreement effective is sufficient in itself to base jurisdiction upon, regardless of the agreement.[1]

2. *Argument for the Validity of the* Clause Contraire

Against the line of argument followed above stands the other viewpoint which sees that nothing in the nature of the Court or in its Statute deprives the parties of the right to reserve to themselves or to any other organ the power to determine whether the Court has jurisdiction over questions that arise in cases referred to the Court by their mutual agreement. In this view, the rule provided for in Article 36(6) is not absolute.[2] It is a general rule which the Court itself found to be applicable only "in the absence of any agreement to the contrary."[3] To insert such an agreement in the treaty conferring jurisdiction on the Court will not therefore be in violation of any obligation under the Statute. Nor would this necessarily be so even if Article 36(6) was expressing a binding rule. For it could always be maintained that the real value of the *clause contraire* depends on its invocation in practice. If it is invoked in a case before the Court this means that the Court's jurisdiction over this case was never accepted. If it is not invoked at

[1] See this argument as developed in Lauterpacht's Separate Opinion in *Certain Norwegian Loans*, [1957] *I.C.J. Rep.* 9, 62. And *cf.* the Swiss Observations in *Interhandel Case*, Pleadings, Oral Arguments and Documents 382, 408 (*I.C.J.*, 1959).

[2] See Rosenne, *The International Court of Justice* 341 (1957). *Cf.*, Hudson, *supra*, p. 50, note 2.

[3] *Nottebohm Case*, *supra*, p. 49, note 1 at 119. But notice that the Court made this reserve while stating the general principle *in international arbitration*. To say that the Court meant to extend it also to the principle as it stands in the Statute (as thought by Gross, *supra*, p. 49, note 5 at 379) could hardly be concluded from the wording of the judgment.

all, the Court is left free to exercise over the case the power covered by Article 36(6).

Thus, regardless of whether Article 36(6) is binding on the parties, the insertion of the clause in the agreement is, according to the above analysis, not incompatible with the Statute. As a result, all arguments raised against the validity of the clause on the basis of its incompatibility with the Statute loose ground. Despite the fact that it is not in conformity with Article 36(6), it is argued in this view that the *clause contraire* is either tolerated by the Article or is meant to allow the application thereof in the limits to which jurisdiction has really been accepted by the respondent. Yet, the *clause contraire* can be deduced only from the most explicit stipulation, due to the very fact of its departure from a principle "strong enough to outweigh all presumptions to the contrary."[1] Consequently, a stipulation that runs counter to the rule of Article 36(6) of the Statute is subject, in this argument, to strict interpretation.

An important observation presents itself in connection with the above arguments. Even if the latter view is upheld, the Court could not declare the validity of the *clause contraire* except after it actually examines its terms and its compatibility with its judicial nature and its Statute. By carrying this very examination it will be in fact exercising the first and indeed the inevitable part of the *compétence de la compétence* from which it could not be deprived. This most preliminary aspect of the power – in a sense the judicial review of the jurisdictional instruments involved, their *clause contraire* included – applies, therefore, regardless of the content of the parties' agreement. Through this review the Court will be able to pronounce on the validity of the conventional stipulations taking away from it the full power to determine its jurisdiction. The course expected to be followed by the Court in this respect is considered in detail in a later part of this study.[2]

C. THE POWER IS GENERALLY INVOKED AND EXERCISED PRELIMINARILY

The Court's *compétence de la compétence* is one of many incidental powers provided for by the Statute in order to enable the Court to do justice in the claims submitted to it.[3] But unlike most of the other

[1] Rosenne, *supra*, p. 51, note 2.

[2] See Chapter VI, *infra* at 294–97.

[3] Other incidental powers are conferred on the Court, as will be shown, by virtue of Articles 41, 48, 53, 60, 61, 62 and 63 of the Statute, and Article 63 of the Rules.

incidental jurisdictional powers possessed by the Court, this power could, except in a few circumstances, be invoked in practice only in a preliminary stage of the proceedings. This is not because of any inherent formalistic requirement but simply because the Court's substantive jurisdiction is primarily based on the parties' consent and unless they object timely to it the Court will be inclined to assume that its competence over the case has been accepted. It is, in other words, a practical matter rather than one of abstract theory. In fact, when the issue was first discussed hypothetically there was some disposition within the Permanent Court to allow the making of objections to jurisdiction in the course of the proceedings on the merits.[1] But when the first practical occasion for pronouncing on the matter arose, the Court, with three judges dissenting on this point, concluded that it had jurisdiction from the fact that the respondent state objected to jurisdiction only in the rejoinder and after submitting its counter-memorial that was dealing solely with the merits.[2] Acceptance of jurisdiction was assumed to have existed at the time of the submission of the counter-case and a later objection was not considered an adequate reason to invalidate it. The dissenting opinions were, however, strongly against the concept that objections to jurisdiction ought to have been in that case, or ought to be in general, preliminary in character.[3] Although no other case since has led to a serious discussion of the issue, the principle of the *Minority Schools Case* (1928) is normally recognized, with perhaps some reservations which the detailed study of the rule of *forum prorogatum* will later reveal.

Nothing in the above principle entails, however, that an objection to jurisdiction has to be formulated in a way to exclude any reference to the merits of the dispute. The Permanent Court considered in the *German Interests in Polish Upper Silesia Case* (1925) an objection that

[1] See *P.C.I.J.*, ser. D., No. 2 (Add.) at 88 (1926) (Judge Moore's statement).

The arbitral practice gives, on the other hand, the impression that the time of presenting objections to jurisdiction was a matter left to the rules of each arbitral tribunal and was not subject to any rigid general rule. See examples in [U.N. Secretariat] *Commentary on the Draft Convention on Arbitral Procedure Adopted by the International Law Commission in its Fifth Session*, U.N. Doc., A/CN.4/92 at 227–9 (1955) (U.N. Pub. Sales No. 1955, v. 1).

For the rule in domestic courts, see a comparison between its different aspects and the practice before the Permanent Court in [Institut für ausländisches öffentliches Recht und Völkerrecht] *Statut et Règlement de la Cour Permanente de Justice Internationale* 269, 270–71 (1934).

[2] See *Minority Schools in Upper Silesia Case*, *P.C.I.J.*, ser. A, No. 15 at 22–9 (1928).

[3] See *id.* at 48–54 (Diss. Op. of Judge Huber); at 56–9 (Diss. Op. of Judge Nyholm); and at 67–73 (Diss. Op. of Deputy Judge Negulesco). Judge Huber thus stated the rule in an opposite manner: "The disputes as to the jurisdiction provided for under the last paragraph of Article 36 of the Statute are not necessarily, except in particular circumstances, preliminary pleas." *Id.* at 50.

dealt also with arguments on the merits noting that it was "submitted at a time when no document of procedure on the merits had been filed."[1] On a later date, it considered in the *Pajzs, Csàky, Esterházy* case (1936) objections to jurisdiction that were included in the counter-memorial itself as valid and timely objections pointing out that "the Statute and Rules of Court lay down no formal conditions which must be fulfilled by documents submitting a preliminary objection... which are not satisfied by the Counter-Memorial." Hence, it regarded that counter-memorial as "lodging a preliminary objection."[2] Not very different from this attitude was that of the present Court in the first phase of the *Ambatielos Case* (1952). Although the respondent Government did inform the Court of its intention to contest the Court's jurisdiction in the very document in which it acknowledged the receipt of the application,[3] only the counter-memorial of that Government pleading to the merits contained a preliminary objection "under Article 62 of the Rules of Court."[5] The President of the Court did not object to this attitude,[5] which was described by the respondent's Counsel himself as a "somewhat unusual course."[6]

What, then, does the practical requirement of raising objections to jurisdiction in the earliest stage of the procedure amount to?

Before 1926 nothing in the Rules of Court referred to preliminary objections despite the fact that the question was discussed at the preliminary session of the Permanent Court when the 1922 Rules were drafted.[7] On that occasion Article 36 of the draft prepared by the Drafting Committee (as well as Article 36 of the revised text of the Secretariat's draft) provided that:

> The parties may raise objections. An objection to the jurisdiction of the Court may however only be raised *in limine litis*, or as soon as possible, and in any case before the commencement of the oral proceedings, unless the Court shall decide otherwise.[8]

This Article was later dropped, leaving the Rules silent on the treatment of objections. However, two contentious cases arising under the 1922 Rules provided occasions for objections to jurisdiction. In the *Mavrommatis Palestine Concessions Case* (1924) after the Greek

[1] *P.C.I.J.*, ser. A, No. 6 at 15 (1925).
[2] See *P.C.I.J.*, ser. C, No. 80 at 1451, 1452 (Order of March 10, 1936).
[3] See *Ambatielos Case*, Pleadings, Oral Arguments and Documents 522 (*I.C.J.* 1953).
[4] *Id.* at 132.
[5] See *Ambatielos Case*, [1952] *I.C.J. Rep.* 16 (Order).
[6] Statement of Sir Eric Beckett, in Pleadings, *op. cit.* note 3 at 281.
[7] See *P.C.I.J.*, ser. D, No. 2 at 203, 214 (1922).
[8] See *id.* at 434 (The Drafting Committee's draft); *id.* at 408 (the Secretariat's draft).

application and case were filed, the respondent (Great Britain) informed the Court of its intention to present a plea to jurisdiction, whereupon the President of the Court fixed a time-limit for "filing the British plea raising a *preliminary objection* to the jurisdiction of the Court."[1] Again in the *German Interests in Polish Upper Silesia Case* (1925) after the Court was notified of an agreement between the parties as to the filing of the written pleadings, it was orally informed by the respondent (Poland) that it intended to file "a preliminary objection." This was later included in the "Memorial," opening the door for an interlocutory procedure on the jurisdictional issue which was concluded even before the applicant state had filed its first pleadings.[2]

In 1926 a new Article added to the Rules (Article 38) provided for the possibility of the filing of "any preliminary objection" when proceedings are instituted by an application. This was enlarged in Article 62 of the 1936 Rules to allow such objections regardless of the way proceedings were instituted, and the latter Article became after slight modifications Article 62 of the Rules of the present Court. None of these provisions speak categorically of objections to jurisdiction, though in their drafting the attention of the Court was chiefly directed to these latter objections.[3] They speak of preliminary objections that "must be filed by a party at the latest before the expiry of the time-limit fixed for the delivery of its first pleading." This has been interpreted by the Permanent Court to cover "any objection of which the effect will be, if the objection is upheld, to interrupt further proceedings in the case, and which it will therefore be appropriate for the Court to deal with before enquiring into the merits."[4]

[1] *P. C. I. J.*, ser. C. No. 5–I at 479 (1924) (Emphasis added).

[2] See *P.C.I.J.*, ser. C, No. 9–I at 119–25 (Response Exceptionnelle du Gouvernement Polonais, dated June 26, 1925), *id.* at 20–1 (Order of August 25, 1925 including the suit concerning the subject matter of the objections on the list).

[3] See *P.C.I.J.*, ser. D, No. 2 (Add.) at 78–94; *id.* (3rd Add.) at 84–97, 148–50, 644–9, 705–8. Judge Hudson found furthermore, in his dissent in the *Panevezys-Saldutiskis Railway case, P.C.I.J.*, ser. A/B, No. 76 at 42 (1939), that, "objections which have been the subject of adjudication have related almost invariably to the jurisdiction or competence of the Court" (*id.* at 44) and that the Court "may hesitate to admit the preliminary character of certain types of objections which do not raise questions of jurisdiction." *Id.* at 45.

[4] The *Panevezys-Saldutiskis Railway Case, P.C.I.J.*, ser. A/B, No. 76 at 16.

See also the Separate Opinion of De Visscher and Count Rostworowski in the same case: "[A]n objection is *prima facie* preliminary when, by its nature or its purpose, it appears directed against the judicial proceedings, that is, against the law on which they rest." *Id.* at 24. And see Anzilotti's definition given in his Separate Opinion in the *Electricity Company of Sofia and Bulgaria Case* (Prel. Obj.), *P.C.I.J.*, ser. A/B, No. 77 at 95: "A preliminary objection is an objection of which the purpose and the effect are to prevent the continuance of proceedings before the Court, without prejudging the question whether the right claimed by the applicant exists or not."

No problem relating to the timing of the preliminary objection arose under the present Court as no party seemed to be particularly dilatory in filing its objections. Two observations are, however, pertinent in this respect:

First, some objections to jurisdiction cannot be preliminary in character as the occasion for their presentation does not arise except in a later stage of the proceedings. For these, the Court's *compétence de la compétence* could be invoked even after the delivery of the first pleadings as long as they are filed before the court can assume, by virtue of the principle of *forum prorogatum*, that they were relinquished. An example of this type of objection in the work of the present Court is the Albanian objection to the Court's jurisdiction to assess the amount of compensation due from Albania to Great Britain in the second phase of the *Corfu Channel Case* (1949).[1]

Second, if the application submitted to the Court does not rely on any jurisdictional title, that is, if it is obvious that the Court lacks all jurisdiction, it cannot reach the conclusion that it has jurisdiction as long as this is not clearly acquiesced to by the defendant. In such a case the Court will not have even the incidental power to determine its jurisdiction. It will merely make an "administrative" order to remove the case from the list. Jurisdiction, even the most incidental jurisdiction, assumes, as will be shown, a proper seisin of the Court. If the Court is not properly seized, it has no jurisdictional powers.[2]

D. THE POWER SHOULD, IN THE FIRST PLACE, BE INVOKED BY THE PARTIES, UNLESS IT COVERS ISSUES NOT RELATED TO THEIR ACCEPTANCE OF THE COURT'S JURISDICTION

If neither of the parties disputes the jurisdiction of the Court, can the Court, nevertheless, raise the issue *proprio motu* and exercise its *compétence de la compétence* to decide whether or not it has jurisdiction? Most writers answer this question in the affirmative, without making any distinction as to the type of the jurisdictional issue involved. To substantiate their stand they rely on certain constructions of the Statute and the Rules of Court, on statements of individual

[1] The Albanian Government questioned the Court's jurisdiction to assess the amount of compensation for the first time only in the last oral statement submitted in its name by M. Pierre Cot in the second phase of the case related to the merits. See 4 *Corfu Channel Case* Pleadings, Oral Arguments and Documents 613, 633 (*I.C.J.*). This objection was not subject to further discussions between the parties but the Court dealt with it extensively. See [1949] *I.C.J. Rep.* 4, 23–6. And see *infra* at 75–76.

[2] See details on this point in Chapter III, *infra* at 84–89.

judges, and cite cases in which the Permanent Court is alleged to have exercised this power *proprio motu*.

1. Article 53 of the Statute and Article 32(2) of the Rules

The first argument is based on Article 53 of the Statute and Article 32(2) of the Rules. The first of these articles allows the Court to decide the cases in which "one of the parties does not appear before the Court or fails to defend its case" only after satisfying itself that it has jurisdiction in accordance with Articles 36 and 37 of the Statute. This provision clearly clothes the Court with the power to determine its jurisdiction *proprio motu* in the case provided for in it. But is it, as is often alleged,[1] an "indirect expression" of a general rule that the Court can apply in all cases? This is doubtful. The Court's jurisdiction is derived from the consent of the parties as manifested in the instruments and facts involved. Such a consent could not be presumed from the mere absence of the party or from its failure to defend its case. Thus, the Statute empowers the court before pronouncing on the facts and law (the merits) to ascertain whether the parties have consented to its jurisdiction. Such a situation should not be analogized to the case where both parties are present and have defended their cases. By doing so without objecting to the Court's jurisdiction they have made possible a conclusion to the effect that they have consented to such a jurisdiction at least by conferring it on the Court according to the principle of *forum prorogatum*. There is no reason that the Court should ignore this acceptance of its jurisdiction and go far to investigate other instruments or facts assimilating this clear case to the case of the absence of the parties where the presumption is to the contrary.

Article 32(2) of the Rules of Court provides, on the other hand, that when a case is brought before the Court by means of an application, this application must, *inter alia*, "as far as possible, specify the provision on which the applicant founds the jurisdiction of the Court..." This Article has been mentioned to support the argument that if the requirement provided for in it is not met, "the Court should at once raise the question of its jurisdiction" and "even if the requirement be met, it ought to be possible for the Court acting *proprio motu* to

[1] See, *e.g.*, Fitzmaurice, "The Law and Procedure of the International Court of Justice," 34 *Brit. Yb. Int'l L.* 1, 28–9 (1958); Maus, *supra* p. 50, note 2 at 33. And see *Electricity Company of Sofia and Bulgaria Case, P.C.I.J.*, ser. A/B, No. 77 at 103 (Diss. Op. of Judge Urrutia).

examine the sufficiency of the basis of jurisdiction set out before the application is transmitted to the intended respondent."[1]

Such an argument goes, however, directly against the Statute (article 40(2)), the Rules (Article 33), and the practice of the Court. According to the two Articles cited the Registrar of the Court "shall *forthwith* communicate the application to all concerned," before the Court can carry any investigation as to its contents.[2] And according to the practice of the Court, its attitude will depend on the reaction of the respondent state. If this refuses to submit to the jurisdiction of the Court, the Court will either remove the case from the list by an order (if the application lacks all bases of jurisdiction),[3] or initiate the preliminary objection proceedings (if the respondent submits any such objections), or act in accordance with Article 53 of the Statute (if the respondent fails to attend, or to defend its case). In the first of these situations the Court will not exercise the *compétence de la compétence;* in the second its exercise of it will not be *proprio motu;* and in the third the Court will be complying with a clear provision of the Statute.

2. *Individual opinions*

The argument for the exercise of the Court's power to determine its jurisdiction *proprio motu* relies also on individual opinions of some judges of the Court, particularly those who were themselves writers of international law. However, among all the judges of the present Court only Lord McNair and Judge Lauterpacht took pains to emphasize this view in explicit terms. Thus, dissenting in the *Anglo-Iranian Oil Company Case* (Prel. Obj.) (1952), Judge McNair wrote that:

> An international tribunal cannot regard a question of jurisdiction solely as a question *inter partes*. That aspect does not exhaust the matter. The Court

[1] Hudson, *The Permanent Court of International Justice* 419 (2d ed. 1943).

[2] This procedure was justified by the fact that the State against which the application is filed may accept the Court's jurisdiction thus saving the Court any further effort of enquiry. See *P.C.I.J.*, ser. D, No. 2 (3d Add.) 67–9, 845 (1936). The argument in the text based on this procedure was also considered by Hudson, *supra*, note 1.

[3] This attitude was followed by the present Court in the eight cases in which the application lacking all bases of jurisdiction was not met with acceptance by the intended respondent. See Orders removing the following cases from the list: *Treatment in Hungary of Aircraft and Crew of U.S.A.* (*U.S.A. v. Hungary*), [1954] *I.C.J. Rep.* 99; *Same* (*U.S.A. v. U.S.S.R.*), [1954] *I.C.J. Rep.* 103; *Aerial Incident of March 10th, 1953*, [1956] *I.C.J. Rep.* 6; *Aerial Incident of October 7th, 1952*, [1956] *I.C.J. Rep.* 9; *Antarctica Case* (*United Kingdom v. Argentina*), [1956] *I.C.J. Rep.* 12; *Antarctica Case* (*U.K. v. Chile*), [1956] *I.C.J. Rep.* 15; *Aerial Incident of Sept. 4th, 1954*, (1958] *I.C.J. Rep.* 158; *Aerial Incident of Nov. 7, 1954*, [1959] *I.C.J. Rep.* 276.

itself acting *proprio motu*, must be satisfied that any State which is brought before it... has consented to the jurisdiction.[1]

Judge Lauterpacht, also dissenting in the *Case concerning Certain Norwegian Loans* (1957), declared that the Court "must have before it as a basis of its jurisdiction a valid text [and that] it must ascertain the existence of that text" even when the respondent did not question its validity.[2]

As to the Permanent Court the alleged principle was pronounced with more frequency in individual opinions though they were also generally in the dissent.

Judge Moore dissenting in the *Mavrommatis Palestine Concessions Case* (1924) cited the French repository of jurisprudence by Dalloz as saying that "jurisdiction is essentially a question of public order [Fr. *d'ordre public*]" and that "even though the Parties be silent the tribunal, if it finds that competence is lacking, is bound of its own motion to dismiss the case..."[3] This was, however, a description of French domestic law and was mentioned in that respect to prove a different point.

The first individual opinion affirming the exercise *proprio motu* of the *compétence de la compétence* was, therefore, Judge Huber's dissent in the very case in which the Court widely affirmed the principle of *forum prorogatum* – the *Minority Schools Case* (1928). Yet, Judge Huber did not pronounce this opinion without reservation as it is sometimes wrongly quoted. He developed the following distinction:

When a case has been referred to the Court under a clause conferring compulsory jurisdiction and no objection to the jurisdiction is raised, the Court is not called upon, except under Article 53 of the Statute, *ex officio* to consider whether it has jurisdiction; it will assume that it has jurisdiction in the absence of an objection. But, when giving judgment in virtue of jurisdiction implicitly or explicitly recognized by the Parties, it must *ex officio* ascertain on what legal foundation it is to base its judgment upon the claims of the parties. *Jura novit curia*. The Court's jurisdiction is determined by the treaty or special agreement establishing that jurisdiction, and not by the contentions maintained by the Parties in the particular case.[4]

[1] [1952] *I.C.J. Rep.* 93, 116 (Diss. Op. of Judge McNair).

[2] [1957] *I.C.J. Rep.* 9, 61 (Diss. Op. of Judge Lauterpacht). And see an aside envisaging the possibility of a decision on jurisdiction reached *proprio motu* in Judge Read's dissent in the *Judgments of the International Tribunal of the I.L.O. Case* (Adv. Op.), [1956] *I.C.J. Rep.* 77, 143, and a dictum in the dissent of Judge Morelli in the *South-West Africa Cases* (Prel. Obj.), [1962] *I.C.J. Rep.* 319, 565, to the effect that the absence of a "genuine dispute" between the parties "would require to be found by the Court *proprio motu*."

[3] *P.C.I.J.*, ser. A, No. 2 at 58 (1924) (Diss. Op. of Judge Moore).

[4] *P.C.I.J.*, ser. A, No. 15 at 53–4 (1928) (Diss. Op. of Judge Huber). In this case, the Court in the course of differentiating between the jurisdiction of domestic courts and its own explained that domestic courts have an obligation to ensure the observance of their juris-

This distinction does not explain why there should be a difference, in this respect, between the "compulsory jurisdiction" of the Court and its *ad hoc* jurisdiction, and in particular, why the *ante hoc* agreement of the parties should be differentiated from their *post hoc* agreement as concluded from their contentions before the Court.

Again, in his observations on the Court's Order of December 6th, 1930, in the *Free Zones Case* (Second phase), Judge Kellogg wrote that it was not necessary that the question of jurisdiction be raised by one of the litigant parties. "It may and should be raised by the Court on its own initiative, as was done in the Eastern Carelia case."[1] The citation of this last case could hardly be helpful in this respect, not merely because this was an advisory case but because, assimilated to the contentious procedure, this would be a typical case to which Article 53 of the Statute applies, as one of the parties did not appear before the Court. On the other hand, the objections which Judge Kellogg was talking of did not relate in any way to the consent of the parties but rather to the ability of the Court to deal with questions explicitly submitted to it by the parties.

In a less clear language, but also in a situation where the consent of the parties was beyond doubt, Judge Negulesco stated in his dissent in the case of the *Free Zones* (Judgment) (1932), that if one of the parties was no longer entitled to raise an objection against a certain power of the Court, "it could still have been raised, as of right, in virtue of the Statute, at any time during the procedure."[2]

Finally, Judge Urrutia dissenting in the *Electric Company of Sofia and Bulgaria Case* (Prel. Obj.) (1939), after defending the freedom of the Court to base its judgment on the legal ground it sees fit even if both parties defend another ground, concluded that: "It is not only the right but the duty of the Court *ex officio* to make sure of its jurisdiction [Fr. *de s'assurer, même d'office, de sa compétence*]..."[3]

This latter case provided, however, two other dissenting opinions in which the power of the Court to investigate its jurisdiction despite the accord of the parties was doubted by Anzilotti,[4] and was found to be usually unnecessary by Hudson.[5] It should also be noted that,

diction *ex officio*, *id.* at 23, which may imply *a contrario* that the Court viewed itself as not under such an obligation.

[1] *P.C.I.J.*, ser. A, No. 24 at 43 (1930) (Observations of Judge Kellogg).

[2] *P.C.I.J.*, ser. A/B, No. 46 at 193 (1932) (Diss. Op. of Judge Negulesco).

[3] *P.C.I.J.*, ser. A/B, No. 77 at 102–3 (Diss. Op. of Judge Urrutia).

[4] *Id.* at 89. Compare, Anzilotti's dissent in *the Interpretation of the Statute of the Memel Territory Case* (*Merits*), *P.C.I.J.*, ser. A/B, No. 49 at 294, 349–50 (1932).

[5] *P.C.I.J.*, ser. A/B, No. 77 at 118, Compare, Hudson, *supra* p. 58, note 1 at 419.

with the exception of the opinions given in the *Free Zones Cases* and possibly the *Minority Schools Case*, all the above statements were mere *dicta* as objections to jurisdiction were already filed by some party in each of these cases.

3. Practice of the Court

The third ground for allowing the Court to inquire *proprio motu*, in all cases, whether it has jurisdiction, is based on an alleged practice of the Court itself.[1]

No precedent could be cited in the work of the present Court where a judgment has openly discussed this problem. Only in the *Haya de la Torre Case* (1951) did the Court refuse to answer a question contained in the submissions of the parties, because doing so was "not part of the Court's judicial function."[2] This refusal was in fact based on considerations of propriety, derived from the Court's concept of its discretionary powers, which, as will repeatedly be shown, is technically a different question than that of jurisdiction. And, at any rate, the objection was not related to the parties' consent to adjudicate the point but to the inability of the Court to pronounce on it.

As to the Permanent Court, it is here maintained that its decisions do not provide an adequate and clear authority for the suggestion they are often cited to support. None of these decisions has raised objections related to the parties' acceptance of jurisdiction in the absence of objections to the same effect advanced by the parties.

In its first judgment, the Permanent Court discussed whether each of the Applicant Governments had a clear legal interest to justify the institution of the proceedings. This, it is true, was undertaken in the absence of a challenge to the admissibility of the claim on this ground. But it should not be forgotten that this very question was, as the

[1] Arbitral cases could also be cited in this context. As early as in the case of *Henry E. Kenney* before the United States-Peruvian claims commission established by the Convention of 12.1.1863, the Umpire "withheld his opinion" because he "perceived he had no authority" to decide on the merits and refused later to amend his conclusion when the commissioners requested him to "withdraw his decision on the ground that it was made upon a point not submitted to him." 2 Moore, *Arbitrations* 1626–7. See also the *Morerie case* before the Brazilian-Bolivian Arbitral Tribunal, cited in Ralston, *The Law and Procedure of International Tribunals* 47 (1926); the *Ottoman Dept Arbitration*, 1 *U.N. Rep. Int'l Arb. Awards* 529, 565 1925). Reviewing the arbitral practice, on this point, two authors concluded, however, that: "It is questionable ... whether the International Court of Justice has power to raise, of its own accord, a question concerning its jurisdiction, where it is not disputed by the parties." Simpson and Fox, *International Arbitration* 69 n. 16 (1959).

[2] [1951] *I.C.J. Rep.* 71, 79. See a criticism of this part of the decision in Rosenne, *supra*, p. 51, note 2 at 76.

Court explained, left by the respondent to the appreciation of the Court,[1] and is not, at any event, a question of consent.

In the *Chorzow Factory Case* (Jurisdiction) (1927), the Court wrote that it "will, in the event of an objection – or when it has automatically [Fr. *d'office*] to consider the question – only affirm its jurisdiction provided that the force of the arguments militating in favor of it is preponderant."[2] Although this statement gives room for the possibility of the Court considering its jurisdiction *ex officio,* that part of it was a mere dictum, as the Court was already examining some objections presented by the respondent against its jurisdiction. Besides, the Court itself has qualified its statement by adding after a few lines that: "The question as to the existence of a doubt nullifying its jurisdiction need not be considered when [the parties'] intention can be demonstrated in a manner convincing to the Court."[3] Such a demonstration – it should always be recalled – was found a year later in the mere absence of objections to jurisdiction in an early stage of the proceedings in the *Minority Schools Case* (1928).[4]

In the *Serbian Loans Case* (1929) and the *Brazilian Loans Case* (1929), both of which were submitted by special agreements, the Court after ascertaining that the dispute was strictly between the states concerned, discussed whether it was proper to decide the questions submitted to it which were governed exclusively by municipal law.[5] In the words of the Court, it was engaged in the process of defining "with reference to the provisions governing its jurisdiction and functions, the task entrusted to it by the Special Agreement."[6] There is no doubt that the Court has always the power to ascertain the question it is required to answer, but this is not to say that it can always investigate whether this question has been submitted to it by the parties when none of them disputes this point. Therefore, even the two dissents in the *Serbian Loans Case,*[7] and the one in the *Brazilian Loans Case,*[8] which found that the character of the dispute was such that would render the Court without jurisdiction to decide the cases, do not indicate that the *compétence de la compétence* could always be

[1] *The S.S. Wimbledon, P.C.I.J.*, ser. A, No. 1 at 20 (1923).

[2] *P.C.I.J.*, ser. A, No. 9 at 32 (1927).

[3] *Ibid.*

[4] *P.C.I.J.*, ser. A, No. 15 at 26 (1928).

[5] See *Serbian Loans Case, P.C.I.J.*, ser. A, Nos. 20/21 at 16–7; *Brazilian Loans Case, id.* at 101–2 (1929).

[6] *Id.* at 16.

[7] *Id.* at 62–63 (Diss. Op. of Judge Pessôa); *id.* at 76–80 (Diss. Op. of Judge *ad hoc* Novacovitch).

[8] *Id.* at 139–142 (Diss. Op. of Judge Pessôa).

exercised *proprio motu*. In these two cases both the Court and the dissenting judges raised no point as to the unquestioned acceptance of jurisdiction. Their investigation related only to the identification of the real parties to the dispute, and to the problem of whether the Court's jurisdiction could be exercised over disputes governed by municipal law.[1]

Another noted case where the Court discussed the propriety of taking a certain measure requested by both parties is the *Free Zones Case* (1929). The parties asked the Court in this case to communicate to them "unofficially" the result of the deliberations upon a question submitted to it for decision, and the Court refused to do so finding this to be in conflict with its Statute.[2] This can hardly be an exercise *proprio motu* of the *compétence de la compétence.* Though given in the form of an "Order," the Court's refusal was, in fact, an interlocutory judgment [3] based on considerations of propriety rather than a pronouncement on jurisdiction in the proper sense. This same remark applies also to the Court's finding in a later phase of the dispute that it was "incompatible with it Statute, and with its position as a Court of Justice, to give a judgment which would be dependent for its validity on the subsequent approval of the Parties."[4]

In the *Legal Status of the South Eastern Territory of Greenland* (1932) the Court discussed in its order of August 3rd, 1932, whether or not to indicate interim measures of protection. There was a request for such measures submitted by one of the parties which the Court refused, before examining whether there was ground for proceeding *proprio motu* to indicate these measures.[5] To discuss whether interim measures could be indicated is certainly, as seen before, an exercise of the *compétence de la compétence*. But the Permanent Court was categorically authorized to do this by Article 41 of the Statute in every case

[1] Although these two Loans cases are usually cited as evidence of the Court's power to raise *proprio motu* objections to its jurisdiction, that had, nonetheless, been relied upon to prove the opposite view. Commenting on the Court's assumption of jurisdiction in them Bruns found that, as a result, it would not ever be possible for a question of jurisdiction *ratione materiae* to arise when the case is submitted to the Court by a *compromis*. This conclusion runs against the alleged general power of the Court to raise this issue *proprio motu*. See, Bruns, "La Cour Permanente de Justice Internationale, son Organisation et sa Compétence," 62 *Recueil des Cours* 551, 637 (1937–IV). *Accord*, Vineuil, "La Cour Permanente de Justice Internationale en 1929," 11 *Rev. Dr. Int'l & Lég. Comp.* 749, 776 (1930 – 3me sér.) who openly contended that the examination of jurisdiction *ex officio* is limited to questions of jurisdiction *ratione personae*.

[2] *P.C.I.J.*, ser. A, No. 22 at 12 (Order of August 19th, 1929).

[3] *Accord*, Separate Opinion of Judge Nyholm, *id.* at 23.

[4] *Case of the Free Zones of Upper Savoy and the District of Gex* (Judgment), *P.C.I.J.*, ser. A/B, No. 46 at 161 (1932).

[5] See *P.C.I.J.*, ser. A/B, No. 48 at 287–9 (1932).

where "it considers that circumstances so require," and not only at the request of a party (a rule that has been clearly emphasized later in Article 61(6) of the 1936 Rules of the Permanent Court and of the Rules of the present Court). Added to this, the exercise of the *compétence de la compétence* was not done strictly *proprio motu* in that particular case, as a request to indicate the measures was made by one of the parties. If the power of the Court to determine its jurisdiction is invoked, it is agreed that it will not be confined to the issues raised by the parties but will allow the Court a full judicial freedom in basing its decision on the ground it sees most convincing. So in the case concerning the *Administration of the Prince Von Pless* (Prel. Obj.) (1933) the Court felt free, *after its jurisdiction was objected to*, to raise, of its own initiative, another jurisdictional question not mentioned by the respondent.[1] On raising this question the Court used again the term "*proprio motu*," thus allowing an extensive reliance, on the part of writers, on this decision to affirm the right of the Court to determine its jurisdiction *ex officio*. It should, however, be recalled that in the latter case the initiative of the Court was limited to discussing "another" objection in connection with the objection raised by the respondent. This new objection was not, on the other hand, directly related to the question of the consent of the parties to adjudicate the case.

Admittedly, the situation was different in *the Appeal from a Judgment of the Hungaro-Czechoslovak Mixed Arbitral Tribunal* (The *Peter Pazmany University Case*), which, incidentally, was decided in the same year (1933). Here the Court discussed its proper jurisdiction to find whether it was *ratione personae* entitled to entertain the suit,[2] despite the fact that neither party questioned this point. On dealing with this case the Court was no doubt conscious of the discussions raised about its jurisdiction in two other appeal cases submitted to it a year earlier under the same jurisdictional title.[3] It, therefore, followed a cautious attitude from the outset by specifying in its Order, fixing the time-limits for the written proceedings that that Order did not affect the question whether the application was admissible or whether the Court had jurisdiction.[4] It, then, asked the parties to

[1] See *P.C.I.J.*, ser. A/B, No. 52 at 15 (1933). The question raised by the Court related in fact to the nationality of the claim as a condition to its admissibility.

[2] *P.C.I.J.*, ser. A/B, No. 61 at 220–1 (1933).

[3] The Court specifically alluded in its judgment to the observations on its jurisdiction submitted by the parties in these previous cases. See *id.* at 212. And see these observations in, *P.C.I.J.*, ser. C, No. 68 at 209–26.

[4] *P.C.I.J.*, ser. C, No. 73 at 1414, 1415 (Order of May 8, 1933).

confine their first observations in the oral hearings to "the question of the nature of the jurisdiction conferred on the Court."[1] As a result, the parties submitted their oral observations on this very question and the Court, after hearing the arguments on the merits, established its jurisdiction in the first part of the Judgment, without, however, referring to the question in the latter's operative clause.

For at least three factors the *Peter Pazmany University Case* can have but little value in proving the Court's alleged all comprehensive power to raise jurisdictional issues *proprio motu*. The first is the particular circumstance related to the two previous cases which, based on the same ground, had created jurisdictional controversies that made the Court particularly conscious of the issue. The second factor is that despite the lack of jurisdictional objections from the parties, the issue was in the air from the beginning and was discussed in detail by the parties. The third and most important factor is that the problem involved was whether the Court had jurisdiction *ratione personae*. The Court would certainly be violating its Statute if it were to decide a controversy submitted to it by parties other than states. Its role in examining whether the dispute covered "a distinct point... between two states" could therefore be easily defended.[2] It does not, however, justify an *ex officio* determination of the completely different point of the acceptance of the Court's jurisdiction by parties each of which is clearly a *legitima persona*.

Finally, in the *Société Commerciale de Belgique Case* (1939) the Court discussed whether a serious transformation in the character of the case during the proceedings was permissible under the Statute.[3] Granted that this was an invocation on the part of the Court of a question that would have affected the Court's jurisdiction, the Court did not

[1] *Supra*, p. 64 note 2 at 212.

[2] Although this decision, as well as the judgments in the *Serbian Loans* and *Brazilian Loans* cases, *supra*, p. 62, note 5, support the invocation *proprio motu* of the Court's jurisdiction *ratione personae*, an earlier case might, however, testify to the contrary. In the *German Interests in Polish Upper Silesia Case*, ser. A, No. 6 (1925), the applicant (Germany) was not a party to the Statute and had not complied with the requirements of the League Council Resolution of May 17, 1922, on the access to the court for non-parties to the Statute. The Court, passing over this fact, was content to state that "the Polish Government does not dispute that the suit has been duly submitted to the Court in accordance with Article 35 ... of the Statute." *Id.* at 11. This case is yet different from the above cases in that no doubt arose in it concerning the fact that both parties were states. It may also be argued that it fell under the exception provided for in Article 35 as will later be seen. It was sharply criticised, however, as disposing of the requirement of the *legitima persona* which it is the duty of the Court to examine. See, *e.g.*, Bos, *Les Conditions du Procès en Droit International Public* 283–4 (1957). And see Hudson, *The Permanent Court of International Justice* 391–2 (2d ed. 1943).

[3] *P.C.I.J.*, ser. A/B, No. 78 at 173 (1939).

proceed with the inquiry any further and was content to take a "broad view" by not regarding the proceedings as irregular because of "the special circumstances of this case... and more especially the absence of any objection on the part of the Agent for the [respondent] Government."[1]

The attitude of the Permanent Court could, therefore, be summed up in two points. First, the Court has never thoroughly discussed whether its jurisdiction was accepted or not when the parties were silent on this point. Second, the Court felt free, in case its jurisdiction was objected to, to discuss the question broadly even by raising issues on which the parties were silent. This latter point could also be traced, though less clearly, in the practice of the present Court. Faced, in the *Interhandel Case* (Prel. Obj.) (1959), with an objection to its jurisdiction *ratione temporis* which did not clarify whether it was meant to apply also to the alternative claim in the application, the Court discussed this question on its own initiative and applied the objection to the alternative claim.[2]

This undogmatic attitude can hardly support a general principle according to which, as Fitzmaurice wrote, "the tribunal may raise any question of jurisdiction *proprio motu*, irrespective of whether the parties do so, and even if neither party disputes the jurisdiction."[3] Such a principle goes not only directly against the clear text of Article 36(6) of the Statute, but also against the unequivocal stand of the present Court in the *Norwegian Loans Case* (1957). Article 36(6) does, above all and despite its law-declaring character, provide explicitly that the *compétence de la compétence* is to be exercised by the Court "in the event of a dispute" [Fr. "*en cas de contestation*"]. And this condition was maintained in the provision despite an early reminder in the proceedings of the Advisory Committee of Jurists (1920) that it ran counter to the power of the Court to determine its jurisdiction *ex officio*.[4] On the other hand, the present Court, in circumstances that will later be expounded, refused in the *Norwegian Loans Case* (1957) to discuss the serious question of the validity of the "self-judging reservation" in the French declaration of acceptance of juris-

[1] *Ibid.*

[2] See [1959] *I.C.J. Rep.* 6, 22.

[3] Fitzmaurice, *supra*, p. 57, note 1 at 28. The writer added, however, that "the Court will not be astute itself to query the common intention [of the parties] if neither party denies it." *Id.* at 29. And *cf.* Rosenne, *The World Court* 89 (1962).

[4] See the proposal of Mr. Hagerup [Norway] to suppress the words "*en cas de contestation*" from Article 29(2) of the draft before the Advisory Committee in, *Procès Verbaux of the Proceedings of the Advisory Committee of Jurists* 654 (1920).

diction, the reason being that:

> [T]he Court has before it a provision which both parties to the dispute regard as constituting an expression of their common will relating to the competence of the Court. The Court does not therefore consider that it is called upon to enter into an examination of the reservation in the light of considerations which are not presented by the issues in the proceedings. The Court, without prejudging the question, gives effect to the reservation as it stands and as the parties recognize it.[1]

The question of raising objections to jurisdiction *proprio motu* is, then, one in which the practice of the Court and the theory expressed in standard writings are at variance. Some writers, influenced by domestic analogies, attempted to reconcile the two views by developing some distinctions. According to the most popular distinction the civil law concept of *ordre public* is introduced in the international procedure. The Court can examine its jurisdiction *ex officio* only when the requirements violated by the parties are related to the *ordre public*, that is to the structure of the tribunal as a court of justice or to requirements imposed by the Statute.[2] Avoiding the French term the distinction was expressed to allow the exercise *proprio motu* of the power "where the limits of jurisdiction are binding upon the parties" but not "where the parties have the power to confer jurisdiction upon the tribunal or to extend it."[3]

This distinction is certainly sound in theory. Yet, any wide application of it in practice is conditioned by a judicial structure similar to that known in domestic systems where there is a hierarchy of courts each invested with a binding jurisdiction which the parties cannot violate even by their mutual agreement.[4] Far from this picture is that of the jurisdiction of the Court where the parties' consent provides the primary test of validity for most of the Court's actions. Even when

[1] [1957] *I.C.J. Rep.* 9, 27. In that case, it should be noticed, objections to jurisdiction were already presented by the respondent on other grounds. The Court was therefore theoretically able to raise other objections. Refusing, however, to discuss the validity of the self-judging reservation, it declined jurisdiction on the basis of the invocation of this very reservation in the case. See an appraisal of this attitude in Chapter VI, *infra*. And *cf.*, *German Interests in Polish Upper Silesia Case, supra*, p. 65, note 2; *Haya de la Torre Case*, [1951] *I.C.J. Rep.* 78.

[2] See Bos, *supra*, p. 65, note 2 at 274–5 (citing decisions of Mixed Arbitral Tribunals to the same effect).

[3] Bin Cheng, *General Principles of Law as applied by International Courts and Tribunals* 266 (1953). *Accord*, 2 Guggenheim, *Traité de Droit International Public* 147–8 (1954). But see the Dutch author Dolleman, *Preliminaire excepties voor het Internationaal Gerechtshof* 44 (1949), as cited by Bos, *supra*, at 275–6, n. 3. He maintained that the Court has also the power to examine *ex officio* the limits of its jurisdiction imposed by the parties, founding this on Art. 32 of the Rules of Court.

[4] See *Minority Schools in Polish Upper Silesia Case, P.C.I.J.*, ser. A, No. 15 at 23 (1923).

the two parties accept the "compulsory" jurisdiction of the Court, they can, at any moment, by their mutual agreement limit or extend this jurisdiction without being accused of violating the Statute or infringing on the nature of the Court. On the other hand, the concept of prorogated jurisdiction which assumes the acceptance of the Court's jurisdiction when this is not timely objected to is difficult to reconcile with the suggested criterion. When the judicial jurisdiction is of *ordre public* not only the tribunal but also the parties maintain the right to raise and discuss jurisdictional issues at any time before the judgment on the merits.

True, the Court may be said to have always the power to ask the parties to specify their views on the jurisdictional issues involved.[1] If neither of the parties disputes the jurisdiction of the Court over the case, the Court is not expected to raise, on its own initiative, objections related to the acceptance of such jurisdiction. This, however, does not stop the Court from applying the objective rules related to the limits of its judicial action. Such limits constitute a part of the law of the Court's jurisdiction (in a broad sense) which the Court is always assumed to know and to be able to apply. This part could however be technically distinguished in most cases from jurisdiction in the strict sense. In practice the questions raised *proprio motu* related to the "ability to appear before the Court" (commonly referred to as jurisdiction *ratione personnae*), and to the "propriety of the Court's actions." Yet, even in invoking such questions the International Court proved, as seen above, to be influenced by the absence of objections from the parties. Only rarely has the Court been more strict than the parties in viewing the limitations on its judicial action.

E. THE POWER IS RELATIVE – EFFECT OF THE EXCESSIVE EXERCISE OF THE POWER

The power of international tribunals to determine their own jurisdiction has, since it was first alleged to exist, been conceived as subject to limitations that stem from the judicial nature of the tribunal and from the instruments that enable it to handle the dispute. The rule

[1] An example of this is shown in the case concerning *appeals from certain Judgments of the Hungaro-Czechoslovak Mixed Arbitral Tribunal,* (1933) where the Permanent Court asked the parties, after the submission of preliminary objections by the respondent, to explain their views on the effect of a certain Article in the agreement that conferred an appellate jurisdiction on the Court in relation to the statutory provisions governing the Court's jurisdiction. See the text of the letter of the Registrar to the Agents of the parties including this request, in *P.C.I.J.*, ser. C, No. 68 at 262.

of the *compétence de la compétence* has, therefore, been always subject, in theory, to another rule according to which a tribunal's decision becomes null if reached as a result of an excessive exercise of jurisdiction.[1] *Extra compromissum arbiter nihil facere potest.* However, the simultaneous existence of the two rules in theory,[2] did not always lead in fact to an adequate interapplication thereof due to the absence of an organized procedure for the verification of the existence and extent of any alleged *excès de pouvoir.*[3] This practical shortcoming led to the situation where, short of an agreement between the parties for adjudicating the question of *excès de pouvoir,*[4] or for a diplomatic

[1] See Commissioner Gore's Opinion in the *Betsey case* (1797) (quoted in Chapter I, *supra* at 14), 3 Moore, *Arbitrations* 2290. And see, "Projet de Règlements pour la Procédure Arbitrale Internationale (1875)," 1 *Annuaire* 126, 133 (1877); Creasy, *First Platform of International Law* 395–6 (1876); de Card, *Droit International, L'Arbitrage Internationale Dans le Passé, Le Présent et L'Avenir* 53 (1877); Heffter, *Le Droit International de L'Europe* 240 (Trad. par Bergson, 1883); Bluntschli, *Le Droit International Codifié* 289 (4th ed., Lardy Trans. 1886); 6 Pradier-Fodéré, *Traité de Droit International Public* 433 (1894); 2 Rivier, *Principes du Droit des Gens* 185 (1896); 3 Calvo, *Le Droit International* 485 (5th ed. 1896); Taylor, *A Treatise on International Public Law* 379 (1901); Audry, *La Révision de la Sentence Arbitrale* 44 (1914); Hall, *A Treatise on International Law* 420 (8th ed. Higgins 1924); Lauterpacht, "The Legal Remedy in case of Excess of Jurisdiction," 9 *Brit. Yb. Int'l L.* 117 (1928); Verdross, "L'Excès de Pouvoir du Juge Arbitral dans le Droit International Public," 9 *Rev. Dr. Int'l & Lég. Comp.* 225, 231 (1928, 3me sér.); Guermanoff, *L'Excès de Pouvoir de l'Arbitre* 64 (1929); Bishop, *International Arbitral Procedure* 242 (1931); Castberg, "L'Excès de Pouvoir dans la Justice Internationale," 35 *Recueil des Cours* 357, 388–9 (1931–I); Wittenberg et Desrioux, *L'Organisation Judiciaire, La Procédure et La Sentence Internationale* 368 (1937); Balasko, *Causes de Nullité de la Sentence Arbitrale en Droit International Public* 201 (1938); Carlston, *The Process of International Arbitration* 140 (1946); Bin Cheng, *supra*, p. 66, note 3 at 261; Ch. Rousseau, *Droit International Public* 496–7 (1953); Berlia, "La Jurisprudence des Tribunaux Internationaux en ce qui concerne leur Compétence," 88 *Recueil des Cours* 109, 129 (1955); Simpson and Fox, *supra*, p. 61, note 1 at 252; Delbez, *Les Principes Généraux du Contentieux International* 32–3 (1962); Brierly, *The Law of Nations* 350–1 (6th ed. Waldock 1963). See also the same view expressed in the individual opinions of Judges Winiarski and Alvarez in the *Awards of Administrative Tribunal*, [1954] *I.C.J. Rep.* 47, 65, 74. And see the present Court's review of whether an arbitral award was made beyond the authority of the arbitrator in *The Arbitral Award Made by the King of Spain on 23 December 1906*, [1960] *I.C.J. Rep.* 192, 214–5.

[2] See this simultaneous operation of the two rules particularly emphasized in, Rolin-Jaequemyns, "Quelques Mots sur la Phase Nouvelle du Différend Anglo-Américain," 4 *Rev. Dr. Int'l & Lég. Comp.* 127, 137–9 (1872); Berlia, *supra*, note 1 at 129; Simpson and Fox, *supra*, p. 61, note 1 at 252. But *cf.*, Lapradelle, "L'Excès de Pouvoir de l'Arbitre," 2 *Rev. Dr. Int'l* 5, 14, 32, 56–7 (Paris, 1928).

[3] The term "*excès de pouvoir*", adapted from French law, is generally used to indicate a wider meaning that is not necessarily limited to the excessive exercise of jurisdiction. See, *e.g.*, Carlston, *supra*, note 1 at 83, 140. It is used above, however, in the strict sense confined to jurisdictional issues. *Accord*, Balasko, *supra*, note 1 at 153. The power the exercise of which is in excess is not, therefore, as used in this context, any power of the tribunal other than its power to determine its jurisdiction.

[4] As, *e.g.*, in the *Orinoco Steamship Company Case* (*U.S. v. Venezuela*) (Agreement of Feb. 13, 1909), Second Award, 11 *U.N. Rep. Int'l Arb. Awards* 227, 239 (1910) (Perm. Ct. Arb.); *Boundary Case between Costa Rica and Panama* (Agreement of March 17, 1910), Second Award, *id.* at 519, 540 (1914); *L'Affaire des Limites entre la Colombie et le Vénézuela* (Agreement of Nov. 3, 1915), Second Award, 1 Lapradelle et Politis, *Recueil* 106, 119 (1922) (Conseil Fédéral Suisse); *The Arbitral Award Made by the King of Spain on 23 December 1906* (Agreement of July 21, 1957), [1960] *I.C.J. Rep.* 192.

settlement of it,[1] the decision remains unexecuted.[2] With such an unsatisfactory result, some modern writers suggested that an arbiter's decision on his jurisdiction should be respected in all cases,[3] leaving no chance for the allegation of nullity because of execessive exercise of jurisdiction. Others have tried to fill in the gap by devising a rule according to which every *compromis* should include a reference to the procedure to be followed in case a party alleges an *excès de pouvoir* in the tribunal's decision.[4] In practice, however, little concern has been given to the problem due to the rarity of the cases in which a decision was refused execution under the sole argument that the tribunal had no jurisdiction to pronounce it.

Does the same controversy apply to the International Court? There is no doubt that this Court's power to determine its jurisdiction is neither absolute nor arbitrary. Moreover, the discretionary powers of the Court are under limitations in the Statute and may be subject to others devised by the parties. Such limitations, statutory and conventional, should in principle be respected by the Court. But does it follow that nullity would be the only sanction of their violation? What, in any event, is the organ that would decide that a violation has occurred and that it is of such a nature as to nullify the decision in whole or in part?

Neither the Permanent Court nor the present one had the occasion to deal squarely with these questions that are "post-adjudicative" in nature, and are, according to the Washington Committee of Jurists

[1] As, *e.g.*, in *L'Affaire des Gisements Diamantifères du Griqualand Occidental* (1871), 2 Lapradelle et Politis, *Recueil* 676, 691. Settlement reached in the Convention signed on July 13, 1876. See Stuyt, *Survey of International Arbitration* 97 (1939); *Northeast Boundary Case* (U.S. *v.* Great Britain) (1831), 1 Moore, *Arbitrations* 132–8. Settlement reached in the treaty signed on August 9, 1842, 1 Malloy, *Treaties* 650. See Stuyt, *op. cit.*, *supra*, at 29; *Boundary Case between Bolivia and Peru* (1909). Settlement reached in treaty signed on Sept. 15, 1909, 3 Martens, *R.G.T.* (3e sér.) 59. See Stuyt, *supra*, at 261.

[2] As, *e.g.*, in *The Honduran-Nicaraguan Arbitration under the Treaty of Corinto* (1907), Carlston, *supra*, p. 69, note 1 at 111–3 (notice difference between the order given in this case and the Arbitral Award made by the King of Spain, *supra*.) And see *Cases before the Central American Court of Justice Involving the Bryan-Chamorro Treaty* (Costa Rica *v.* Nicaragua) (1916); (El Salvadore *v.* Nicaragua) (1917), *id.* at 127–40.

[3] See *e.g.*, Salvioli, "Sul Potere dell'Arbitro a Pronunciarsi sulla Competenza," 13 *Diritto Internazionale* 119, 121 (1959).

[4] See Report of the Committee Appointed by the Council, Submitted on September 5th, 1930, *League of Nations Off. J.*, 16th sess. (annex) 1359–65 (1930) (proposing the conferment on the Permanent Court of an appellate jurisdiction over Arbitral awards). See also on this point, Hudson, *The Permanent Court of International Justice* 431–2 (2d ed. 1943); Rundstein, "La Cour Permanente de Justice Internationale comme Instance de Recours," 43 *Recueil des Cours* 1–113 (1933-I). And see the International Law Commission's first Draft on Arbitral Procedure, Arts, 30–31, *U.N. Gen. Ass. Off. Rec.*, 7th Sess., Supp. 8 at 10 (Doc. No. A/2163) (1952), and its final Model Rules on Arbitral Procedure, Arts. 35–36, *U.N. Gen. Ass. Off. Rec.*, 13th Sess., Supp. No. 9 at 9 (Doc. No. A/3859) (1958).

(1945), not the business of the Court.[1] In fact, the Permanent Court did indicate from the very beginning that it neither could nor should contemplate the contingency that the parties will not comply with its judgment.[2] It did not need to deal with an actual case of non-compliance as none of its decisions was refused execution by the mere will of the judgment debtor.[3] On the other hand, the power of the Council of the League of Nations in relation to noncompliance with judicial decisions was invoked only in one case related to an arbitral award.[4] This Council had, according to the Covenant, the power to "propose," in the event of any failure to carry out an international arbitral award or judicial decision, the steps to be taken to give effect thereto (Article 13(4)). The Covenant indicated also that the judgment creditor might resort to war to enforce the decision only after the expiration of a period of three months after the judicial decision or the Council's report (Article 12). Neither the Covenant nor the Statute of the Permanent Court referred to any special treatment of the issue if the noncompliance was based on an allegation of an excessive exercise of jurisdiction on the part of the Court. Nor did this particular point arouse much discussion in the writings dealing with the work of the Court due, perhaps, to the absence of an actual case to necessitate it. Such a case arose, however, in the practice of the present Court. After three phases of adjudication of the *Corfu Channel Case* the judgment debtor (Albania) refused to comply with the decision on the ground that it was passed in *excès de pouvoir*. No further action was taken in the case.[5] The judgment creditor (the United Kingdom) did not even invoke Article 94(2) of the Charter [6], and thus deprived the

[1] See [Basdevant] Report on Draft of Statute of an International Court of Justice, Doc. No. Jurist 86, G. 173, 14 *U.N. Conf. Int'l Org. Docs.* 821, 853 (1945).

[2] See *S.S. Wimbledon, P.C.I.J.*, ser. A, No. 1 at 32 (1923); *Chorzow Factory Case* (Indemnity-Merits), *P.C.I.J.*, ser. A, No. 17 at 63 (1928). Compare, Chapter V, *infra* at 186–87.

[3] In the *S.S. Wimbledon Case* (1923) Germany was required to pay certain indemnities to France but the Guarantee Committee of the Reparation Commission did not enable it to do so. See the letter of this committee communicated by Germany to the Court on Dec. 6, 1923, in *P.C.I.J. Ann. Rep.*, ser. E, No. 1 at 167–8 (1922–1925). In the *Interpretation of the Treaty of Neuilly Case* (1924) the respondent's objections to the judgment resulted only in a request for interpretation that was refused by the Court. See, *P.C.I.J.*, ser. A, No. 4 at 7 1925). See generally, Carlston, *supra*, p. 69, note 1 at 113–6.

[4] This was the Award in the case concerning the *Forests of Rhodope* (Greece *v.* Bulgaria), 3 *U.N. Rep. Int'l Arb. Awards* 1405 (1933). Greece sought the Council's intervention under Article 13(4) of the Covenant; see letter of the Greek Government of Sept. 6, 1934 in *League of Nations Off. J.*, 15th Ass. 1477 (1934); but no such intervention was needed as the Bulgarian Government indicated its intention to carry out the award when its financial position would enable it to do so. *Id.* at 1432.

[5] See Chung, *Legal Problems Involved in the Corfu Channel Incident* 274 (1959).

[6] Art. 94(2) of the Charter of the United Nations provided that: "If any party to a case fails to perform the obligations incumbent upon it under a judgment rendered by the Court,

Security Council of the opportunity of discussing the question. The United Kingdom tried, however, to make use of this Article in the context of another case. It resorted to the Security Council in an attempt to have it enforce an Order indicating interim measures of protection in the *Anglo-Iranian Oil Company Case.*[1] The discussions in the Council were not particularly revealing, however. Not only the Council's competence to deal with the issue was disputed, but also the binding effect of orders indicating interim measures was said to be doubtful in principle. Thus, it was found convenient to postpone the discussion until the Court pronounced on its own jurisdiction to deal with the merits.[2] The undecided questions, therefore, remain. Does it make a difference if the noncompliance is based on an allegation that the Court has violated its jurisdictional limits? Who is to decide?

Apart from the Court itself – whose power could be invoked under the Articles of its Statute related to interpretation and revision in the proper limits of each – it is doubtful that there is any other organ that can investigate whether the Court has excessively exercised its jurisdiction. The Court has once doubted that the General Assembly of the United Nations can act as an appellate judicial organ for the United Nations Administrative Tribunal.[3] There is no reason to assume that this Assembly or even the Security Council can exercise any judicial review over the Court's action. The Security Council, it is true, may, if the judgment creditor resorts to it and if it deems necessary, "make recommendations or decide upon measures to be taken to give effect to the judgment" (Article 94(2) of the Charter), but this in itself assumes that the Council's action must be based on the validity and enforceability of the decision. Therefore, it would be *ultra vires* for the Council to discuss the Court's jurisdiction in the case submitted to it for enforcement purposes, regardless of whether the arguments invoked in the Council against the Court's jurisdiction were raised before the Court or are new arguments. It may, however, be argued, and rightly so, that nothing in the Charter or the Statute or in the doctrine of *res judicata,* should prevent the Council, if it deems

the other party may have recourse to the Security Council, which may, if it deems necessary, make recommendations or decide upon measures to be taken to give effect to the judgment."

[1] See *U.N. Security Council Off. Rec.*, 6th year, 559th Meeting, at 1 *et seq.* (S/PV 559) (1951).

[2] *Id.* at 565th meeting at 12, (Vote on the French proposal) (S/PV 565) (1951). And see for the binding effect of orders indicating interim measures, Dubisson, *La Cour Internationale de Justice* 228–30 (1964).

[3] *Effect of Awards of Compensation Made by the United Nations Administrative Tribunal*, [1954] *I.C.J. Rep.* 47, 56 (Adv. Op.).

it necessary, to direct a request to the Court for an advisory opinion as to the meaning of its contested judgment.[1] Yet it is doubtful that the Court, through an advisory opinion to this effect, could change its attitude toward the jurisdictional issue involved in the original judgment. It must, therefore, be submitted that once a decision is passed there is no way to have it reconsidered by any organ other than the Court itself. The validity of the judgment could not be affected by a mere assertion by one of the parties to the effect that it was done in excess of the Court's jurisdiction. The Court, it is true, must act only within the proper limits of its jurisdiction. But if one party alleges that the Court violated these limits, this is no way of invalidating the judgment, and this party is still under the obligation to comply with the allegedly invalid decision.[2] If both parties agree that the Court's jurisdiction was excessively exercised, then there is nothing in the present structure of international adjudication to prevent them from reaching a different settlement through diplomatic means or by submitting the same dispute to another tribunal.

The above discussion does not arise, in law, in regard to the advisory competence of the Court. If the organ requesting the opinion finds that the Court has answered another question than the one submitted to it or has violated in any way its jurisdictional limits, such organ is not, at any event, under a legal obligation to comply with the opinion, unless, of course, it is otherwise stipulated in the instrument enabling the organ to make the request.[3] However, as a matter of propriety, the requesting organ should not question the manner in which the Court exercised its *compétence de la compétence* or enter into discussions related to this delicate topic. The opinion is advisory. If it could not be followed, it should simply be set aside.

F. FINALITY OF THE EXERCISE OF THE POWER – IS THE DECISION ON JURISDICTION *RES JUDICATA*?

Assuming that the Court has given a decision affirming its jurisdiction, can this be overruled at any time before the judgment on the merits or in this judgment itself?

Two questions are involved. If the Court dismisses the objections

[1] *Accord*, Rosenne, *The International Court of Justice* 84 (1957).

[2] But *cf.*, Lauterpacht, *The Function of Law in the International Community* 210 (1933).

[3] *E.g.*, with respect to requests related to the validity of judgments of the Administrative Tribunal of the I.L.O. See, *Case concerning Judgments of the Administrative Tribunal of the I.L.O.*, [1956] *I.C.J. Rep.* 77, 84 (Adv. Op.).

to its jurisdiction, would it still be open to the objecting party to invoke anew the Court's *compétence de la compétence* by raising new arguments against this jurisdiction? Could the Court itself overrule its previous judgment on jurisdiction if it discovers, on dealing with the merits, that it was mistaken in affirming its jurisdiction? These are admittedly difficult questions. There is no doubt, however, that if the first judgment on jurisdiction disposes only of some objections and postpones judgment on the rest of them until the Court considers the merits,[1] the argument of *res judicata* does not arise, thus leaving both the Court and the parties free to raise and discuss new arguments against the Court's competence to deal with the case. It should also be admitted that even when the judgment on jurisdiction covers all the objections invoked, the parties can, in principle, still introduce new pleas in bar if such a judgment results in transforming the case, as when the objections are partly admitted and partly dismissed.[2]

Apart from these two situations, the attitude of the Court does not suggest unqualified solutions. The question presented itself first in the *German Interests in Polish Upper Silesia Case* before the Permanent Court. In the first phase of this case the Court affirmed the admissibility of a question submitted by the applicant, despite the respondent's objection to it on the basis that it constituted in fact a request for an advisory opinion.[3] Yet, in a later stage the Court found itself unable to give judgment on this issue. This reversal of attitude was not, however, presented by the Court as a correction of its prior judgment. Rather it was said to be the result of the subsequent failure of the applicant to take the steps anticipated by that first judgment:

> The Court... did not at the outset declare that it had no competence to deal with this submission, in spite of the fact that the Applicant had couched it in the form of a question. In proceeding thus, however, the Court supposed that the latter would, in his Case on the merits of the dispute, formulate properly set out claims in regard to [this] submission. But in the proceedings on the merits, the data anticipated by the Court have not been furnished, and the point in question remained in its purely interrogative form. In these circumstances, the Court is not in a position to give judgment on this submission, for though it can construe the submissions of the Parties, it cannot substitute itself for them and formulate new submissions simply on the basis of arguments and facts involved.[4]

[1] *E.g.*, in the *Case concerning Right of Passage over Indian Territory* (Prel. Obj.), [1957] *I.C.J. Rep.* 125.

[2] *Accord*, Rosenne, *supra*, p. 73, note 1 at 354.

[3] See *P.C.I.J.*, ser. A, No. 6 at 21–2 (1925).

[4] *P.C.I.J.*, ser. A, No. 7 at 34–5 (1926).

By imparting the Court's inability to deal with an issue found admissiable in a prior judgment to subsequent factors extrinsic to that judgment, the Court has practically deprived this precedent from the influence it could have had on the question in discussion. This question was directly raised for the first time in the *Corfu Channel Case* before the present Court. After the Court's first decision affirming its jurisdiction on the case,[1] and after the conclusion of a special agreement between the parties, the respondent (Albania) objected in the last oral statement of its Agent (in the second phase of the case) to the Court's jurisdiction to assess the amount of compensation[2] – an objection that was discussed by the Court, though not by the parties, and was dismissed in its second judgment in the case.[3] Then, instead of submitting its observations regarding the amount of compensation due from it, Albania objected again to the Court's jurisdiction to assess this amount.[4] The applicant Government (the United Kingdom) subsequently submitted its observations to the effect that that question "has been decided affirmatively by the Court and is now *res judicata*," and that Albania was bound by the prior decision on jurisdiction by virtue of its prior consent and of Articles 36(6) and 60 of the Statute.[5] The Court, thus confronted with the problem of the bearing of the doctrine of *res judicata* on its decision on jurisdiction,[6] answered emphatically in its third judgment in the case, that:

> The Albanian Government disputed the jurisdiction of the Court with regard to the assessment of damages. The Court may confine itself to stating that this jurisdiction was established by its judgment of April 9th, 1949, that in accordance with the Statute (Article 60) which, for the settlement of the present dispute, is binding upon the Albanian Government, that judgment is final and without appeal, and that therefore the matter is *res judicata*.[7]

This statement does not, however, dispose completely of the problem. First, it should be noted that the objection raised by Albania was exactly the same objection that the Court dismissed in its previous judgment and that no new argument against the Court's jurisdiction was advanced, which made it an easier case for the application of the

[1] See [1947–1948] *I.C.J. Rep.* 15.
[2] See 4 *Corfu Channel Case*, Pleadings, Oral Arguments and Documents 613, 663 (*I.C.J.*).
[3] See [1949] *I.C.J. Rep.* 4, 23–6.
[4] 2 *Corfu Channel Case, supra*, note 2 at 400.
[5] *Id.* at 390.
[6] See the problem generally discussed in *Interpretation of Judgments Nos. 7 and 8 (the Chorzów Factory)*, *P.C.I.J.*, ser. A, No. 13 at 23 (Diss. Op. of Judge Anzilotti). He maintained that Art. 60 of the Statute gives the Court's judgment "the formal value of *res judicata*," and Art. 59 determines "the material limits of *res judicata*."
[7] The *Corfu Channel Case* (Assessment), [1949] *I.C.J. Rep.* 244, 248.

doctrine of *res judicata*. It will be recalled that when this very objection was first raised it was not dismissed on the same basis, though it was invoked after a decision affirming the Court's jurisdiction to deal with the case generally. Second, the Court's statement mentioned above makes no reference to Article 36(6) of the Statute relied upon by the applicant Government – an attitude that led some to conclude an "unexpressed desire [on the part of the Court] that the issue of *res judicata* should remain within the orbit of Chapter III of the Statute, relating to procedure, and not be brought into the scope of Chapter II which relates to the competence of the Court."[1]

This uncertainty has prompted a more cautious practice followed by respondent states in subsequent cases. Thus, the United States Government, on submitting what it deemed to be an interpretative objection to the Court's jurisdiction in the *U.S. Nationals in Morocco Case* (1951), reserved the right to file further preliminary objections.[2] Such a "right" was not, however, exercised. Instead, the first objection was withdrawn and a statement was made in the counter-memorial announcing the intention of that Government not to raise any further jurisdictional issues in that case.[3] The occasion for taking advantage of a similar reservation came in the *Nottebohm Case*. Guatemala, the respondent, pleaded that the Court was without jurisdiction *ratione temporis* and suggested that if the Court dismissed this plea, it might raise further objections in exercising its right to reply.[4] The plea was dismissed in the judgment on the preliminary objection,[5] and Guatamala followed by submitting in its counter-memorial, which dealt alternatively with the merits, three conclusions on the inadmissibility of the claim.[6] The applicant did not in turn raise the argument of *res judicata* and was content to allude to the fact that at least one of these three grounds might have been invoked with the first objections to jurisdiction.[7] This attitude was probably due to the con-

[1] Rosenne, "*Res Judicata:* Some Recent Decisions of the International Court of Justice," 28 *Brit. Yb. Int'l L.* 365, 367 (1951).

[2] 1 *The U.S. Nationals in Morocco Case*, Pleadings, Oral Arguments and Documents 238 (*I.C.J.* 1952).

[3] *Id.* at 262.

[4] 1 *Nottebohm Case*, Pleadings, Oral Arguments and Documents 162, 168 (*I.C.J.* 1955).

[5] See [1953] *I.C.J. Rep.* 111.

[6] See 1 *Nottebohm Case, supra*, note 4 at 184 *et seq.* The three conclusions related to the absence of prior diplomatic negotiations, the absence of a tie of nationality between the applicant and Mr. Nottebohm and the non-exhaustion of local remedies. *Id.* at 186, 188, 198.

[7] *Id.* at 373, 377. (The ground alluded to was the alleged absence of the tie of nationality.) And see the oral presentation of M. Sauser-Hall (Counsel for Liechtenstein) at 2 *id.* at 65, 66, who, mentioning that Guatemala was not allowed to present new objections after the expiry of the period fixed in Art. 62 of the Rules, added that Liechtenstein nevertheless

viction that the new objections were not related to jurisdiction proper, and had a direct bearing on the merits. The preliminary objection procedure provided for in Article 62 of the Rules was not followed in this new phase and was, on the contrary, asserted by the Counsel of Guatemala himself to be capable of invocation only once.[1] The Court, on its part, considered the new objections, recognizing in the circumstances the correctness of the procedure.

Again, this case does not solve the problem of the successive invocation of objections to jurisdiction after a judgment on the first objection. It could be argued that the new objections in this case were not directed against the jurisdiction of the Court but, as mentioned above, against the admissibility of the claim. It could also be said that the Court's competence to deal with the new objections was perfected by prorogation.[2] In fact, an occasion for a clear answer to the problem presented itself in this case when a Guatemalan representative put to the President of the Court, in an interview before the first hearing, the plain question of whether his Government could present further objections should the Court decide it had jurisdiction. The President replied that he could not make any commitment as to the course of the procedure,[3] thereby leaving the question unanswered.

If the practice of the Court could not thus provide a decisive solution for the problem, it may be helpful to approach it from a different aspect, i.e., the nature of the decision on jurisdiction. Is it a final decision of a constitutive nature or rather a declaratory decision subject to corrections that may become necessary in the further development of the case? Only one of the Permanent Court's judges dealt with this matter. Judge Rostworowski, dissenting in the case concerning *Certain German Interests in Polish Upper Silesia* (1925), wrote:

> Such a decision [settling the question of jurisdiction] which, if taken, can clearly be based only on the objective law [Fr. *droit objectif*] applicable in the particular case, is of a purely declaratory nature, and it can never create a right [Fr. *sans pouvoir jamais revêtir le caractère constitutif*], i.e., bestow on the Court itself a jurisdiction which is not supported by applicable rules of law either general or particular.[4]

"s'abstient de formuler une contre-exception d'irrecevabilité; elle s'en remet à la haute sagesse de la Cour."

[1] See 2 *id.* at 159, 162 (statement of M. Rolin).

[2] See Rosenne, *supra*, p. 73, note 1 at 354.

[3] See Letter of the Deputy Registrar to the Guatemalan Chargé d'Affaires at Paris, dated Nov. 11, 1953 in, 2 *Nottebohm Case, supra*, p. 76, note 4 at 617, 618.

[4] *P.C.I.J.*, ser. A, No. 6 at 32 (Diss. Op. of Count Rostworowski).

It follows from this characterization that if the Court, after affirming its jurisdiction in a case, discovers *ex officio* or after a new objection, that it lacks such jurisdiction, a new decision declining jurisdiction becomes mandatory. The same concept was affirmed in the *Von Tiedmann* case (1926) before the Polish-German Mixed Arbitral Tribunal. In this case the tribunal, which had previously found itself competent to deal with the merits, reversed its decision and reached the new conclusion that it was without jurisdiction.[1] Reversal of previous judgments, the tribunal admitted, cannot be the rule in the judicial process, but interlocutory judgments on jurisdiction can justifiably be excepted particularly as the rules of the tribunal did not provide otherwise. As to the doctrine of *res judicata* the tribunal found that in order to apply it to such a situation, it would necessarily be committing a manifest *abus de pouvoir*.[2] To avoid such an abuse it explained that only valid judgments can acquire the status of *res judicata*. A decision made in excess of jurisdiction could be refused execution by the parties and for this reason the tribunal should be able to remedy its error if it realized it in time.[3]

This latter decision, though unrepeated in practice,[4] was found by some to be "entirely justified"[5] – a belief that led its holder to deny the application of Article 60 of the Statute to the preliminary decisions of the International Court.[6] It allowed others to go as far as to state that "a tribunal should... also be prepared to reverse a ruling that it had no jurisdiction, if it is shown to be erroneous,"[7] without limiting this to the strict procedure of "revision."

If conclusions are to be drawn from this analysis one can at least emphasize three points:

First, that after a decision on jurisdiction is rendered, the invocation of the same objection supported by the same arguments or without arguments, could not ordinarily lead to a reopening of the issue (*Corfu Channel Case*).

[1] See *Von Tiedmann c. Etat polonais et sept autres affaires*, 6 *Rec. des déc. des trib. arb. mixtes* 997, 1003 (1926).

[2] *Id.* at 1001.

[3] *Ibid.*

[4] Compare, Salvioli, "Les Rapports entre le Jugement sur la Compétence et celui sur le Fond dans la Jurisprudence Internationale," 36 *Rev. Gén. Dr. Int'l Pub.* 108, 115 (1929) where he contends, without citing specific examples, that, "il ne manque toutefois pas de sentences qui, tout en confirmant le principe de l'irrévocabilité de la décision sur la compétence, reconnaissent dans le jugement sur le fond que la matière en question était en dehors de leur juridiction pourtant peu avant affirmée."

[5] Bos, *Les Conditions du Procès en Droit International Public* 320 (1957).,

[6] See *id.* at 321.

[7] Simpson and Fox, *International Arbitration* 234 (1959).

Second, that a decision affirming jurisdiction might not be a barrier against raising new objections to the admissibility of the claim or to the standing of a party, particularly if the party raising them had reserved from the beginning its right to advance further objections (*Nottebohm Case*).

Third, that the Court relying on the declaratory nature of its pronouncements on jurisdiction can, in the future, reverse a decision affirming its competence to deal with a case if it later finds beyond doubt that its prior decision was erroneous, and provided that a decision on the merits was not yet pronounced. If this would happen, Article 60 of the Statute would not then apply to decisions on the preliminary objections related to jurisdiction. This is, however, a mere possibility that cannot be based on the standing practice.

PART TWO

THE SUBJECT MATTER OF THE POWER – AN OPERATIONAL ANALYSIS

CHAPTER III

THE PROCESS OF THE COURT'S DETERMINATION OF ITS SUBSTANTIVE JURISDICTION

The power of the International Court to determine its jurisdiction, as any other judicial power, cannot be analyzed in depth except in the context of the subject matter on which it is exercised. By defining this subject matter one is in fact answering the question: "What does this power mean, both to the Court and to the parties to any given dispute of which the Court is seized?" It is for this reason that an attempt to ascertain such a subject matter is carried out in this part of the study, which will however, be limited to such details as will help clarify the significance of the power in the work of the Court. In other words, the only questions that are to be raised here are those which the Court may need to answer in the course of the exercise of its power to determine its jurisdiction. This proposed limitation is subject, however, to one observation. Whereas the Court, being a judicial entity, is under no duty to give general definitions or comprehensive analyses of its jurisdictional powers, this part of the study is mainly concerned with these fundamental problems.

Put in its simplest form the subject matter of the Court's power to determine its jurisdiction, is this jurisdiction itself. To differentiate it from the power (which is a jurisdiction of a more preliminary character), this subject matter will always be referred to as the Court's "substantive jurisdiction." The Court determines whether such substantive jurisdiction exists by examining the instruments and facts expressing the intention of the parties in the context of the framework of its role under the Statute. On so doing the Court has not always been a mere executor of the will of the parties. It considered, however, such will as the major foundation of its substantive jurisdiction, and, relying on it and on its constituent instrument, built for this jurisdiction a complicated structure that was made possible and became more refined by the continued exercise of the very *compétence de la compétence.*

A. SEIZING THE COURT OR THE INSTITUTION OF PROCEEDINGS

Both the Statute (Article 40(1)) and the Rules of Court (Article 32), along with the Court's own practice, indicate that there are only two ways through which a case could be brought before the Court – the unilateral application and the notification of a special agreement. Each of these methods presents different problems.

1. Seizing the Court by the Notification of a Special Agreement

The institution of proceedings by the notification to the Registrar of a special agreement concluded between the parties to confer jurisdiction on the Court over the specific dispute indicated in it, is much similar to the institution of proceedings before an arbitral tribunal. It does involve fewer problems before the Court than the case of instituting the proceedings by a unilateral application. Yet it is the least practiced method,[1] due mainly to the political difficulty of getting the parties to agree *ad hoc* to submit a specific standing dispute to the decision of the Court.

The joint notification of a special agreement [2] – which should indicate the subject of the dispute and the parties to the case – seizes the Court and provides it with the substantive power to deal with the case. It does not, however, preclude either party from objecting to the Court's jurisdiction.[3] In case such objections are presented, the preliminary *compétence de la compétence* will practically be confined to the interpretation of the agreement's terms and may extend occasionally to the examination of the compatibility of such terms with the Court's judicial function.

[1] 12 cases (the *Borchgrave Case* being counted twice) were submitted to the Permanent Court by means of notification of a special agreement, and 6 cases (including the two phases of the *Corfu Channel Case* dealing with the merits and assessment) have so far been submitted to the present Court on the basis of special agreements. Two of these latter cases, other than the *Corfu Channel Case*, were instituted however by applications. See Appendix III (Remarks).

[2] Notification normally includes the deposit of a copy of the agreement. When it is made by one party only "the Registrar shall forthwith notify the other party that it has been so filed" (Art. 32(a) of the Rules of the present Court). If the latter party fails to raise objections, it will be assumed that it acquiesces in the notification. See examples of this, a normal practice under the present Court, in Appendix III.

[3] Such a possibility took place in the *Borchgrave Case* (Prel. Obj.), *P.C.I.J.*, ser. A/B, No. 72 (1937), and could particularly be envisaged when a party to the agreement objects not to jurisdiction in the strict sense but to the admissibility of a specific claim as is shown *infra*.

2. *Seizing the Court by a Unilateral Application*

This is the method which clearly distinguishes the Court as a judicial institution different from *ad hoc* arbitral tribunals.[1] Its exercise is subject to some important distinctions:

(a) When the unilateral application relies on a prior jurisdictional title, it is then as capable of seizing the Court as the notification of a special agreement. This, of course, assumes that the application is a valid instrument indicating the parties and the subject of the dispute.

The Court's subsequent attitude in this situation will depend on the attitude of the party against whom the claim is brought. If the latter submits a preliminary objection, the proceedings on the merits shall be suspended and the preliminary objection procedure will take place.[2] If it confines its defense to the merits, then the Court's substantive jurisdiction will normally be assumed to have been accepted and the Court will directly deal with the merits. If it fails to attend, or to defend its case, the Court will *proprio motu* look into its competence before dealing with the merits (Article 53 of the Statute).

(b) The difficulty arises, however, when the unilateral application does not rely on any prior instrument conferring pre-established jurisdiction on the Court. Such an application amounts only to a mere invitation to the other party to accept the Court's jurisdiction *ad hoc*. It is now established that this is a valid way to *attempt to seize* the Court. Its invalidity was advocated by dissenting judges in both the *Minority Schools Case* (1928),[3] and the *Corfu Channel Case* (Prel. Obj.) (1948).[4] They argued that a unilateral application is necessarily the formal instrument to bring before the Court the matters

[1] It resembles, on the other hand, the institution of proceedings before municipal courts particularly in the form of "*recours*" known in Civil Law. See Scerni, "La Procédure de la Cour Permanente de Justice Internationale," 65 *Recueil des Cours* 565, 628–9 (1938–III).

[2] 13 out of the 14 cases in which objections to the Permanent Cout's jurisdiction were submitted were introduced by unilateral applications. As to the present Court the record shows no exception: the eighteen cases in which the preliminary objection procedure was followed were introduced by applications. This includes the *Corfu Channel Case*. See Appendix II.

[3] See *P.C.I.J.*, ser. A, No. 15 at 69–70 (Diss. Op. of Judge Nyholm). In that case, it should however be noticed, the application did rely on a pre-existing treaty but it was quite doubtful that the latter would have made a valid basis of jurisdiction.

[4] See [1947–1948] *I.C.J. Rep.* 15, 35–6 (Diss. Op. of Judge *ad hoc* Daxner). And see, Argument of M. Vochoč, Counsel for Albania in 3 *Corfu Channel Case*, Pleadings, Oral Arguments and Documents 33–8 (*I.C.J.* 1949). In this case also the application relied on an alleged prior basis of jurisdiction. See text of application in 1 *id.* at 8. And see further details in Chapter IV, *infra* at 131.

of *compulsory* jurisdiction, and could not therefore be used when this latter type of jurisdiction was not existing. The Court, however, indicated in both cases that an application not based on any prior jurisdictional title can still be capable of instituting the proceedings, and will confer jurisdiction on the Court if met by the acceptance of the other party. As to the argument that seizing the Court by means of an application is "only possible where compulsory jurisdiction exists," the present Court found that this was "a mere assertion" not justified by either Article 40(1) of the Statute or Article 32(2) of the Rules.[1]

This does not, however, mean that a unilateral application of this kind is in itself sufficient for seizing the Court. It all depends on the later developments and in particular on the reaction of the other party. In this respect four hypotheses could be conceived:

(i) The other party may refuse the offer to submit to the Court's jurisdiction. By such a refusal it prevents the seisin of the Court, and the latter will have to dismiss the application by an administrative order. This procedure was applied in eight cases before the present Court.[2]

(ii) The other party may explicitly accept the offer implied in the unilateral application allowing, therefore, the proper seisin of the Court, and perfecting its jurisdiction through the new agreement made *post hoc*. This was the Court's conclusion as to the attitude of Albania in the *Corfu Channel Case* (1948).

(iii) The other party may directly submit its defense on the merits of the claim without raising at that stage any objection against jurisdiction. This will more likely be taken as an implicit acceptance of the Court's jurisdiction and will thus lead to the same result reached

[1] *Corfu Channel Case*, [1947–1948] *I.C.J. Rep.* 15, 27. See also, *Minority Schools Case*, *P.C.I.J.*, ser. A, No. 15 at 23–6. Both Articles 40(1) of the Statute and 32(2) of the Rules require the indication in the application of the parties involved and the subject of the dispute. The latter Article adds, *inter alia*, that the application "must also, *as far as possible*, specify the provision on which the application founds the jurisdiction of the Court . . ." (Emphasis added). This was taken by the dissent in the *Corfu Channel Case* (first phase) as an evidence that the application must be based on an existent jurisdiction but was found by the Court as implying that "the institution of proceedings by application is not exclusively reserved for the domain of compulsory jurisdiction." *Ibid.* This was in agreement with the British Observations to the Albanian Preliminary Objection. See 2 *Corfu Channel Case*, Pleadings at 18. But see, *Aerial Incident of 27 July 1955*, Pleadings, Oral Arguments and Documents 265, 273–6 (*I.C.J.* 1959) (third preliminary objection of Bulgaria against the U.S. application).

[2] See a list of these cases in Chapter II, *supra*, p. 58, note 3. Surprisingly enough Lauterpacht cited the first of these cases (*Treatment in Hungary of Aircraft and Crew of U.S.A.*) as an example of the examination of questions of jurisdiction *proprio motu*. See Lauterpacht, *The Development of International Law by the International Court* 348 (1958)

in hypothesis (ii). The Permanent Court's attitude in the *Minority Schools Case* (1928) supports this conclusion.

(iv) The other party may give no answer. This is merely a theoretical hypothesis with no precedent in the practice of the International Court. No consent could of course be derived from the mere failure to comment on receiving a copy of an application not based on any pre-established title of jurisdiction. Because such an application is not in itself capable of seizing the Court and therefore of allowing the application of Article 53 of the Statute which assumes a valid seisin, this hypothesis should be dealt with as hypothesis (i) and the case should normally be dismissed by an order.

B. THE SEISIN OF THE COURT

When the procedural steps explained above are duly followed, the Court becomes seized of the dispute, but this is not to say that it necessarily acquires by such seisin a substantive jurisdiction over the case.[1] Seisin, the first result of a valid seizing of the Court,[2] confers, however, on the latter by force of the Statute many jurisdictional powers which are all incidental to substantive jurisdiction and which are meant to enable the Court to function as a judicial institution.[3] First and foremost among these powers is, as explained earlier, the *compétence de la compétence*.

Beyond such incidental jurisdictions resulting directly from a valid seisin, substantive jurisdiction may be obtained in the same time and by the same acts which create the seisin. This has already been shown in two situations; namely, when the Court is seized by means of a valid notification of a special agreement covering the dispute, and when an attempt to seize the Court by a unilateral application not based on any pre-established jurisdiction is met directly by the other party's acceptance to adjudicate the case before the Court. At the moment this latter acceptance reaches the Court, its seisin is validated

[1] Accord, *Nottebohm Case* (Prel. Obj.), [1953] *I.C.J. Rep.* 111, 122. And see Briggs, "La Compétence Incidente de la Cour Internationale de Justice en tant que Compétence Obligatoire," 64 *Rev. Gén. Dr. Int'l Pub.* 217, 222 (1960); Fitzmaurice, "The Law and Procedure of the International Court of Justice, Questions of Jurisdiction, Competence and Procedure," 34 *Brit. Yb. Int'l L.* 1, 14–5 (1958); Reuter, *Les Modes de Solution des Conflits Internationaux* (Cours de Droit International Public – Doctorat) 300 (1958); Rosenne, *The International Court of Justice* 257 (1957).

[2] "Seizing" and "seisin" are, therefore, not identical terms. See Fitzmaurice, *supra*, note 1 at 14, n. 2. Compare the English text of the first judgment in the *Nottebohm Case* where both terms are used as equivalent to the French term "*saisine*" [1953] *I.C.J. Rep.* 111, 120, 122.

[3] See Briggs, *supra*, note 1 at 222–7. And see details on incidental jurisdiction in Chapter IV, *infra* at 169.

and its substantive jurisdiction is simultaneously established.[1] Such a coincidence should not, however, cause a confusion between "seisin" and "jurisdiction" as each has completely different effects on the powers of the Court.

However, seisin has a direct relationship with substantive jurisdiction, for it establishes the critical date for the efficacy of the jurisdictional titles involved in any given case.[2] This general rule found clear applications in the present Court's work, and was generally assumed in the work of its predecessor.

In both the *Losinger Case* (1936) and the *Phosphates in Morocco Case* (1938) before the Permanent Court, the period for which the defendants' declarations of acceptance were to run expired after the seisin. Yet, neither these defendants nor the Court itself raised any objections based on this fact, though other objections to the Court's jurisdiction were involved.[3] The same example was followed before the present Court in the *Anglo Iranian Oil Co. Case* (1952) where the termination of the Declaration of Iran after the seisin was not relied upon as basis of lack of jurisdiction. An argument to this effect was raised, however, for the first time in Guatemala's objections to the Court's jurisdiction in the first phase of the *Nottebohm Case.*[4] This argument described by the applicant as resulting in consequences "bordering on absurdity"[5] was sharply rejected by the Court which declared that:

> Once the Court has been regularly seised, the Court must exercise its powers, as these are defined in the Statute. After that, the expiry of the period fixed for one of the Declarations on which the application was founded is an event which is unrelated to the exercise of the powers conferred on the Court by the Statute...[6]

It is to be noticed that the Court has first worded the principle in the most general terms, thus suggesting its application regardless of

[1] Accord Reuter, *supra*, p. 87, note 1 at 302.

[2] See Fitzmaurice, *supra*, p. 87, note 1 at 15–21 and particularly at 18.

[3] See *Losinger Case, P.C.I.J.*, ser. A/B, No. 67 (1936) (declaration of defendant expired at midnight of the day of filing the application); *Phosphates in Morocco Case, P.C.I.J.*, ser. A/B, No. 74 (1938) (the period for which declarations of both applicant and defendant were to run expired in the course of the proceedings but declaration of respondent was renewed as from the date of the expiry of that period. See Appendix VI, Nos. 47, 48, 74.)

[4] See 1 *Nottebohm Case*, Pleadings, Oral Arguments and Documents 162, 165 (*I.C.J.* 1955). The Government of Guatemala contended that from the moment of the expiry of its declaration of acceptance the Court had no jurisdiction, unless Guatemala so accepted, notwithstanding the fact that the expiry of the declaration took place after the seisin.

[5] Statement of the Observations of the Government of the Principality of Liechtenstein, *id.* at 172–7 and particularly at 175.

[6] *Nottebohm Case*, [1953] *I.C.J. Rep.* 111, 122.

the type of instrument on which jurisdiction is allegedly based.[1] Restated in similar terms in the *Right of Passage Case* (1957),[2] the principle has, however, been recently subjected to an important qualification in the *Northern Cameroons Case* (1963). This latter case was brought before the Court on the basis of a compromissory clause in a trusteeship agreement terminated two days after the seisin. The Court finding that adjudication would be "devoid of purpose" as a result of the termination of the whole trusteeship system over the territory involved, refused to exercise jurisdiction on the case despite the validity of the seisin, justifying this attitude, in part, by the argument that the judicial protection provided for in the agreement cannot survive "when all of the concomitant elements to which it was related had disappeared."[3] This conclusion clearly suggests that the effectivity of jurisdictional titles may be greatly influenced by events subsequent to seisin. The impact of such events pertains however to considerations of propriety rather than to the technical rules of jurisdiction, as will later be shown.

Finally, if the effect of jurisdictional titles is to be judged at the moment of seisin regardless of subsequent developments, the same does not apply to the *facts* that have a bearing on the Court's jurisdiction. A change in a relevant jurisdictional fact after the seisin of the Court may lead to a completely different attitude at least in relation to the question of the admissibility of the claim.[4]

C. ABILITY TO APPEAR BEFORE THE COURT

All states parties to the Statute accept the jurisdiction of the Court only in the sense that they have access to the Court, or, to use the language of Article 34 of the Statute, that the Court is "open" to them.[5] This general ability to appear before the Court should not, therefore, be confused with jurisdiction as related to the subject

[1] See the principle applied to a treaty in Hudson's Dissenting Opinion in the *Electricity Company of Sofia and Bulgaria, P.C.I.J.*, ser. A/B, No. 77 at 123. In that instance, however, the treaty involved had a provision to the same effect.

[2] See [1957] *I.C.J. Rep.* 125, 142.

[3] See [1963] *I.C.J. Rep.* 15, 36. See further details of this case in Chapter V, *infra* at 235–36.

[4] A clear example of this is the change of the nationality of the person in whose favor a state pursues the case, when such a change occurs after the institution of proceedings and before the judgment. But see *Administrative Decision No. V* (United States-German Mixed Claims Commission), 7 *U.N. Rep. Int'l Arb. Awards* 119 (1924).

[5] See the expression "the Court shall be open to the states ..." as used in Art. 35 of the Statute, and the expression "states entitled to appear before the Court" as used in Arts. 40 and 66 of the Statute and in Arts. 34, 44, 75 of the Rules of Court.

matter of a given dispute, despite the fact that the term "jurisdiction" covers both concepts when used in its broad sense.[1]

The ability to appear before the Court is now ruled by Article 93 of the United Nations Charter, Articles 34, 35 of the Statute, Article 36 of the Rules, and the Security Council Resolution of October 15, 1946. According to these provisions states members of the United Nation (and non-members if they comply with the conditions to be determined *in each case* by the General Assembly upon the recommendation of the Security Council) are parties to the Statute, and parties to the Statute are *ipso facto* able to appear before the Court. Other states will, "subject to the special provisions contained in treaties in force," have this ability only after fulfilling the conditions required by the Council's Resolution. Both the Permanent and the present Courts have been, however, rather lenient in examining the adherence to this latter requirement.

In the *S.S. Wimbledon Case* (1923) the defendant state, Germany, was not as yet a member of the League or a party to the Statute and had not deposited the declaration required by the League Council Resolution of May 17, 1922 which determined the conditions under which the Permanent Court was to be open for states not parties to the Statute. Germany was not, however, asked to deposit such a declaration because, as the application pointed out, the case came within Article 37 of the Permanent Court's Statute, and was thus covered by the reservation in Article 35 which made its application "subject to the special provisions contained in treaties in force."[2] In the *German Interests in Polish Upper Silesia Case* (1925), Germany was the applicant, and was again allowed to pursue the case without fulfilling the requirements in the League Council Resolution. This attitude was justified by the fact that that case too was based on treaty provisions, and particularly because the defendant did not dispute the fact that the suit had been duly submitted in accordance with Article 35 of the Statute.[3]

The present Court faced the problem squarely in the *Corfu Channel*

[1] See *Corfu Channel Case*, [1947–1948] *I.C.J. Rep.* 15, 38–9 (Diss. Op. of Judge *ad hoc* Daxner). And see, Simpson and Fox, *International Arbitration* 48 (1959); Fitzmaurice, "The Law and Procedure of the International Court of Justice; International Organization and Tribunals," 29 *Brit. Yb. Int'l L.* 1, 41–2 (1952); Hudson, *International Tribunals* 67 (1944).

[2] See the application instituting proceedings in the *S.S. Wimbledon Case* in *P.C.I.J.*, ser. A, No. 1 at 6–7. And see a discussion on the proper scope of the reservation provided for in Art. 35 of the Statute, in Chapter IV, *infra* at 142–43.

[3] See *P.C.I.J.*, ser. A, No. 6 at 11 (1925). As to the question whether this was an indication hat the Court would not review the issue *proprio motu*, see Chapter II, *supra*, p. 65, note 2.

Case (1948) where Albania, the respondent, was not a party to the Statute and had not made any declaration in accordance with the Security Council Resolution of October 15, 1946. In that case, however, there was involved a Security Council recommendation to submit the dispute to the Court and a note of the Albanian Government containing its acceptance to appear before the Court.[1] The President of the Court stated, in an order fixing the time-limits, that "having regard to the Resolution of the Security Council [recommending the submission of the dispute to the Court] the said note of the Albanian Government may be regarded as constituting the document mentioned in Article 36 of the Rules of Court."[2] By this it was obviously suggested that the Security Council Resolution of October 15, 1946 is not the only instrument through which the Security Council may authorize non-parties to the Statute to appear before the Court.[3] The Yearbook of the Court re-emphasized this view when it treated the Albanian note as a "particular declaration" on the part of that Government to become a party before the Court.[4]

This attitude of the International Court is undoubtedly a result of a liberal exercise of its power to determine its jurisdiction *ratione personae*. As such, it was met with different reactions in jurisprudential writings[5]. It has also led some to conclude that the international judge may presume the *ligitima persona* of the parties if the applicant's contentions do not testify to the contrary and provided that the absence of such a requirement was not invoked by the defendant and was not previously known to the judge.[6]

D. JURISDICTION PROPER – THE INTERACTION OF JURISDICTIONAL INSTRUMENTS WITH JURISDICTIONAL FACTS

After being duly seized of a dispute between parties to which it is open, the Court confronts the problem of determining its substantive

[1] See the text of this note in 2 *Corfu Channel Case*, Pleadings, Oral Arguments and Documents 25 (*I.C.J.* 1949).

[2] [1947–1948] *I.C.J. Rep.* 4, 5 (Order of July 31, 1947).

[3] *Accord*, Rosenne, *supra*, p. 87, note 1 at 238–9.

[4] See [1947–1948] *I.C.J.Y.B.* 34.

[5] Compare, *e.g.*, Kelsen, *The Law of the United Nations* 537n. (1951) with Jully, "Le Premier Arrêt de la Cour Internationale de Justice," 48 *Friedens-Warte* 144, 148–149 (1948).

[6] See Bos, *Les Conditions du Procès en Droit International Public* 275 (1957). The same writer refers to another authority (Dolleman, *Preliminaire Excepties voor het Internationaal Gerechtshof* 48 (1949)) as saying that the Court should examine the judicial capacity of the parties only "when its absence is obvious and seems probable." See Bos, *id.* at 284–5 n. 9

jurisdiction. This jurisdiction is created and ruled by certain instruments or by the interaction of such instruments with given facts. It is, therefore, of central importance to analyze these two elements (the jurisdictional instruments and the jurisdictional facts) which provide the criteria according to which the Court determines whether or not it is legally qualified to hear and decide the dispute.

1. The Jurisdictional Instruments

a. What are the Jurisdictional Instruments?

The term "jurisdictional instrument" is used here in the widest sense to cover all the written acts affecting the Court's jurisdiction in a given case. The first instrument that governs the Court's jurisdiction is, of course, the Statute. By itself it does not, however, enable the Court to exercise any substantive jurisdiction, but it allows the Court, after a valid seisin, to look into the other instruments involved. These other instruments differ according to the type of jurisdiction conferred, and range from unilateral declarations to multilateral and organizational conventions. According to the Statute the structure is as follows:

(i) The advisory jurisdiction is conferred in a given case by the combined effect of the Statute, the Charter of the United Nations (besides, in some cases, the act according to which another organ is authorized to make a request), and the specific resolution submitting the request to the Court.

(ii) The jurisdiction in contentious cases between parties to the Statute is conferred by the Statute and either a special agreement followed by a notification thereof, or a treaty containing a clause accepting the jurisdiction of the Court followed by an application, or a declaration accepting the continued jurisdiction of the Court followed by an application against a state which has made another declaration of acceptance covering the same case.

(iii) The jurisdiction in contentious cases where a non-party to the Statute is involved requires in addition to the instruments enumerated above, an authorization to the non-party by the Security Council (Resolution of October 15, 1946, or any other authorization found adequate by the Court, as in the *Corfu Channel Case*), and a declaration by the non-party in accordance with this authorization.

These are, therefore, the instruments which *confer* jurisdiction on the Court, but they do not cover all the instruments that *affect* this jurisdiction. The Rules of Court, agreements between the parties and even some of their unilateral acts may also constitute jurisdictional instruments in this context. Moreover, the Permanent Court considered as instruments affecting its jurisdiction "the documents preparatory to the Special agreement,"[1] and the present Court has consulted in the process of determining its jurisdiction documents preparatory to a declaration of acceptance.[2]

A relevant question which has presented itself in the practice of both the Permanent and the present Courts is whether the Court can deal with acts taking place subsequent to the seisin as instruments contributing in shaping the Court's jurisdiction. The answer is obvious in relation to such instruments as may contain a "counter-claim" or a "withdrawal of the case" for the direct effect of such instruments on the Court's jurisdiction is beyond doubt. In addition, the Permanent Court had no difficulty in deriving the consent of the parties to adjudicate a particular question from acts or omissions which took place after the institution of proceedings.[3] However, it may be argued that reliance on instruments related to the proceedings was not always accepted by that Court. In the *S.S. Lotus Case* (1927) the Court noticed that "it is rather to the terms of [the special] agreement than to the submissions of the parties that the Court must have recourse in establishing the precise points which it has to decide."[4] Yet, in the *Territorial Jurisdiction of the International Commission of the River Oder Case* (1929) the Court defined the point it had to decide not only by referring to the special agreement but also to the "terms of the submissions admitted in the conclusions of the Polish Case and... implicit in... the Polish Counter-Case."[5] There does not seem, however, to be a difference in principle between the Court's stand in each of these cases. When the case is submitted on the basis of a special agreement it is only natural that this agreement, being the expression of the common will of the parties, will provide the major terms of

[1] See *Lighthouses Case between France and Greece, P.C.I.J.*, ser. A/B, No. 62 at 13 (1934).

[2] See *Anglo-Iranian Oil Company Case* (Prel. Obj.), [1952] *I.C.J. Rep.* 93, 106–7. And see for the significance of the practice followed in this case Rosenne, *supra*, p. 87, note 1 at 314–5.

[3] See *e.g., Mavrommatis Palestine Concessions Case* (Merits) *P.C.I.J.*, ser. A, No. 5 at 27 (1925); *Minority Schools Case, P.C.I.J.*, ser. A, No. 15 at 23–6 (1928); *Chorzów Factory Case* (Merits), *P.C.I.J.*, ser. A, No. 17 at 37 (1928); *Société Commerciale de Belgique Case, P.C.I.J.*, ser. A/B, No. 78 at 174 (1939). And see further details of jurisdiction completed by instruments or facts subsequent to the initiation of proceedings in *infra* at 100–1 and in Chapter IV at 128–34.

[4] *P.C.I.J.*, ser. A, No. 10 at 12 (1927). The statement quoted above related to the definition of the dispute submitted rather than to the Court's jurisdiction to deal with it.

[5] *P.C.I.J.*, ser. A, No. 23 at 17–8 (1929).

reference for the Court. If the terms of the agreement are not clear, further clarifications will ordinarily be sought in the parties' submissions.[1]

Apart from the cases brought under special agreements, the Permanent Court left no doubt as to its attitude when it inferred its jurisdiction in the *Minority Schools Case* (1928) from a memorial that dealt exclusively with the merits.[2] This particular conclusion, it is to be noticed, was reached despite the argument expressed in Judge Huber's dissent in the following terms:

> As the jurisdiction of international tribunals is almost always derived from treaties or other instruments expressly declaring the intention of the State, it is difficult to conceive that new jurisdictional powers – even in regard to a particular case only – could be indirectly inferred from the line of conduct of agents.[3]

The problem of conferring "new jurisdictional powers" in the course of the proceedings arose before the present Court in the *Ambatielos Case* (1952). The dispute before the Court was confined to the question of the arbitrability before a certain commission of the Greek claim against the United Kingdom. Yet the Greek Government suggested in its memorial that it had the right to seize the Court of the merits of the claim.[4] The Court, however, did not assume jurisdiction over such merits on the sole expressed basis that the applicant's offer was not followed by a clear acceptance on the part of the defendant.[5] This holding implies *a contrario* that an unequivocal agreement between the parties in the course of the proceedings will normally be taken into consideration in determining the Court's jurisdiction. To this latter conclusion Judge Levi Carneiro added that even the declarations of Counsel may suffice, in principle, to establish new jurisdictional powers for the Court. But this, he found, could not have been so in the case at hand:

> ... the Court could not agree to any derogation from the clause contained in [the] inter-governmental agreement [which provided for resort to a commission

[1] See a view based on the Court's statement in the *S.S. Lotus Case* to the effect that the Court distinguished between cases brought by a notification of a special agreement and cases brought by application, and considered subsequent submissions irrelevant in the former cases only, in Feller, "Conclusions of the Parties in the Procedure of the Permanent Court of International Justice," 25 *Am. J. Int'l L.* 490, 492 (1931).

[2] *P.C.I.J.*, ser. A, No. 15 at 26 (1928).

[3] *Id.* at 53.

[4] See *Ambatielos Case*, Pleadings, Oral Arguments and Documents 24 (Mémoire Hellénique of August 30, 1951) (*I.C.J.* 1953).

[5] See [1952] *I.C.J. Rep.* 28, 39. And see further details on this case in Chapters IV and V *infra*.

of arbitration] on the basis of the mere declarations of Counsel; nor could it admit that jurisdiction to adjudicate on the dispute has been transferred to it by virtue of such declarations.[1]

The limits to which the Counsel binds his Government is, of course, a matter that the Court can decide. Once it reaches the decision which imputes the Counsel's declarations to the Government he defends, such declarations could very well be considered as jurisdictional instruments affecting the Court's jurisdiction one way or the other. The same applies to all documents duly presented by the parties in the course of the proceedings.[2] Even when the dispute is submitted by the notification of a special agreement, there is no reason why the Court should ignore the modification of such an agreement by the subsequent mutual accord of the parties as shown by their further submissions.[3]

Ascertaining the jurisdictional instruments involved in a given case constitutes the first step in the Court's exercise of its power to determine its jurisdiction. The steps that follow are mainly concerned with the examination of these instruments with the purpose of measuring their effect on the Court's substantive jurisdiction.

b. Form of the Jurisdictional Instruments

Should jurisdictional instruments be molded in any given form? The instrument instituting the proceedings should no doubt fulfill the requirements of the Statute (Article 40) and the Rules (Article 32). An application made by the Peruvian delegate to the League of Nations by means of a letter to the President of the Court [4] was not entered in the Court's list. Such an entry was postponed pending, as the Ninth Annual Report of the Permanent Court explained, "the filing of an application fulfilling the *formal* conditions laid down by the Statute and Rules."[5]

Apart from this requirement as to the instrument instituting the proceedings, no particular form is required in the jurisdictional instru-

[1] *Id.* at 51. And *cf.*, *The Monetary Gold Case*, [1954] *I.C.J. Rep.* 19, 34.

[2] *Cf.*, Rosenne, *The Time Factor* 38–9 (1960).

[3] See details on the effect of the modification of the case in the course of the proceedings in Chapter V.

[4] This letter was confined to the following: "Pursuant to the instructions of my Government, I have the honour to submit to the jurisdiction of the Court under Article 36 of the Statute, the Salomon-Lozano Treaty concluded between the Governments of Peru and Colombia, this treaty not having been executed in the latter country, as will be established by evidence provided by my Goverment in due course." *P.C.I.J. Ann. Rep.*, ser. E, No. 9 at 76 n. 2 (1933).

[5] *Ibid.* (Emphasis added).

ments composed by the parties.[1] The Permanent Court, it is true, declared once that special agreements conferring *ad hoc* jurisdiction on it should be "formulated with due regard to the forms in which the Court is to express its opinion according to the precise terms of the constitutional provisions governing its activities."[2] But this is not to say that special agreements should be cast in any particular form. It only suggests that the *contents* of the special agreement, like, indeed, the contents of all jurisdictional instruments composed by the parties, should not go so far as to ask the Court to act beyond the limits of its judicial powers.

c. Characterization of the Jurisdictional Instruments

As the Court's jurisdiction is primarily conferred by the specific categories of instruments enumerated in subdivision "a" above, the question may arise as to whether the alleged title of jurisdiction in a given case is of the category that normally confers the type of jurisdiction invoked. The actual instance where this question assumed particular importance is the *South West Africa Cases* (1962). According to the applications in these cases jurisdiction was based on the Mandate over South West Africa, this being considered "a treaty or convention in force" in the sense used in Article 37 of the present statute. Such a characterization was questioned by the respondent state which did not see in the Mandate – ostensibly a resolution of the League Council – a treaty subject to the prolonging effect of Article 37. The Court, as a result, had to determine the nature of the jurisdictional instrument and found that, "in fact and in law" it was "an instrument having the character of a treaty or convention and embodying international engagements..."[3]

The question of characterization was also involved in the *Corfu Channel Case* where, as seen above, the Albanian note accepting the appearance before the Court was regarded as "constituting the document mentioned in Article 36 of the Rules of Court."[4] Some existing

[1] See *infra*, Chapter IV at 128, and Chapter V at 201–2. And see *Temple of Preah Vihear Case* [1961] *I.C.J. Rep.* 17, 31 where the Court added only one observation: "The only formality required is the deposit of the acceptance [by means of a declaration] with the Secretary General of the United Nations under paragraph 4 of Article 36 of the Statute."

[2] *Free Zones Case*, *P.C.I.J.*, ser. A, No. 22 at 13 (1929).

[3] [1962] *I.C.J. Rep.* 319, 330. See also *id.* at 416 (Sep. Op. of Judge Jessup).

[4] [1947–1948] *I.C.J. Rep.* 4, 5.

jurisdictional instruments may also raise important problems of characterization if invoked in future cases.[1]

d. Registration of the Jurisdictional Instruments

Article 102 of the Charter of the United Nations made the registration of "every treaty and every international agreement" a prerequisite to be fulfilled before a party "may invoke that treaty or agreement before any organ of the United Nations." Could a jurisdictional instrument *characterized by the Court as a treaty or an international agreement* be invoked before the Court (the principal judicial organ of the United Nations) even if it has not been registered in conformity with Article 102? This question, though most pertinent, has not been examined in detail in any case except very recently in the *South West Africa Cases* (1962).

The Permanent Court operating in the context of Article 18 of the Covenant of the League, which required registration under even a greater sanction that gave no binding effect to non-registered treaties between members of the League, did not seem to recognize the general scope of that Article. Only three of the eleven special agreements invoked before the Permanent Court were registered.[2] Yet, the fact of the non-registration of the agreement was never raised before that Court as an obstacle against the conferment of jurisdiction, nor did the Court hesitate to base its jurisdiction upon unregistered agreements. In fact an insistence by the Permanent Court on the fulfilment of the requirement of registration would have been totally inconsistent with its attitude, particularly in the *Minority Schools Case* (1928), to the effect that an agreement conferring jurisdiction upon the Court need not be written or even explicit.[3]

Similarly, the present Court has not shown much interest in im-

[1] See *e.g.*, the declaration of Egypt (U.A.R.) [Appendix VI, No. 34]. Whether this is a declaration proper under the Optional Clause system or an addition of a compromissory clause to the Suez Canal Convention (made by an offer from the Government of Egypt and tacitly accepted by the other parties to the Convention) has a clear effect on the Court's jurisdiction. Only when it is characterized as a declaration would the declaring state be able to require the other parties in a given case to have adhered to the Optional Clause system and to invoke the reservations in these parties' declarations.

[2] See Appendix III A. As to *treaties* invoked as basis of jurisdiction they were all registered except the Mandates and the treaties concluded before the establishment of the League of Nations. See Appendix IV.

[3] For the operation of the principle of *forum prorogatum* as a perfecting element of non-registered agreements, see Rosenne, *The International Court of Justice* 273 n. 1 (1957). And see, generally, Broches and Boskey, "Theory and Practice of Treaty Registration," Part II, 4 *Nederlands Tijdschrift voor Internationaal Recht* 277–92 (1957).

posing the requirement of registration as regards jurisdictional titles. It was satisfied to base its jurisdiction on an *ad hoc* acceptance imputed to Albania in the first phase of the *Corfu Channel Case* (1948), and then established further proceedings in the case on a special agreement that was not registered. It assumed jurisdiction in the *Asylum Case* (1950) on the basis of an unregistered special agreement. It also extended its jurisdiction in the *Haya de la Torre Case* (1951) because the *conduct* of the parties was sufficient to confer jurisdiction on the Court,[1] without even relying on the unregistered treaty cited by the applicant. The question of registration was however briefly raised in the pleadings in the *Monetary Gold Case* (1954) but was not carried any further as the instrument involved proved to have been registered.[2] The instance that shed stronger light on the issue was therefore the *South-West Africa Cases* (1962). After characterizing the League of Nations' Mandate as a treaty, the Court had to discuss whether, so characterized, the Mandate ought to have been registered under Article 18 of the Covenant. Understandably, the Court avoided any broad treatment of the issue and confined itself to the question of the lack of registration of the Mandate involved, concluding that Article 18 of the Covenant had no application in that case.[3] Two separate Opinions, however, dealt more extensively with the requirement of registration; one by adding more arguments for the validity of the

[1] See [1951] *I.C.J. Rep.* 71, 78.

[2] Judge Armand-Ugon put to the Agents of the parties in the *Monetary Gold Case* (1954) the question whether the Washington Statement in which the U.S.A., the U.K. and France accepted the Court's jurisdiction over the issue, was registered with the Secretariat of the U.N. Pending information on this question, Sir Gerald Fitzmaurice, then Agent of the U.K., submitted in his "Rejoinder" that he was not sure "that it has been the usual habit of countries to register agreements in the nature of a *compromis* whose specific object it is to provide for the submission of some question to an international tribunal." He then doubted, as an example, that the special agreement for the submission of the *Minquiers Case* (1953) was registered. *Case of the Monetary Gold Removed From Rome in 1943*, Pleadings, Oral Arguments and Documents 165 (*I.C.J.* 1954). (In fact the special agreement for the submission of the *Minquiers Case* was registered in the course of the proceedings in that case. See 118 *U.N.T.S.* 149.) The question was not pursued in the *Monetary Gold Case* as it was later proved that the Washington Statement was duly registered. See Pleadings, *op. cit.* at 210.

[3] See [1962] *I.C.J. Rep.* 319, 332. The Court based this conclusion on three grounds: a) that if the mandate was *ab initio* null and void because of non-registration "it would follow that the Respondent has not and has never had such a title for its administration of the territory," b) that Art. 18 provided for registration of "every treaty or international engagement entered into *hereafter* by any member of the League" whereas the Mandate involved was agreed upon in fact before the Covenant took effect, and c) that "Article 18, designed to secure publicitly and avoid secret treaties, could not apply in the same way in respect of treaties to which the League of Nations itself was one of the Parties as in respect of treaties concluded among individual Member States."

non-registered Mandate,[1] and the other by emphasizing that registration of jurisdictional instruments in general has not been required in the previous practice of the Court.[2]

It remains to be noticed that the unregistered jurisdictional titles relied upon by the Court were by no means secret instruments. This has in fact allowed some writers to justify the attitude of the Court in ignoring the requirements of Article 102 of the Charter in this context by saying that the publication of the jurisdictional instrument covers the main purpose of the requirement of registration.[3] A further distinction may be relevant in this respect. If the Court's jurisdiction is not disputed by the parties, which is usually, though not necessarily, the situation when the case is based on a special agreement, the Court need not base its jurisdiction on the unregistered written agreement, as it can always base it on the parties' implicit acceptance of jurisdiction.[4] It could, therefore, be safely stated that registration is not a necessary prerequisite in such a situation for allowing the Court to exercise its jurisdiction. As to the situation where the Court's jurisdiction is disputed despite the unregistered agreement, reliance on this latter instrument can still be justified by the fact that in such circumstances the objective of Article 102 of the Charter (securing publicity for the instrument) is by no means defeated.[5] Furthermore, the Court can always restate its argument that in regard to its jurisdiction little concern should be attached to matters of form, and that once the consent of the parties to this jurisdiction is proved beyond doubt, it need not be molded in any particular form, not to mention an official registration. One, therefore, tends to conclude, despite the absence of any clear pronouncement from the Court, that the requirement provided for in Article 102 of the Charter will not be applied by the Court in relation to agreements conferring jurisdiction on it.[6]

[1] *Id.* at 372 (Sep. Op. of Judge Bustamante). This opinion added four grounds to the reasoning of the Court, most important among which is the argument that "the exact meaning of Article 18 of the Covenant does not ... extend to nullifying unregistered treaties *ipso jure* but simply creates for one of the parties the right *if it wishes* of raising the objection of inadmissibility of the obligation to perform the treaty. Any other interpretation will destroy the principle of good faith."

[2] *Id.* at 421 (Sep. Op. of Judge Jessup).

[3] See *e.g.*, [Lauterpacht] International Law Commission, Report on the Law of Treaties, U.N. Doc. A/CN.4/63 at 217–8 (1953).

[4] *Accord*, Broches and Boskey, *supra*, p. 97, note 3 at 290–1.

[5] See *id.* at 291–2; Lauterpacht, *supra*, note 3 at 218.

[6] But see, Broches and Boskey, *supra*, p. 97, note 3 at 291–2. Although they submitted that non-registration is unlikely in most cases to defeat the objective of Article 102, they concluded that: "It is another matter to assert that that objective can never demand registration of a Special Agreement. Consequently one cannot conclude that Special Agreements as a category are not required to be registered."

The ineffectiveness of the requirement of registration is not confined to bilateral or multilateral instruments. As far as the declarations of acceptance of the continued jurisdiction are concerned, the Court has considered the date of their deposit with the Secretary General of the United Nations, and not the date of the *ex officio* registration which takes place as a result,[1] to be the crucial date for the proper invocation of such declarations.[2]

e. Validity of the Jurisdictional Instruments

A jurisdictional instrument invalid in its inception has been recognized in international arbitration as a good title of jurisdiction if the complaining party has taken part in the procedure without objecting to its defects.[3] This very concept goes far to account in part for the emergence of the principle of *forum prorogatum* before the International Court. It explains why the Permanent Court adopted the rule according to which all applications would *directly* be transmitted to the adverse party (Article 33 of the 1936 Rules), as the latter's acquiescence corrects the defects that may be involved in the application.[4] This question was particularly raised in the first phase of the *Corfu Channel Case* (1948) before the present Court. The Albanian Counsel suggested in this case a distinction between invalid instruments the defects of which could later be overcome, and instruments which are absolutely invalid where the irregularity might be *"si complète, que l'acte est inexistant de plein droit."*[5] Assuming the British application to be of the latter character, he argued that the letter by means of which Albania accepted jurisdiction could not eliminate the question of the validity of the application.[6] The same

[1] The Secretary General of the U.N. is required *ex officio* to register the declarations made under Art. 36(2) of the Statute *after they have entered into force*. See 5 *Repertory of United Nations Practice*, Art. 102, paras. 24, 47 at 293, 299 (U.N. Pub. Sales No. 1955, v. 2. (vol. V)).

[2] See *Right of Passage Case* (Prel. Obj.), [1957] *I.C.J. Rep.* 125, 146.

[3] See, *e.g.*, Goldschmidt, "Projet de Règlement pour Tribunaux Arbitraux Internationaux" (Présenté à l'Institut de Droit International), Art. 32(1), 6 *Rev. Dr. Int'l & Lég. Comp.* 421, 447, (1874); Revon, *L'Arbitrage International, Son Passé – Son Présent – Son Avenir* 518 (1892); Acrement, *La Procédure dans les Arbitrages Internationaux* 157 (1905); Carlston, *The Process of International Arbitration* 64–6 (1946).

[4] See *P.C.I.J.*, ser. D, No. 2 (3d Add.) 67–9, 845. Defects in the application may also be rectified by subsequent documents submitted by the applicant itself. See *Interpretation of the Statute of the Memel Territory*, *P.C.I.J.*, ser. A/B, No. 49 at 351 (1932) (Diss. Op. of Judge Anzilotti). On the other hand, if the application was not invalid at the time when it was filed it "must be considered as real and as remaining real unless it is formally withdrawn." *Monetary Gold Case*, [1954] *I.C.J. Rep.* 19, 29, 30.

[5] 3 *Corfu Channel Case*, Pleadings, Oral Arguments and Documents 47 (Exposé de M. Vochoč).

[6] *Id.* at 49.

argument seems to appear in the dissenting opinion of the Albanian Judge *ad hoc* Daxner, who declared the British application *prima facie* irregular and added that the Albanian letter "could not and did not by itself, in any way affect the position regarding the admissibility of [this] application."[1] The Court did not, however, agree with this attitude, which by declaring the application incapable of subsequent correction amounts in fact to denying the principle of *forum prorogatum.*[2]

On the other hand, the present Court has attempted to develop another distinction as to the defects in the instruments carrying consent to its jurisdiction. In the *Temple of Preah Vihear Case* (1961) the declaration of acceptance made by Thailand in 1950 was asserted by it to have been devoid of object as it was in fact a renewal of a declaration made in 1940 and expired with the dissolution of the Permanent Court. The Court, finding that Thailand had no other intention in making its 1950 declaration than to recognize the compulsory jurisdiction of the present Court, added that:

> [T]he Court could not accept the plea that this intention had been defeated and nullified by some defect involving any flow in the consent given, unless it could be shown that this defect was so fundamental that it vitiated the instrument by failing to conform to some mandatory legal requirement... it is the duty of the Court not to allow the clear purpose of a party to be defeated by reason of possible defects which, in the general context, in no way affected the substance of the matter and did not cause the instrument to run counter to any mandatory requirement of law.[3]

This doctrine which may become subject to further refinements in the future, emphasizes again that the concern of the Court is directed to the intention of the parties. Such intention will be respected regardless of the instrument in which it is expressed, unless a "mandatory requirement of law" is violated. No further elaboration on what constitutes such a requirement is given in the case. Yet, it is clear that a requirement of this sort can be imposed only by the Court's constituent instrument (the Statute) or by its judicial character, as will shortly be seen.

[1] [1947–1948] *I.C.J. Rep.* 15, 45 (Diss. Op. of Judge *ad hoc* Daxner).

[2] *Accord,* Chung, *Legal Problems Involved in the Corfu Channel Incident* 83–4 (1959).

[3] [1961] *I.C.J. Rep.* 17, 34. And see Separate Opinion of Judge Morelli, in *id.* at 45 to the effect that invalidity "could reside only in a genuine nullity, a nullity absolute and *ipso jure* [Fr. *nullité absolue et de plein droit*]. See also, *Mavrommatis Palestine Concessions Case P.C.I.J.*, ser. A, No. 2 at 34 (1924).

f. Multiplicity of Instruments Conferring Jurisdiction on the Court

In a given case there may be involved more than one instrument conferring jurisdiction on the Court as when two states bound by mutual declarations of acceptance submit a case by means of a special agreement or in accordance with a treaty in force.[1] An illustrative example is found in particular in the *Borchgrave Case* (1937) before the Permanent Court. In that case both parties, Belgium and Spain, were subject to the Court's continued jurisdiction through their declarations of acceptance, both had also adhered to the Geneva General Act of 1928, both had accepted the jurisdiction of the Court in a prior treaty between them, and, above all, they submitted this particular case through a special agreement.[2]

In such cases it is clear that a special agreement made for the submission of a specific case to the Court is intended to prevail over the other general instruments. Apart from this, there is no reason to assume that one instrument has priority over the other unless an intention to this effect is proved.[3] The Permanent Court acted on this assumption when it stated in the *Electricity Company of Sofia and Bulgaria Case* (1939) that:

> In its opinion, the multiplicity of agreements [Fr. *engagements*] concluded accepting the compulsory jurisdiction is evidence that the contracting parties intended to open up new ways of access to the Court rather than to close old ways or to allow them to cancel each other out with the ultimate result that no jurisdiction would remain.[4]

The application in this case relied upon two jurisdictional titles, a treaty between the parties and their mutual declarations of acceptance. The Court examined first the objections raised against its jurisdiction under the treaty. Reaching the conclusion that such objections were well founded, it then considered "the other source of jurisdiction invoked separately and independently from the first" to conclude that

[1] This obviously presents a problem different from the problem of *litispendence* when different instruments confer jurisdiction over a given question on the Court as well as on *other* organs. This latter problem is dealt with in Chapter V, *infra* at 257–61. The problem discussed above is also different from the problem created when one or more instruments confer two types of jurisdiction, one advisory and one contentious, in relation to the same subject matter. This problem is dealt with in Chapter IV, p. 125, note 1.

[2] See *P.C.I.J.*, ser. C, No. 83 at 10, 67, 83, 116, 129. And see, Hudson, *The Permanent Court of International Justice* 475–6 (2d ed. 1943).

[3] See examples of treaties made subsequent to declarations free from the reservations included in the latter, of treaties that have been modified to take account of declarations made by the parties thereto, and of the possibility of the modification of declarations by means of bilateral instruments in Hudson, *id.* at 468, 473–5.

[4] *P.C.I.J.*, ser. A/B, No. 77 at 76 (1939).

"the attempt to prove that the Court lacks jurisdiction under the Optional Clause is thus unsuccessfull..."[1]

This attitude of the Permanent Court suggests that when the Court's jurisdiction is alleged to be based on more than one source the Court will carry out the examination of such sources until it becomes certain of the grounds on which it can deal with the merits. If the first source dealt with (which would normally be the title relied upon first by the applicant) proves to be adequate for this purpose the Court will be under no obligation thereafter to pursue the examination of the other sources. It is not certain, however, that the present Court will respect this course when the different titles of jurisdiction are not directly invoked as such before it.

In *Certain Norwegian Loans Case* (1957) the applicant (France) relied in its application on the declarations of acceptance of the parties as the only basis of jurisdiction. The respondent (Norway) objected to jurisdiction on different grounds one of which was based on a reservation in the applicant's declaration. Consequently, the applicant explained in its Observations that the parties had previously agreed in two conventional instruments in force to submit their disputes to arbitration or judicial settlement in certain circumstances including the case at hand.[2] The Court refused, however, to consider these newly invoked instruments as an alternate basis of jurisdiction because, as it stated it, "if the French Government had intended to proceed upon that basis it would expressly have so stated."[3] This conclusion which was generally unquestioned by the dissenting judges[4] is not easy to reconcile with the doctrine derived from the attitude of the Permanent Court in the *Electricity Company of Sofia and Bulgaria Case* (1939). Such a doctrine was particularly understood to negate in case of plurality of jurisdictional titles any presumption to the effect that the parties have opted for one particular title as the basis of jurisdiction,

[1] *Id.* at 77, 80, 83. But see, *id.* at 90 (Diss. Op. of Judge Anzilotti), at 103–5 (Diss. Op. of Judge Urrutia), at 109–12 (Diss. Op. of Judge Van Eysinga), and at 123–32 (Diss. Op. of Judge Hudson). All these dissenting judges agreed that the treaty should have prevailed. But whereas Judge Anzilotti found the effect of the treaty to be "not the abrogation of the Declarations but its temporary suspension," *id.* at 93, Judge Urrutia denied that the treaty had cancelled, abrogated or suspended the legal effects of the declarations finding instead that it made them "subject to such conditions that, during the term of the treaty, the Court's jurisdiction may only be exercised in accordance with those conditions." *Id.* at 105.

[2] *Certain Norwegian Loans Case*, Pleadings, Oral Arguments and Documents 163, 173 (*I.C.J.* 1957).

[3] [1957] *I.C.J. Rep.* 9, 25.

[4] But see *id.* at 71–3 (Diss. Op. of Judge Basdevant).

unless they so indicate.[1] It was even interpreted to mean that "an application will not necessarily fail because it is brought in reliance on one title when it might have been brought under another."[2] The present Court's attitude was therefore criticized not only on the ground that the Court should always look for the proper basis of its jurisdiction when this is disputed, but also because it chose not to do so despite the invocation by the applicant, hesitant though it was, of possible bases of jurisdiction other than the one to which it confined its judgment.[3] Yet, it should be recalled that there is a clear difference between the circumstances in which the other basis of jurisdiction was invoked in the *Electricity Company Case* and in the *Norwegian Loans Case*. Only in the first did the application mention more than one basis of jurisdiction. Moreover, in the second case, the Court clearly indicated that it would have considered other bases of jurisdiction had they been expressly relied upon as such by the applicant. This may suggest that the Court's reluctance to consider the treaties mentioned in the French Observations was due to the unclear stand of France as regards these treaties. Had France clearly relied upon them as basis of jurisdiction in the case, the Court would have felt obliged to consider them, notwithstanding the time at which they were invoked. It has already been shown that acts taking place subsequent to the application can very well serve as basis of jurisdiction. The same should *a fortiori* hold true in relation to jurisdictional instruments made prior to the seisin but invoked thereafter.

True as this conclusion may be, it has no bearing on another important rule upheld by the Court since 1924:

> If a State has recourse to the Court under a clause establishing the latter's compulsory jurisdiction, it must be prepared for the contingency that the other Party may cite agreements entered into between the opposing Parties which may prevent the exercise of the Court's jurisdiction.[4]

g. *Hierarchy between the Jurisdictional Instruments*

Among all jurisdictional instruments the Court's Statute assumes a special importance. It is an integral part of the Charter of the United Nations (Article 92 of the Charter) and as such, a multilateral con-

[1] See Charles de Visscher, *Problèmes d'Interprétation Judiciaire en Droit International Public* 214 (1963).

[2] Rosenne, *supra*, p. 87, note 1 at 274. The statement quoted above clearly supports the Court's power to consider a jurisdictional title not raised by the applicant.

[3] See generally, Verzijl, "Affaire Relative à Certains Emprunts Norvégiens," 4 *Nederlands Tijdschrift voor Internationaal Recht* 373, 395 (1957).

[4] *Mavrommatis Palestine Concessions Case, P.C.I.J.*, ser. A, No. 2 at 29–30 (1924).

vention which provides for an institution that can hardly function if it were up to the parties to modify its structure by their unilateral or bilateral instruments. As a result, the Statute has been recognized in the work of the Court as composed of higher norms with which other instruments must agree. The Permanent Court thus refused to depart, on the proposal of the parties, from what it understood to be the terms of its Statute.[1] And the present Court reviewed in both its contentious [2] and advisory [3] jurisdictions the compatibility of certain jurisdictional instruments with the Statute in a manner not very different from the judicial review of the constitutionality of laws known in some domestic systems.[4]

This principle should not, however, be overestimated. It has been demonstrated that within the strict limits of its material jurisdiction, the Court is not expected to raise jurisdictional issues *proprio motu*. In fact, the Permanent Court almost denied the possibility that an instrument would be incompatible with the Statute because of the dispute it invites the Court to solve, when it emphasized that "there is no dispute which states entitled to appear before the Court cannot refer to it."[5] This would leave the problem of incompatibility confined in practice to two categories of questions: i) questions of jurisdiction *ratione personae* that is, whether the parties to the dispute are states entitled to appear before the Court according to Articles 34 and 35 of the Statute; and ii) questions of propriety, that is, whether in deciding the case the Court will be acting in accordance with its judicial nature and its role under the Statute. As to the compatibility of instruments that attempt to deprive the Court of the powers conferred on it by the Statute, particularly the power provided for in

[1] See *Free Zones Case, P.C.I.J.*, ser. A, No. 22 at 12, 15 (Order of August 19, 1929); *id.*, ser. A, No. 46 at 161 (1932).

[2] See *e.g., Right of Passage Case,* [1957] *I.C.J. Rep.* 125, 141–4.

[3] See *e.g., Judgments of the Administrative Tribunal of the I.L.O.*, [1956] *I.C.J. Rep.* 77, 84 (Adv. Op.) (The decisive factor in assuming jurisdiction in this case was, in fact, the compatibility of the instrument conferring jurisdiction (Statute of the Administrative Tribunal of the I.L.O., Rule XII) with the Statute of the Court.) And *cf., The Voting Procedure of the General Assembly in the Matter of Petitions from South-West Africa*, [1955] *I.C.J. Rep.* 67, 76 (Adv. Op.) where, speaking of the General Assembly, the Court affirmed the principle that an organ cannot act except in accordance with its constituent instrument.

[4] See the statutory rules described as "constitutional provisions" in the *Free Zones Case, P.C.I.J.*, ser. A, No. 22 at 13 (1929). And see the term as used in Hudson, *supra*, p. 102, note 2 at 413; Reuter, *Les Modes de Solution des Conflits Internationaux* 289 (1958).

[5] *Minority Schools Case, P.C.I.J.*, ser. A, No. 15 at 22 (1928); *Chorzów Factory Case* (Merits), *P. C.I.J.*, ser. A, No. 17 at 37 (1928). The Court acted upon this principle when it exercised its jurisdiction on matters governed by municipal law in the *Serbian Loans* and the *Brazilian Loans* cases (ser. A, No. 20/21 (1929)). But see, Bruns, "La Cour Permanente de Justice Internationale, son Organisation et sa Compétence," 62 *Recueil des Cours* 551, 632–6 (1937–IV).

Article 36(6), this problem along with the effect of incompatibility, if established, on the whole instrument, is dealt with elsewhere in this study.[1]

2. *The Jurisdictional Facts*

If jurisdictional instruments are such instruments as will confer on the Court substantive jurisdiction (jurisdictional titles) or will affect a jurisdiction previously conferred, jurisdictional facts play both of these roles, by substituting for a lacking instrument, or by standing as an evidence of a certain prerequisite for the Court's exercise of its proper jurisdiction. To quote a statement given in the context of international arbitration, "[t]he *compromis* [in this context, the major jurisdictional instrument] is the best evidence of the scope of the powers intended to be conferred upon the tribunal by the parties, but it is not the only means for the conferment of jurisdiction, for *by their conduct* the parties can by tacit consent enlarge the powers of the tribunal."[2] Examples have already been given for cases where the jurisdiction of the International Court has been conferred or extended by the mere fact of the defendant's failure to object to it at the right time. This simple fact, a mere inaction, has, therefore a great jurisdictional value transforming an application into a special agreement upon which the Court exercises its jurisdiction. Similarly, if the jurisdiction is conferred by an instrument in which a party reserves the power to decide whether the dispute is within the jurisdiction of the Court, and if such a reservation is deemed valid, the invocation or non-invocation of the reservation becomes a fundamental jurisdictional fact.

On the other hand, jurisdictional facts are not always related to the question of the parties' consent. They may form certain requirements necessary for the exercise of the Court's jurisdiction such as the fact of the nationality of the claim, the existence of a dispute or the exhaustion of local remedies, etc. With respect to this type of facts, which are required on the whole by general rules of international law, certain points should particularly be kept in mind. Because they do not directly relate to the consent of the parties to submit the dispute to the Court, they mainly relate to the problem of admissibility of the claim rather than that of jurisdiction in its strict sense. They are

[1] See Chapter II, *supra*, at 47–52, and Chapter VI, *infra*.

[2] Carlston, *The Process of International Arbitration* 169–70 (1946). (Emphasis added).

also closer to the merits than the facts related directly to consent, which make their joinder to the merits more frequent as will shortly be shown. A strict proof of these facts is usually required,[1] and, as said above, a change in them after the seisin is relevant and may affect the ability of the Court to continue dealing with the case. Finally, although the Court may rely only on such facts as the parties consider in their presentation, the Court remains free in evaluating jurisdictional facts, as indeed it is with regard to all facts presented, and controls the conclusions drawn from them.[2]

By ascertaining the jurisdictional instruments and the jurisdictional facts involved in a case, the Court becomes able to find whether it has jurisdiction or not. It may reach this conclusion by a simple study of the jurisdictional instruments,[3] and it may have to apply such instruments to the jurisdictional facts before it becomes able to determine the question of jurisdiction.[4] The latter cases usually cover problems of admissibility and may involve a study of the merits before a decision on jurisdiction.

E. ADMISSIBILITY OF THE CLAIM

Although the admissibility of the claim and the jurisdiction of the Court are not exactly the same thing, the distinction between the two has never been laid on clear grounds, nor has it been accorded its full effect, in the work of the Court. In many domestic systems an objection to jurisdiction [Fr. *exception d'incompétence*] is directed against the tribunal's power to hear and determine the dispute involved whereas an objection to the admissibility [Fr. *fin de non-recevoir ou de non-valoir ou de non-proceder*] does not question the existence of the tribunal's power but challenges the right of the applicant to invoke it in the circumstances of the case.[5] The distinction might not always

[1] For the Court's attitude in the ascertainment of jurisdictional facts, see Chapter V, *infra*, at 239–57. And see Simpson and Fox, *International Arbitration* 198–9 (1959) for the attitude of arbitral tribunals.

[2] See Smith, *The Relation between Proceedings and Premises* 110 (1962).

[3] See *e.g.*, *Nottebohm Case* (First Phase), [1953] *I.C.J. Rep.* 111, *The Anglo-Iranian Oil Co.*, [1952] *I.C.J. Rep.* 93; *Aerial Incident of 27 July 1955* (Israel *v.* Bulgaria), [1959] *I.C.J. Rep.* 127; *Temple of Preah Vihear Case* (Prel. Obj.), [1961] *I.C.J. Rep.* 17.

[4] See *e.g.*, *Mavrommatis Palestine Concessions Case*, *P.C.I.J.*, ser. A, No. 2 (1924); *Pajzs, Csáky, Esterházy Case*, *P.C.I.J.*, ser. A/B, No. 68 (1936); *Panevezys-Saldutiskis Railway Case*, *P.C.I.J.*, ser. A/B, No. 76 (1939); *Electricity Company of Sofia and Bulgaria*, *P. C.I.J.*, ser. A/B, No. 77 (1939); *Nottebohm Case* (Second Phase), [1955] *I.C.J. Rep.* 4; *Interhandel Case*, [1959] *I.C.J. Rep.* 6, *South-West Africa Cases*, [1962] *I.C.J. Rep.* 319.

[5] See generally, Parisot et Jauffret, *Manuel de Procédure Civile* 17–18 (7th ed. 1962); 1 Solus et Perrot, *Droit Judiciaire Privé* 290–1 (1961); Tunc, *Cours de Procédure Civile* 57–9 (1961).

mean the same in the international procedure but it has been in the air from the very beginning of the work of the Court. In its judgment No. I (*The S.S. Wimbledon Case*) the Permanent Court stated that the first question it had to consider was "whether proceedings could be instituted by the four [applicant] Governments." It then expressed the view that:

> The Court has no doubt that it can take cognizance [Fr. *recevabilité*] of the application instituting proceedings in the form in which it has been submitted. It will suffice to observe for the purposes of this case that each of the four Applicant Powers has a clear interest in the execution of the provisions relating to the Kiel Canal...[1]

In terms of the distinction made above and with due regard to the French version of the judgment this was clearly a question of admissibility rather than jurisdiction. It is, therefore, interesting to notice that the English version referred to this concept by using a third term – "cognizance." In its second judgment the Court more directly declared its uninterestedness in exacting this terminology, stating that "it need not consider whether 'competence' and 'jurisdiction,' *incompétence* and *fin de non recevoir* should invariably and in every connection be regarded as synonymous expressions."[2] The preliminary objection raised in the case covered, however, the two conceptions. As the Court itself put it:

> ... the preliminary question to be decided is not merely whether the nature and subject of the dispute laid before the Court are such that the Court derives from them jurisdiction to entertain it, but also whether the conditions upon which the exercise of this jurisdiction is dependent [i.e., conditions of admissibility] are all fulfilled in the present case.[3]

In the following year the Court dealt with the case concerning *Certain German Interests in Polish Upper Silesia* (1925) where separate objections were made against the "jurisdiction of the Court" and the "admissibility of the suit." The Court dealt with each of these categories separately, but preferred to take one of the objections to its jurisdiction together with the objections to admissibility because it found that "it rather affects the question whether the suit can be entertained [Fr. *soulève plutôt une question d'irrecevabilité*]."[1] However, on dealing, in the same case, with the objection based on the fact that

[1] *The S.S. Wimbledon, P.C.I.J.*, ser. A, No. 1 at 20 (1923).

[2] *Mavrommatis Palestine Concessions Case, P.C.I.J.*, ser. A, No. 2 at 10 (1924).

[3] *Ibid.*

[4] *P.C.I.J.*, ser. A, No. 6 at 13. This was the contention that a submission in the application was equivalent to a request for an advisory opinion.

the dispute was pending before an arbitral tribunal (which the defendant considered a reason for the inadmissibility of the claim), the Court found no practical value in ascertaining the nature of such an objection:

> Whether this submission, should be classified as an "objection" or as a *fin de non recevoir,* it is certain that nothing, either in the Statute or Rules which govern the Court's activities, or in the general principles of law, prevents the Court from dealing with it at once, and before entering upon the merits of the case...[1]

The attitude of the Permanent Court in this last case, i.e., differentiating between objections to jurisdiction and objections to admissibility without deriving any clear consequences from such a distinction, is probably typical of its stand on this issue throughout its history,[2] despite a few individual opinions which attempted to give the distinction some practical value.[3]

As to the present Court, it confronted the problem – as well – in the first case submitted to it. After the British application in the *Corfu Channel Case,* Albania replied, first, that it was prepared "notwithstanding this irregularity in the action taken by the United Kingdom to appear before the Court," emphasizing that "its acceptance of the Court's jurisdiction for this case cannot constitute a precedent for the future."[4] It then presented, within the time-limit fixed for the presentation of the counter-memorial, a preliminary objection entitled "*L'Exception préliminaire de non-recevabilité de la requête du Gouvernement du Royaume Unie*" which it ended by requesting that the Court should find the case "inadmissible" (*n'est pas recevable*) because it was based on an invalid application.[5] As Albania developed this objection later to be a challenge to the very jurisdiction of the Court, the latter, after establishing in its first judgment the acceptance on the part of Albania of its jurisdiction, disposed of the question of admissibility. This it did by simply adding that the Albanian Government's first

[1] *Id.* at 19.

[2] See *e.g., Losinger Co. Case, P.C.I.J.,* ser. A/B., No. 67 at 23–24 (Order of June, 27 1936, joining both the objections against jurisdiction and those against admissibility to the merits); *Pajzs, Csáky, Esterházy Case, P.C.I.J.,* ser. A/B No. 68 at 51 (1936).

[3] See *e.g., Electricity Company of Sofia and Bulgaria, P.C.I.J.,* ser. A/B, No. 77 at 141 (1939) (Sep. Op. of Judge Erich). And *cf., Minority Schools Case, P.C.I.J.,* ser. A, No. 15 at 69 (1928) (Diss. Op. of Judge Negulesco, who, however, wanted to assimilate the plea against jurisdiction before the Court to the *fin de non-recevoir* so that it could be raised at any stage of the proceedings.)

[4] 2 *Corfu Channel Case,* Pleadings, Oral Arguments and Documents 25–6 (Original French text in 5 *id.* at 136-138).

[5] 2 *id.* at 9–12.

reply "cannot be understood otherwise than as a waiver of the right subsequently to raise an objection directed against the admissibility of the application found on the alleged irregularity of that instrument."[1]

The subsequent work of the present Court presents a clearer picture of the distinction than the one found in the Permanent Court's, though the new picture in itself is not crystal clear. In the *Anglo-Iranian Oil Co. Case* (1952), after reaching the conclusion that it had no jurisdiction, the Court found that "it need not examine any arguments put forward by the Iranian Government against the admissibility of the claims of the United Kingdom Government."[2] Later in the *Ambatielos Case* (Second phase) (1953) after the Court had decided the arbitrability of the dispute under the treaty involved, it refused to express any view on the "arguments in defense directed to the admissibility of the Ambatielos Claim,"[3] as these related in fact to the merits of the claim which were beyond the question submitted to it. The clearest case, however, where the distinction arose and produced important practical consequences was the *Nottebohm Case*. After rejecting the objection against its jurisdiction in the first phase of this case, the Court was faced anew with a series of objections to the admissibility of the claim. The applicant did not raise the argument of *res judicata* and the Court found it possible to deal with the question of admissibility as a matter different from the question it disposed of in the judgment on the preliminary objection, as was expounded above in detail.[4] Nothing in this attitude seems to be in contradiction with the earlier judgment in the case, as the latter clearly differentiated admissibility as a question independent from both jurisdiction and merits.[5]

In the *Interhandel Case* (1959) the Court characterized the respondent's third objection based on the non-exhaustion of local remedies as an objection to admissibility (and not, as the respondent made it, an objection to jurisdiction), and therefore proceeded to consider ahead of it the fourth objection which related to jurisdiction proper.[3] However, the Court disposed of the case on the basis of the inadmissibility of the claim, finding that it was not necessary to settle

[1] *Corfu Channel Case* (Prel. Obj.), [1947–1948] *I.C.J. Rep.* 27.

[2] [1952] *I.C.J. Rep.* 93, 114.

[3] [1953] *I.C.J. Rep.* 10, 23.

[4] See Chapter II, *supra*, at 76–77.

[5] "Once this condition has been satisfied – wrote the Court referring to the condition of a valid seisin – the Court must deal with the claim; it has jurisdiction to deal with all its aspects, whether they relate to jurisdiction, to admissibility or to the merits." [1953] *I.C.J. Rep.* 111, 123.

[6] See [1959] *I.C.J. Rep.* 6, 23–4. And see details of this case in Chapter VI.

the jurisdictional question raised by the fourth preliminary objection.[1] This attitude amounts to saying that the Court has to *discuss* the objections to jurisdiction before those against admissibility without, however, being necessarily obliged to dispose of all objections to jurisdiction before reaching a decision on the inadmissibility of the claim. Four dissenting judges rejected such a conclusion as they argued that any judgment on admissibility assumes that the Court has jurisdiction and therefore this latter issue ought to have been completely solved before dealing with the admissibility of the claim.[2]

The same question arose again in the *South-West Africa Cases* (1962) where at least two of the four grounds of the Preliminary Objection presented by South Africa could be characterized as related to the admissibility of the claim rather than to jurisdiction.[3] In these cases, President Winiarski, dissenting, recalled the observation of the dissenting judges in the *Interhandel Case* to the effect that the consideration of a question of admissibility assumes a finding of jurisdiction, but did not agree on its validity in all cases.[4] In fact, in these very *South-West Africa Cases* the Court referred first of all to the third objection relating to the existence of a dispute between the parties, which if upheld would have led to "a conclusion of incompetence or *fin de non recevoir*."[5] Judge Morelli went even further in his dissent when he conceded that this problem (the existence of a dispute) was a matter of admissibility that "arises prior to any question of jurisdiction" concluding that "if the Courts finds that no dispute exists between the parties, it will not be called upon to pass upon its jurisdiction itself; it must, in that case, confine itself to a finding that the claim is inadmissible."[6] He then followed by expounding a thesis, that is not completely alien to international jurisprudence,[7] by stating that:

[1] *Id.* at 29–30.

[2] See *id.* at 54 (Sep. Op. of Judge Spender); at 78–9 (Diss. Op. of J. Klaestad); at 85 (Diss. Op. of Judge Armand-Ugon); and at 95–100 (Diss. Op. of Judge Lauterpacht). It is interesting to observe here that in his dissenting opinion in the *Norwegian Loans Case,* [1957] *I.C.J. Rep.* 9, 34, Judge Lauterpacht dealt first with the objection related to the character of the dispute, *id.* at 35–8, then with the question of the exhaustion of local remedies, *id.*, at 39–41, and finally with the objection to jurisdiction founded on the "self-judging" reservation, *id.* at 43–66.

[3] See [1962] *I.C.J. Rep.* 319, 349, 386 (Sep. Op. of Judge Bustamante).

[4] See *id.* at 449.

[5] *Id.* at 328. The use of the preposition "or" demonstrates again the uninterestedness of the Court in characterizing the issue one way or the other. However, this point was generally dealt with in the individual opinions as a matter of admissibility. See Chapter V, *infra* for further details on the requirement of a dispute between the parties to the case.

[6] *Id.* at 565.

[7] See *e.g.*, Wittenberg et Desrioux, *L'Organisation Judiciaire, la Procédure et la Sentence Internationales* 103 (1937); Bos, *Les Conditions du Procès International* 256 (1957).

> Admissibility can relate only to conditions lack of fulfilment of which prevents a decision on the merits. Within these terms, however, it is quite possible to give the term a very wide meaning so as to refer to all the conditions having that character, *including jurisdiction.*
> ... [A]mong the conditions for admissibility there are others than those related to jurisdiction. But what is above all of interest here is the fact that among these latter conditions there are some which must be considered before the question of jurisdiction is considered. [Two examples of these are] the condition of validity of the application... [and] the condition of the existence of a dispute...[1]

This opinion denies in fact the distinction between jurisdiction and admissibility. In it, jurisdiction is only a part of the conditions of admissibility, and, as such, it is not necessarily the most preliminary part. The practice of the Court does not, however, support such a conclusion. This practice has recognized, though with little concern, that objections to jurisdiction form a category different from objections to admissibility. This recognition led to two consequences. The first is that the Court tends to deal with objections to jurisdiction before dealing with objections against admissibility, with perhaps an exception as to the question of the existence of a dispute which the Court may be persuaded to handle in the very beginning even though it may be characterized as a condition of admissibility. The second conclusion relates to the problem of successive objections, as the Court is expected to be less willing to allow new objections to jurisdiction after the failure of earlier objections belonging to this category than in the case where the new objections assume the existence of jurisdiction but relate to the admissibility of the claim.[2] Except in these two spheres, it is difficult to discover any major difference that may generally ensue from the distinction between jurisdiction and admissibility.[3]

[1] [1962] *I.C.J. Rep.* 319, 574 (Emphasis added.) It should be noticed that the validity of the application is commonly dealt with as a condition of a valid seisin of the Court (that comes before jurisdiction) and not as a condition of the admissibility of the claim. But see, *Corfu Channel Case* (Prel. Obj.) [1947–1948] *I.C.J. Rep.* 15, 27.

[2] *Accord*, Fitzmaurice, "The Law and Procedure of the International Justice ...," 34 *Brit. Yb. Int'l L. 1*, 12–13 (1958); Rosenne, *The International Court of Justice* 354 (1957). And see Chapter II, F, *supra.*

[3] A less significant consequence may, however, result from the differentiation; if the question of jurisdiction is agreed upon between the parties each can still raise objections against admissibility. But see the *Borchgrave Case, P.C.I.J.*, ser. A/B, No. *72* (1937), where Spain objected to both the jurisdiction of the Court and the admissibility of the claim though the case was submitted by means of the notification of a special agreement between the parties. Another practical difference arises, as will be shown, in regard to the question of the joinder of the preliminary objection to the merits.

F. JOINDER OF THE PRELIMINARY OBJECTIONS (AGAINST JURISDICTION OR ADMISSIBILITY) TO THE MERITS

It has already been said that substantive jurisdiction is conferred on the Court through the mutual consent of the parties as derived from the relevant instruments and facts. If the existence of such a consent is disputed by a party's assertion that the instruments relied upon are invalid or are not in force, a decision on this objection scarcely requires an investigation of the facts of the original dispute or of the substantive law governing it. On the other hand, if the objection to jurisdiction is based, not on an alleged vice related to the instruments in themselves, but on the contention that such instruments are not applicable to the facts of the dispute, or even on an allegation related exclusively to these facts, the Court may very well find it impossible to reach a decision on its jurisdiction before a detailed consideration of the merits of the case. This is exactly the situation envisaged by Article 62(5) of the Rules of Court that permits the Court, after hearing the parties in the preliminary objection procedure, to "join the objection to the merits." This provision was first introduced in the 1936 amendment of the Rules of the Permanent Court. However, the Court followed this logical practice [1] even before that date. The problem first arose in the case concerning *Certain German Interests in Polish Upper Silesia* (1925) where no joinder took place, however. There, the Court found that Poland (the defendant) took some of the arguments supporting its objection to the Court's jurisdiction from the very merits of the case. It then simply added that:

> [T]he Court cannot in its decision on this objection in any way prejudge its future decision on the merits. On the other hand, however, the Court cannot on this ground alone declare itself incompetent; for, were it to do so, it would become possible for a party to make an objection to the jurisdiction – which could not be dealt with without recourse to arguments taken from the merits – have the effect of precluding further proceedings simply by raising it in *limine litis*; this would be quite inadmissible.[2]

Only in 1933 did the Court feel the necessity of joining the pre-

[1] It is "logical" because the alternative solutions lead to unacceptable results. As Lauterpacht put it, "if in such cases the [Court] declines jurisdiction there is the danger that it may have done so by reference to pleadings which lack completeness, [and if] it declares itself competent it may do so in reliance upon a reasoning which prejudges some of the aspects of the case upon the merits." Lauterpacht, *The Development of International Law by the International Court* 113 (1958).

[2] *P.C.I.J.*, ser. A, No. 6 at 15 (1925).

liminary objection to the merits. This was in the case concerning the *Administration of the Prince Von Pless*. Besides the objection that the defendant presented in this case, the Court felt called upon to raise a related question and as this was closely connected with the merits, the Court ordered it to be joined to the latter and justified its order by the fact that it could not pass upon the question of jurisdiction "until the case has been argued upon the merits."[1] This practice, codified after three years in the Rules, was then followed by the Permanent Court in three cases during the short period of two years.[2] By contrast, the present Court has found so far only two occasions for applying it.[3]

The procedure according to which preliminary objections are to be joined to the merits, though required by "the interests of the good administration of justice,"[4] is nonetheless an exceptional course. It was followed only in six cases out of the thirty two cases in which preliminary objections were filed before the two Courts.[5] This might be an evidence of the existence of a criterion of "absolute necessity" which Judge Levi Carneiro required for a joinder of this sort.[6] In fact, the Court has, except when the parties agreed on the joinder, insisted that no joinder would take place unless the examination of the facts of the dispute was 'essential" to a decision on the objection, or, to use Judge Badawi's words, when "jurisdiction can only be established by reasons which are bound up [Fr. *se rattachent*] with the merits."[7] Hence, it becomes understandable why the Court should be reluctant to join to the merits an objection directed exclusively against the

[1] *P.C.I.J.*, ser. A/B, No. 52 at 15 (Order of 4 February 1933).

[2] See *Pajzs, Csáky, Esterházy Case, P.C.I.J.*, ser. A/B, No. 66 at 9 (Order of 23 May 1936); *Losinger Co. Case, P.C.I.J.*, ser. A/B, No. 67 at 23 (Order of 27 June 1936); *Panevezys-Saldutiskis Railway Case, P.C.I.J.*, ser. A/B, No. 75 at 56 (Order of 30 June 1938). It was in this "frequency of the joinder of jurisdictional objections to the procedure on the merits" that Lauterpacht found "an instructive example of the attitude of caution in the matter of jurisdiction." See Lauterpacht, *supra*, p. 113, note 1, at 113.

[3] The preliminary objection was joined to the merits by the agreement of the parties in the *Norwegian Loans Case* (See [1957] *I.C.J. Rep.* 9, 12) and two of the six bases of the Indian objection in the *Right of Passage Case* were joined to the merits by the Court's decision dismissing the other four grounds (see [1957] *I.C.J. Rep.* 150, 152).

[4] *Panevezys-Saldutiskis Railway Case*, note 2 at 56.

[5] See Appendix II. (*The South-West Africa Cases* (1962) are counted as two cases.)

[6] See *Ambatielos Case*, [1952] *I.C.J. Rep.* 28, 48 (Indiv. Op. of Judge Levi Carneiro).

[7] *Judgment of the Administrative Tribunal of the I.L.O.* (Adv. Op.), [1956] *I.C.J. Rep.* 77, 123 (Diss. Op. of Judge Badawi, referring to the jurisdiction of the Administrative Tribunal). *Cf.*, *Acquisition of Polish Nationality Case* (Adv. Op.), *P.C.I.J.*, ser. B. No. 7 at 22 (Observations by Lord Finlay): "The question of relevancy is in its nature preliminary, but if it depends on a point which is also decisive of the merits, both questions may most properly be considered together."

validity of the jurisdictional title.[1] This also explains why the issue of joinder arises, in particular, when the objection engages the very facts of the dispute by asserting, for instance, that there is no dispute justifying jurisdiction (as in the *South-West Africa Cases* (1962)), or that the dispute does not have an international character (as in the *Norwegian Loans Case* (1957)), or that the dispute is within the limits of the domestic jurisdiction or the reserved domain of the defendant state (as in the *Anglo-Iranian Oil Co. Case* (1952) and the *Right of Passage Case* (1957)), or that the local remedies have not yet been exhausted (as in the *Interhandel Case* (1959)), etc. In such cases, "a joinder or a refusal of it may – as concluded by Fitzmaurice – be inspired by basically the same sort of motive – in the one case not to prejudice issues of merits before these have been fully heard; and in the other not to prejudge issues of merits which may never arise at all, or need to be heard."[2]

It is not, on the other hand, an easy question to tell in advance how far would the Court, after a joinder of the objection to the merits, probe into the facts and law of the original controversy between the parties. If one is to uphold Judge Read's concept of jurisdiction that covers even the question of what kind of judgment can the Court give on the merits,[3] one can hardly see how the Court can decide on "jurisdiction" and still refrain from prejudicing and prejudging the merits. Indeed, such a concept is bound to invite the conclusion that Salvioli reached much earlier when he wrote that "the objection to jurisdiction *ratione materiae* is necessarily a defense on the merits."[4] However, the problem will perhaps lose much of its difficulty when one recalls the proper limits of the *compétence de la compétence*. This is a preliminary function directed to the question of whether the Court's jurisdiction has been accepted by the parties in such circum-

[1] In this light one can easily understand the insistence of Judge Lauterpacht, in the *Interhandel Case*, that the question of the validity of the U.S. declaration could not be joined to the merits. See [1959] *I.C.J. Rep.* 99, 100.

[2] Fitzmaurice, *supra*, p. 112, note 2 at 25.

[3] See Judge Read's dissent in the *Judgment of the International Tribunal of the I.L.O.* (Adv. Op.), [1956] *I.C.J. Rep.* 77, 143 where he wrote that the notion of jurisdiction "applies at all stages of proceedings: commencement; pleadings; oral proceedings; and above all, at the crucial stage, delivery of judgment," and that "it is the duty of every tribunal ... to satisfy itself that it is competent to deliver the judgment ..." As a result, Judge Read defined the merits to be "the question whether the decision is right or wrong."

[4] Salvioli, "Les Rapports entre le Jugement sur la Compétence et celui sur le Fond dans la Jurisprudence Internationale," 36 *Rev. Gén. Dr. Int'l Pub.* 108, 112 (1929). This conclusion was based on the assumption that an objection against jurisdiction amounts to an assertion that the act in dispute was not committed in violation of the rule the violation of which confers jurisdiction on the Court. "Ainsi, inévitablement, en tranchant la question de compétence on préjuge le fond." *Id.* at 111.

stances as to fulfill the requirements of the admissibility of the claim at hand, and without asking the Court to exceed the limits of its judicial function. When the Court is exercising such a power, any point beyond this question (which relates to the consent to adjudicate the dispute rather than to get a particular remedy) will belong to the merits and should not, therefore, be prejudged by a decision given in the preliminary phase of the dispute concerned with the jurisdiction of the Court, or the admissibility of the claim.

CHAPTER IV

PATTERNS OF THE JURISDICTION OF THE INTERNATIONAL COURT

The jurisprudential attempts to classify the substantive jurisdiction of the Court are many.[1] The criterion followed in each relates in most cases to the form, character, or timing of the consent of the parties to submit the dispute to the Court. In this study a classification based on the nature of the different patterns of substantive jurisdiction is suggested. Though objective in character, this suggested classification is clearly established on the differences that result from the involvement of different jurisdictional instruments in each pattern. Consequently, the easier method of distinguishing the suggested patterns would follow a "formal" criterion (examining the instruments) to reach the "objective" distinction.

The jurisdiction of the International Court is divided into advisory jurisdiction and contentious jurisdiction. The latter covers original or primary jurisdiction and incidental jurisdiction. The original jurisdiction forms two patterns: *ad hoc* jurisdiction and continued jurisdiction, each of which has at least two subdivisions. The *ad hoc*

[1] See *e.g.*, 2 Oppenheim, *International Law* 58–65 (7th ed. Lauterpacht 1952) where jurisdiction is classified into voluntary, obligatory and advisory, the second being conferred either by special clauses in treaties other than those referring specifically to pacific settlements, or by clauses in treaties of pacific settlement, or by the so-called "Optional Clause." This classification, found also in many standard writings, is subject to criticism. Jessup suggested the term "automatic jurisdiction" instead of the term "compulsory" jurisdiction. See Jessup, "The International Court of Justice of the United Nations", 21 *Foreign Policy* 56 (August, 1945). And Schwarzenberger suggested instead the trichotomy of *ad hoc*, limited and general jurisdiction. See his "Trends in the Practice of the World Court," 4 *Current Legal Problems* 2, 22 (1951). Briggs was content with the dichotomy of jurisdiction based on *ad hoc* consent and jurisdiction based on general consent. See his "La Compétence Incidente de la Cour Internationale de Justice ...," 64 *Rev. Gén. Dr. Int'l Pub.* 217, 221 (1960). See also Rosenne, *The International Court of Justice* 273–4 (1957) where he classifies contentious jurisdiction into conventional, prorogated and compulsory. And see this latter classification criticized in Fitzmaurice, "The Law and Procedure of the International Court of Justice ...," 34 *Brit. Yb. Int'l L.* 1, 70 (1958) where another classification is made dividing the contentious jurisdiction according to the time in which the consent is given, into *ante hoc*, *ad hoc* and *post hoc*.

jurisdiction covers jurisdiction conferred by special agreements and jurisdiction assumed in accordance with the principle of *forum prorogatum.*[1] The continued jurisdiction is conferred either through treaties or by means of mutual declarations of acceptance.

Following are the details of this seemingly complicated picture.

A. ADVISORY JURISDICTION

Despite the call of Judge Azevedo in his separate opinion in the *Peace Treaties Case* (1950) that "we must build a wall between the contentious and the advisory functions,"[2] the practice of the International Court has been generally toward the assimilation of the two procedures.[3] As seen above,[4] the Permanent Court exercised from the outset the *compétence de la compétence* with regard to its advisory jurisdiction despite an interpretation of Article 14 of the Covenant to the opposite effect. Since 1936, however, the Statute made it clear that the Court "may", but does not have to, give the opinion requested. Beyond this point, the question now arises as to how the Court decides whether or not to answer the request. What are the factors that the Court considers in determining its (substantive) advisory jurisdiction?

The first point to be made in this respect is the general scope of the advisory jurisdiction of the Court. By both Article 96 of the Charter and Article 65 of the Statute, this scope covers "any legal question" requested by a competent organ.[5] Under the Permanent

[1] It also covers in one view the jurisdiction supposedly conferred by a resolution of the Security Council requesting the parties to a dispute to refer it to the Court. See details of this view *infra* at 135–9.

[2] [1950] *I.C.J. Rep.* 65, 88 (Sep. Op. of Judge Azevedo). See also *Judgments of the Administrative Tribunal of the I.L.O.*, [1956] *I.C.J. Rep.* 77, 159 (Diss. Op. of Judge Cordova).

[3] This assimilation is particularly emphasized when the case involves a standing dispute. See the report of the Committee composed of Judges Loder, Moore and Anzilotti made in connexion with the first revision of the Rules of the Permanent Court, in *P.C.I.J., Ann. Rep.*, ser. E, No. 4 at 76 (1927). And see the Separate Opinion of Judge Winiarski in the *Judgments of the Administrative Tribunal Case, op. cit., supra,* note 2 at 105–6. Some writers went as far as to assimilate the advisory jurisdiction, in some circumstances, to the "compulsory" jurisdiction. See *e.g.*, Hambro, "Some Observations on the Compulsory Jurisdiction of the International Court of Justice," 25 *Brit. Yb. Int'l L.* 133, 155 (1948); Lauterpacht, *The Development of International Law by the International Court* 357 (1958) (using the term "quasi-compulsory"); Anand, *Compulsory Jurisdiction of the International Court of Justice* 281 (1961). Others have assimilated it to prorogated jurisdiction. See Rosenne, "The Advisory Competence of the International Court of Justice," 30 *Rev. Dr. Int'l* I, 10, 31. (Geneva, 1952).

[4] Chapter II, *supra* at 42–47.

[5] Compare Judge Winiarski's Separate Opinion in the *Judgments of the Administrative Tribunal Case*, [1956] *I.C.J. Rep.* 77, 106, where he stated that the advisory function of the Court was provided in respect of two categories of questions only; namely: abstract questions, and questions actually pending between two or more states. He concluded from this limitation, contrary to the holding of the Court, that a case involving a judicial appeal from the

Court the wording was more elaborate. Article 14 of the Covenant extended to the Court the advisory function over "any dispute [Fr. *différend*] or question [Fr. *point*] referred to it by the Council or the Assembly."[1] However, the possibility of requesting an advisory opinion on a dispute pending between two states was always subject to controversy. This could be traced back to the discussions in the Advisory Committee of Jurists which drafted the first Statute,[2] and is found even in the work of the present Court.[3] The fear was commonly expressed that by submitting disputes to the Court through a request for an advisory opinion, the latter may be used as a circuitous route for imposing compulsory jurisdiction upon states which did not accept the interference of the Court.[4] This becomes particularly true when it is recalled that the Court's opinion, although theoretically not binding and directed only to the requesting organ, may very well have a decisive effect on the relations between the parties. However, in view of the broad terms of the provisions governing the Court's advisory jurisdiction, almost every question submitted to the Court for an advisory opinion has related, at least indirectly, to a dispute, though the Court has managed in many cases to deal with the issue as one of an abstract interpretation of texts.[5] This latter tendency which was allowed to grow particularly after the present Court stated in its first Opinion that it "may give an advisory opinion on any legal question, abstract or otherwise,"[6] contradicted the argument upheld

Administrative Tribunal of the I.L.O. "was certainly not contemplated by the draftsmen of the Charter and the Statute of the Court."

[1] Originally, Art. 14 of the text agreed upon by Wilson and Cecil on March 18, 1919 provided that the Court was competent to hear and determine "*any issue* referred to it by the Executive Council or Body of Delegates." (The same was suggested by the French delegate M. Larnaude as to "*toute question*..."). This was then explained by the British Delegation, in its note on the redraft submitted by the drafting committee as a power that "will be indispensable for the settlement of *some classes of disputes*." The text was later redrafted by the same Delegation on April 1, 1919 to read "and also to advise upon *any dispute or question* referred to it by the Council or by the Body of Delegates." This latter draft was the direct source of the above quoted phrase in Art. 14 of the Covenant. See 1 Miller, *Drafting of the Covenant of the League of Nations* 416 (1928); 2 *id.* at 585, 670 (Emphasis added.)

[2] See *Procès-Verbaux of the Proceedings of the Advisory Committee of Jurists* 584–5 (1920) (Comments of Mr. Root and M. De Lapradelle).

[3] See *e.g.*, *Interpretation of the Peace Treaties Case*, [1950] *I.C.J. Rep.* 65, 84–5 (Sep. Op. of Judge Azevedo); *id.* at 111 (Diss. Op. of Judge Krylov).

[4] See generally, A. Hammerskjöld, "Quelques Aspects de la Fonction Consultative de la Cour Permanente de Justice Internationale," in his *Juridiction Internationale* 283, 284 (1938); Fitzmaurice, *supra*, p. 117, note 1 at 142–3.

[5] See *e.g.*, *Admission of a State to the United Nations*, [1947–1948] *I.C.J. Rep.* 57, 61; the *Competence of the General Assembly*, [1950] *I.C.J. Rep.* 4, 6; *Reservations to the Genocide Convention*, [1951] *I.C.J. Rep.* 15, 21; the *United Nations Administrative Tribunal*, [1954] *I.C.J. Rep.* 47, 50–1.

[6] *Admission of a State to the U.N.*, [1947–1948] *I.C.J. Rep.* 57, 61.

by many writers and expressed before the Court in that very case that the Court may not comply with requests for advice on purely abstract questions.[1] A dissenting judge in the same case has actually insisted that the Court should have answered the abstract question submitted to it only "by dealing with the concrete case from which the question arose; especially as there are legal elements in that case which, when separated from the political elements would permit of the giving of a reply based on law."[2]

Yet, if the Court can, when duly requested, exercise its advisory jurisdiction on pending disputes as well as on abstract questions, the treatment of each differs in some respects. In particular a request related directly to a dispute, being closely assimilated to an application invoking the contentious jurisdiction of the Court, raises the question of whether the consent of the parties would be required for the exercise of the advisory function.[3] Such a requirement was first invoked in the *Eastern Carelia Case* (1923), but there the Court avoided giving a general pronouncement on this very question.[4] It preferred instead to base its inability to answer the request on the lack of competence of the Council of the League to make it, as one of the parties (Russia) was not a member of the League. Noting, however, that Russia had also openly challenged the Court's jurisdiction to deal with the specific question submitted, the Court added that:

> The submission, therefore, of a dispute between them [the Russian Government] and a Member of the League [Finland] for solution according to the methods provided for in the Covenant, could take place only by virtue of their consent. Such consent, however, has never been given by Russia... The Court therefore finds it impossible to give its opinion on a dispute of this kind.[5]

The Court recalled also the difficulty of examining the facts without the participation of Russia, finding in this a subsidiary reason for not answering the request. Such an answer, said the Court, "would be substantially equivalent to deciding the dispute between the parties"

[1] See *Conditions of Admission of a State to Membership in the United Nations*, Pleadings, Oral Arguments and Documents 80 (Exposé de M. Bartos), 99–100 (Statement by Dr. Lachs). Both argued that the question submitted was not a legal question but hypothetical and abstract. See also, Rosenne, *supra*, p. 117, note 1 at 455.

[2] [1947–1948] *I.C.J. Rep.* 57, 105 (Diss. Op. of Judge Zoričić). And see *Admissibility of Hearings of Petitioners by the Committee on South-West Africa Case*, [1956] *I.C.J. Rep.* 23, 36 (Individual Op. of Judge Lauterpacht).

[3] See A. Hammarskjöld, *supra*, p. 119, note 4, for the view that the power of the Court to determine its jurisdiction is confined in advisory cases to ascertaining the consent of the parties, and therefore, has no practical significance in cases where the request covers abstract issues (*points*). *Id.* at 288.

[4] *P.C.I.J.*, ser. B, No. 5 at 27 (1923).

[5] *Id.* at 27–8.

– a step which could not, under the circumstances, be performed by a "court of justice."[1]

Later in the same year the Court emphasized anew, in the *German Settlers in Poland Case* (1923), the dependence of its advisory competence on the competence of the Council of the League to make the request. It said:

If... the subject matter of the controversy is not within the competency of the League, the Court would not be justified in rendering an opinion as to the rights of settlers.[2]

The question of consent was again directly involved in the *Frontier between Turkey and Iraq Case* (1925) where one of the parties to the dispute, Turkey, was not a member of the League. After the Council of the League resolved to refer two primary questions – related to the way in which the Council was to handle this dispute – to the Court, Turkey which objected in the first place to the making of this request informed the Court that the questions referred to it "are of a distinctly political character and... cannot form the subject of a legal interpretation," and – as a result – refused to be represented before the Court.[3] The Court, however, proceeded to the examination of the questions submitted and gave its opinion on them. Yet, this attitude was not considered a reversal of the doctrine of the *Eastern Carelia Case*. On the contrary, it was pointed out that unlike the situation in the latter case, the questions involved here related to matters of procedure (the competence of the Council and the vote in it) and that Turkey, at any rate, did not openly boycott the Court, but had cooperated with it by submitting documents, after it had in fact tacitly consented to its dealing with the case.[4]

The three cases mentioned above demonstrate, therefore, a tendency but not a clear doctrine of the Permanent Court to the effect that if

[1] *Id.* at 29. This was, however, "an overstatement of the effect of an advisory opinion." See Hudson, *The Permanent Court of International Justice* 500 (2d ed. 1943).

[2] *P.C.I.J.*, ser. 8, No. 6 at 19 (1923).

[3] See the text of the telegram sent by the Turkish Foreign Minister to the Registrar of the Court in *P.C.I.J.*, ser. B. No. 12 at 8–9 (1925); ser. E, No. 2 at 166–7 (1925–1926). Earlier in the League Council, Turkey's objection to referring the dispute to the Court was also based on the "extremely political" character of the questions involved. See *League of Nations Off. J.* 1381 (1925).

[4] See generally, Philipse, *Les Fonctions Consultatives de la Cour Permanente de Justice Internationale* 47 (1928). In his Separate Opinion in the *Peace Treaties Case*, [1950] *I.C.J. Rep.* 65, 81, Judge Azevedo discussed the *Frontier between Turkey and Iraq Case*. Denying that it was a departure from the Eastern Carelia doctrine, he invoked the principle of *forum prorogatum* as "Turkey, inspite of the objections she had signified to the Council, did not meet the Court with a refusal but, on the contrary, gave an unmistakable tacit consent."

the request for an advisory opinion was directly related to a pending dispute, the Court would exercise its jurisdiction only in the absence of an unequivocal opposition from the parties, particularly if such parties were not members of the League.[1] This is the very tendency that the present Court seems to have reversed in its noted Opinion in the *Peace Treaties Case* (1950). For in this latter case the three states directly concerned were not then members of the United Nations and had openly objected to any action by the Court on the request submitted to it by the General Assembly. The Court, nevertheless, after admitting that the consent of the parties is the "basis" of its jurisdiction in contentious cases, added that:

> The situation is different in regard to advisory proceedings even where the Request for an opinion relates to a legal question actually pending between States. The Court's reply is only of an advisory character: as such it has no binding force. It follows that no State, whether a Member of the United Nations or not, can prevent the giving of an Advisory Opinion which the United Nations considers to be desirable in order to obtain enlightenment as to the course of action it should take. The Court's Opinion is given not to the States, but to the Organ which is entitled to request it; the reply of the Court, itself an "organ of the United Nations", represents its participation in the activities of the organization, and, in principle, should not be refused.[2]

This clear statement can hardly be reconciled with the Permanent Court's holding in the *Eastern Carelia Case* (1923), notwithstanding the attempt made in the Opinion to differentiate between the two cases.[3] As Judge Krylov explained in his dissent, the differences referred to by the Court (that only a question of procedure is involved in the new case; that no practical difficulties arise in relation to the question of evidence; and that the present Court is an organ of the United Nations) could not normally justify a departure from the

[1] In relation to members of the League it was argued that the mere fact of their membership implies their acceptance "*d'avance et eo ipso*" of the right of the Council and the Assembly to make requests related to disputes. See A. Hammarskjöld, *supra*, p. 119, note 4 at 288–93. On the other hand, a strong argument was made under the League to the effect that a request for an advisory opinion should be adopted by a unanimous vote, which would safeguard the consent of all members, See *e.g.*, McNair, "The Council's Request for an Advisory Opinion from the Permanent Court of International Justice," 7 *Brit. Yb. Int'l L.* 1–13 (1926). Though this question was left undecided some writers argued that it would present a problem of admissability as a request adopted by a method unacceptable to the Court would be inadmissible, even if the subject matter was otherwise within the Court's jurisdiction. See Hammarskjöld, *op. cit.* at 293–5. Compare, Hudson, *The Permanent Court of International Justice* 444 (1934). The requirement of unanimity was generally justified by the substantive rather than procedural nature of the decision to make a request and its effect on the rights of the parties involved. The same reasoning could be used at present to substantiate the view that the Security Council of the U.N. can make such a request only by a majority of seven votes including those of the Permanent members.

[2] [1950] *I.C.J.P. Rep.* 65, 71.

[3] See *id.* at 74.

previous tendency if this was still respected. The same applies to the distinguishing element suggested by Lauterpacht, namely, that the treaty whose interpretation was requested in the *Eastern Carelia Case* conferred no function at all upon the League of Nations while the peace treaties involved in the 1950 case did so, by express reference to the Secretary General of the United Nations and otherwise.[1] This possible distinction could not be supported by the broad reasoning of the Court in the *Peace Treaties Case* cited above; a reasoning which indeed makes it clear that the consent of the parties had no place in the Court's advisory function. This being so, the *Eastern Carelia Case,* as Lauterpacht himself concluded, "can no longer be regarded as a precedent of authority."[2]

Not less importantly, the *Peace Treaties Case* (1950) laid the foundation of a new doctrine that is now solidly established, according to which a presumption exists to the effect that the request for an advisory opinion should not in principle be refused.[3] This doctrine was categorically reenunciated in the *Reservations to the Genocide Convention Case* (1951)[4] and was again emphasized in the *Judgments of the Administrative Tribunals Case* (1956) [5] and the *United Nations Expenses Case* (1962).[6] The *Judgments of the Administrative Tribunals Case* had in fact put the doctrine in the standard wording in which it is usually expressed at present: Only "compelling reasons" should lead the Court to refuse to give a requested advisory opinion.[7]

Such a doctrine seems to imply, as noticed by Rosenne,[8] two presumptions – one related to the competence of the requesting organ (that the request is *intra vires* this organ), and the other related to the subject matter of the request (that such subject matter constitutes

[1] See Lauterpacht, *The Development of International Law by the International Court* 355 (1958).

[2] *Id.* at 248. Lauterpacht, like Hammarskjöld before him, argued however that: "Members of the United Nations, in giving the Court the general power of rendering Advisory Opinions, thereby consented to its advisory jurisdiction on any legal question ..." *Id.* at 356–7. But see, Fitzmaurice, *supra*, p. 117, note 1 at 142–3.

[3] See [1950] *I.C.J. Rep.* 65, 71.

[4] [1951] *I.C.J. Rep.* 15, 19.

[5] [1956] *I.C.J. Rep.* 77, 86.

[6] [1962] *I.C.J. Rep.* 151, 155.

[7] Could it be said in this respect that the Court has been more conscious of its "duty" to comply with requests for opinions when these requests were in fact appeals from judgments of another international (administrative) tribunal? Indeed, the Court has expressed in the above case its concern not to adopt a negative attitude towards its jurisdiction that would "imperil the working of the régime established by the Statute of the Administrative Tribunal ..." *Op. cit.*, note 5. Yet the pronouncements of the Court in the other advisory opinions would not warrant at present the distinction between different types of advisory cases in this regard. Such a distinction may very well be developed in the future work of the Court.

[8] See Rosenne, *The International Court of Justice* 467 (1957).

a legal question). The first presumption is supported by the fact that the determination of the competence of the requesting organ is in principle a matter left to the exclusive power of that organ, and not to the Court. This fact by no means indicates, however, that any request falls *ipso facto* within the competence of the Court; for again this is a matter that the Court decides independently of the decision of any other organ. The Court's own competence is assumed in fact by the addition of the other presumption according to which the request is supposed to cover a legal question. Such an assumption finds its normal basis in most cases in the Court's characterization of the request as presenting a problem of interpretation of conventional legal provisions.[1]

These presumptions which have led the Court to describe its advisory function as a "duty"[2] are however rebuttable. In no case, it is true, did the present Court reach the conclusion that a request was *ultra vires* the requesting organ, or that the subject matter of the request was not a legal question, but the Court did discuss its advisory jurisdiction whenever this was challenged, and answered the request in such cases only after positively stating that its jurisdiction had been established.[3]

However, despite the rebuttability of the presumptions, and the limits of the Court's "duty" to answer the requests, it seems in fact doubtful that the tendency expressed in the *Eastern Carelia Case* (1923) will be revived in the work of the present Court.[4] This Court can always safely decline to discuss whether the requesting organ was competent to make the request, thus escaping an important reason for its own incompetence, or rather for the inadmissibility of the request. As to the subject matter of the request, the Court developed, as seen before, a great tendency toward treating the latter as an abstract question[5] of interpretation of legal texts thus facilitating its

[1] See Dubisson, *La Cour Internationale de Justice* 295–99 (1964) for a general explanation of the process through which different issues have been dealt with by the Court as legal questions, by isolating the question submitted from related issues and by defining the elements involved in this question through the analysis of its subject-matter.

[2] See *e.g.*, *Peace Treaties Case*, [1950] *I.C.J. Rep.* 65, 71.

[3] It is true that the Court does not follow a separate procedure in case of preliminary objections to its advisory jurisdiction as it does in the contentious procedure, but this is merely a matter of convenience not imposed by the Statute or the Rules. Such an attitude should not, at any rate, be understood to imply that preliminary objections are treated more carefully in the contentious procedure.

[4] But see, Fitzmaurice, *supra*, p. 117, note 1 at 142.

[5] Compare *id.* at 149 where Sir Fitzgerald criticizes the call for abstraction and contends that: "The Court has been right to keep its hands, and those of potential requesting entities, free in this matter." And see Dubisson, *supra*, note 1 at 300–301.

characterization as a legal question. In this way the Court was able to undertake its advisory function even when related to a pending dispute between states opposing the Court's interference, and regardless of whether or not this latter dispute was such as could be brought within the Court's contentious jurisdiction.[1]

This is not intended to suggest that the Court will answer every request duly submitted to it. For in exercising the *compétence de la compétence* in the context of its advisory function the Court may be met with considerations of propriety that could persuade it to decline the giving of an opinion in pursuance of a request which it otherwise finds within its competence. This particular problem will, however, be dealt with in detail in the following chapter in relation to the judicial techniques involved in the determination of the Court's jurisdiction.

B. CONTENTIOUS JURISDICTION

1. Original or Primary Jurisdiction

The Basis of the Court's Original Jurisdiction

International arbitration has laid down the principle that "jurisdiction is purely a matter of agreement between the interested nations."[2] Considering itself bound by the same principle, the Permanent Court affirmed in its second judgment, as in fact on every subsequent

[1] In the *German Settlers in Poland Case, P.C.I.J.*, ser. B, No. 6 (1923), the Permanent Court referred to the fact that the question submitted to it in the request for an advisory opinion could be brought within its contentious jurisdiction established under another paragraph of the same treaty which allowed the Council to make the request. Then it added that: "If the Court should refuse to take cognizance of a question presented under either paragraph on the ground that it conceivably might have been or might be presented in a different way under the other, the result might be to make both paragraphs practically ineffective." *Id.* at 23. The same conclusion was reached by the present Court in the *Reservations to the Genocide Convention Case.* [1951] *I.C.J. Rep.* 15, 20. On the other hand, in the *Interpretation of the Greco-Bulgarian Agreements Case, P.C.I.J.*, ser. A/B, No. 45 (1932) (Adv. Op.), the Court was confronted by an agreement between the Agents and Counsel of the two Governments concerned made during the proceedings and directing the Court to ignore a condition in the request for the advisory opinion. The Court refusing to adhere to such an agreement, found it unnecessary to say "whether it is possible for an understanding between the representatives of the interested Governments, reached in the course of the proceedings [in an advisory case] to serve as a kind of 'special agreement,' initiating a contentious proceeding before the Court." *Id.* at 78.

The problem does not have an agreed-upon solution in doctrinal writings. Compare *e.g.*, Salvioli, "La Jurisprudence de la Cour Permanente de Justice Internationale," 11 *Recueil des Cours* 1, 41–4 (1926–II) with Hudson, *supra*, p. 121, note 1 at 373; Philipse, *supra*, p. 121 note 4 at 51.

[2] *Administrative Decision No. V*, United States – German Mixed Claims Commission, 7 *U.N. Rep. Int'l Arb. Awards* 119, 141 (1924).

occasion, that "its jurisdiction is limited, that it is invariably based on the consent of the respondent and only exists insofar as this consent has been given."[1] The same general principle, conceived of as the *norme procédurale fondamentale* in international adjudication,[2] was also invariably upheld by the present Court whenever its jurisdiction was objected to.

Consent, as Fitzmaurice elucidated, does not, however, mean in this respect the "willingness" to have recourse to the Court;[3] otherwise, an objection to jurisdiction would have always been sufficient in itself to take the case out of the Court's jurisdiction. Consent, therefore, means the acceptance of the jurisdiction of the Court, even when such an acceptance is followed by the respondent's reluctance to admit its relevance to the actual case. Yet, because consent as a reality imparted to the intention of the parties can always be disputed, it is consent "as determined by the Court" that really constitutes the basis of jurisdiction. The differentiation between the hypothetical "real consent" and the factual "consent as determined by the Court" will be elaborated later on,[4] but it should be borne in mind, as an inevitable consequence of the court's search in the "intentions" of states.

Ad Hoc Jurisdiction and Continued Jurisdiction

By examining the instruments and facts that enable the Court to determine the existence and scope of the consent of the parties one is apt to discern two types of contentious jurisdiction: *a jurisdiction conferred in relation to one specific case,* and a jurisdiction established without relevance to a given case but which *is meant to continue through a period of time, or even indefinitely and to cover any case that may arise within the defined scope of such continued acceptance.* The first is termed here "*ad hoc* jurisdiction" and the other is termed "continued jurisdiction." This latter appellation serves two purposes: to manifest the continuation of this jurisdiction for a period of time regardless of any one particular case, and to avoid the expression "obligatory" or

[1] *The Mavrommatis Palestine Concessions Case, P.C.I.J.*, ser. A, No. 2 at 16. See also, *P.C.I.J.*, ser. A, No. 5 at 27 (1925); ser. A, No. 9 at 32 (1927); ser. A, No. 12 at 24 (1927); ser. A, No. 15 at 22–3 (1928), etc.

[2] See the term as used in Morelli, "La Théorie Générale du procès International," 61 *Recueil des Cours* 257, 286 (1937–III); Bruns, "La Cour Permanente de Justice Internationale," 62 *id.* at 551, 623, 639 (1937–IV); Scerni, "La Procédure de la Cour Permanente de Justice Internationale," 65 *id.* at 565, 611 (1938–III).

[3] See Fitzmaurice, *supra*, p. 117, note 1 at 86, where he illustrated the distinction by assimilating the situation of a consenting state to a man who "may agree to undergo an operation" where "it does not follow that he actually undergoes it willingly."

[4] See Chapter V, *infra*, at 205–6.

"compulsory" jurisdiction which may not, as will be shown, cover the same field.

Each of these two types of jurisdiction is exercised in more than one pattern and raises different legal problems.[1]

a. Ad Hoc *Jurisdiction*

The conferment on the Court of jurisdiction to deal with one particular case results ordinarily from a special agreement made between the parties to this effect. Added to this normal procedure anticipated in Article 36(1) of the Statute, the practice of the Court allows the extension of its jurisdiction over a case by successive acts (by virtue of the principle of *forum prorogatum*). Finally, *ad hoc* jurisdiction could, according to a rather weak argument, be conferred by a resolution of the Security Council made under Article 36(3) of the Charter of the United Nations.

(i) *Ad Hoc* Jurisdiction Established by Means of a Prior Special Agreement (Compromis):

This pattern of jurisdiction has been exercised in twelve cases before the Permanent Court and in six before the present Court.[2] In some of these cases this pattern was particularly chosen despite the possibility of invoking some other pattern of the Court's jurisdiction. The reason is clear. A special agreement contains an agreed-upon statement of the issues involved, and a notification of it will make of neither party a complainant nor a respondent and will give both "an equal opportunity reciprocally to discuss their respective contentions..."[3] Yet, the cases based on special agreements are relatively few because of the difficulties involved in reaching such agreements in the first place.

Cases based on special agreements raise many problems related in particular to the Court's powers in relation to the issues contained in the agreement, as is expounded in detail in the following Chapter.

[1] Though most feared by states, continued jurisdiction is generally favored by theoreticians. Not only does it make the resort to the Court in a particular case an easier political decision by the Governments concerned (as it will not be a completely new decision but an implementation of a standing acceptance, and as the case, being brought before the dispute is aggravated by time and emotions, will cover a small issue on which an unfavorable decision could be less reluctantly accepted), but also it would, as a result, facilitate the task of the Court itself. On the other hand, *ad hoc* jurisdiction is more difficult to confer as it has to be created in relation to each particular case in the heat of the dispute.

[2] See Appendix III.

[3] *Case Relating to the Territorial Jurisdiction of the International Commission of the River Oder, P.C.I.J.*, ser. A, No. 23 at 45 (Order of August 15, 1929). Compare *South Eastern Territory of Greenland Case*, ser. A/B, No. 48 at 270 (1930).

Mentioning one aspect of these problems the Permanent Court required, in the first phase of the *Free Zones Case* (1929), that "special agreements... should... be formulated with due regard to the forms in which the Court is to express its opinion according to the precise terms of the constitutional provisions governing its activity..."[1] This, as was noticed in the previous Chapter, refers to the contents of the special agreement and by no means indicates that such an agreement should itself be molded in any particular form. In fact, the following pattern of jurisdiction testifies that the agreement of the parties to confer jurisdiction on the Court was at no time required to be formal, written, or even explicit.

(ii) *Ad Hoc* Jurisdiction Established on the Basis of *Forum Prorogatum* (Prorogated Jurisdiction):

Unlike the previous pattern, prorogated jurisdiction assumes necessarily the existence of a standing tribunal as it could be conferred only subsequent to an attempt to institute the proceedings. The concept, known since Roman Law, was not however completely alien to the arbitral experience where jurisdiction was sometimes extended to issues not contained in the *compromis* due to the explicit or tacit acceptance by one party of their submission by the other.[2] Yet, the Permanent Court was the first international tribunal to provide an institution capable, at least in theory, of exercising a jurisdiction established by prorogation *ab initio*, that is, with regard to an entire case which had no other basis of jurisdiction. This was not, however, the clear intention of the drafters of the Statute of that Court.[3] Its practice, on the other hand, recognized the principle in many cases,

[1] *P.C.I.J.*, ser. A, No. 22 at 13 (1929).

[2] A relatively recent example is the case of *Taussig et Wippler c. Etat serbe-croate-slovène*, 9 *Rec. des déc. des trib. arb. mixtes* 396, 398–9 (1930). Some arbitral tribunals refused, however, to deduce consent to their jurisdiction from the mere silence of the respondent. See an early example in *Bozano Case* (Italy *v.* Chile) (1888), cited in Ralston, *Supplement to the Law and Procedure of International Tribunals* 29 (1936).

[3] Article 36(1) of the Statute which provides that the jurisdiction of the Court comprises "all cases which the parties refer to it" was clearly drafted with joint submission by *compromis* in mind. To interpret it otherwise would be, as Judge Huber showed in his dissent in the *Minority Schools Case*, "difficult to reconcile with the conceptions which, at the time of the preparation of the Statute, were current in Government circles in regard to compulsory arbitration, and it is itself contradicted by the records of the preparatory work." *P.C.I.J.*, ser A, No. 15 at 52. The question "whether a suit could be brought before the Court by means of an application when the parties had not accepted compulsory jurisdiction" was particularly raised by Huber on the occasion of the first amendment of the Rules of the Permanent Court (1922), and there he held the view that this was not possible. See *P.C.I.J.*, ser. D, No. 2 at 201 (1922).

but presented no occasion where jurisdiction over the whole case was exercised in the absence of any basis thereof in the application.

The first case in which the Permanent Court enunciated the principle that its jurisdiction, even if lacking at the time of the initiation of proceedings could be perfected in the course of the latter, was the *Palestine Mavrommatis Concessions Case* (1924). This was not exactly a case of prorogated jurisdiction, however. One of the bases of jurisdiction in that case was a certain treaty text which, it was alleged, was not yet applicable at the moment of instituting the proceedings but entered into force on a later date. In relation to this argument, the Court noticed that:

> Even if the grounds on which the institution of proceedings was based were defective for the reason stated, this would not be an adequate reason for the dismissal of the applicant's suit. The Court whose jurisdiction is international, is not bound to attach to matters of form the same degree of importance which they might possess in municipal law. Even, therefore, if the application were premature because the Treaty of Lausanne had not yet been ratified, this circumstance would now be covered by the subsequent deposit of the necessary ratifications.[1]

Later, in its Judgment No. 4 related to the interpretation of Judgment No. 3 the Court preferred to avoid the question of whether its jurisdiction was validly based on the unilateral request for interpretation; and was able to do so only because it found that the respondent Government had submitted observations regarding the request "without disputing the Court's jurisdiction to give such interpretation." Therefore, the Court concluded that it had jurisdiction "as the result of this agreement between the parties..."[2]

The first clear case allowing the extension of jurisdiction during the proceedings to an issue not covered in advance by the application is the second *Mavrommatis Case* (1925). There, the Court felt juristfied to reply to a question "not by reason of the jurisdiction conferred on the Court under Article 26 of the Mandate, but in consequence of an agreement between the Parties resulting from the written proceedings."[3] Then, it clearly indicated that "by virtue of a further agreement could other disputes... be dealt with by the Court."[4]

All the above cases were, however, only an introduction to the leading case in this field to which reference has already been exten-

[1] *P.C.I.J.*, ser. A, No. 2 at 34 (1924). Judges Finlay, Moore, Bustamante and Oda dissented on this point.

[2] *P.C.I.J.*, ser. A, No. 4 at 5–6 (Decision of the Chamber of Summary Procedure).

[3] *P.C.I.J.*, ser. A, No. 5 at 27.

[4] *Id.* at 28.

sively made – the *Minority Schools Case* (1928). The proceedings in this case were initiated on the assumption that the Court had a continued jurisdiction based on a treaty in force. The respondent Government did not at first object to such an assertion and had actually argued in its counter-memorial on the merits of the case, without however explicitly acknowledging the Court's jurisdiction. Later on, it raised objections against this jurisdiction in its "Rejoinder.' But the Court found that the earlier attitude of the respondent "must be regarded as an unequivocal indication of the desire of [that] State to obtain a decision on the merits..."[1] This desire, the Court argued constituted a foundation for an agreement between the parties to confer jurisdiction on the Court to deal with the case at hand, and an "agreement" of this sort is perfectly valid. In the Court's own words:

> ... there is nothing... in the principles governing the Court's jurisdiction to prevent questions not falling within the category of those in respect of which compulsory jurisdiction is established, from being submitted to the Court by agreement between the parties, notwithstanding the fact that the suit has been brought on the basis of the clause conferring compulsory jurisdiction.[2]

The same principle was recalled and was partly applied in the second phase of the *Chorzow Factory Case* (1928).[3] The question was then extensively argued in the discussions between the members of the Court on the occasion of the last revision of its Rules. This came in connection with the proposal requiring unilateral applications instituting proceedings to mention the basis of jurisdiction in the case – a requirement that would have had a direct effect on the application of the principle which was then referred to, for the first time in the work of the Court, as the doctrine of *forum prorogatum*.[4] Such a proposal did not, however, pass and the condition it included was finally redrafted to be required only "as far as possible."[5] Thus the

[1] *P.C.I.J.*, ser. A, No. 15 at 24 (1928). (Judges Huber, Nyholm and Negulesco dissenting.)

[2] *Ibid.*

[3] *P.C.I.J.*, ser. A, No. 17 at 37 (1928).

[4] See *P.C.I.J.*, ser. D, No. 2 (3rd Add.) at 69 (1936) (Comment of Judge Schucking). This comment referring to the doctrine as "in the interests of the good administration of justice" was followed by other statements using the same term, and the whole discussion is listed in the above publication under the title: *Forum Prorogatum.* And see a discussion of the accuracy of this term in relation to the work of the Court in Winiarski, "Quelques Réflexions sur le Soi-Disant *Forum Prorogatum* en Droit International," in [Constantopoulos et al.] *Grundprobleme des Internationalen Rechts* 445–52 (1957).

[5] The origin of this formula is found in the suggestion of Judge Formageot which was more explicit in maintaining the doctrine of *forum prorogatum.* This suggestion was to the effect that the original proposal be amended to require the application to specify the provision on which it is founded ' if any" [Fr. *éventuellement*]. See *P.C.I.J.*, ser. D., No. 2 (3rd. Add.). at 154 (1936).

doctrine was maintained and in fact was again applied in the *Société Commerciale de Belgique Case* (1939) where the Court found it sufficient to observe "that [the respondent] has raised no objection; on the contrary it has submitted arguments on the merits and has asked for a decision on the merits" as evidence that the parties were "in agreement" on the question of jurisdiction.[1]

The doctrine of *forum prorogatum* presented itself again in the very first case the present Court dealt with. The United Kingdom instituted the proceedings by an application against Albania in the *Corfu Channel Case*, though the latter was not bound by any prior acceptance of the Court's jurisdiction. The application, it is true, did mention as the basis of jurisdiction the resolution of the Security Council recommending that the parties resort to the Court, describing it as binding under Article 25 of the Charter and, therefore, a "matter specially provided for in the Charter" in the sense meant in Artical 36(1) of the Statute.[2] Yet, the reliance on such a basis was unprecedented and, as shortly will be seen, its validity is too doubtful. It was clear, therefore, that a subsequent acceptance of Albania would make the case only one of *ab initio* prorogated jurisdiction. In fact this was the conclusion of the Court which founded its jurisdiction exclusively on the acceptance it imparted to Albania as expressed in a letter sent by it to the Court after the institution of the proceedings. This basis is closer to the concept of *forum prorogatum* than even the special agreement alleged by the applicant to have resulted from the Albanian acceptance of the Security Council resolution,[3] or from the mere appearance of both parties before the Court.[4] Although it is only an advanced application of the principle already settled in the work of the Permanent Court, it was no doubt a significant contribution which some have rightly considered a "highly important innovation."[5]

After the *Corfu Channel Case* (1948) the Court had at least four occasions to shed more light on the doctrine which it then found applicable only in one case. This was the *Haya de la Torre Case* (1951) in which one of the parties to the prior *Asylum Case* (1950) asked the

[1] *P.C.I.J.*, ser. A/B, No. 78 at 174 (1939).

[2] 1 *Corfu Channel Case*, Pleadings, Oral Arguments and Documents 8 (*I.C.J.* (1949)).

[3] See 2 *id.* at 18.

[4] See 3 *id.* at 57.

[5] Simpson and Fox, *International Arbitration* 64 (1959). Compare, Schwarzenberger, "Trends in the Practice of the World Court," 4 *Current Legal Problems* 1, 24 n. (1951). See generally on the significance of the doctrine in the work of the present Court, Dubisson, *La Cour Internationale de Justice* 198–204 (1964).; Rosenne, "The *Forum Prorogatum* in the International Court of Justice," 6 *Rev. Hellénique* 1–26 (1953).

Court to indicate the manner of, and the steps required for, the execution of the judgment in the latter. The new case was brought by application in which no basis of jurisdiction of clear relevance to the case was elucidated, yet the respondent made no objection to jurisdiction. As a result, the Court in a manner very similar to that of its predecessor was content to state that:

> The parties have in the present case consented to the jurisdiction of the Court. All the questions submitted to it have been argued by them on the merits, and no objection has been made to a decision on the merits. This conduct of the parties is sufficient to confer jurisdiction on the Court.[1]

This was, therefore, the second, and so far the only other incident in which the present Court by applying the principle of *forum prorogatum* has transformed a unilateral application into a special agreement (a *contrat judiciaire,* as Reuter put it)[2] made after the initiation of the proceedings and considered as a proper basis of jurisdiction. However, when the United Kingdom alleged in the *Anglo-Iranian Oil Co. Case* (1952) despite the clear objection to jurisdiction by Iran, that a similar acceptance could be concluded from the fact that the respondent Government had presented objections to the admissibility of the claim, the Court found in this weak contention, which was not pressed in fact, an occasion to explain the limits of the doctrine:

> The principle of *forum prorogatum*... would have to be based on some conduct or statement of the Government of Iran which involves an element of consent regarding the jurisdiction of the Court. But that Government has consistently denied the jurisdiction of the Court.... It is true that it has submitted other Objections which have no direct bearing on the question of jurisdiction. But they are clearly designed as measures of defense which it would be necessary to examine only if Iran's Objections to the jurisdiction were rejected. No element of consent can be deduced from such conduct on the part of the Government of Iran. Consequently, the Submission of the United Kingdom on this point cannot be accepted.[3]

A stricter application of the doctrine was in fact implemented in the *Ambatielos Case* (1952) decided a little earlier in the same year. The merits of the case related to the question whether there was an obligation on the part of the United Kingdom to accept the resort to arbitration before a certain commission in regard to a certain claim made by Greece. The Court's power to deal with this issue was objected to by the respondent. But before the filing of the preliminary objection

[1] [1951] *I.C.J. Rep.* 71, 78.
[2] See Reuter, *Les Modes de Solution des Conflits Internationaux* 306 (1958).
[3] [1952] *I.C.J. Rep.* 93, 114.

the applicant Government went in its memorial beyond the question of arbitrability asserting that it was "en droit de saisir la Cour du fond du differend existant entre les deux Gouvernements sans même être tenu d'avoir recours au prealable a l'arbitrage..."[1] Although such a contention was twice met with a hesitant acceptance by the United Kingdom (once in its counter-memorial [2] and once by its Counsel in the oral hearings),[3] the Court, noting that the acceptance was made in each case under conditions that were somewhat different and, in the case of the Counsel's acceptance were "not very clear," it concluded that:

> This discrepancy throws some doubt on the existence of any unequivocal agreement between the parties on this matter. The Court has, however, no doubt that in the absence of clear agreement between the parties in this respect, the Court has no jurisdiction to go into all the merits of the present case as a commission of arbitration could do.[4]

This attitude was probably more cautious and conservative than what the previous work of the Court could have suggested as a prediction of what the Court's conclusion would have been. Moreover, this degree of caution seems now hard to reconcile with the example of boldness the Court itself showed in the same case in determining its jurisdiction to deal with the question of arbitrability.[5]

The final instance to be mentioned here relates to the argument which evolved in the course of the proceedings in the second phase of the *Nottebohm Case* (1955). Liechtenstein argued that Guatemala, having by a letter of its Foreign Minister suggested negotiations with Liechtenstein with a view to arriving at an amicable solution, had accepted the jurisdictional fact that the claimant was a national of Liechtenstein and therefore accepted the title of the latter state to espouse the claim and to seize the Court. This argument was, however, completely refuted by the Court which could not find in the mentioned letter any acceptance to that effect.[6] No other occasion has since arisen where the argument was made to extend an *ad hoc* prorogated

[1] *Ambatielos Case*, Pleadings, Oral Arguments and Documents 24 (*I.C.J.* 1953).

[2] *Id.* at 180.

[3] *Id.* at 284. (Oral argument of Sir Eric Beckett). The Counsel made it clear in this respect that the acceptance takes place only if the Court finds itself competent to deal with the case. "Consequently – he added – in this case there is no question of the Court acquiring jurisdiction on the basis of *forum prorogatum*."

[4] *Ambatielos Case* (Prel. Obj.), [1952] *I.C.J. Rep.* 28, 39.

[5] For a comparison between the attitude of the Court toward the two issues, see Fitzmaurice, "The Law and Procedure of the International Court of Justice ...," 34 *Brit. Yb. Int'l L.* 1, 92–5 (1958).

[6] See [1955] *I.C.J. Rep.* 4, 19–20.

jurisdiction over a given case or even over an issue related to a pending case.

The principle of prorogated jurisdiction could, therefore, be said to require a clear, unequivocal and valid acceptance of the respondent,[1] given after the attempt of seizing the Court by the applicant, in order to allow the Court to adjudicate on the case or on an issue involved in it, with which it would not otherwise be able to deal. Such a principle can be fully applied in practice only when Articles 40(1) of the Statute and 32(2) of the Rules are interpreted as not requiring that the application instituting the proceedings be based on a prior jurisdictional title.[2] It also was considered an illustration of the general principle of estoppel as applied to the international procedure,[3] a principle that was asserted to be also capable of expanding to confer an *ad hoc* jurisdiction on the Court whenever it is possible to prove an "implied agreement of the parties reached *before* the institution of the proceedings."[4]

[1] What if the consent given by the respondent in the course of the proceedings was based on an error? The question of error as a vice in the consent expressed in international instruments was discussed in the *Temple of Preah Vihear Case* (Merits), though in a completely different context. The general principle laid in that case may, however, be useful in this respect: "It is an established rule of law – wrote the Court – that the plea of error cannot be allowed as an element vitiating consent if the party advancing it contributed by its own conduct to the error, or could have avoided it, or if the circumstances were such as to put that party on notice of a possible error." [1962] *I.C.J. Rep.* 6, 26.

[2] See *Corfu Channel Case*, [1947–1948] *I.C.J. Rep.* 27. But see, *Minority Schools Case, P.C.I.J.*, ser. A, No. 15 at 69 (Diss. Op. of Judge Nyholm). And see, Waldock, "*Forum Prorogatum* or Acceptance of a Unilateral Summons to Appear before the International Court," 2 *I.L.Q.* 377, 387 (1948) where he distinguishes between Art. 36(1) of the Statute which deals with "the substance and not the procedure of jurisdiction," and which regards the consent of both parties as "essential before the Court could be seised of a case," and Article 40(1) which deals with a question of procedure and includes no requirement to the effect that an application should be made jointly or be necessarily based on a previously established jurisdiction. See also, Chung, *Legal Problems Involved in the Corfu Channel Incident* 93–4 (1959).

[3] See Rosenne, *The International Court of Justice* 267–8, (1957); Simpson and Fox, *supra*, p. 131, note 5 at 66. *Cf.*, Reuter, *supra*, p. 132, note 2 at 305. (The latter author refers to the principle of estoppel as itself an application of the principle of good faith.) Compare, Delbez, *Les Principes Généraux du Contentieux International* 62 (1962) where he based prorogated jurisdiction on an asserted "right" of members of the U.N. to seize the Court, the latter being an organ of the United Nations.

[4] Rosenne, *supra*, note 3 at 268 (Emphasis added). No case was ever based on such a ground, however. If the application instituting proceedings in a case specifies the basis of jurisdiction as a prior implied special agreement and the Court finds the documents attached to it of a relevant value there is no reason why it should not consider itself properly seized and open an investigation of its jurisdiction if the other party objects to it. If the alleged implied agreement is proved beyond doubt, the fact that it was made before, rather than after, the institution of proceedings should not prevent the Court from exercising an *ad hoc* jurisdiction over the case. This, however, could take place only when the implied agreement is proved to have meant the direct submission of the case to the Court and not merely to "arbitration" or to "a judicial settlement" or even to the Court under conditions not yet fulfilled.

The *ad hoc* prorogated jurisdiction has, moreover, as elaborated elsewhere in this study, important effects particularly on the timing of the preliminary objection,[1] and on perfecting the Court's jurisdiction even when it is originally based on invalid instruments.[2]

(iii) *Ad Hoc* Jurisdiction Alleged to Be Based on Resolutions of the Security Council

It is recalled that the application of the United Kingdom in the *Corfu Channel Case* relied on an alleged joint effect of Article 36(3) of the Charter and Article 36(1) of the Statute, according to which the Security Council would have the power to confer jurisdiction on the Court by recommending to the parties that they should refer their legal disputes to the Court. As a recommendation of this sort was already made with respect to the dispute with Albania, the applicant contended that the latter was under an obligation to accept the Court's jurisdiction which was established by the Security Council's resolution. Such a contention simply meant that the Statute together with the Charter allow the Security Council to create a pattern of *ad hoc* jurisdiction that is truly compulsory; for unlike any other pattern of original jurisdiction this would be established regardless of the will of the respondent and only by a "recommendation" from the Security Council.[3]

Despite the novelty and importance of this contention the Court, by an eight-to-seven vote, did not consider it necessary to express an opinion on the subject, content as it was to found its jurisdiction on the safer basis of the respondent's acceptance. Not less than seven judges, however, made it clear that they were not convinced by the United Kingdom's argument, their reasons being that:

In particular, having regard (1) to the normal meaning of the word recommendation, a meaning which this word has retained in diplomatic language..., (2) to the general structure of the Charter and the Statute which founds the jurisdiction of the Court on the consent of States, and (3) to the terms used in Article 36, paragraph 3, of the Charter and to its object which is to remind the Security Council that legal disputes should normally be decided by judicial

[1] See Chapter II, *supra* at 52–53.

[2] See Chapter III, *supra* at 100–101.

[3] It could be argued that this pattern of jurisdiction is not *ad hoc* but continued, accepted in advance by ratifying the Charter; the recommendation of the Security Council being merely a necessary precondition for submitting a particular case. However, it is preferred to treat it as a pattern of *ad hoc* jurisdiction because, as in the case of a special agreement, no jurisdiction is conferred before the recommendation of the Security Council is made and this recommendation supposedly confer jurisdiction over one specific case only. The fact that the jurisdiction will be conferred regardless of the will of the respondent is irrelevant in this respect. It makes jurisdiction "compulsory" but not necessarily "continued".

methods, it appears impossible to us to accept an interpretation according to which this Article, without explicitly saying so, has introduced more or less surreptitiously, a new case of compulsory jurisdiction.[1]

This opinion, which was met with widely different reactions by the writers who have commented on it,[2] negates, therefore, that Article 36(3) of the Charter has introduced a new pattern of *ad hoc* jurisdiction, at least in the case at hand. The argument, however, is still voiced for and against this contention. In fact, since the *Corfu Channel Case* Article 36(3) of the Charter was twice relied upon, independently of any resolutions from the Security Council, to substantiate subsidiary bases of the Court's jurisdiction.[3]

Historically, Article 36(1) of the Statute was drafted before the making of the Charter and had provided for the inclusion in the jurisdiction of the Court of "all matters specially provided for in the Charter" on the assumption that such matters would be specified in the future Charter.[4] During the drafting of the latter, the question was raised whether a provision should be made to enable the Security Council to recommend that justiciable disputes should be referred to the Court.[5] Such a proposal was later adopted as Article 5 of the draft chapter on Pacific Settlement of Disputes, but the Rapporteur of the sub-committee in charge of drafting this article made it clear that it "definitely did not involve the principle of compulsory jurisdiction," and that the Council was merely reminded that "as a general rule justiciable disputes should normally be referred to the Court."[6] Besides, the sub-committee followed by adding the words "by the parties"

[1] *Corfu Channel Case*, [1947–1948] *I.C.J. Rep.* 31–2 (Separate Opinion by Judges Basdevant, Alvarez, Winiarski, Zoričić, De Visscher, Badawi, and Krylov).

In his dissenting opinion Judge *ad hoc* Daxner went further to say that even the acceptance by the parties of the Security Council recommendation would not create jurisdiction but will only make a "*pactum de contrahendo.*" *Id.* at 37.

[2] Compare, *e.g.*, Schwarzenberger, *supra*, p. 131, note 5 at 23; Jessup, "The International Court of Justice and Legal Matters," 42 *Ill. L. Rev.* 273, 285 (1948); Jully, "Le Premier Arrêt de la Cour Internationale de Justice," 48 *Friedens Warte* 144, 151–2 (1948), with Johnson, "The Effect of Resolutions of the General Assembly of the United Nations," 32 *Brit. Yb. Int'l L.* 97, 108 (1956); Jones, "Corfu Channel Case – Jurisdiction," 35 *Transact. Grot. Soc'y* 91, 109–11 (1949).

[3] See *Ambatielos Case*, Pleadings, Oral Arguments and Documents 25 (*I.C.J.* 1953); *Anglo-Iranian Oil Co. Case*, Pleadings, Oral Arguments and Documents 17–8 (*I.C.J.* 1952). The Court expressed no opinion on this point in either case.

[4] See the two alternate provisions of Article 36 of the final Draft Statute in the Report of the Washington Committee of Jurists, April 25, 1945, in Doc. No. Jurist 86, J/73, 14 *U.N. Conf. Int'l Org. Docs.* 821, 841 (1945)

[5] See Doc. No. 674, III/2/24, 12 *id.* at 96–7.

[6] See Doc. No. 992, III/2/27, *id.* at 105, 108. The report added in explicit words, "The Council was not authorized to insist that the parties to such a dispute must refer it to the Court." *Id.* at 108–9.

after the word "referred" in the text of the Article so that it may be clear that the Council had no right or duty to refer justiciable disputes to the Court.[1] However, only a day later, another commission (the Commission on Judicial Organization) discussed a proposal to delete the words "in the Charter of the United Nations or" from Article 36(1) of the Statute, but declined to undertake such a deletion after a view was expressed to the effect that "paragraph 6 of Chapter VIII A [now Article 36(3)] of the Charter related to compulsory references of cases to the Court by the Security Council."[2]

Such uncertainty as to what could be concluded from the preparatory works left many writers unclear as to what Article 36(1) of the Statute meant by the "matters provided for in the Charter." Some wrote that "the only provision which comes into consideration is that of Article 36, paragraph 3 of the Charter."[3] Some found that the phrase envisages the advisory jurisdiction of the Court provided for in Article 96 of the Charter.[4] Others went as far as to suggest that the reference is to the other texts of Article 36 of the Statute itself, the latter being an integral part of the Charter.[5] And still others found the reference "of doubtful effect" adding that "it might become useful if the Charter were amended to confer some jurisdiction on the Court."[6]

The same question could be approached from the side of Article 36(3) of the Charter. Does this provision entitle the Security Council to adopt a decision binding on the parties asking them to refer the dispute to the Court?[7] The Article, it is recalled, forms part of Chapter VI of the Charter dealing with the pacific settlement of disputes, and enables the Council to recommend in legal disputes the "procedure" of resorting to the Court instead of laying down itself the "terms" of a settlement. In fact, all that the provision says is that the Council "in making *recommendations*" as to the procedures or methods of

[1] See Doc. No. 1029, III/2/33, *id.* at 134, 137.

[2] Doc. No. 828, IV/1/67, 13 *id.* 282, 284.

[3] Kelsen, *The Law of the United Nations* 517 (1951). The writer added however that "this interpretation, according to which Article 36, paragraph 3, would provide a kind of compulsory jurisdiction of the Court, is doubtful."

[4] See Jully, *supra*, p. 136, note 2 at 152–3.

[5] See Maus, *Les Réserves dans les Déclarations d'Acceptation de la Juridiction Obligatoire de la Cour Internationale de Justice* 29 (1959).

[6] Hudson, "The Twenty-Fourth Year of the World Court," 40 *Am. J. Int'l L.* 1, 32 (1946). See also Hambro, "Some Observations on the Compulsory Jurisdiction of the International Court of Justice," 25 *Brit. Yb. Int'l L.* 133 (1948); Lawson, "The Problems of the Compulsory Jurisdiction of the World Court," 46 *Am. J. Int'l L.* 219, 220 n. 3 (1952).

[7] For an early discussion of the possible relations between the Council and the Court in this respect and a proposal covering the situation where the Council's resolution would confer obligatory jurisdiction on the Court, see Sohn, 'E'xclusion of Political Disputes From Judicial Settlement," 38 *Am. J. Int'l L.* 694, 699–700 (1944).

adjustment "should also *take into consideration* that legal disputes should as a general rule be referred *by the parties* to the International Court of Justice *in accordance with the provisions of the Statute of the Court.*" It has always been disputed whether the Security Council can adopt binding decisions under Article 36 of the Charter as a whole.[1] Stronger reasons arise particularly against the binding effect of a recommendation to refer a dispute to the Court in accordance with the last paragraph of that Article, due to the wording of this paragraph (as revealed in the underlined parts above). Moreover, the mere reference of the dispute by one party, or even by all parties, to the Security Council does not in itself imply an acceptance of the Court's jurisdiction to handle the case. It may, on the contrary, imply that the parties want to avoid a judicial solution and seek a political one through the Council. To say that each party, when it refers the dispute to the Council, knows in advance that the latter has the power to bind the parties to refer the dispute to the Court, and therefore, accepts the jurisdiction of the Court over this matter, is to beg the question, for it is this very power of the Council that is in dispute.

Finally it has been suggested that the Joint Dissenting Opinion in the *Corfu Channel Case* (1948), though "not without a degree of pursuasiveness" fails to justify the reference in Article 36(1) of the Statute to "matters specially provided for in the Charter" and was based on the meaning of the word "recommend" used in the Security Council's resolution related to that case. As a result, it was concluded that that opinion is not conclusive on the general power of the Council in this respect, particularly as the latter can still use in future cases stronger wording ordering the parties to resort to the Court.[2] Such a conclusion is, however, based on the doubtful assumption that the Security Council has the power to bind the parties to refer the dispute to the Court while it is by no means clear that Article 36(3) of the Charter allows it to do so.

Nevertheless, if, the case arising, the Security Council arrogates to itself such a power and "decides" that the parties "must" submit their dispute to the Court, in the absence of any other basis of jurisdiction this will admittedly put the Court in the embarrassing situation

[1] See generally, 2 *Repertory of Practice of the United Nations Organs* 286–98 (1955) (U.N. Pub. Sales No. 1955. V. 2 (vol. II)).

[2] See Rosenne, *The International Court of Justice* 284 (1957); Chung, *supra*, p. 134, note 2 at 75. And see Farmanfarma, *The Declared Jurisdiction of the International Court of Justice* 17 (1952).

of either assuming jurisdiction or declining it in a judgment that would amount in fact to declaring the Council's decision *ultra vires*. Fortunately, the Council can always avoid bringing about this difficult situation by requesting the Court directly to give an advisory opinion on the case and then undertaking itself to lay down the final terms of settlement in accordance with the given opinion.

b. Continued Jurisdiction

Whereas the *ad hoc* jurisdiction covers, regardless of its pattern, a dispute already existing and known to the parties at the time of accepting the submission to the Court, an acceptance of continued jurisdiction is given in advance of the rise of any specific dispute to cover whatever future cases may fall within its limits. This latter type of jurisdiction needs, in order to be conferred on the Court, some voluntary acts to be taken by the parties, such as a treaty accepting the resort to the Court as a method for adjudicating the disputes that may arise under it or reciprocal declarations made in accordance with the Optional Clause system. Jurisdiction accepted by means of such declarations is usually referred to in standard writings, including those of the Court, as "compulsory jurisdiction." No strong justification stands behind this use of the term, however. If by "compulsory" it is meant that jurisdiction is conferred in advance and therefore allows the bringing of a party before the Court without need for its approval in each specific case, then the term should be equally used whenever the respondent's acceptance is given in advance, be it by means of a declaration or otherwise (i.e., by means of a prior treaty). The term "compulsory" is, at any rate, imprecise; for in all, such cases the Court cannot exercise jurisdiction unless it is beyond doubt that both parties have consented to it through their previously-made instruments.

Granted, however, that the continued jurisdiction of the Court could be created by treaties as well as by declarations of acceptance, the question arises as to whether the two patterns are subject in all respects to the same rules. The Statute, it is noticed, makes a slight differentiation in the wording of the texts dealing with each. Article 36(1) speaking, *inter alia*, of the continued jurisdiction by means of treaties, provides that "the jurisdiction of the Court comprises... *all matters* specially provided for... in treaties and conventions in force." On the other hand, the second paragraph of the same Article dealing with continued jurisdiction by means of declarations confines such jurisdiction to "all *legal* disputes *concerning*" one of the four categories designated in it.[1] A comparison between the two provisions shows that the latter pattern of jurisdiction was meant to be narrower in scope in at least two respects. First, it is confined to legal disputes, which is due to the fact that it covers questions as yet unknown, so it becomes necessary that the character of these questions shall justify and permit a strictly legal settlement.[2] Second, among legal disputes it covers only the categories designated in Article 36(2). Yet, this differentiation should not be overestimated. On the one hand, only a few treaties have conferred on the Court jurisdiction on all disputes, legal or not,[3] and, on the other hand, the categories enumerated in Article 36(2) are broad enough to cover almost all international disputes. Suffice it to recall that such categories include, among other things, "any question of international law."[4]

Apart from the above differentiation, it is true, as Rosenne noticed, that "the Court has not, and generally speaking does not, see major differences *of principle* between one or other basis for its jurisdiction,"[5] and that the general tendency is to assimilate the two mutual declarations of acceptance in a given case to a treaty to the same effect. Yet differences between the two patterns exist and are caused on the whole by the special difficulties involved in the situation in which jurisdiction is conferred by means of declarations.

[1] See text in Appendix V. The corresponding provision in the Statute of the Permanent Court mentioned "all *or any* of the classes of legal disputes concerning" the same four categories. The deletion of the words "or any" in the new Statute was considered in its preparatory work "not only to be an improvement in form but is also favorable to the jurisdiction of the Court." See Doc. No. 702, IV/1/55, 13 *U.N. Conf. Int'l Org. Docs.* 558 (1945). This is not, however, to say that the new Statute does not allow the exclusion from the acceptance in the declaration of some categories of disputes. See Thévenaz, "La Nouvelle Cour Internationale de Justice," 45 *Friedens-Warte* 406, 411 (1945).

Originally, the draft prepared by the Drafting Committee of the Committee of Jurists (1920) provided in Art. 29 for the acceptance of jurisdiction over "cases concerning" the four categories, but on the suggestion of the President of the Committee, the text was amended to cover "cases of a legal nature, that is to say, concerning ..." The words "that is to say" were later omitted by a vote in the Committee. See *Procès-Verbaux of the Proceedings of the Advisory Committee of Jurists* 582, 604 (1920).

[2] See Bustamante, *The World Court* 204 (Trans. by Read 1925).

[3] See examples of this practice in *Systematic Survey* 3–4. And see League of Nations Off. Docs., *Records of First Assembly, Committees*, I, at 382 (1920) where it was explicitly envisaged in the discussions that the (proposed) Permanent Court would have jurisdiction over "non-juridical questions which the parties might chose to submit to it."

[4] See generally Hudson, *The Permanent Court of International Justice* 459 (2d ed. 1943). Compare, 1 Miller, *The Drafting of the Covenant* 327–31 (1928); Sir John Fischer Williams, "The Optional Clause," 11 *Brit. Yb. Int'l L.* 63, 68 (1930).

[5] Rosenne, *The Time Factor* 12 (1960).

(i) Continued Jurisdiction by Means of Treaties

Compromissory clauses in bilateral and multilateral treaties stipulating for the reference of disputes between the parties to adjudication are found in agreements that date far beyond the establishment of the Permanent Court.[1] But most of these clauses were merely instances of a *pactum de contrahendo* that required a special agreement to be reached before resorting to arbitration in each specific case. Although this practice has been followed occasionally under the International Court, "continued jurisdiction" is created by treaties only when these confer directly on the Court the power to deal with a dispute arising under the treaty and brought before the Court, if necessary, by means of a unilateral application.[2] Such treaties may be concluded solely for this purpose (treaties of pacific settlement of disputes enabling the parties to refer them to the Court), and may be concluded for other purposes while providing in a compromissory clause for the competence of the International Court in case of a dispute between the parties as to the interpretation or application of the treaty.[3] Under treaties which are mostly of the latter type 19 cases were dealt with by the Permanent Court (besides two cases of interpretation of judgments brought under the Statute, a treaty), and 15 cases were similarly dealt with by the present Court on the same basis (besides one case of interpretation of a prior judgment).[4] Not all the instruments involved in these cases were clearly treaties, however. *The Mavrommatis Cases* before the Permanent Court and the *South-West Africa Cases* before the present Court (all counted here as 7 cases) were based on Mandates made by the Council of the League of Nations. The *Monetary Gold Case* (1954) was partly based on a "statement" accompanying an agreement between three states which accepted the Court's jurisdiction as defendants in a designated dispute. And the *Northern Cameroons Case* (1963) was based on a Trusteeship Agreement. The consideration of these cases as instances of continued jurisdiction based

[1] See generally, Wilson, "Reservation Clauses in Agreements for Obligatory Arbitration," 32 *Am. J. Int'l L.* 68–93 (1929), and his *International Agreements for Obligatory Arbitration*, Doctoral Thesis (Harvard) 36–128 (1927).

[2] See lists of treaties of this category in *P.C.I.J.*, ser. D, No. 6 (4th ed. 1932); ser. E, No. 16 at 406–43; [1962–1963] *I.C.J.Y.B.* 260–71. And see a comprehensive study of these treaties in Jenks, *The Prospects of International Adjudication* 24–68 (1964).

[3] See a proposed model clause to this effect in Guggenheim, "L'Elaboration d'une Clause Modèle de Compétence Obligatoire de la Cour Internationale de Justice," 44 *Annuaire* 468 (1952–I). The proposed clause makes the reference of a dispute to the Court subject to two conditions: that it was not possible to solve the dispute by diplomatic means, and that the parties have not agreed to resort to another method of settlement.

[4] See Appendix IV. In some of these cases other bases of jurisdiction were also involved and were at times relied upon by the Court as the only or the primary basis of its jurisdiction.

on "treaties" comes through a process of characterization that constitutes, as seen in the preceding Chapter, a part of the substance of the Court's power to determine its jurisdiction.

Besides the general reference in Article 36(1) of the Statute to this pattern of jurisdiction, further references to it are made in Articles 35 and 37, each of which raises a multitude of questions.

Article 35(2) provides that the conditions under which the Court shall be open to states not parties to the Statute shall be laid down by the Security Council "subject to the special provisions contained in treaties in force." The question has been touched above as to whether this provision opens the Court to such states even if they do not adhere to the conditions laid down by the Security Council in every case where they are parties to a treaty conferring jurisdiction on the Court. It should now be noticed that an unqualified affirmative answer to this question would deprive the requirement of complying with the conditions laid down by the Council of its practical value, as it would be always possible for states to which the Court is not otherwise open to escape such conditions by concluding a treaty conferring jurisdiction on the Court. A strong opinion therefore found that the corresponding text in the Statute of the Permanent Court ought to have been understood as confined to treaties related to the liquidation of the war of 1914–18.[1] Yet, as revealed by the discussions between the members of the Permanent Court on the first occasion for the revision of the Rules, a state not party to the Statute which had not complied with the conditions required by the [League] Council's resolution, could still, it it was a party to a treaty in force, appear before the Court which would decide in each case on any objections raised against the Court's jurisdiction on that ground.[2] The practice of that Court has also shown, as seen before, a lenient attitude in this

[1] See *P.C.I.J.*, ser. D, No. 2 (Add.) at 105–6 (1926) (Comment of Judge Anzilotti in which the Court's President concurred). See also, Hudson, *supra*, p. 140, note 4 at 391–2. The reason behind the limitation of the exception to the peace treaties of 1919 and related treaties is apparently that these treaties provided for the reference to the future Court of many categories of disputes which might arise between the parties thereto. If the Court was to refuse access to a party of these treaties on the ground that it was not a party to its Statute, this would have amounted to amending the treaties.

[2] See *P.C.I.J.*, ser. D, No. 2 (Add.) at 107 (1926). See also the Report of M. Hagerup submitted on behalf of a sub-committee of the Third Committee of the First Assembly of the League and approved by the Assembly, commenting on Art. 35 by saying that: "The access of other states to the Court will depend either on the special provisions of the treaties in force (*for example* the provisions of the treaties of peace concerning the right of minorities, labor, etc.) or else on a resolution of the Council." League of Nations Docs., *Records of First Assembly, Plenary* 462 (1920) (Emphasis added.)

respect in both the *S.S. Wimbledon Case* (1923) and the *German Interests in Upper Silesia Case* (1925).[1]

Nothing in the Statute or the practice of the present Court serves as a new clue to the problem. It, therefore, still presents the dilemma of either respecting the broad wording of the reservation in Article 35(2), thus sacrificing greatly the requirement imposed by this paragraph, or else considering such requirement as a condition to be fulfilled in all cases by states not parties to the statute, thus rendering the reservation a dead letter (except in such cases as could still arise under the treaties related to World War I). In the absence of a third solution giving the reservation an arbitrary limitation, the second attitude should be favored. As the choice is between the general rule and an exception thereto, the first should be saved at the expense of the latter, not *vice versa*. The practice of states non-parties to the present Statute seems to be in conformity with this conclusion.[2]

Article 37, on the other hand, has a prolonging effect on any "treaty or convention in force [Fr. *en vigueur*]," which had provided for reference of a matter to "a tribunal to have been instituted by the League of Nations or to the Permanent Court." According to this Article, such a matter shall "as between the parties to the present Statute, be referred to the International Court of Justice." As this provision raises problems similar to those raised under Article 36(5) in relation to the continued jurisdiction by means of declarations, it will be soon treated in conjunction with the latter.

(ii) Continued Jurisdiction by Means of Mutual Declarations of Acceptance

The idea of creating a continued jurisdiction to be optionally accepted by means of declarations was reached as a compromise in the committee of the Assembly of the League of Nations charged with studying the draft-scheme of the Statute of the Permanent Court.[3] Again it was maintained in the present Statute after being proposed by the Washington Committee of Jurists alternatively with a provision

1 See Chapter III, *supra*, at 90. It is noticed that the first of the above cases was based on the Peace Treaty of 1919, and the second on the Geneva Convention concerning Upper Silesia of 1922, which is closely related to the liquidation of World War I.

2 Both the Federal Republic of Germany and the Republic of Viet Nam (non-parties to the Statute) have filed general declarations under the Resolution of the Security Council only to obtain access to the Court for disputes as to which they accepted the jurisdiction of the Court *by means of treaties in force*. See [1952–1953] *I.C.J.Y.B.* 200; [1954–1955] *id.* at 217; [1955–1956] *id.* at 215; [1960–1961] *id.* at 219.

3 See generally, Hudson, *The Permanent Court of International Justice* 126–7 (2ed d. 1943).

for a general compulsory jurisdiction.[1] According to this idea, better known as the "Optional Clause system," the states parties to the Statute (and the non-parties if they make a general declaration in accordance with the Security Council resolution of October 15, 1946) may at any time declare that they recognize "as compulsory *ipso facto* and without special agreement, in relation to any other state accepting the same obligation" the jurisdiction of the Court in all legal disputes concerning the four categories enumerated in Article 36(2) of the Statute.

Since the entry into force of the Statute of the Permanent Court till the end of the year 1964, at least 148 declarations and renewals were made under this system, though many of these never became effective.[2] On the other hand, declarations in force were invoked as alleged bases of jurisdiction, sometimes along with other jurisdictional instruments, in twelve cases before the Permanent Court and sixteen cases before the present Court.[3] In such cases and in many other hypothetical ones controversial questions present themselves, many peculiar to this pattern of jurisdiction and some common to the two patterns of continued jurisdiction. Following is a treatment of the most relevant among these questions:

(a) Legal Nature of the Declaration of Acceptance

An extensive study of writings relating to the legal nature of declarations of acceptance is not needed to justify the obligatory effect of what is seemingly a unilateral act. Such an effect results directly from the Statute, a conventional instrument which accounts for the obligations based on its text.[4] This by no means suggests that the inquiry related to the legal nature of these declarations is merely an academic exercise. The classification of that nature has a direct influence on at least seven problems concerning the continued jurisdiction by means of declarations. These are: the determination of the moment in which a declaration becomes effective, the requirement of registration, the possibility and process of modification, the termina-

[1] See the two texts proposed by the Washington Committee of Jurists as presented in its final report in Doc. No. Jurist 86, J/73, 14 *U.N. Conf. Int'l Org. Docs.* 821, 841 (1945). And see the report of the special subcommittee appointed at the San Francisco Conference for the study of this question in Doc. No. 702, IV/1/55, 13 *id.* 557–9, and see the text adopted at the Plenary meeting of the Conference in its present form, in Doc. No. 1210, P/20, 1 *id.* at 627.

[2] See a detailed table of these declarations in Appendix VI.

[3] See Appendix V.

[4] *Accord*, Biscottini, *Contributo alla Teoria degli Atti Unilaterali nel Diritto Internazionale* 158–9 (1951). See also Maus, *supra*, p. 137, note 5 at 92.

tion of the declaration, its interpretation, the possibility of maintaining a declaration after holding that a reservation attached to it is invalid, and the question of whether a declaration is subject, from the viewpoint of domestic law, to the procedure required for the ratification of treaties.[1]

The Permanent Court had first dealt with the problem of the legal nature of the declarations of acceptance in the *Phosphates in Morocco Case* (1935) where it seemed to have stressed simultaneously the unilateral element in the making of the declaration and the reciprocal element in its effect.[2] However, when the Court dealt with this issue the second time, it put the whole emphasis on the bilateral element, calling the relationship established under the Optional Clause "an agreement" between the parties.[3] The present Court on the other hand, considered first in the *Anglo-Iranian Oil Co. Case* (1952) that the text of a declaration is not a "treaty text resulting from negotiations" but "the result of unilateral drafting" and derived from this conception certain conclusions related to the interpretation of the declaration.[4] In the same case some individual judges held more specific views. McNair saw in the Optional Clause "a standing invitation made on behalf of the Court,"[5] thus suggesting that a declaration creates a bilateral relationship between the declarant state and the Court. Alvarez, on the other hand, found the declaration "a multilateral act of a special character... the basis of a treaty... with the States which had already adhered and with those which would subsequently adhere to the provisions of Article 36, paragraph 2, of the Statute of the Court."[6] And Read emphasized that the legal relationships created by declarations are "consensual in their character."[7] The bilateral element became clearer in the Court's judgment in the *Norwegian Loans Case* (1957) where the Court referred to its jurisdiction under mutual declarations of acceptance as the result of "the common will of the

[1] In relation to this last problem it may be noted that ratification was mostly required in old declarations, and that the practice is to the effect that this matter is left to each declarant state. See Appendix VII, No. 1. And see Delbez, *Les Principes Généraux du Contentieux International* 71 (1962).

[2] *P.C.I.J.*, ser. A/B, No. 74 at 23 (1938).

[3] See *Electricity Company of Sofia and Bulgaria Case, P.C.I.J.*, ser. A/B, No. 77 at 87, 89 (1939). And see the dissenting opinion of Judge Urrutia in the same case where he found the "adherence of the two parties to Article 36 of the Statute ... equivalent in law to an international agreement between them ..." *Id.* at 103.

[4] [1952] *I.C.J. Rep.* 93, 105.

[5] *Id.* at 116.

[6] *Id.* at 125.

[7] *Id.* at 142.

parties."[1] But a strong separate opinion of Judge Lauterpacht preferred another characterization, seeing in the declaration an act of accession to a multilateral treaty, i.e., the Statute.[2] The bilateral element was further emphasized, however, in the *Right of Passage Case* (1957), where the Court described the optional clause system as a "contractual relation" and a "consensual bond."[3] Yet this did not lead the Court in that case to determine the moment in which a declaration becomes effective as the moment of the knowledge, real or constructive, of its contents by the other declarant parties, but rather as the moment of the deposit of the declaration in the Secretariat of the United Nations. For this reason Judge Badawi dissented, writing the strongest opinion for the contractual nature of the relationship established by declarations. This relationship, he argued, should be viewed as nothing but "a contract by correspondence between the declarant state and the other states through the agency of the Secretary General [of the United Nations] as an intermediary," a contract that "has nothing in common with a collective convention" and "is not a contract of adhesion."[4]

These characterizations expressed by the Court and by some of its individual members were adopted along with almost every other possible thesis on the subject in the different jurisprudential writings. Some found in every two declarations an international agreement;[5] some a treaty only if the acceptance included in them was unconditional;[6] some unilateral acts creating a legal bond essentially contractual and partly institutional;[7] some acts that are unilateral in form but contractual in substance,[8] some an engagement between the

[1] [1957] *I.C.J. Rep.* 9, 23–4.

[2] *Id.* at 48–9. And see Lauterpacht, *The Development of International Law by the International Court* 345 (1958).

[3] [1957] *I.C.J. Rep.* 125, 146.

[4] *Id.* at 156, 157–8.

[5] See *e.g.*, Fachiri, *The Permanent Court of International Justice* 99 (2d ed. 1932); Salvioli, "La Corte Permanente di giustizia Internazionale," 15 *Rivista di Diritto Internazionale* 11, 19 (1923). The latter found in the acceptance of jurisdiction by means of declarations "un vero trattato di arbitrato."

[6] See Farmanfarma, *supra*, p. 138, note 2 at 54–5.

[7] See Maus, *supra*, p. 137, note 5 at 59–60. See also, Dubisson, *La Cour Internationale de Justice* 192 (1964).

[8] See Fitzmaurice, "The Law and Procedure of the International Court of Justice, 1951–4: Treaty Interpretation and Other Treaty Points," 33 *Brit. Yb. Int'l L.* 203, 230–1 (1957). The same author wrote, a year later, that: "These declarations are not treaties, but they give rise to a quasi-treaty by creating a network of bilateral relationships between the various declarants." 34 *id.* at 1, 75 (1958).

declarant state and the United Nations;[1] some a contract of adhesion *sui generis*;[2] some a general offer to all other states accepting the same;[3] and some seeing in them a "consensual relation which is *sui generis*," that is "for most purposes bilateral [but] also has a multilateral aspect."[4]

The confusion, it is appreciated, is due to the simultaneous existence of three elements in every relationship resulting from two declarations of acceptance:

(1) The *unilateral* element which presents itself in the drafting of the declaration and which must be taken into consideration particularly in interpreting its terms;

(2) the *bilateral* element which presents itself in the actual cases brought before the Court on the basis of declarations where jurisdiction will be established only to the extent to which the declarations of the parties coincide; and,

(3) the *multilateral* element which is based on the fact that each declaration derives its legal value from the Statute, and which leads to the assumption that in the absence of an evidence to the contrary declarations will be considered as made within the framework designated by the Statute.

These three elements should all be given their full weight and effect in estimating with respect to each specific issue the possible attitude of the Court. The characterization of the relationship in terms of one of these elements to the exclusion of the others might facilitate the theoretical treatment of the subject but will hardly be consistent with the very nature of the Optional Clause system.

(b) The Reciprocal Effect of Declarations of Acceptance

(1) Meaning and Effect of Reciprocity – Paragraphs 2 and 3 of Article 36 of the Statute. Much of the confusion related to the meaning and effect of the principle of reciprocity as applied to declarations of acceptance may be derived from the ostensible discrepancy between Paragraphs 2 and 3 of Article 36 of the Statute. Whereas the first assumes that every declaration accepts the Court's jurisdiction

[1] See Rosenne, *The International Court of Justice* 317–8 (1957). He also argued that a bilateral agreement exists between each two states *in a concrete case* brought on the basis of declarations only after a legal dispute "is concretized by the filing of an application."

[2] See Ténékides, "Les Actes Compromissoires Concurrents," 17 *Rev. Dr. Int'l & Lég. Comp.* 719, 721 (3me sér. 1936).

[3] See Briggs, "Reservations to the Acceptance of Compulsory Jurisdiction of the International Court of Justice," 93 *Recueil des Cours* 229, 244–5 (1958–I).

[4] Waldock, "Decline of the Optional Clause," 32 *Brit. Yb. Int'l L.* 244, 254 (1955–1956).

only "in relation to any other state accepting the same obligation," Paragraph 3 explicitly provides that declarations "may be made unconditionally or on condition of reciprocity." The latter text, however, was first suggested for the purpose of enabling the declarant state to suspend, if it wishes, the entry into force of its acceptance until certain other states (specified by name or by number) have accepted the same pattern of jurisdiction.[1] Thus relying on the preparatory work of the Statute, and also in order to maintain consistency between the two texts, most writers found in Paragraph 2 a genuine and indispensable requirement of reciprocity and in Paragraph 3 only a permission for inserting a "suspensive condition" for the entry into force of the declaration.[2] Under this prevalent interpretation Paragraph 3 could, therefore, be read to mean that the operation of declarations "may be made immediate or suspended on the acceptance of other states."[3] In this sense a declaration made "on condition of reciprocity" as provided for in Paragraph 3, will not be an effective declaration binding on its declarant in relation to any other State, unless and until the condition be fulfilled. But once this takes place, the declaration enters into force producing a reciprocal effect "in relation to any other state accepting the same obligation."

Such an interpretation, it was noticed, extends the requirement of reciprocity in Paragraph 2 at the expense of the permissive provision of Paragraph 3. Furthermore, it gives the word "reciprocity" as used in the latter paragraph a meaning alien to the normal sense of the term. As a result, it was not satisfactory to those writers who, in particular, saw no reason why a state should not be able to make, if it wants, its acceptance not subject to any condition.[4]

[1] See League of Nations Docs., *Records of First Assembly, Committees I* at 553 (1920). (Proposal of M. Fernandes).

[2] See *e.g.*, Sir John Fischer Williams, "The Optional Clause," 11 *Brit. Yb. Int'l L.* 63, 73 (1930); Perassi, "I Caratteri Formali della Clausola Facoltativa sulla Giurisdizione Obligatoria della Corte Permanente de Giustizia Internazionale" (note), 24 *Rivista di Diritto Internazionale* 127, 131 (1932); Hudson, *The Permanent Court of International Justice* 451, 465 (2d ed. 1943); Vulcan, "La Clause Facultative," 18 *Acta Scandinavia Juris Gentium* 30, 39–40 (1947–1948); Waldock, *supra*, p. 147, note 4 at 254–6; Rosenne, *supra*, p. 147, note 1 at 316; Briggs, *supra*, p. 147, note 3 at 240–1, 266; Maus, *supra*, p. 137, note 5 at 75, 91, 109–10.

[3] According to this interpretation, the declaration of Brazil (Appendix VI, No. 15)is the only general declaration made "on condition of reciprocity" in the sense meant in Art. 36(3) of the Statute.

[4] See *e.g.*, Enrique, "L'Acceptation sans Réciprocité de la Juridiction de la Cour Permanente de Justice Internationale," 13 *Rev. Dr. Int'l & Lég. Comp.* 834, 842–56 (3me sér. 1932). See also, Verzijl, "Cour Internationale de Justice – Affaire Relative à Certains Emprunts Norvégiens," 4 *Nederlands Tijdschrift voor Internationaal Recht.* 373, 381 (1957); Farmanfarma, *supra*, p. 138, note 2 at 50; Hambro, "Some Observations on the Compulsory Jurisdiction of the International Court of Justice," 25 *Brit. Yb. Int'l L.* 133, 136–7 (1948).

In practice, reciprocity was explicitly mentioned in all declarations but seven.[1] Among these seven declarations only three were made without conditions of any kind. Two of these three declarations are still in force though only one mentions that it is made "unconditionally."[2] The question of whether the declarant state can, even in this situation, take advantage of the "condition" of reciprocity as provided for in Paragraph 2 is, therefore, still alive. Neither the Permanent Court nor the present Court had the occasion to pronounce on this question which presents only one part of a broader problem the different aspects of which are exposed in the following hypotheses:

First: If the declaration mentions that it is made on condition of reciprocity (and 141 of the 148 declarations enumerated in Appendix VI do), this should be understood to be a reference to the reciprocal effect meant in Paragraph 2 of Article 36, and as this condition is already included in the Statute its addition in the declaration does not have any independent legal effect.[3]

Second: If the declaration is silent on this matter; that is, if it does not mention whether it is made on condition of reciprocity or unconditionally, the principle of Paragraph 2 prevails, limiting the effect of the declaration to other states accepting the same obligation. For, it should be assumed in the absence of evidence to the contrary, that declarations are made within the framework of Article 36(2).

Third: If the declaration states that it is made "unconditionally" [Fr. *purement et simplement*,] this will more likely be understood to be a use of the term as it appears in Paragraph 3 of Article 36; for it is in this context that a state would normally be expected to refer to the term. Here "unconditionally" would mean "immediately" and would not exclude the application of the condition of reciprocity in Paragraph 2. This is the meaning the term was meant to serve and also the meaning it has acquired in most writings.

Fourth: If the declaration uses clearer language to the effect that it contains an acceptance of the Court's continued jurisdiction regardless of the acceptance by other parties to future cases of the same obligation, this will be clearly an attempt to go beyond the condition of reciprocity in Paragraph 2, and, it seems, could be judged regardless

1 See Appendix VII, No. 2.

2 Compare declaration of Nicaragua [Appendix VI, No. 97] with declaration of Haiti [No. 58]. The declaration of Paraguay [No. 107] provided also that it was made "unconditionally" but was denounced unilaterally on April 26, 1938. On the effect of this denunciation, see *infra* at 164–8.

3 *Accord*, Hudson, *supra*, p. 148, note 2 at 465; Waldock, *supra*, p. 147, note 4 at 254–5; Briggs, *supra*, p. 147, note 3 at 267, etc.

of the provision of Paragraph 3. A declaration made in accordance with Paragraph 2 could, and in fact normally does, contain limitations which do not exist in Article 36 and which confine the acceptance to narrower limits. If this is so, why could not a declaration provide for the acceptance of the Court's jurisdiction in a broader manner than the one anticipated in that Article? A state should be able, if it clearly wants it, to accept this jurisdiction without the condition of reciprocity, that is, in relation to all other states to whom the Court is open. This, it is true, will go beyond what is envisaged in Article 36(2), but it can hardly be called a "violation" of that Article.[1] If this is true regardless of the provision of Article 36(3), the existence of the latter could not affect this conclusion. If its terms, taken in their historical context, do not support it, they certainly do not contradict it.

A provision in a declaration dispensing with the condition of reciprocity should, however, be drafted in the clearest terms; it is not enough, as seen above, to provide in the declaration that it is made "unconditionally." As a result, it could safely be stated that despite the possibility envisaged in the last hypothesis none of the declarations that have ever been made could qualify as accepting the Court's jurisdiction regardless of the condition of reciprocity as expressed in Paragraph 2 of Article 36.

What then does the reciprocal effect provided for in Article 36(2) mean? Clearly, it does not mean, as was once contended, that each state making a declaration is confined to the terms of its own declaration and cannot avail itself of reservations made by other states.[2] Furthermore, it does not mean, as the earliest historical origin of the text may imply,[3] that each acceptance will produce its effects only in relation to other acceptances covering the same "categories" of disputes. As the Court declared on many occasions, this condition means that in a specific case the Court will have jurisdiction "only to the extent to which the two Declarations coincided in conferring it,"[4] that is to say, in the area where the two declarations overlap.

[1] *Cf.* Hudson, *supra*, p. 148, note 2 at 450.

[2] See Kelsen, *The Law of the United Nations* 526–7 (1951). This interpretation comes as a result of understanding the words "accepting the same obligation" in Art. 36(2) as meaning merely the making of a declaration under the same Article regardless of its content. This, Kelsen admits, is only one interpretation among others, but he suggests that it ensures a more effective compulsory jurisdiction.

[3] See an account of the roots of the Optional Clause traced to the work of the Second Peace Conference at the Hague (1907) in Waldock, *supra*, p. 147, note 4 at 256–7.

[4] *Anglo-Iranian Oil Co. Case*, [1952] *I.C.J. Rep.* 93, 103. *Accord*, *id.* at 116 (Diss. Op. of Judge McNair); *Phosphates in Morocco Case*, *P.C.I.J.*, ser. A/B, No. 74 at 22 (1938); *Electricity Company of Sofia and Bulgaria Case*, *P.C.I.J.*, ser. A/B, No. 79 at 81 (1939); *Nottebohm Case*, [1952] *I.C.J. Rep.* 111, 122; *Case of Certain Norwegian Loans*, [1957] *I.C.J. Rep.* 9, 23–4.

(2) Reciprocity and the Time-Limits in Declarations – Double Effect of Reciprocity Denied. The first judgment in the *Right of Passage Case* (1957) made it clear that the crucial date for the entry into force of a declaration is the date of its deposit in the Secretariat of the United Nations.[1] No reciprocal effect can alter this date, though the temporal scope of the obligation covered by the declaration can of course be affected by reciprocity. If, for example, state A accepts jurisdiction only for disputes arising after January 1960, state B whose declaration is deposited in 1950 and includes no similar reservation can, if sued by state A on a dispute arising before the latter's exclusion date, invoke the reservation in the declaration of state A.[2] In this case the declaration of state B though entering into force in 1950 becomes, by reciprocity, limited in scope so that it may cover, in relation to state A, only disputes arising after January 1960.

If reciprocity has nothing to do with the entry into force of a declaration, it does not affect its duration either. The fact that state A's declaration is made for 5 years does not entitle state B whose declaration is made for 10 years to conclude that in relation to state A the period of its acceptance of jurisdiction is shortened to 5 years.[3] The period for which a declaration runs is governed by this instrument itself. If at the time the Court is seized of a case the respondent's declaration has not yet expired according to its own terms or otherwise, its end could not be brought by virtue of reciprocity.

Nor would reciprocity enable a state to terminate its declaration in regard to a case of which the Court has already been seized on the ground that the other party reserved the right to denounce its declaration. Once the Court is seized no change in the jurisdictional title can in principle affect its ability to deal with the case. It had been argued, however, that apart from the situation where seisin already took place, as some declarations provide for the right to terminate them and some do not, "reciprocity would seem to demand that in

[1] [1957] *I.C.J. Rep.* 125, 146. But see, *id.* at 154, 156 (Diss. Op. of Judge Badawi); *id.* at 166, 170 (Diss. Op. of Judge *ad hoc* Chagla).

[2] This is the situation the present Court envisaged in its *dictum* in the *Interhandel Case*, [1959] *I.C.J. Rep.* 6, 23: "Switzerland, which has not expressed in its Declaration any reservation *ratione temporis*, while the United States has accepted the compulsory jurisdiction only in respect of disputes subsequent to August 26th, 1946, might, if in the position of Respondent, invoke by virtue of reciprocity against the United States the American reservation if the United States attempted to refer to the Court a dispute with Switzerland which had arisen before August 26th, 1946. This is the effect of reciprocity in this connection."

[3] But see, Waldock, *supra*, p. 147, note 4 at 278. And see for a differentiation between the principle of "equality", on which Waldock relied, and that of "reciprocity," Rosenne, *The Time Factor* 50–1 (1960).

any given pair of States each should have the same right as the other to terminate the juridical bond existing between them under the optional clause."[1] Such an opinion is clearly motivated by the desire to maintain equality between states, and is based on the assumption that bilateral relationships exist between each given pair of declaring states even before the rise of a particular case. Its acceptance by the Court seems, however, to be most doubtful. The termination of a declaration, like its entry into force, is subject to the general rules governing them regardless of any reciprocal effect.[2] And, at any rate, reciprocity operates only in relation to a specific case already before the Court, as seisin establishes the crucial date for the efficacy of jurisdictional titles and their practical significance in general.

Finally, if reciprocity allows a state to limit the scope of its acceptance *ratione temporis* because of a limitation in the applicant's declaration, it certainly does not permit the respondent to benefit from a reservation which does not exist in the applicant's declaration on the pretext that the latter would have benefited from such a reservation had it been the respondent. This problem was first raised in the *Phosphates in Morocco Case* (1938) though no decision was needed on it.[3] In the *Interhandel Case* (1959), however, the respondent (the United States) having in its declaration a limitation making its acceptance confined to disputes "hereafter arising" (i.e. after August 26, 1946), argued that as the applicant whose declaration entered into force in 1948 without a similar limitation could benefit by reciprocity from the exclusion, the United States should, again by reciprocity, invoke this exclusion not as dated in its declaration but "from the date it entered into force in relation to Switzerland." In other words, the United States argued that as regards Switzerland, the acceptance of the United States covers only disputes arising after the entry into force of the Swiss declaration; that is, almost two years after the date of the entry into force of the American declaration. This assertion was unanimously rejected by the Court along with the objection based on it:

[1] Waldock, *supra*, p. 147, note 4 at 278. The same argument was the basis of the second objection submitted by India in the *Right of Passage Case*. See [1957] *I.C.J. Rep.* 125, 132.

[2] *Accord*, Briggs, *supra*, p. 147, note 3 at 246; Rosenne, *supra*, p. 151, note 3 at 50. For the "general rules" applicable to the termination of declarations, see *infra*.

[3] See *P.C.I.J.*, ser. A/B, No. 74 at 25. France, the respondent in that case, argued that the exclusion in its declaration operated, in relation to the applicant (Italy) not from the date of the entry into force of the French declaration [Appendix VI, No. 47], but from the date of the entry into force of the declaration of Italy [No. 74] which did not include a similar reservation.

Reciprocity – said the Court – enables the State which has made the wider acceptance of the jurisdiction of the Court to rely upon the reservations to the acceptance laid down by the other Party. There the effect of reciprocity ends. It cannot justify a State, in this instance the United States, in relying upon a restriction which the other Party, Switzerland, has not included in its own Declaration.[1]

This clear statement amounts to saying that reciprocity is capable of producing its effect only once by limiting jurisdiction to the common ground accepted by both parties, but could not be invoked for any further double effects that would result in fact in permitting one party to benefit from non-existent reservations in the declaration of the other.[2]

The principle of reciprocity, though it forms part of the system of the Optional Clause, is therefore limited to defining the scope of the obligation accepted and has little to do with the time-limits of the declarations involved.

(c) The Reservations to Declarations of Acceptance

The freedom of the declarant state to attach reservations to its acceptance of the continued jurisdiction of the Court is, in principle, guaranteed. The Statute provided for such a freedom (Article 36(3)); the League of Nations repeatedly confirmed it;[3] the preparatory works of the present Statute provided further evidence for it;[4] and the state practice has, from the outset, left no doubt as to the possibility of its exercise in the widest latitude.[5] Only twelve declarations, in a total of 148, could be said to have been drafted without reservations, though seven of them mentioned the condition of reciprocity [declarations Nos. 18, 25, 61, 106, 111, 134, 146 in Appendix VI] and two required also ratification [Nos. 25, 32] thus leaving only three [Nos. 58, 97, 107] which were drafted without any condition whatsoever. All these declarations but two [Nos. 61, 134] were made under the Permanent Court. Standard reservations, initiated usually by big powers, are now

[1] [1959] *I.C.J. Rep.* 6, 23. And see *id.* at 74 (Sep. Op. of Sir Percy Spender).

[2] See generally, Briggs, *supra*, p. 147, note 3 at 249; Rosenne, *supra*, p. 151, note 3 at 51.

[3] See League of Nations Docs., *Records of Fifth Assembly, Committees, III*, at 198–9 (1924) (Politis, Rapporteur); *id. Plenary* 225 (Resolution of October 2, 1924); *op. cit.*, *Records of Ninth Assembly, Plenary* 183 (Resolution of September 26, 1928).

[4] See Doc. No. 702, IV/1/55, 13 *U.N. Conf. Int'l Org. Docs.* 559 (1945).

[5] But see the view that Art. 36(3) of the Statute "specifies the only conditions which states may impose," expressed in *The Anglo-Iranian Oil Co. Case*, [1952] *I.C.J. Rep.* 93, 154 (Diss. Op. of Judge Levi Carneiro). *Accord*, Quincy Wright in 48 *Annuaire* 159 (1959–II) (his suggestion to that effect in the "Institut de Droit International" was defeated by 48 votes against 4 and one abstention. *Id.* at 164); Vulcan ,"La Clause Facultative," 18 *Acta Scandinavia Juris Gentium* 30, 41 (1947–48); Thévénaz, "La Nouvelle Cour Internationale de Justice," 45 *Friedens-Warte* 406, 410–1 (1945).

copied in most declarations along with reservations made for the purpose of excluding specific areas of disputes that the declarant state may not be ready to adjudicate before the Court.[1] All the reservations which have been made are divided in Appendix VII to this study into twenty categories (including the condition of reciprocity), some of which are further divided into as many as four sub-categories. Reference is made, therefore, to this Appendix for the number of states subscribing to each reservation and other relevant observations. Particularly to be mentioned here are two types of reservations which have the most serious effect on the power of the Court to exercise its jurisdiction. The first comprises the reservations which give the declaring state the right to terminate the declaration immediately on notice, and these will be dealt with in connection with the termination of declarations. The second type includes the reservations which entitle the declaring state to decide, itself, whether a certain matter is within or without the jurisdiction of the Court. This latter type, being a clear challenge to the Court's *compétence de la compétence*, will be dealt with independently in the last Chapter of this work.

(d) Continuity of Jurisdiction Accepted Under the Permanent Court

Article 36(5) of the Statute attempts to secure for the present Court the continuity of the jurisdiction accepted under the Permanent Court by means of declarations. Along with Article 37 which has the same purpose in relation to the jurisdiction conferred by treaties, these texts were in fact adopted to enable the new Court to exercise a wide range of jurisdiction despite the retention of the Optional Clause system in the new Statute.[2] Although the principle was applied without difficulty in regard to both patterns of continued jurisdiction it caused a great controversy in the case where its applicability was first challenged – *Aerial Incident of July 27th, 1955* (*Israel v. Bulgaria*) (1959).[3]

The problem arose in this case as to the scope of the principle of continuity in relation to jurisdiction conferred by declarations. In this respect Article 36(5) provides that:

Declarations made under Article 36 of the Statute of the Permanent Court of International Justice and which are still in force [Fr. *pour une durée qui n'est*

[1] See *e.g.*, the third declaration of Australia, Appendix VI, No. 6.

[2] See generally, Doc. No. 759, IV/1/59, 13 *U.N. Conf. Int'l Org. Docs.* 246–50 (1945); Doc. No. 913, IV/1/74(1), *id.* at 381, 390–2; Doc. No. 702, IV/1/55, *id.* at 557–9.

[3] [1959] *I.C.J. Rep.* 127. Two other cases arising from the same incident were initiated against Bulgaria but were discontinued after the judgment in the case brought by Israel. See *Case Concerning the Aerial Incident of July 27th, 1955* (*United Kingdom v. Bulgaria*), [1959] *I.C.J. Rep.* 264; *U.S.A.* v. *Bulgaria* [1960] *I.C.J. Rep.* 146.

pas encore expirée] shall be deemed, as between the parties to the present Statute, to be acceptances of the compulsory jurisdiction of the International Court of Justice for the period which they still have to run and in accordance with their terms.

Bulgaria, whose declaration [No. 18] entered into force on August 12, 1921, became a member of the United Nations and consequently a party to the Statute only as late as December 14, 1955. Sued by Israel in 1957 on the basis of the mutual declarations of both parties, Bulgaria objected to the Court's jurisdiction, *inter alia*, on the ground that its declaration had lapsed before it was admitted to the United Nations and, therefore, could not be subject to the rule of continuity provided for in Article 36(5) which applies only to declarations "still in force." The Court, conceiving this to be a justiciable question under Article 36(6) of its Statute, made a clear differentiation between two types of states accepting the jurisdiction of the Permanent Court, according to whether or not they were signatories of the Charter of the United Nations. "This difference – the Court agreed – is not expressed in the text of Article 36, paragraph 5, but is derived from the situation which that text was meant to regulate, namely the transfer to the International Court of Justice of declarations relating to the Permanent Court of International Justice which was on the point of disappearing when the Statute was drawn up."[1] The signatories of the new Statute were in such a situation able only to extend the effect of their own declarations. They could not through Article 36(5) preserve the declarations of nonsignatories and transfer them to the jurisdiction of the present Court. This distinction is particularly based, according to the Court, on the following interrelated grounds:

(1) The purpose of Article 36(5) was to provide "a transitional provision" for the transitory situation to the regulation of which it is confined. Such a situation assumes the institution of a new Court "just when the old Court was being dissolved," which is entirely different from the situation of a nonsignatory (like Bulgaria) that becomes a party to the new Statute after the old Court and the acceptance of its jurisdiction have long since disappeared.

(2) At the date when Bulgaria became a member of the United Nations, its declaration of 1921 was no longer in force in consequence of the dissolution of the Permanent Court in 1946. "The acceptance set out in that Declaration... was thereafter devoid of object since

[1] [1959] *I.C.J. Rep.* 127, 136. The distinction made by the Court in this respect was not presented by the respondent, nor argued by the parties.

that Court was no longer in existence."[1] As a result, Article 36(5) cannot apply in this respect, for its application is made subject not only to the condition *ratione personae* that the declarant state should be a party to the Statute, but also to the further requirement *ratione temporis* that the declaration of that state should be still in force.

(3) If any doubt remained, Article 36(5) should be interpreted by the Court only in its proper context, bearing in mind "the general scheme of the Charter and the Statute which founds the jurisdiction of the Court on the consent of States." To hold that Bulgaria had consented to the Court's continued jurisdiction by its mere admission to the United Nations would be "to regard its request for admission as equivalent to an express declaration by that State as provided for by Article 36, paragraph 2, of the Statute." This runs counter to the latter provision and regards as sufficient a consent which is merely presumed.[2]

(4) Finally, if it were decided that Article 36(5) applied to declarations made by nonsignatories, the date of the transfer of jurisdiction in such situations can scarcely be determined in any satisfactory manner. In particular, the date of admission to the United Nations of the nonsignatory "might be very distant from the entry into force of the Statute, and this would hardly be in harmony with the spirit of a provision designed to provide for the transition from the old to the new Court by maintaining something of the former regime."[3]

The Court's argument is, therefore, that Bulgaria's declaration of 1921 accepting the jurisdiction of the Permanent Court became "dead" or "devoid of object" with the dissolution of that Court. No later event could resurrect it. The admission of Bulgaria to the United

[1] *Id.* at 143. Does this mean that Art. 36(5) would not cover the declaration of a state which did participate in the San Francisco Conference and signed the Charter but ratified it only after the dissolution of the Permanent Court? On the one hand, such a state is a signatory of the Charter and therefore its declaration is, according to one argument of the Court, covered by Art. 36(5). But, on the other hand, as this state becomes a party to the Statute after the dissolution of the old Court, its declaration was, according to another argument of the Court, devoid of object at the time of ratification. The Court's doctrine is not therefore clear on this point, which seems, however, to have been in the mind of the judges who wrote the joint dissenting opinion arguing in part that the Court's doctrine would have led to a complete frustration of the purpose of Art. 36(5) had the Permanent Court been dissolved prior to the entry into force of the Charter. See *id.* at 167.

[2] See *id.* at 142.

[3] *Id.* at 139. Judge Zafrulla Khan who concurred in the Court's judgment interpreted Art. 36(5) as requiring only that the declaration made under the Permanent Court should still be in force when the declaring state becomes a party to the Statute. In relation to the members of the U.N., this would make the paragraph applicable only to states signatories of the Charter. See *id.* at 146.

Nations could not in particular bring into effect Article 36(5) of the Statute which deals exclusively with declarations "in force."

Besides this argument in which the Court has strictly followed a "logical approach" in interpreting the text, two individual judges added in their respective separate opinions an argument based on a "literal interpretation" of Article 36(5) in its French version. Judges Badawi and Armand-Ugon expressed the view that the phrase "still in force" appearing in the French version as "pour une durée qui n'est pas encore expirée"[1] (for a period which has not yet expired) assumes that the text applies only to declarations made for a given period of time. As the Bulgarian declaration was made without any time-limit, they found that it was not, at any rate, subject to Article 36(5).[2]

On the other hand, a joint dissenting opinion by Judges Lauterpacht, Koo and Spender, strongly objected to the Court's interpretation. Reviewing in detail the preparatory work of Article 36(5) and the connotations of the principle of continuity, they agreed that the Bulgarian declaration ceased to be applicable when the Permanent Court was dissolved, but added that:

> However, in relation to the International Court of Justice, the dissolution of the Permanent Court was precisely the situation envisaged by the framers of the new Statute as a reason for the adoption of paragraph 5, and its full operation in consequence of, and subsequent to the dissolution of the Permanent Court. It was for the purpose of preserving for the new Court the compulsory jurisdiction which had been conferred upon the old Court and whose period of validity had not expired that paragraph 5 was adopted and inserted in Article 36 of the present Statute and that Article 37 was introduced.[3]

Thus, holding this view on the purpose of the text, they concluded that its effect covered, though not in the same manner, declarations of both signatories and nonsignatories.[4] As to the declarations of the signatories the effect was to transform them immediately into acceptances of the jurisdiction of the new Court. And as to the nonsignatories, "declarations of acceptance which were still in force were not to be extinguished and forgotten. Their operation was *suspended* until such time as the declarant state became a party to the Statute by

[1] The French equivalent of the term "in force" in both Articles 36(1) and 37 is, however, "*en vigueur*." This was also the case in the first French version of Art. 36(5) as suggested in Committee IV/1 of the San Francisco Conference. It was changed at the request of the French delegation into the present wording in French. See Doc. No. 947, IV/1/60, 13 *U.N. Conf. Int'l Org. Docs.* 486 (1945).

[2] See [1959] *I.C.J. Rep.* 148, 149 (Sep. Op. of Judge Badawi); *id* at 152, 153 (Sep. Op. of Judge Armand-Ugon).

[3] *Id.* at 166.

[4] Compare, Doc. No. 796, IV/1/59(1), 13 *U.N. Conf. Int'l Org. Docs.* 266 (1945) (Statement of the Australian representative).

being admitted to the United Nations or by virtue of Article 93(2) of the Charter."[1]

The "suspensive effect" of Article 36(5) in regard to nonsignatories was also subscribed to by the Israeli national judge in his separate dissent. Using the metaphoric expressions which characterized the pleadings in this case, he argued that the declarations in force at the time of the enactment of the Statute "might 'die' with the 'death' of the Permanent Court, were they not kept 'alive' by Article 36(5)."[2] As to the argument that the agreement of the signatories of the Charter could not legitimately bind the nonsignatories, he found that this question was not of great relevance to the case as "Bulgaria ratified what had been done there [i.e., in the San Francisco Conference] when she became a member of the United Nations without denouncing her declaration."[3]

Such arguments as the dissenting judges developed have probably found a greater response in the comments of writers than had the arguments of the Court.[4] However, the principle pronounced in this decision is still the Court's doctrine on the issue, subject to the further refinement it underwent in the *Temple of Preah Vihear Case* (1961).

[1] [1959] *I.C.J. Rep.* 127, 166 (Emphasis added). Furthermore, the jointly dissenting judges disagreed sharply with the argument presented by Judges Badawi and Armand-Ugon. Nothing in the wording of Art. 36(5), they argued, precludes the application of this text to declarations of indefinite durations, "for, in strict logic, these have still to run for such indefinite time as they may last." Besides, if the view of Judges Badawi and Armand-Ugon prevails many a declaration considered now in force would not be so. The declaration of Iran of 1930 would not either have had any validity before the present Court on this ground – an assertion which was not invoked in the *Anglo-Iranian Oil Co. Case* (1952). See *id.* at 192–3.

[2] *Id.* at 200, (Diss. Op. of Judge *ad hoc* Goiten). This was apparently the answer of Judge Goiten to the Bulgarian argument that the declaration of Bulgaria was attached to the Statute of the Permanent Court like "a branch is to the tree" and as the "tree" was cut down in 1946, the "branch" fell with it and could not be restored to life in 1955. See *Aerial Incident of 27 July 1955*, Pleadings, Oral Arguments and Documents 383, 388, 393.

[3] [1959] *I.C.J. Rep.* 127, 202.

[4] See *e.g.*, Dubisson, *supra*, p. 146, note 7 at 179–80; Shachor-Landau, "The Judgment of the International Court of Justice in the Aerial Incident Case between Israel and Bulgaria," 8 *Archiv des Völkerrechts* 277, 286, 289–90 (1960); Conac, "L'Affaire Relative à l'Incident Aérien du 27 Juillet 1955 Entre Israël et la Bulgarie devant la Cour Internationale de Justice," 64 *Rev. Gén. Dr. Int'l Pub.* 711, 721, 729 (1960); Caflisch, "The Recent Judgment of the International Court of Justice in the Case Concerning the Aerial Incident of July 27, 1955," 54 *Am. J. Int'l L.* 855, 864 (1960) (Author, nevertheless, termed the effect of Art. 36(5) a process of *novation*," which coincides with the Court's thesis that this Article constituted "a new obligation" [1959] *I.C.J. Rep.* 127, 143). See also, L. Gross, "The Jurisprudence of the World Court: Thirty-Eighth Year (1959)," 57 *Am. J. Int'l L.* 751, 766 (1963). And see earlier writings to the same effect of the dissenting opinions in the case in Hudson, "The Twenty Fourth Year of the World Court," 40 *Am. J. Int'l L.* 1, 34 (1946); Engel, "The Compulsory Jurisdiction of the International Court of Justice," 40 *Geo. L.J.* 41, 49–50 (1951–1952). But see Verzijl, "The International Court of Justice in 1959" Part II, 7 *Nederlands Tijdschrift voor Internationaal Recht* 1, 8–10 (1960).

Thailand, the respondent in this latter case, first accepted the jurisdiction of the Permanent Court by a declaration made in 1929 [No. 128] for ten years and renewed it in 1940 for a similar period. Thailand, furthermore, was not an original member of the United Nations and was admitted as a member of this organization only on December 16, 1946, almost eight months after the dissolution of the Permanent Court. However, after the expiration of the period designated in the renewal of 1940, Thailand again "renewed" on May 20, 1950, its declaration for another ten years. This latter renewal, made at a time when Thailand was already a member of the United Nations, allowed the Court to differentiate this case from that of Bulgaria. By the renewal of 1950, Thailand was thus found by the Court to have "at least purported to accept and certainly intended to accept, the compulsory jurisdiction of the present Court."[1] Yet, as the argument was raised that Thailand could not in 1950 renew a declaration that was, according to the *Aerial Incident Case*, "devoid of object" since the dissolution of the Permanent Court, the Court had to deal with the issue in detail. First, it defined the problem in the following terms:

> The real question in the present case... is not: Could Thailand by her 1950 Declaration renew or revive her 1929 and 1940 Declarations despite the fact that these had lapsed and were no longer in force; the question is, what was the effect of her Declaration of 1950: did she thereby merely revive obligations that could no longer operate because they related to a no longer existent object, or were they revived in such a way as to relate to the present Court?[2]

Then, admitting that the language used in the 1950 declaration (depicting it as a "renewal" of the declaration of 1929 as renewed in 1940) was "inadequate to achieve the purpose for which that Declaration was made," the Court refused to consider this issue as one of "error." And, as error would, at any rate, be judicially relevant only if it could affect the reality of the consent supposed to have been given, the Court concluded by saying that:

> The Court cannot however see in the present case any factor which could, as it were *ex post* and retroactively, impair the reality of the consent Thailand admits and affirms she fully intended to give in 1950. There was in any case a real consent in 1950, whether or not it was embodied in a legally effective instrument.[3]

Therefore, according to the doctrine of the *Aerial Incident Case* (1959) as refined in the *Preah Vihear Case* (1961) the actual application

[1] *Temple of Preah Vihear Case*, [1961] *I.C.J. Rep.* 17, 29.

[2] *Id.* at 30.

[3] *Ibid.* And see *id.* at 48 (Sep. Op. of Judge Morelli): "... renewal does not presuppose the initial validity of the declaration renewed."

of Article 36(5) will afford the distinction between the following categories of declarations:

(1) The declarations made under the Permanent Court which had still to run at the time of the dissolution of that Court (i.e., on April 18, 1946, and *a fortiori* at the time of the entry into force of the new Statute; October 24, 1945) and which were made by states which became original members of the United Nations: These declarations were equally valid under the present Court. This category covered the declarations of the following states (given in their numbers in Appendix VI):

Australia [5] (replaced in 1954 [6]); Bolivia [13] (replaced in 1948 by a declaration that ran for 5 years [14]); Brazil [16] (renewed for 5 years in 1948 [17]); Canada [20]; Colombia [24] (no time-limit); Denmark [29] (followed by a declaration in 1946 [30] and another in 1956 [31]); Dominican Republic [32] (no time-limit); El Salvador [35] (no time-limit); Haiti [58] (no time-limit); India [66] (followed by declarations in 1956 [67] and 1959 [68]); Iran [69] (denounced in 1951); Luxemburg [87]; The Netherlands [92] (renewed in 1946 [93] and replaced by another in 1956 [94]); New Zealand [96]; Norway [100] (renewed twice in 1946 [101] and 1956 [102]); Panama [106] (no time-limit); Union of South Africa [136] (replaced in 1955 [137]); United Kingdom [139] (denounced in 1955 and followed by declarations in 1955 [140; 141], 1957 [142], 1958 [143] and 1963 [144]); and Uruguay [146] (no time-limit).

The declaration of Paraguay [107] could also have been added to this list except that it was denounced on April 26, 1938. The effect of its denunciation will later be discussed.

(2) The declarations made under the Permanent Court and which still had to run at the moment of its dissolution, but were made by states which ceased to exist as independent states: This category covers the declarations of Estonia [38] and Latvia [78] and does not raise any problems at present.

(3) Declarations made under the Permanent Court and which still had to run at the time of its dissolution but which expired before the declaring states became members of the United Nations or parties to the statute: This category covers the declarations of Finland [44]; Ireland [71]; Sweden [120] and Switzerland [125]. These declarations could not be covered by the provision of Article 36(5) of the Statute even as interpreted by the dissenting opinions in the *Aerial Incident Case* (1959). New declarations were thus made under the present Statute by Finland, Sweden and Switzerland.

(4) Declarations made under the Permanent Court which still had to run at the time of its dissolution, and which did not yet expire at the time the declaring states became *subsequent* members of the

United Nations: This is the only category which creates problems as to the application of Article 36(5). Fortunately, it covers only three declarations: those of Bulgaria [18], Portugal [111] and Thailand [128]. The first and third of these declarations have already been studied by the Court as seen above. As to the declaration of Portugal, it was replaced by another after that state was admitted to the United Nations and this latter declaration [112] has since been in force.

This categorization makes it clear that *no further problem is expected to arise in the future as to the proper scope of Article 36(5)* except in one of two situations, both of which are rather unlikely to occur. The first is the case in which a suit is brought against Bulgaria on the basis of its declaration, nothwithstanding the Court's previous ruling. The second situation is where the argument advanced by Judges Badawi and Armand-Ugon in the *Aerial Incident Case* is revived in a case brought against an original member of the United Nations whose declaration was made under the Permanent Court without a time-limit.[1]

The question remains as to whether similar problems may arise under Article 37 of the Statute, that is to say, in regard to the jurisdiction accepted under the Permanent Court by means of treaties. As said before, this Article was meant to secure for the present Court the range of jurisdiction that was conferred on its predecessor by treaties in force. As the reference in the text was to "a treaty or convention in force [Fr. *en vigueur*]," it has been suggested that the binding force of this provision for *subsequent* parties to the Statute can hardly be questioned in most cases, the reason being that the treaty as a whole, unless it normally expired according to its terms, would remain "in force" in the period between the dissolution of the Permanent Court and the admission of the parties to the treaty to the United Nations.[2] Yet, an accurate analysis of the situation requires the differentiation between two cases:

First: If the treaty was made for the sole purpose of conferring

[1] This covers the declarations of the following states: Colombia [24], Dominican Republic [32], El Salvador [35], Haiti [58], Panama [105] and Uruguay [142]. It is to be recalled that the Joint Dissenting Opinion in the *Israel* v. *Bulgaria Case* (1959) mentioned the possibility of having these declarations nullified as a dangerous result of the view held in that case by Judges Badawi and Armand-Ugon. See [1959] *I.C.J. Rep.* 127, 192–3.

[2] See Caflisch, *supra*, p. 158, note 4 at 862; Engel, *supra*, p. 158, note 4 at 50. But see Cecchetto, "La Posizione dell' Italia Rispetto all'Art. 37 dello Statuto della Corte Internazionale di Giustizia," 39 *Rivista di Diritto Internazionale* 339, 343 (1956). And see a detailed attempt to interpret Art. 37 with little regard to the impact of the doctrine of the *Israel* v. *Bulgaria case* in Siorat, "L'Article 37 du Statut de la Cour Internationale de Justice," 8 *Annuaire Français de Droit International* 285–330 (1962).

jurisdiction on the Permanent Court (a treaty of judicial settlement), the situation would certainly be very close to that regulated by Article 36(5). No problem arises if all the parties to the treaty were original members of the United Nations. The same holds true if only some parties to the treaty were original members as long as the case arises exclusively between them. As to the parties which are not original members, Article 37 cannot extend its effect to them before they become parties to the Statute, for it applies only "as between the parties to the present Statute." On the other hand, when these states become parties to the Statute, the treaty – under the doctrine expressed in the *Aerial Incident Case* in relation to the declarations of acceptance – would have been already "devoid of object" as far as these parties are concerned. Consequently, their admission to the United Nations could not have the effect of resurrecting their old obligation under the Permanent Court. The same should be held, *a fortiori*, if *all* the parties to such a treaty are not original members of the United Nations.

Second: If the treaty was dealing ordinarily with other matters but included a compromissory clause according to which disputes arising under the treaty would be referred to the Permanent Court, the question should be decided as to whether the term "in force" in Article 37 refers to the treaty as a whole or to the compromissory clause in it. This question is of course irrelevant when all the parties to the treaty are original members of the United Nations for both the treaty and the compromissory clause would in this situation remain effective after the dissolution of the Permanent Court. But if none of the parties to the treaty is an original member of the United Nations, it could be argued, as an extension of the present doctrine of the Court, that the compromissory clause becomes devoid of object after the dissolution of the Permanent Court and that it could not be revived by a later event, even though the rest of the treaty may still be in force. This will not however be possible to maintain if the intention of the parties is proved to have been directed to keeping the compromissory clause in effect in case the Permanent Court was to be replaced by another court.

A further complication is introduced in case of multilateral treaties when some parties to the treaty are original members of the United Nations and some are not. Those which are not yet parties to the Statute cannot be brought before the Court on the basis of the treaty as Article 37 does not extend its effect to them in this stage. Similarly, such parties would not be able to bring the parties who are original members before the Court on the sole basis of the treaty. This latter conclusion is justified first by the fact that the continuity providəd for in Article 37 is limited to the parties to the Statute, and is also based on the absence of consent on the part of the defendant in such a situation. For although the condition of reciprocity is mentioned in the Statute only in regard to declarations, the respondent in this situation had in the first place accepted jurisdiction on the assumption that the acceptance was mutual between all parties to the treaty, and therefore cannot be held as accepting jurisdiction in relation to a party which is no longer bound by the compromissory clause.

What would happen if after a period of time one of those parties to the treaty which did not become original members of the United Nations was admitted to this organization and became a party to the Statute as well? Would Article 37 revive automatically in regard to such a party the compromissory clause that was kept "in force" only between the parties which are original members? Here again the doctrine of the *Aerial Incident Case* can, with some persuasiveness, be invoked to support the argument against reviving an obligation that has long disappeared. Yet, the fact that the compromissory clause has been uninterruptedly kept in force (though only between some parties) may prove relevant in giving Article 37 a broader interpretation to justify its application to parties to the treaty which became parties to the statute only after the dissolution of the Permanent Court.

As to bilateral treaties, it is clear that this analysis requires for the application of Article 37 that both parties be original members of the United Nations (e.g., in the *Haya de la Torre Case* and the *Ambatielos Case*). This is not, however, the situation in regard to the treaty invoked by Belgium as the basis of the Court's jurisdiction in the case concerning the *Barcelona Traction Light and Power Company* (now pending).[1] It is expected, therefore, that the Court will not be satisfied to have its jurisdiction in the case based solely on this treaty.*

Finally, it should be mentioned that the Yearbook of the present

[1] The application of Belgium bases the Court's jurisdiction over this case on articles 2 and 7 of the Treaty of Conciliation, Judicial settlement and Arbitration, signed at Brussels on July 19, 1927 [See text in 80 *L.N.T.S.* 18–27 (1928)]. This bilateral treaty concluded between Belgium and Spain provides, *inter alia*, that all disputes between the parties that it has not been possible to settle amicably "shall be submitted for decision to an arbitral tribunal or to the Permanent Court of International Justice" (Art. 2). Belgium is an original member of the U.N. but Spain became a member only on December 14, 1955.

* The judgment in the above case rendered on July 24, 1694 (and published after this book was printed) reached, however, a different conclusion. By 10 votes to 6 the Court rejected the second preliminary objection of Spain, depicted the *Israel v. Bulgaria Case* as "in a certain sense *sui generis*", and refused to apply the principle embodied in it to art. 37 of the Statute. See [1964] *I.C.J. Rep.* 6, 28–39.

Court, giving in its last issue a list of the treaties that provide for the jurisdiction of the Court, mentions only two treaties made under the Permanent Court, both of which are bilateral and were made by original members of the United Nations.[1]

e. The Termination of Declarations of Acceptance

Reference has already been made occassionally to the "general rules governing the termination of declarations of acceptance." It is time now to ask what these rules are.

The Statute does not speak of the termination of declarations. Nor has this question raised a problem before the Court except in the *Nottebohm Case* (1953) where it emphasized that the expiry of the declaration of the respondent, after the seisin of the Court, will have no effect on the Court's jurisdiction. As seen before, this was also manifested in fact in the *Losinger Co. Case* (1936), the *Anglo-Iranian Oil Co. Case* (1952) and the *Right of Passage Case* (1957). In all these cases the declarations of the respondents either expired (the first case) or were denounced (the other two cases) during the proceedings, this fact having no effect on the Court's jurisdiction. Apart from this settled question, the effect of a modification or a termination of a standing declaration is still an open issue.

Some writers, influenced by the "compulsory" effect of the declaration, argued that the declarant state cannot validly denounce or modify its declaration immediately on notice, even if the declaration authorizes it to do so. Their argument is based on the ground that a declaration should remain in effect for the period designated in it or else indefinitely except when there is an express reservation of unilateral termination *after a reasonable period of notice*. If the reservation does not provide for such a period, it will be incompatible with the Statute as it will enable the declarant state to escape the Court's jurisdiction whenever this is about to be invoked. Some writers went even to the extent of holding any reservation of termination as incompatible with the Statute because with such a reservation the declaration will not be made "for a *certain* time" contrary to the authorized limits of reservation provided for in Article 36(3).[2] Other

[1] See [1962–1963] *I.C.J.Y.B.* 260. In previous issues of this Yearbook only one more treaty was occasionally cited. This is the Constitution of the International Civil Aviation Organization signed at Chicago on December 7, 1944.

[2] See *e.g.*, Briggs, *supra*, p. 147, note 3 at 278; Delbez, *Les Principes Généraux du Contentieux International* 74, 76 (1962); Maus, *Les Réserves dans les Déclarations d'Acceptation de la Juridiction* 78–80 (1959). Briggs, however, added that "it is most improbable that the Court would declare [such declarations] invalid."

writers relied on the "bilateral element" in the relationship created by declarations to reach the conclusion that "there is no right of unilateral termination of a declaration under the Optional Clause unless the right has been expressly reserved in the declaration," conceding that a reservation permitting a state to terminate or vary its declaration immediately on notice would not, despite its dangerous effect, be invalid.[1]

A study of the 148 declarations made under the International Court yields the following conclusions (expounded in figures in Appendix VII, No. 3):

(1) Eighty-two declarations were made for a certain period without automatic renewal. Only one of these declarations is now in force, this is the declaration of Turkey which has recently been renewed for five years as from May 23, 1962 [No. 133a].

(2) Seven declarations were made each for a certain period to be renewed automatically for similar periods until it is terminated on a six-months' notice. Six of these declarations [Nos. 31, 45, 87, 94, 102, 122] are still in force. The seventh (declaration of Pakistan [103]) was denounced according to the reservation in it without objection from other states. More than five months after its denunciation a new declaration [104] took its place.

(3) Twenty-five declarations were made for a certain period "and thereafter until terminated." Twelve of these declarations [Nos. 12, 19, 20, 22, 50, 75, 80, 88, 96, 109, 112, 145] are still in force; three of them [22, 88, 145] have conditioned the termination by a requirement of a six-months' notice; and one [112] permitted the unilateral exclusion from the scope of the declaration of "any given category or categories of disputes."[2]

In September 1939, six of the declarations falling into this category [Nos. 4, 20, 65, 95, 135, 138], along with one declaration of category (1) (declaration of France [48]), underwent an amendment excluding

[1] See Waldock, "The Decline of the Optional Clause," 32 *Brit. Yb. Int'l L.* 244, 265–7, (1955–1956).

[2] This is the declaration of Portugal made on December 19, 1955. In the *Right of Passage Case* India attacked the above reservation in this declaration, as "incompatible with the object and purpose of the Optional Clause." The Court, which found that the exclusion anticipated in the declaration cannot have retroactive effect so as to cover cases already pending, concluded that the reservation was not inconsistent with the Statute. As to the element of uncertainty which this reservation introduces in Portugal's acceptance, it was not, the Court argued, any greater than the uncertainty present in the Indian declaration which included a reservation allowing its termination immediately on notice. See [1957] *I.C.J. Rep.* 141–4. Clearly, the Court acted in that case on the assumption that despite the reservations in the Portuguese and Indian declarations both constituted a valid basis for the Court's jurisdiction.

from the acceptance disputes arising out of events during the war.[1] Although this unilateral modification was alleged to have been based on the change in circumstances (thus invoking the doctrine *rebis sic stantibus*) many objections were made against it,[2] to the extent that four of the six states that had introduced it preferred to make, after the expiry of the first period of their declarations, new ones in which they incorporated the war exclusion.

All the other declarations of category (3) which are not now in force were – with the exception of the declaration of Iraq [70] which was never ratified – denounced without objection, but they were all followed by new declarations from the same states.

(4) Eighteen declarations were made for an unlimited period to be in force until they are denounced. Only one of these conditions the termination on one-year's notice [No. 126]. At present ten of the eighteen declarations are in force [Nos. 6, 68, 73, 82, 105, 115, 116, 126, 136, 144], leaving eight that were denounced without objection, though they were all replaced by new declarations. Two of the declarations in force [Nos. 115, 144] reserve, moreover, the right of unilateral modification.

(5) Sixteen declarations were made for an unlimited period without any conditions as to their termination. Three of these [Nos. 25, 56, 79] were never ratified; one (declaration of Bulgaria [18]) has, according to the *Aerial Incident Case* (1959), lapsed with the dissolution of the Permanent Court, and another (declaration of Colombia [23]) was replaced by a new declaration. Among the remaining eleven, ten are in force but one (declaration of Paraguay [107]) was unilaterally terminated in 1938. It was sought to justify this termination by the fact that Paraguay ceased to be a member of the League of Nations, and that its acceptance was not made for any stated period.[3] Six states objected, however, to this practice, two of them (the Netherlands and Czechoslovakia) indicating that the question should be governed by the law relating to the termination of treaties.[4] No further development took place except that the Yearbook of the present Court has,

[1] See *League of Nations Off. J.*, 20th Ass., 407–10 (1939); *id.* 21st Ass. 44 (1940).

[2] See the observations of Belgium, Brazil, Denmark, Estonia, Haiti, the Netherlands, Norway, Peru, Sweden, Switzerland and Thailand, in *P.C.I.J. Ann. Rep.*, ser. E, No. 16 at 333–43 (1939–1945).

[3] See *League of Nations Off. J.*, 19th Ass., 650–2 (1938). And see, for a discussion of the grounds on which the withdrawal was based, Farmanfarma, *The Declared Jurisdiction of the International Court of Justice* 79–87 (1952); Engel, *supra*, p. 158, note 4 at 54–9; Fachiri, "Repudiation of the Optional Clause," 20 *Brit. Yb. Int'l L.* 52–7 (1929). They were all of the opinion that the withdrawal was based on unsound grounds.

[4] See *League of Nations Off. J.*, 19th Ass., 686–7, 1180–2 (1938); *id.* 20th Ass., 235–6 (1939); *P.C.I.J. Ann. Rep.*, ser. E, No. 14 at 57 n. 2; *id.*, No. 15 at 227 n. 2.

till its issue of 1959–1960, kept citing the declaration of Paraguay as one of the declarations in force, with, however, a reference to the incident of withdrawal in 1938 and the comments it invoked. In the later issues of that Yearbook no similar citation is made of the declaration of Paraguay, and no reason is expressed for this omission.[1]

The practice reviewed above bears, therefore, evidence that a termination of a declaration, made even immediately on notice, does not arouse objections if it is anticipated in the declaration itself. Declarations containing reservations to that effect were normally relied upon as valid bases of the Court's jurisdiction.[2] As to the only declaration denounced in the absence of a reservation allowing such action (the declaration of Paraguay), it may be significant that this declaration has never since been invoked. The fact that the Court insists always that its jurisdiction must be based on the consent of the parties makes it rather unrealistic for states to resort to the Court against a party which has already denounced its instrument of acceptance which was made for an indefinite period. One tends, therefore, to agree with Rosenne in saying that the question whether an unqualified declaration can be withdrawn or denounced must largely be "relegated to the realm of theory."[3] But even in this realm the insistence on applying the rules relating to the termination of treaties, and therefore of invalidating any unilateral termination not anticipated in the instrument, is not always justified. It has been explained before that the "bilateral element" is not the only element in the relationship created by the declarations of acceptance, and that this element becomes particularly important only after the seisin of the Court of a given case. All agree that a unilateral termination will then have no effect on the Court's jurisdiction. Before the Court is seized, however, the vague relationship between each two declaring states, with its three elements present, can hardly be called a treaty subject to the rules governing the termination of treaties. If the application of such rules

[1] In a letter to this writer dated Dec. 10, 1963, by Mr. Stanislas Aquarone, the Deputy Registrar of the present Court, it was explained that "the omission was not inadvertent." Mr. Aquarone however pointed out that he had no knowledge "of any communication from the Government of Paraguay in this connection." Referring to the introductory passage preceding the texts of declarations in the I.C.J. Yearbooks and citing the *Israel* v. *Bulgaria* and the *Temple of Preah Vihear* cases, he concluded that "the Registry had to decide whether it would be more misleading to include Paraguay in the list of States accepting the compulsory jurisdiction, and thereby to appear to adopt the view that the 1933 declaration is to be regarded as binding on Paraguay for all time, or to omit it, and appear to adopt the contrary view that, at all events at the present day, the denunciation must be regarded as having had some effect. No doubt a legal argument could be advanced for either view . . ."

[2] See Appendix V as compared with Appendix VII, No. 3.

[3] Rosenne, *The Time Factor* 26 (1960).

is found "desirable" as it results in widening the Court's scope of continued jurisdiction, it may at best be suggested as an instance of the "should be" as compared with the "is" in the realm of international adjudication.

f. Declarations Made by States not Parties to the Statute

The question of the conditions under which the Court is open to states not parties to the Statute has been discussed on two occasions above.[1] Such conditions, it was explained, consist of making a declaration in conformity with the Security Council resolution of October 15, 1946, and depositing it with the Registrar of the Court (rather than with the Secretary General of the United Nations who only receives a certified copy from the Registrar). This declaration may be either *particular* (accepting the jurisdiction of the Court in respect only of a particular dispute or disputes which have already arisen) or *general* (accepting jurisdiction generally in respect of all disputes or of a particular class or classes of disputes). In neither case does the declaration create jurisdiction in the strict sense. It merely "opens" the Court to the declaring state thus conferring on the latter the "ability to appear before the Court." But in making a *general* declaration, the declaring state is authorized by the resolution of the Security Council (paragraph 2) to recognize, in accordance with Article 36(2) of the Statute "as compulsory *ipso facto* and without special agreement, the jurisdiction of the Court." This latter declaration which is capable of creating continued jurisdiction is, however, subject to the serious condition that it "may not, without explicit agreement, be relied upon *vis-à-vis* states parties to the Statute, which have made the declaration in conformity with Article 36, paragraph 2 of the Statute of the International Court of Justice." Such a condition, inherited from the corresponding resolution of the Council of the League (Resolution of May 17, 1922) and found then to be "indeed curious,"[2] puts a heavy limitation on the effect of a declaration of acceptance made in pursuance of the resolution. If the declaring state will not be able by virtue of such a declaration to bring before the Court a state party to the Statute which made a declaration in conformity with Article 36(2), then by force of reciprocity it could

[1] See Chapter III, at 90–91 and this Chapter, at 192–3. Notice the difference between states not parties to the Statute and states not members of the U.N. which became parties to the Statute in accordance with Art. 93(2) of the Charter, i.e. ,on the conditions determined in each case by the General Assembly upon the recommendation of the Security Council.

[2] Hudson, *The Permanent Court of International Justice* 351 (1934).

not be sued either by the latter state. The result is to limit the effectiveness of the declaration made by a nonparty to other nonparties filing similar declarations, which will give it a narrow scope indeed. Under the Permanent Court only two states made such declarations: Liechtenstein (declaration of March 22, 1939 [81]) and Monaco (declaration of April 22, 1937 [89]). Neither of them had an occasion to sue the other, but the first attempted to bring a state party to the Statute (Hungary) before the Court in the *Gerliczy Case*. The Application in this case, filed on June 17, 1939, was met on the part of Hungary with an expressed intention to object to it on the ground that the jurisdictional title on which Liechtenstein relied was not effective *vis à vis* Hungary, but the case did not proceed any further due to the outbreak of the Second World War.[1] No new declaration of acceptance of the "continued jurisdiction" was made under the present Court by a state not party to the Statute. This is not a surprising reaction and is probably bound to be the case as long as the Security Council resolution renders such declarations without effect in relation to the parties to the Statute. No state nonparty to the Statute is expected to take the initiative of making a declaration that will be practically meaningless.

It may finally be relevant to add in this respect that the resolution of the Security Council of October 15, 1946 expressly empowers the Court to decide "all questions as to the validity or the effect of a declaration made under the terms of this resolution" (Paragraph 5), which is a specified aspect of the Court's general *compétence de la compétence*.

2. *Incidental Jurisdiction*

Patterns of Incidental Jurisdiction

The patterns of jurisdiction so far dealt with are all primary or original in the sense that they relate to the merits of the dispute between the parties and are directly based on their consent. However, once the Court is seized in an attempt to establish its primary jurisdiction some questions may arise as incidents of the proceedings before the Court. The power to determine such questions constitutes the "incidental jurisdiction" which the Court acquires by virtue of its judicial nature and in accordance with the provisions regulating its activities. As these questions often arise before, and at times for the purpose of, a decision whether the primary substantive jurisdiction

[1] See *P.C.I.J. Ann. Rep.*, ser. E, No. 16 at 154–8 (1939–1945).

exists, it is clear that, if they are to be timely decided, the Court must be able to exercise its incidental jurisdiction independently of the question of its jurisdiction over the merits of the dispute. Rather than being based on the consent of the parties, incidental jurisdiction is, therefore, founded on institutional instruments (The Statute or the Rules of Court or both) and the jurisdictional fact of a valid seisin of the Court. Only because the Statute may be considered for this purpose as a treaty accepted in advance by the parties the principle of consent is formally complied with. Incidental jurisdiction is, otherwise, more of an inherent and objective character. It need not be always exercised in the first phase of the proceedings. For, as Fitzmaurice explained, there may be a "preliminary exercise" and a "consequential exercise" of incidental jurisdiction.[1] The first takes place before, or regardless of, the determination of the substantive jurisdiction of the Court, such as the jurisdiction to determine jurisdiction (Article 36(6)), the jurisdiction to indicate interim measures of protection (Article 41), and the jurisdiction to allow third-party intervention (Articles 62 and 63). As to the "consequential" exercise of incidental jurisdiction, it presupposes a determination of the question of substantive jurisdiction and is consequential upon it. This is particularly so in case of the jurisdiction to interpret or revise a judgment, and the jurisdiction to decide on counter–claims.

Among all these patterns the jurisdiction which is most preliminary and general in character is that provided for in Article 36(6) of the Statute. As already explained, it covers even the other patterns of incidental jurisdiction, both preliminary and consequential. With respect to these other patterns, two of them present in particular jurisdictional problems of controversy and interest: the jurisdiction to indicate interim measures of protection and the jurisdiction to decide on counter-claims. Only the first pattern is dealt with here as the latter is considered along with some aspects of other incidental jurisdictions in the following Chapter.

Jurisdiction to Indicate Interim Measures of Protection

The request for the indication of interim measures of protection presents, in theory, two questions as to the time in which it may be considered by a judicial tribunal. The first question is whether the tribunal is competent to pronounce on the request before the filing

[1] See Fitzmaurice, "The Law and Procedure of the International Court of Justice ...," 34 *Brit. Yb. Int'l L.* 1, 108–9 (1958).

of the suit instituting proceedings, and the second is whether the interim measures can be indicated before the tribunal's jurisdiction to deal with the merits is established. Only the latter problem arises before the International Court. The first, though answered in the affirmative in some municipal codes and in the rules of procedure of arbitral tribunals, is clearly disposed of by Article 61(1) of the Rules of Court. According to this provision a request for the indication of interim measures "may be filed at any time *during* the proceedings in the case in connection with which it is made." It is not surprising, therefore, that in the whole history of the International Court no request for interim measures was made independent of a pending case.[1]

As to the question of the stage of the proceedings at which the jurisdiction to indicate interim measures could validly be exercised, a careful answer must be preceded by a review of the practice of the International Court in this regard.[2]

The first occasion on which a request for interim measures was made before the Permanent Court was the case concerning the *Denunciation of the Treaty of November 2nd, 1865 between China and Belgium* (1927). In the very application instituting proceedings in this case on the basis of mutual declarations of acceptance made by the parties under Article 36(2) of the Statute, Belgium requested the Court to indicate, pending judgment, "any provisional measures to be taken for the preservation of rights which may subsequently be recognized as belonging to Belgium or her nationals." The request was accordingly considered by the Court's President before the question of substantive jurisdiction was settled and even before the lapse of the time-limit for lodging preliminary objections. The President noticed in his order that both parties had recognized the continued

[1] In the *South Eastern Territory of Greenland Case* (1932) the Permanent Court noted that, "it is in principle arguable that such a power [to indicate interim measures] on the part of the Court exists only in respect of a dispute already submitted to it." Ser. A/B, No. 48 at 283 (1932). In the *Polish Agrarian Reform Case* (1933) the same Court indicated, however, that "the essential condition which must necessarily be fulfilled ... is that such measures should have the effect of protecting the rights forming the subject of the dispute *submitted to the Court.*" Ser. A/B, No. 58 at 177 (Emphasis added). In this last case the German Government had notified the Registrar, before the institution of proceedings, that interim measures would be requested, but the actual request was filed with the application instituting proceedings. See *P.C.I.J.*, ser. C, No. 71 at 136–7 (1933).

[2] See for the treatment of this question before arbitral tribunals, Fitzmaurice, *supra*, p. 170, note 1 at 115–24; Cocatre-Zilgien, "Les Mesures Conservatoires en Droit International," 11 *Revue Egyptienne* 73, 90–3 (1955); Bin Cheng, *General Principles of Law as Applied by International Courts and tribunals* 268–70 (1953); Guggenheim, "Les Mesures Conservatoires dans la Procédure Arbitrale et Judiciaire," 40 *Recueil des Cours* 649, 698–743 (1932–II); Dumbauld, *Interim Measures of Protection in International Controversies* 125–144, 186 (1932).

jurisdiction of the Court by means of declarations which ordinarily would cover the dispute in question "if the treaty of November 2nd, 1865 were recognized as still operative," and that the subsequent infractions of this treaty "could not be made good by the payment of an indemnity or by compensation or restitution." As a result he concluded by indicating some measures of protection that were made "provisionally, pending the final decision of the Court... by which decision the Court will either declare itself to have no jurisdiction or give judgment on the merits..."[1] This order given in the absence of any objection, or in fact any pleadings related to the Court's incidental jurisdiction, was soon to be revoked on the request of Belgium in pursuance of an agreement reached with China.[2] No objection to the Court's substantive jurisdiction was later submitted by China, and the case was finally withdrawn.[3]

The second request for interim measures was made in the *Chorzów Factory Case* (1927) after the Court had established its substantive jurisdiction and had reserved the claims for judgement on the merits. There was, therefore, no problem involved as to whether the Court had jurisdiction to indicate interim measures at that stage of the proceedings. No such measures were indicated, however, as the Court found that the request "cannot be regarded as relating to the indication of measures of interim protection, but as designed to obtain an interim judgment in favor of a part of the claim formulated in the application."[4]

A request was again made by Norway in its application instituting proceedings in the case concerning the *Legal Status of the South Eastern Territory of Greenland* (1932) in which it asked the Court to indicate provisional measures that would apply to both parties. The request was objected to by the other party, Denmark, thus providing the first discussion in the pleadings before the Permanent Court on the Court's jurisdiction to indicate interim measures.[5] The Court on its part found first that the circumstances mentioned in the Norwegian request and the oral statements did not require such measures to be taken, then proceeded to discuss whether it might indicate interim measures *proprio motu*.[6] This latter discussion ended also by a refusal

[1] *P.C.I.J.*, ser. A, No. 8 at 7 (Order of January 8, 1927).
[2] *Id.* at 9–11 (Order of February 15, 1927).
[3] *P.C.I.J.*, ser. A, No. 18/19 (Order of May 25, 1929).
[4] *P.C.I.J.*, ser. A, No. 12 at 10 (Order of November 21, 1927). (The request was made for the immediate payment of a certain sum of money).
[5] See a summary of the arguments of both parties reproduced in the Court's order in *P.C.I.J.*, ser. A/B, No. 48 at 278–83 (1932).
[3] *Id.* at 287.

to indicate any measures. The substantive jurisdiction in the case, based on mutual declarations of acceptance, was never disputed, and the case itself was later withdrawn.[1]

In the *Prince von Pless Case* (1933) a request for the indication of certain provisional measures was made after the Court's jurisdiction was disputed by the respondent and the objection was joined to the merits. However, due to the attitude subsequently adopted by the respondent and agreed to by the applicant, the Court declared the request to have ceased to have any object, but was careful to indicate that this "must in no way prejudge either the question of the Court's jurisdiction to adjudicate upon the... Application instituting proceedings... or that of the admissibility of that Application."[2]

In the same year the Court had to consider a request for interim measures made by Germany together with its application instituting proceedings in the *Polish Agrarian Reform and the German Minority Case* (1933). As this request was objected to by the defendant Government, a lengthy discussion took place in three oral hearings on the issue of the Court's jurisdiction to indicate the measures requested.[3] It is instructive that in this discussion no argument was ever made to the effect that the Court lacked the incidental jurisdiction because its substantive jurisdiction was not yet certain. The Court finally refused to indicate the measures requested only because they could not be regarded as "solely designed to protect the subject of the dispute and the actual object of the principal claim,"[4] reiterating again the principle that its order was given without in any way prejudging the question of its own jurisdiction or the admissibility of the claim. Three judges dissented finding that the request should have been answered. Judge Anzilotti concurred in the Court's conclusion but was unable to base it on the same grounds. To him, the refusal to indicate interim measures in the case should have been based on "the uncertainty which the application instituting the main proceedings allows to subsist as to what the [applicant] seeks to obtain from the Court, and, in consequence as to the extent of any rights which the interim measures would have to protect."[5] Nothing, therefore, was mentioned in regard to the certainty or uncertainty of the

[1] See *P.C.I.J.*, ser. A/B, No. 55 (Order of May 11, 1933).
[2] *P.C.I.J.*, ser. A/B, No. 54 at 153 (Order of March 11, 1933).
[3] *P.C.I.J.*, ser. C, No. 71 at 36–59 (1933).
[4] *P.C.I.J.*, ser. A/B, No. 58 at 178 (Order of July 29, 1933).
[5] *Id.* at 181.

jurisdiction on the merits of the case. This latter jurisdiction was not objected to until the case was finally discontinued.[1]

Finally, in the *Electricity Company of Sofia and Bulgaria Case* two separate requests for interim measures were made by the applicant Government. The first, dated July 2, 1938, was made before the Court's substantive jurisdiction in the case was established (and in fact before it was objected to by the respondent). It was later withdrawn before any observations on it were submitted by the respondent.[2] The second request was, on the other hand, made on October 14, 1939, i.e., after the judgment affirming the Court's jurisdiction to deal with the merits of the case. No problem as to the proper timing of the examination of the request was therefore involved. The request was later granted though the Court was able to hear the applicant's argument only.[3]

In summation, seven requests for the indication of interim measures of protection were submitted to the Permanent Court. Two of these requests were subsequently withdrawn, two were requested already after the Court's substantive jurisdiction was established and one after this jurisdiction was objected to (the *Prince Von Pless Case*). Out of the seven requests only two were granted. On the other hand, discussions in the pleadings of the parties on the Court's jurisdiction to indicate the measures requested took place in only two cases, but no where in these discussions or otherwise did the argument arise to the effect that the incidental jurisdiction to indicate interim measures presupposes that the Court's jurisdiction on the merits must be probable or possible.[4] This argument arose by contrast with regard to the first request submitted to the present Court, creating a controversy that has since been the most relevant problem in the question of interim protection.

After filing the application instituting proceedings in the *Anglo-Iranian Oil Co. Case*, the United Kingdom requested the Court to indicate certain provisional measures that it thought should be imposed on the Government of Iran until a decision on the merits is reached

[1] See *P.C.I.J.*, ser. A/B, No. 60 at 33 (Order of December 2, 1933).

[2] See *P.C.I.J.*, ser. C, No. 88 at 475 (1938–1939).

[3] See *P.C.I.J.*, ser. A/B, No. 79 (Order of December 5, 1939).

[4] Commentators on the work of the Permanent Court have therefore agreed that the indication of interim measures was not dependent upon a determination of the Court's substantive jurisdiction. See *e.g.*, Hudson, *The Permanent Court of International Justice* 425 (2d ed. 1943); A. Hammarskjöld, "Quelques Aspects de la Question des Mesures Conservatoires en Droit International Positif," in his *Juridiction Internationale* 299, 313 (1938); Dumbauld, *supra*, p. 171, note 2 at 186.

by the Court. On the communication of the text of this request to Iran, the latter, declining to appear before the Court, sent a note to it asking that the request ought to be dismissed because the Court lacked all jurisdiction over the case. This lack of jurisdiction was based, in the Iranian note, on two grounds – an assertion that the dispute was between a private company and Iran (thus suggesting that the United Kingdom had no *locus standi* in the case), and a contention that the dispute belonged exclusively to Iran's domestic jurisdiction, and was, therefore, outside the scope of any international jurisdiction.[1] The latter contention seems to have struck the Court as presenting the first problem on which the issue of the determination of jurisdiction to indicate interim measures depended. After a brief treatment of the first contention the Court wrote that:

> ... the complaint made in the application is one of an alleged violation of international law by the breach of the agreement for a concession..., and by a denial of justice... and... it cannot be accepted *a priori* that a claim based on such a complaint falls completely outside the scope of international jurisdiction...[2]

Reaching this conclusion, the Court, without seeking any further manifestation of the probability of its acquisition of substantive jurisdiction over the case, added that "the considerations stated in the preceding paragraph suffice to empower the Court to entertain the request for interim measures of protection."[3] Then the Court reiterated the principle long upheld by the Permanent Court to the effect that:

> ... the indication of such measures in no way prejudices the question of the jurisdiction of the Court to deal with the merits of the case, and leaves unaffected the right of the Respondent to submit arguments against such jurisdiction.[4]

Accepting this last principle as valid, Judges Badawi and Winiarski disagreed, however, with the course followed by the majority of the Court. To them interim measures are "exceptional in character, and in derogation of general rights" to the extent that "they may easily be considered a scarcely tolerable interference in the affairs of a sovereign State." Therefore, in order to indicate them the Court should, in their view, "examine the situation as a whole" and in particular

[1] See *Anglo-Iranian Oil Co. Case*, Pleadings, Oral Arguments and Documents 672, 679–80 (*I.C.J.* 1952).

[2] [1951] *I.C.J. Rep.* 89, 93. (Compare the observations of Iran in relation to this order in which the Court was accused of *excès de pouvoir*. Pleadings, *op. cit.*, note 1 at 281–6.)

[3] *Ibid.*

[4] *Ibid.*

"must consider its competence [over the merits of the dispute] *reasonably probable.*"[1] Thus they concluded:

We find it difficult to accept the view that if *prima facie* the total lack of jurisdiction of the Court is not patent, that is, if there is a possibility, however remote, that the Court may be competent, then it may indicate interim measurese of protection. This approach which also involves an element of judgment, and which does not reserve to any greater extent the right of the Court to give a final decision as to its jurisdiction, appears however to be based on a presumption in favour of the competence of the Court which is not in consonance with the principles of international law. In order to accord with these principles, the position should be reversed: *if there exist weighty arguments in favour of challenged jurisdiction, the Court may indicate interim measures of protection;* if there exist serious doubts or weighty arguments against this jurisdiction such measures cannot be indicated.[2]

It is seen from this that both the Court and the dissenting judges agreed only on two points: a) that the Court will have no jurisdiction to indicate interim measures if it was apparent *a priori* that the merits of the dispute fall completely outside the scope of the Court's jurisdiction, and b) that the Court need not be completely certain that it has substantive jurisdiction over the merits in order to be able to indicate interim measures. The difference between the two viewpoints lies in the question of how far the Court should look into its jurisdiction over the merits when it considers a request for the indication of interim measures. The majority sought to establish a negative criterion (that the Court should satisfy itself that the merits are not completely outside the scope of its substantive jurisdiction) while the dissenting judges called for a more positive test – the Court's substantive jurisdiction should be "reasonably probable." When it is recalled in this respect that a valid seisin of the Court cannot take place if the application instituting proceedings does not rely on any prior jurisdictional title,[3] it will be easy to reduce the Court's criterion to the simple statement that a proper seisin (in the sense explained above) is all that is required for the exercise of the Court's jurisdiction to indicate interim measures of protection.[4] Apparently, this was not what some

[1] *Id.* at 96. (Emphasis added.)

[2] *Id.* at 97. (Emphasis added.)

[3] See details in Chapter III, *supra.*

[4] What should the Court do if it is not clear whether the parties are "states" and therefore possess the ability to appear before the Court? When Iran contested the *locus standi* of the applicant in the *Anglo-Iranian Oil Co. Case* as part of its objection to the Court's power to indicate interim measures, the Court emphasized before establishing this power in the case that it appeared to it from the application that the applicant Government "had adopted the cause of a British Company and is proceeding in virtue of the right of diplomatic protection." [1951] *I.C.J. Rep.* 89, 92. This indicates that there should be at least *prima facie* evidence that the parties are *legitimae personae.* Compare, Rosenne, "The *Forum Prorogatum* in the International Court of Justice," 6 *Revue Hellénique* 1, 16 (1953).

writers deduced from the Court's holding in the *Anglo-Iranian Oil Co. Case*. Rosenne, for instance, after agreeing that if the application needs for its perfection a successive step on the part of the respondent and that step has been refused "there will be no 'proceedings' and consequently no inherent jurisdiction to indicate interim measures," added that: "The position might be otherwise so long as it is not clear whether the respondent has refused the invitation to accept the jurisdiction of the Court..."[1] It is submitted here, on the contrary, that even in this last position interim measures could not be indicated,[2] for the simple reason of the lack of any valid seisin which is, as seen above, a prior requirement for the indication of interim measures, and indeed for the exercise of all patterns of incidental jurisdiction. On the other hand, some writers seem to have read in the majority's view in the *Anglo-Iranian Oil Co. Case* a requirement that is, at least theoretically, a little more strict than the condition of a mere valid seisin. Lauterpacht, with whose view on this matter Fitzmaurice concurs, commented on the judgment in that case by saying that the Court can indicate interim measures:

> ... provided that there is in existence an instrument, such as a Declaration of Acceptance of the Optional Clause, made by both Parties to the dispute, which *prima facie* confers jurisdiction upon the Court and provided that there are no reservations to that instrument which clearly exclude the jurisdiction of the Court.[3]

The second condition in the example cited by Lauterpacht clearly goes beyond the simple requirement of a valid seisin. That his understanding of the criterion applied in the *Anglo-Iranian Oil Co. Case* was stricter than that of the Court was in fact proved in the first phase of the *Interhandel Case* (1957). Lauterpacht, by then a member of the Court, applied his conclusion to the circumstances of the new case only to find himself in disagreement with the Court, despite the fact that the latter did not in principle change its stand on the subject.

Two days after filing its application instituting the proceedings in the *Interhandel Case*, the Swiss Government requested the Court to indicate three types of provisional measures to be carried out by the respondent (the United States). The latter responded by filing a preliminary objection under Article 62 of the Rules of the Court to

[1] Rosenne, *The International Court of Justice* 328 (1957).

[2] *Accord*, Fitzmaurice, *supra*, p. 170, note 1 at 114.

[3] Lauterpacht, *The Development of International Law by the International Court* 112 (1958). And see, Fitzmaurice, *supra*, p. 170, note 1 at 113–4. Compare, Ch. de Visscher, *Problèmes d'Interprétation Judiciaire en Droit International Public* 201, n. 3 (1963).

the proceedings instituted by the Government of Switzerland as relating to a particular area of the dispute, which was covered by the request for interim measures. This preliminary objection invoked the "self-judging" reservation in the American Declaration [145] for the purpose of declaring the part of the dispute covered by the objection a matter essentially within the United States domestic jurisdiction. In the oral hearings on the request for interim measures Mr. Guggenheim, the Co-Agent of the Swiss Government, challenged the validity of the reservation in the American declaration that allowed the respondent to submit its objection but agreed that the Court would not wish, in its examination of a request for the indication of interim measures, to adjudicate upon so complex and delicate a question as this.[1] Meanwhile, the United States' Co-Agents argued that the Court, being clearly without jurisdiction on the merits as a result of the invocation of the self-judging reservation, had no incidental jurisdiction to indicate provisional measures of protection.[2] A development then took place outside the Court according to which the United States Government indicated that it "is not taking action at the present time to fix a time schedule for the sale of [the shares in dispute]." This was not, however, found by Switzerland to be an adequate assurance justifying the withdrawal of its request for interim measures which covered, at any rate, other matters as well. The Court, therefore, discussed its power to indicate the measures requested by noting first that both parties had accepted its continued jurisdiction by means of mutual declarations of acceptance made in accordance with Article 36(2) of the Statute within the purview of which "by its subject-matter the present dispute falls."[3] Then referring to the invocation by the respondent of its "self-judging" reservation it noticed that the preliminary objection was submitted under Article 62 of the Rules whereas the request for interim measures could be dealt with only under the procedure indicated in Article 61. It finally added that "the decision given under this procedure in no way prejudges the question of the jurisdiction of the Court to deal with the merits of the case and leaves unaffected the right of the Respondent to submit arguments against such jurisdiction."[4] As a result the Court found that it had jurisdiction to indicate interim measures in that case regardless of the question of the validity of the reservation and of the objection

[1] *Interhandel Case*, Pleadings, Oral Arguments and Documents 462–3 (*I.C.J.* 1959).
[2] See *id.* at 452–8.
[3] [1957] *I.C.J. Rep.* 105, 110.
[4] *Id.* at 111.

that was based on it. No such measures were indicated, however, as the Court found that the only measure formulated in the request in terms fulfilling the requirement laid down in Article 61(1) of the Rules was already taken voluntarily by the respondent. Both Judges Badawi and Winiarski, it should be noted, participated in the majority making this Order which may be an indication that they have found that there was enough basis in the case for a provisional conclusion that the substantive jurisdiction of the Court was "reasonably probable." Yet, in the view of six other judges the circumstances of the case did not seem to warrant in the first place the exercise of the jurisdiction to indicate interim measures.[1] Judge Koo held that the American reservation and its invocation in the case were valid and that the Court was consequently "not competent to deal with the Swiss request for indication of provisional measures and that its decision should be based upon this ground."[2] Judge Klaestad, in whose opinion Judges Hackworth and Read concurred, argued that as a *prima facie* finding, the reservation should be given effect "without entering into an examination of its validity," thus concluding that the Court was without jurisdiction to indicate any provisional measures.[3] Finally, Judge Lauterpacht wrote a longer dissent in which he referred to the importance of taking into consideration "the nature of the request" and the "factor of urgency inherent in the procedure under Article 41 of the Statute," but added that "it is another thing to affirm that the Court can act under Article 41 without any regard to the prospects of its jurisdiction on the merits and that the latter question does not arise at all in connection with a request for interim measures of protection."[4] As to the case at hand, he found no chance of a future affirmative decision on substantive jurisdiction:

If the Court subsequently holds that reservation [i.e. the self-judging reservation in the declaration of the respondent] to be valid that will automatically terminate its jurisdiction with regard to the sale of the shares. Should, on the other hand, the Court eventually declare the reservation in question to be invalid, such invalidity may well entail the invalidity of the Declaration of Acceptance as a whole and thus render impossible altogether the jurisdiction of the Court... on either alternative the Court will be without jurisdiction to entertain the Application so far as it relates to the sale and disposition of the shares.[1]

[1] Five of these wrote or concurred in written separate opinions, while Judge Kojevnikov declared he was unable to agree with the order without giving the reasons for his opinion. See *id.* at 114.

[2] *Id.* at 113.

[3] *Id.* at 116.

[4] *Id.* at 118.

[5] *Id.* at 119.

Thus, Judge Lauterpacht argued, the Court which could not have jurisdiction over the merits in this case, was without jurisdiction to indicate interim measures.

It remains to be said that despite its persuasiveness, the conclusion of Judge Lauterpacht does not reflect the attitude of the Court. In fact, the latter, by excluding the consideration of the preliminary objection on procedural grounds (that is, by saying that the procedure applicable was the one indicated in Article 61(1) and not Article 62 of the Rules), has affirmed the view that a valid seisin in the sense expounded in the previous Chapter is all that is practically required for exercising this incidental jurisdiction (provided of course that the circumstances of the case are such as to justify the measures requested). An interpretation of the Statute by the "systematic method" was found to be in conformity with this conclusion, as Article 41 of the Statute (dealing with the indication of provisional measures) is placed at the beginning of Chapter III of the Statute concerned with "Procedure" and comes immediately after the Article dealing with the institution of proceedings but before the various articles concerned with the actual procedure before the Court.[1]

The attitude of the Court as expounded above is not free from criticism, especially as the jurisdiction to indicate interim measures may be exercised, as both the Rules and the practice of the Court affirm, *proprio motu,* and need not be confined to the measures requested. The noncompliance of Iran in the only case where the present Court has indicated interim measures under its standing criterion, is particularly instructive. One may expect, therefore, that the Court may be persuaded in the future to move in the direction devised by Judges Badawi and Winiarski in the *Anglo-Iranian Oil Co. Case,* adopting a stricter requirement for the exercise of its jurisdiction to indicate interim measures of protection.

[1] See Bin Cheng, *supra,* p. 171, note 2 at 270.

PART THREE

THE EXERCISE OF THE POWER – A CRITICAL ANALYSIS

CHAPTER V

THE TECHNIQUES USED BY THE COURT IN THE EXERCISE OF THE POWER TO DETERMINE ITS JURISDICTION

In the preceding parts of this study the power of the International Court to determine the limits of its jurisdiction has been analyzed both in its inherent qualities and in its application to the different patterns of this Court's jurisdiction. It remains now to probe further into the attitude of the Court in the course of exercising this power, in an attempt to discover the motives that justify this attitude and the techniques that enable the Court to apply it in the specific cases. Through this and similar attempts, it is hoped that the seemingly variable doctrines of the Court on jurisdictional matters will become more readily subjected to predictable standards. It may help determine in general the situations where the Court could be expected to adopt a restricitve view of its jurisdiction and those where it tends to enlarge its limits. It may help clarify in particular the possible alternatives that the Court may have to follow when it is faced anew with the problem of a challenge to its very *compétence de la compétence*. Needless to say, however, any attempt of this sort will inevitably involve a degree of speculation particularly when it comes to interpreting "the mind of the Court" or what has elsewhere been described as its "*imagination juridique.*"[1]

GENERAL FACTORS INFLUENCING JURISDICTION

In general, one may think of at least three factors that could influence a judge's decision on his jurisdiction to deal with a given case, other than the limitations imposed on him by the judicial system in which he works and by the instruments involved in the specific case. These three factors are the previous legal training of the judge,

[1] See Reuter, *Les Modes de Solution des Conflits Internationaux* 295 (1958).

the merits of the case, and the expected degree of compliance in case jurisdiction is exercised:

First: The effect of the legal background of the judge on his views in general (including his attitude towards jurisdictional questions) has been well expressed by Judge Levi Carneiro in his dissent in the *Anglo-Iranian Oil Co. Case* (1952):

> It is inevitable – he wrote – that everyone of us in this Court should retain some trace of his legal education and his former legal activities in his country of origin. This is inevitable, and even justified, because in its composition the Court is to be representative of "the main forms of civilization and of the principal legal systems of the world" (Statute, Article 9), and the Court is to apply "the general principles of law recognized by civilized nations" (Statute, Article 38 (1) (c)).[1]

This "trace" of the judge's legal education, it is submitted, becomes relevant particularly in such areas where no established rule exists and a new solution is to be made. It is only natural that each judge will, in such a situation, tend to employ the techniques and methods he is most familiar with. This may, for instance, explain why judges differ in the degree of the importance they confer on the letter of the texts involved.[2] It may also explain the different attitudes adopted by judges of the present Court as to the time in which the expression of the will of a party becomes effective,[3] or the tendency of some judges to analyze the conformity to the Statute of other jurisdictional instruments in terms of the "constitutionality" of such instruments.

However, the influence of this factor should be viewed with the utmost caution as there is no evidence that a judge having his legal training in a given legal system will always confine his thinking and conclusions to the limits normally observed in such a system. Yet, the composition of the court may be a telling factor in predicting its future attitude particularly in relation to issues where the opinions of individual members have already been pronounced in previous decisions or otherwise. The composition of the Court may involve, it is true, the consideration of other elements besides the prior legal training of the judge, such as his nationality and his outlook toward

[1] [1952] *I.C.J. Rep.* 93, 161.

[2] Compare *e.g.*, the separate opinions of Judges Badawi and Armand-Ugon in the *Aerial Incident of July 27th 1955 Case* (Israel *v.* Bulgaria), [1959] *I.C.J. Rep.* 127, 149, 153, with the joint dissenting opinion of Judges Lauterpacht, Koo and Spender in *id.* at 192–3.

[3] See *e.g.*, *Right of Passage Case* [1957] *I.C.J. Rep.* 125, 156 (Diss. Op. of Judge Badawi). Judge Badawi's conclusion in this respect was reached after an explicit reference to the different positions adopted by municipal legal systems in relations to the formation of contracts by correspondence.

the role of the Court and international adjudication in general. It is preferred, however, to confine the importance of this factor to the element of legal training because this is the least uncertain among these elements in its effect on the legal thinking of the members of the Court.

Second: The merits of the case may be so entangled with the jurisdictional issue that a decision on the latter becomes heavily influenced by them. This is, for example, quite clear in every case where the Court investigates whether a dispute exists and whether it satisfies the requirements imposed by the Statute, and, in fact, in all such cases where a study of the merits is deemed necessary before rendering a decision on jurisdiction.[1] Even apart from such cases, the merits of the case may make the adjudication without purpose, thus rendering it improper for the court to exercise its jurisdiction.[2] However, the popular theme is to the effect that "it is the nature and not the justice of a claim that determines jurisdiction."[3] And the rule expressed in both domestic and arbitral cases has always been to the effect that "matters pleaded in defense with respect to the merits of the case are not relevant to the question of jurisdiction."[4] It is maintained here that although this is valid in theory, the merits of the case may in some situations have a great impact on the judge's attitude toward his jurisdiction. In conformity with this, it has been noticed in the domestic judiciary as "a whole-some instinct among judges" that:

> ...when a tribunal approaches a question, where on one horn of the dilemma is the trained moral sentiment of the judge, and on the other the "hypersensitive nerve of public opinion" it will "shy off" and throw the burden of the decision on other shoulders.[5]

[1] This is particularly so in the situation where the jurisdictional issue is dependent on the law applicable to the merits, *e.g.*, when no jurisdiction will be established unless the merits are governed by international law (a doctrine to which the Court has not so far subscribed). See *infra* at 224–8. See also, 1 *Procès Verbaux of the Proceedings of the Advisory Committee of Jurists* 309–10 (1920), where Mr. Root expressed the view that the Court would have no jurisdiction in case of *non liquet*, i.e., in the absence of rules to govern the merits.

And *cf.* generally, Goyard, *La Compétence des Tribunaux Judiciaires en Matière Administrative* 20 (1962).

[2] See the *Northern Cameroons Case*, [1963] *I.C.J. Rep.* 15, 36, 37–8. The Court's reluctance to entertain that case was based, however, on the fact that a judgment on the merits would be moot, not that the dispute itself was moot. See a criticism of the judgment based on this distinction in Gross, "Limitations upon the Judicial Function," 58 *Am. J. Int'l L.* 415, 430–31 (1964). And see further details on this case *infra* at 235–6.

[3] See 1 *Some Opinions, Articles and Reports Bearing Upon the Treaty of Trianon and the Claims of the Hungarian Nationals with Regard to their Lands in Transylvania* 105, 106 (Opinion of Barthélémy) (1928).

[4] *The International Fisheries Company Case* (U.S.A. *v.* Mexico) (Nielsen's dissent), 4, *U.N. Rep. Int'l Arb. Awards* 691, 716 (1931).

[5] Finkelstein, "Judicial Self-Limitation," 37 *Harv. L. Rev.* 338, 339 (1923–24).

This remark was, however, confined to such questions "which are so bitterly contentious as to be, for the moment, incapable of solution,"[1] and was justified in the main by the "fear of consequences" or "the lack of adequate data."[2] The remark is certainly valid in regard to international adjudication. It is felt that some arbitral tribunals have declined jurisdiction mainly because it seemed clearly unjust to assume it, or have accepted it out of considerations of equity.[3] The International Court was careful not to give this impression though it did rely on arguments related exclusively to the merits to confirm or deny its jurisdiction. The clearest example of this is perhaps the Permanent Court's reluctance to exercise its advisory function in the *Eastern Carelia Case* (1923) based, subsidiarily, on the lack of adequate data on the merits.[4]

It is not, therefore, surprising that in such cases as the *Ambatielos Case*, the respondent Government submitted in its counter-memorial in which it objected to the Court's jurisdiction, a detailed defense to the merits. This particular attitude was partly meant – as explained the Counsel of the respondent in his oral argument – to avoid putting the Court in the position of knowing what the applicant had to say on the merits while ignorant of what the respondent had to say on the merits, too.[5]

Hence, it is with this factor in mind that one can understand the reference of Sir Gerald Fitzmaurice to the "solution" which a finding against jurisdiction may provide "in those cases where the necessity of giving a decision on the merits would involve unusual difficulty or embarrassment for the tribunal."[6]

Third: Related to this latter factor is the judge's fear that if he assumes jurisdiction over the case, his decision on the merits may not be respected. It may be correct in theory that a tribunal should not allow itself "to be influenced by considerations as to whether or not it may be rightly contended that its award will have consequences

[1] *Id.* at 345.

[2] See *id.* at 363.

[3] See the instances discussed at p. 253, note 1 *infra* in relation to the proof of the nationality of claimants. And see the *Rudloff Case* (U.S.A. and Venezuela), 9 *U.N. Rep. Int'l Arb. Awards* 244, 254 (1903) (Opinion of Umpire Barge).

[4] *P.C.I.J.*, Ser. B., No. 5 at 27–8 (1923).

[5] See *Ambatielos Case*, Pleadings, Oral Arguments and Documents 282 (oral argument of Sir Eric Beckett) (*I.C.J.* 1953). Nonetheless, Sir Eric submitted first that the question of jurisdiction "does not depend in any way upon the merits." *Ibid.* See also 2 *Nottebohm Case*, Pleadings, Oral Arguments and Documents 17 (Plaidoirie de M. Sauser-Hall) (*I.C.J.* 1955).

[6] Fitzmaurice, "The Law and Procedure of the International Court of Justice ...," 34 *Brit. Yb. Int'l L.* 1, 12 n. 3 (1958).

which might be looked upon as not desirable."[1] That is, as the Permanent Court itself said, "the Court neither can nor should contemplate the contingency that the parties will not comply with its judgments."[2] But, in fact, this has not been always the case when the respondent is a Government that may or may not comply. One may indeed think that even domestically the development of the whole doctrine of the immunity of the sovereign before judicial tribunals has been partly contributed to by the conscious avoidance by the judiciary of a possibility of a clash with the executive. Tribunals have domestically preferred to adopt a doctrine by which Governments became in principle immune from their jurisdiction rather than to subject them to such jurisdiction and to run the danger of having their decisions neglected by a party they cannot compel to comply. Similarly, an international judge, confronted with a party that in advance expresses its intention not to comply with any potential decision on the merits might prefer to decline jurisdiction, basing this ruling on some technical ground. It is true, however, that the International Court has not followed such an attitude in the *Corfu Channel Case* (Assessment) (1949) and in the first phase of the *Anglo-Iranian Oil Co. Case* (1951). Yet, it should be added that it was specifically in these two cases that the Court's decisions were not complied with – a fact that might influence the future attitude of the Court if the issues involved are to arise again.

Bearing the above-mentioned factors in mind, a detailed study follows concentrating on the actual techniques employed by the International Court in determining its jurisdiction in the cases submitted to it, along with the possible techniques to be used in the future. In fact, the jurisdiction provided for in Article 36(6) of the Statute of the Present Court presents an excellent example of a power which, though limited, involves a wide discretion on the part of the Court. By applying it in individual cases, this Court and its predecessor have provided a rich source material from which it was possible to draw the structure outlined in the preceding chapter. In principle, however, Judge Nyholm's remark in his dissent in Judgment No. 12 of the

[1] *Case of the Interpretation of the London Agreement of August 9, 1924 (Award No. II)*, 2 *U.N. Rep. Int'l Arb. Awards* 885, 888 (1927).

[2] The *S.S. Wimbledon Case, P.C.I.J.*, ser. A, No. 1 at 32 (1923); *Chorzów Factory Case* (Merits), *P.C.I.J.*, ser. A, No. 17 at 63 (1928). Compare, *Northern Cameroons Case* where the present Court refused to entertain the claim submitted partly because the judgment, if rendered, would not be "susceptible of any compliance or execution whatever, at any time in the future." [1963] *I.C.J. Rep.* 15, 37. This was due to the fact that no action or avoidance of action was expected to take place as a result of the requested decision.

Permanent Court expressed a valid norm: "The Court decides whether it has jurisdiction, but it does not lay down its jurisdiction."[1] Yet, the techniques employed by the Court in "deciding whether it has jurisdiction" have not always been within the limits of this statement. The study of such techniques may, therefore, shed light on the areas where the Court could be said to have subjected itself to a process of self-limitation as well as on the areas where it has arrogated to itself a wider scope of jurisdiction than that anticipated in the instruments involved.

A. TECHNIQUES BASED ON THE INTERPRETATION OF INSTRUMENTS RELATED TO THE PARTIES' ACCEPTANCE OF THE COURT'S JURISDICTION

In tracing the development of the power of international arbitral tribunals to determine their proper jurisdiction, it has been pointed out that in most cases such power had one practical manifestation – the interpretation of the *compromis*.[2] As to the International Court, to a lesser extent, this could still be a valid remark if taken to apply to all instruments related to the consent of the parties to the Court's jurisdiction.[3] It is only natural, therefore, that the process of interpretation provides the Court with the richest choice of techniques for the determination of its jurisdiction. In this respect, and quite apart from any controversy as to the Court's attitude on interpretation in general,[4] both the Permanent Court and its successor have made it abundantly clear that the purpose of any interpretation carried in the context of the *compétence de la compétence* is to ascertain the

[1] *Minority Schools Case, P.C.I.J.*, ser. A, No. 15 at 56 (Diss. Op. Judge Nyholm).

[2] See Chapter I, *supra.*

[3] See Berlia, "La Jurisprudence des Tribunaux Internationaux en ce qui concerne leur Compétence," 88 *Recueil des Cours* 109, 118, 135, 139 (1955). And see the oral argument of M. Roman, Counsel of the Spanish Government, in the *Borchgrave Case, P.C.I.J.*, ser. C, No. 83 at 59 (1937).

[4] For the question of whether the "intention of the parties" is in general the dominating factor in treaty interpretation conducted by the International Court, see Charles de Visscher, *Problèmes d'Interprétation Judiciaire en Droit International Public* 50 (1963); Hogg, "The International Court: Rules of Treaty Interpretation," 43 *Minn. L. Rev.* 369, 372–4 (1958–59); Fitzmaurice, "The Law and Procedure of the International Court of Justice: Treaty Interpretation and Certain Other Treaty Points," 28 *Brit. Yb. Int'l L.* 1, 6–7 (1957); Lauterpacht, "Restrictive Interpretation and the Principle of Effectiveness in the Interpretation of Treaties," 26 *id.* 48, 55, 83 (1955); And see a summary of the Court's attitude as to this point in *South-West Africa Cases*, [1962] *I.C.J. Rep.* 319, 576–91 (Diss. Op. of Judge *ad hoc* Van Wyk).

intention of the parties toward the question of its jurisdiction.[1] In this process of ascertaining the existence and scope of such intention, the Court has felt free to resort to the traditional methods of interpretation, either to apply them or to justify its derogation therefrom in the specific case before it.[2]

1. The Court's Approach toward the Traditional Methods and Principles of Interpretation

In determining its jurisdiction, the International Court has never outrightly denied the validity of any traditional method of interpretation. In many cases, however, it mentioned the method only to explain why it was not possible to apply it in the case:

a. Restrictive interpretation

The principle mostly referred to by the parties opposing the Court's jurisdiction, particularly before the Permanent Court, was that jurisdictional instruments should be interpreted restrictively.[3] This was normally based on the following grounds: The Court's exercise of jurisdiction constitutes a limit on, and a derogation from the sovereignty of states and, therefore, should be understood in the strictest sense, particularly as the Court's jurisdiction is exclusively of a voluntary character. Moreover, as a limitation on sovereignty, this jurisdiction is an exceptional procedure that could not be assumed in case of doubt. Finally, doubt in general should be interpreted in favor of the debtor in every specific obligation, including the obligation to submit a dispute to the Court.[4] Regardless of the validity of these grounds, the Permanent Court has nominally subscribed to the above-

[1] See *e.g.*, *Chorzow Factory Case* (Jurisdiction), *P.C.I.J.*, ser. A, No. 9 at 32 (1927); *Minority Schools Case, P.C.I.J.*, ser. A, No. 15 at 22 (1928); *Free Zones Case, P.C.I.J.*, ser. A/B, No. 46 at 153 (1932); *Phosphates in Morocco Case, P.C.I.J.*, ser. A/B, No. 74 at 23–24 (1938); *Ambatielos Case* (Prel. Obj.), [1952] *I.C.J. Rep.* 28, 38; *Anglo-Iranian Oil Co. Case,* [1952] *I.C.J. Rep.* 93, 103; *Ambatielos Case* (Merits), [1953] *I.C.J. Rep.* 10, 44; *Monetary Gold Case* [1954] *I.C.J. Rep.* 19, 32; *Aerial Incident of July 27, 1955* (Israel *v.* Bulgaria) [1959] *I.C.J. Rep.* 127, 142.

[2] Obviously the resort to one or the other of these methods will itself be the result of a prior choice inspired by the general factors referred to above along with the considerations of good faith and of justice. *Accord*, Lauterpacht, *supra*, p. 188, note 4 at 53, 83.

[3] See a distinction between the above principle and the agreed-upon doctrine that the consent of the parties should be strictly proved in Lauterpacht, *The Development of International Law by the International Court* 99, 342 (1958); Fitzmaurice, *supra*, p. 186, note 6 at 88.

[4] For a discussion of these grounds and of their validity see generally, Lauterpacht, *supra*, p. 188, note 4 at 56–67; Hudson, *The Permanent Court of International Justice* 660–1 (2d ed. 1943); 1 Rousseau, *Principes Généraux du Droit International Public* 688 (1944); Balasko, *Causes de Nullité de la Sentence Arbitrale en Droit International Public* 137–8 (1938).

mentioned principle as a general rule that applies equally to jurisdictional instruments. However, in every case in which the argument was raised in relation to jurisdiction, the principle, though confirmed, was not taken into consideration. This was done by using the simple technique of declaring this principle applicable only in the last resort; that is, if all other methods of interpretation fail to help the Court to identify the intention of the parties – a possibility which, understandably, never took place.[1] In conformity with this practice, less concern has been given to the principle in the pleadings before, and the pronouncements of, the present Court, though the rule of interpreting doubt against the existence of jurisdiction was occasionally voiced in some dissenting opinions.[2] It could therefore be concluded that the concept of restrictive interpretation proved to have no significance in the work of the Court related to the interpretation of jurisdictional instruments. This in itself is a phenomenal attitude on the part of the Court for, theoretically, the latter concept is more relevant in this field than perhaps in any other. This may be the reason why some writers still refer to the application by the Court of other principles of interpretation in this respect as a *"correctif"* of the principle of restrictive interpretation.[3]

b. Natural meaning

Another traditional method of interpretation is that according to which words are to be given their normal, natural and unstrained

[1] See *Free Zones Case, P.C.I.J.*, Ser. A/B, No. 46 at 138–9 (1932); *Phosphates in Morocco Case, P.C.I.J.*, Ser. A/B, No. 74 at 23–4 (1938). In both cases the Court was applying the criterion it stated in the *Commission of the River Oder Case* to the effect that resort to restrictive interpretation could take place "[o]nly when in spite of all pertinent considerations, the intention of the parties remain doubtful ..." *P.C.I.J.*, Ser. A., No. 23 at 26 (1929). See also *Polish Postal Service Case, P.C.I.J.*, Ser. B, No. 11 at 39 (1925) (Adv. Op.). In many other cases the Court avoided any reference to restrictive interpretation despite the reliance of respondents on it. The principle was, however, applied by some dissenting judges. See *e.g.*, *Mavrommatis Palestine Concessions Case, P.C.I.J.*, Ser. A, No. 2 at 85 (Diss. Op. of Judge Oda). But see, *The Lighthouses in Crete and Samos Case*, Ser. A/B, No. 71 at 132 (1937) (Diss. Op. of Judge Séfériadis) (calling the restrictive interpretation of the scope of the special agreement "a denial of justice of a special kind.") And see generally, de Visscher, *supra*, p. 188, note 4 at 84–92; Hogg, "The International Court: Rules of Treaty Interpretation II," 44 *Minn. L. Rev.* 5, 19–28 (1959–60).

[2] See *e.g.*, *Corfu Channel Case* (Merits), [1949] *I.C.J. Rep.* 4, 67 (Diss. Op. of Judge Badawi); *id.* at 73 (Judge Krylov); id. at 128 (Judge *ad hoc* Ečer); *South-West Africa Cases*, [1962] *I.C.J. Rep.* 319, 473–4 (Diss. Op. of Judges Spender and Fitzmaurice). Compare, *id.* at 415 where Judge Jessup described the argument that Art. 37 of the Statute should be interpreted strictly, as an "assumption" for which there was no basis. See also the dissenting opinions of Judges Hackworth and Read in *Anglo-Iranian Oil Co. Case*, [1952] *I.C.J. Rep.* 93, 140, 143. Judge Read particularly understood the Court's judgment in that case to be a result of a restrictive interpretation of the declaration of Iran.

[3] See *e.g.*, Berlia, *supra*, p. 188, note 3 at 146, 148. And *cf.*, Reuter, *International Institutions* 228 (1958).

meaning. From the start, this principle was conceived as subject to two conditions: words are to be understood in the context in which they occur (even if this makes their meaning different from the abstract natural meaning); and the normal meaning can be displaced if it leads to an unreasonable or absurd result.[1] This qualified nature of the principle enabled the Court to apply this method and to reject its application according to the circumstances of the case. Thus, when it was contended in the *German Interests in Upper Silesia Case* (1925), that jurisdiction would exist only if the dispute related to both "the construction *and* (*et*) application of" the articles in question, the Permanent Court found in a *dictum* that "in both ordinary and legal language the word *et* may equally have an alternative or a cumulative meaning."[2] On the other hand, the present Court found in the *Anglo-Iranian Oil Co. Case* (1952) that it "cannot base itself on a purely grammatical interpretation of the text" which would have made good the two opposed interpretations of the declaration of Iran that were submitted by the parties. Instead, the Court stated that: "It must seek the interpretation which is in harmony with a natural and reasonable way of reading the text, having due regard to the intention of the government of Iran at the time when it accepted the compulsory jurisdiction of the Court."[3] More boldly the Court rejected the unqualified application of the natural meaning method in its decision in the *South-West Africa Cases* (1962). Referring to the contention that the phrase "another member of the League" in Article 7 of the Mandate on South West Africa, required, by its natural and ordinary meaning, that the applicant should be a member of the League of Nations which could not be the case in a suit brought before the Court long after the disappearance of the League, the Court answered:

> But this rule of interpretation is not an absolute one. Where such a method of interpretation results in a meaning incompatible with the spirit, purpose and context of the clause or instrument in which the words are contained, no reliance can be validly placed on it.[1]

[1] See Lauterpacht, *supra*, p. 188, note 4 at 48–9; Fitzmaurice, *supra*, p. 188, note 4 at 33.

[2] *P.C.I.J.*, Ser. A, No. 6 at 14 (1925). And see generally for the application of this method in the work of the Permanent Court, Hudson, *supra*, p. 189, note 4 at 645–50.

[3] [1952] *I.C.J. Rep.* 93, 104. The Court, therefore, makes a distinction in this decision between the "purely grammatical interpretation" and the "natural and reasonable" interpretation. In other cases the "grammatical" meaning was used as equivalent to the "ordinary and natural meaning." See *e.g., Commission of the River Oder Case, P.C.I.J.*, Ser. A, No. 23 at 26 (1929). See also a distinction between the "literal meaning" and the "natural and ordinary meaning" in the *Peace Treaties Case* (2d phase), [1950] *I.C.J. Rep.* 221, 227. And see the present Court's resort to the "ordinary sense" in the *Right of Passage Case,* [1957] *I.C.J. Rep.* 125, 142, and to the "natural and ordinary meaning in the context" in *Temple of Preah Vihear Case,* [1961] *I.C.J. Rep.* 17, 32.

[4] [1962] *I.C.J. Rep.* 319, 336.

This, was, therefore, a clear case where the apparent natural meaning of the words was sacrificed by means of resorting to other methods of interpretation mentioned again as exceptions from, or corrections of, the general principle. This technique is even clearer, as will shortly be shown, in the argument of the implied meaning of the text. However, the Court would not ignore the "natural meaning" unless it states a justification for this (by saying, for example, that the ordinary meaning is "obscure,"[1] or "absurd,"[2] or "incompatible with the purpose of the instrument").[3] It has also to find the alternative principle or argument according to which words are given a meaning other than the one they ordinarily convey.[4]

c. *Purposive interpretation*

Among these latter alternatives, the concept of the purpose of the text proved to be a helpful device. Teleological interpretation is, therefore, a commonplace in the work of the Court, relating to its jurisdiction and otherwise.[5] In the case of the Court's jurisdiction, the Permanent Court stated the factors to be taken in consideration in interpreting the compromissory clause in the treaty involved, as follows:

[1] *Cf.* the *Brazilian Loans Case, P.C.I.J.*, Ser. A, No. 20/21 at 119 (1929) (interpretation of a contract). Adoption of the "ordinary meaning" is itself normally justified by the fact that the text is clear. Compare, the *Employment of Women During the Night Case, P.C.I.J.*, Ser. A/B, No. 50 at 383 (Adv. Op.) (Sep. Op. of Judge Anzilotti).

[2] See *e.g.*, the *Polish Postal Service in Danzig Case, P.C.I.J.*, Ser. B, No. 11 at 39 (1925); *South-West Africa Cases*, [1962] *I.C.J. Rep.* 319, 341. The test of the absurdity or reasonableness is of course like the test of clarity subject to the understanding of each individual judge. See a discussion of the test of reasonableness applied to jurisdictional instruments in *The Aerial Incident of July 27, 1955 (Israel* v. *Bulgaria) Case*, [1959] *I.C.J. Rep.* 127, 188–92 (Joint Diss. Op. of Judges Lauterpacht, Koo and Spender) where they felt bound "to adhere to the past jurisprudence of the Court which, while consistently treating the element of consent as the decisive factor has applied the test of reasonableness as a motive, not for defeating but for upholding its jurisdiction." *Id.* at 192. And compare this last conclusion with the judgment in the *Anglo-Iranian Oil Co. Case.*

[3] See *e.g.*, *South-West Africa Cases*, [1962] *I.C.J. Rep.* 319, 336.

[4] Related to the question of the natural meaning of texts is the problem that results when two or more authentic versions use words do not convey exactly the same meaning. In this situation the Permanent Court found itself "bound to adopt the more limited interpretation which, as far as it goes, is doubtless in accordance with the common intention of the parties" *P.C.I.J.*, Ser. A, No. 2 at 19 (1924). This interpretation assumed "especial force" in that case because of relevant circumstances, and the rule seems to be otherwise that neither version should be subordinated to the other though the history of them all should be taken into account. See the case concerning the *Competence of the I.L.O. in regard to Regulation of the Conditions of Labor of Persons Employed in Agriculture, P.C.I.J.*, Ser. B, No. 2 at 35–9 (1922) (Adv. Op.). In practice, when the instrument was plurilingual the Court has, on the whole, resorted only to the English and French texts. See generally, Hardy, "The Interpretation of Plurilingual Treaties by International Courts and Tribunals," 37 *Brit. Yb. Int'l L.* 72, 141–6 (1961).

[5] See the relevant cases enumerated in Hudson, *supra*, p. 189, note 4 at 650–2 and in the *South-West Africa Cases*, [1962] *I.C.J. Rep.* 319, 583 (Diss. Op. of Judge Van Wyk).

... account must be taken not only of the historical development of arbitration treaties, as well as of the terminology of such treaties, *but also and more especially* of the function which in the intention of the contracting Parties is to be attributed to this provision.[1]

On the other hand, a declaration made by Thailand in 1950 as a renewal of a prior declaration of acceptance that was not in force at the time of the "renewal," was, nevertheless, found by the present Court to be a valid acceptance of the Court's jurisdiction as Thailand "could have had no other purpose in addressing the Secretary General under Paragraph 4 [of Article 36 of the Statute] than to recognize the compulsory jurisdiction of the present Court under Paragraph 2 – nor does she pretend otherwise."[2] Again in the *South-West Africa Cases* (1962) the literal meaning of a phrase in the compromissory clause of the Mandate was refused because of its incompatibility with "the spirit, purpose and context" of the clause and with the "*raison d'être* of this essential provision."[3]

d. Resort to preparatory works and to subsequent conduct

Would the Court, in ascertaining the purpose of the provision under interpretation, resort to the preparatory work of such provision, or to the manner in which it was applied in subsequent practice?

As to the resort to the *travaux préparatoires*, or more generally the method of historical interpretation, the present Court made it clear in its first advisory opinion, that ' it does not feel that it should deviate from the consistent practice of the Permanent Court of International Justice, according to which there is no occasion to resort to preparatory work if the text of a convention is sufficiently clear in itself."[4] The Permanent Court did, however, resort to the *travaux préparatoires* of texts of jurisdictional instruments under interpretation in at least three cases.[5] Yet, the Permanent Court was usually careful to present its resort to the preparatory work of the text under interpretation as a *subsidiary* method to buttress the conclusions that were already reached on other grounds. This attitude was also followed by the present Court in interpreting jurisdictional instruments pre-

[1] *Chorzow Factory Case, P.C.I.J.*, Ser. A, No. 9 at 24 (1927) (Emphasis added).

[2] *Temple of Preah Vihear Case*, [1961] *I.C.J. Rep.* 17, 33.

[3] [1962] *I.C.J. Rep.* 319, 336.

[4] *Admission of a State to the U.N. Case*, [1947–1948] *I.C.J. Rep.* 57, 63 (Adv. Op.).

[5] See *Palestine Mavrommatis Concessions Case, P.C.I.J.*, Ser. A, No. 2 at 24 (1924); *Lighthouses Case between France and Greece, P.C.I.J.*, Ser. A/B, No. 62 at 13 (1934); *Borchgrave Case, P.C.I.J.*, ser. A/B, No. 72 at 164–7 (1937).

pared by the parties [1] and also in interpreting jurisdictional clauses in its own statute.[2] What remains to be doubted, in actual fact, is whether it is possible that a conclusion could be reached independently of the *travaux préparatoires* (thus allowing the Court to invoke the latter merely to confirm it) when such *travaux* are known to the Court and discussed by the parties before this conclusion is made. One can only agree with Hudson that this doubt "robs the actual formulations by the Court of some of their importance."[3]

On the other hand, resort to the subsequent conduct of the parties under the instrument interpreted was also made in ascertaining the Court's jurisdiction.[4] But this was done again as a subsidiary method and could be said to have served as a rule of evidence rather than one of interpretation.[5] As such, it was particularly resorted to in cases where jurisdiction was said to be conferred on the Court by the mere conduct of the parties (on the basis of *forum prorogatum*).[6]

e. Effective interpretation (interpretation by implication)

In interpreting jurisdictional instruments, the International Court has relied on the principle of effective interpretation, *ut res magis valeat quam pereat*, perhaps more than on any other traditional method. This principle, sometimes referred to in practice as interpretation by necessary implication, has certainly enabled the Court to extend its jurisdiction to certain areas despite lack of proof that the parties specifically accepted the Court's power to adjudicate them. It is particularly responsible for the establishment of jurisdiction over questions incident to the merits of a dispute already within the Court's jurisdiction.[7]

[1] See *e.g.*, *Corfu Channel Case*, [1949] *I.C.J. Rep.* 4, 25 (resort to the circumstances in which the special agreement was made); *Anglo-Iranian Oil Co. Case*, [1952] *I.C.J. Rep.* 93, 106 (resort to the circumstances accompanying the drafting of the declaration of Iran).

[2] See *e.g.*, *Aerial Incident of July 27th 1955* (*Israel* v. *Bulgaria*) *Case*, [1959] *I.C.J. Rep.* 127, 140–1. And see a more extensive resort to the preparatory work of the Statute in *id.* at 158–61 (Joint Diss. Op. of Judges Lauterpacht, Koo and Spender).

[3] Hudson, *supra*, p. 189, note 4 at 654 n. 63.

[4] See *e.g.*, *Corfu Channel Case*, [1949] *I.C.J. Rep.* 4, 25. In the *Israel v. Bulgaria Case* all the dissenting judges referred to the subsequent conduct of Bulgaria as evidence that it did not consider its declaration to have terminated with the dissolution of the Permanent Court. See [1959] *I.C.J. Rep.* 127, 182–4 (Joint Diss. Op.); *id.* at 202 (Diss. Op. of national Judge Goiten). The jointly dissenting judges took pains to review the subsequent attitude of all states not original members of the U.N. which had declarations in force at the time of the dissolution of the Permanent Court. *Id.* at 184. See also, *Temple of Preah Vihear Case*, [1961] *I.C.J. Rep.* 17, 34.

[5] See Fitzmaurice, *supra*, p. 188, note 4 at 21.

[6] See Chapter IV, at 128–35.

[7] Not to be confused with the above is "incidental jurisdiction" treated in Chapter IV, *supra*, which covers issues incident to the proceedings before the Court. Although the term

The extension of jurisdiction by necessary implication (that is, for the purpose of making the original acceptance of jurisdiction fully effective) normally assumes that some substantive jurisdiction has already been conferred on the Court. It has always been relied upon to justify the extension, rather than the original establishment of jurisdiction. And, understandably, it was mainly through this technique that the argument for strict interpretation was defeated.[1]

In its second judgment, the Permanent Court, after stating that it was not competent to interpret and apply the Protocol of Lausanne upon a unilateral application, reserved the jurisdiction to apply this Protocol "insofar as this is made *necessary* by Article 11 of the Mandate" whose interpretation was within its jurisdiction.[2] This practice was pronounced in clearer language in the *German Interests in Polish Upper Silesia Case* (1925):

> ... The interpretation of other international agreements is indisputably within the competence of the Court if such interpretation must be regarded as incidental to a decision on a point in regard to which it has jurisdiction.[3]

A wider application of the principle of effectiveness followed in the *Chorzow Factory Case* (1927) where the Permanent Court understood its jurisdiction over disputes related to the "interpretation or application" of a certain convention to enable it to decree and assess reparation in respect of the breach of the obligations of this convention. "Reparation – the Court argued – is the indispensable complement of a failure to apply a convention, and there is no necessity for this to be stated in the Convention itself."[4] Therefore, the decision whether

incidental is used in many writings to describe both concepts, jurisdiction extended to matters sufficiently related to the merits is distinctively called "implicit jurisdiction" or "jurisdiction by implication." See a wide application of this term in Rouyer-Hameray, *Les Compétences Implicites des Organisations Internationales* (1962).

[1] See a clear pronouncement to this effect in the *S.S. Wimbledon Case, P.C.I.J.*, Ser. A, No. 1 at 24–5 (1923). "Effective interpretation" was itself foresaken through the application of other methods particularly when it was invoked to "establish" a new jurisdiction rather than to extend an existing one. See *e.g., Corfu Channel Case* [1947–1948] *I.C.J. Rep.* 15, 31–2 (Joint Sep. Op.); *Anglo-Iranian Oil Co. Case* [1952] *I.C.J. Rep.* 93, 105. And see generally, *South-West Africa Cases*, [1962] *I.C.J. Rep.* 319, 582–4 (Diss. Op. of Judge Van Wyk). For an arbitral instance of this practice, see *Mariposa Development Company and Others* (U.S.A. *v.* Panama), 6 *U.N. Rep. Int'l Arb. Awards* 338–9 (1933).

[2] *Mavrommatis Palestine Concessions Case, P.C.I.J.*, Ser. A, No. 2 at 28 (1924) (Emphasis added).

[3] *P.C.I.J.*, Ser. A, No. 6 at 18 (1925). Notice that the word "necessary" used in the *Mavrommatis* case is not repeated here, and see the same principle applied in the following advisory cases: *Jaworzina Case, P.C.I.J.*, Ser. B, No. 8 at 50 (1923); *Exchange of Greek and Turkish Population Case, P.C.I.J.*, Ser. B, No. 10 at 25 (1925); *Case Concerning the Competence of the I.L.O. to Regulate Incidentally the Personal Work of the Employer, P.C.I.J.*, Ser. B, No. 13 at 19 (1926).

[4] *P.C.I.J.*, Ser. A, No. 9 at 21 (1927).

there had been a breach of an engagement involved in the mind of the Court "a more important jurisdiction as to the nature or extent of reparation due for a breach of an international engagement, the existence of which is already established."[1]

The tendency towards a wide application of the principle of effectiveness was somewhat restricted in a later phase of the case,[2] and when the occasion came for the resort to this principle in the *Free Zones Case* (1929) the Court felt bound to state it in a rather qualified formula:

> ... in case of doubt, the clauses of a special agreement by which a dispute is referred to the Court must, if it does not involve doing violence to their terms, be construed in a manner enabling the clauses themselves to have appropriate effects.[3]

Yet, the principle of the *Chorzow Factory Case* (1927) was soon to be revived in the work of the present Court, though the circumstances of the new case did not call for as great an extension of jurisdiction. After the first judgment in the *Corfu Channel Case,* the parties made a special agreement asking the Court to decide: whether Albania was responsible under international law and whether there was any duty to pay compensation. The interpretation of the Court was to the effect that its jurisdiction to pronounce on the latter point covers a jurisdiction to assess the amount of compensation due. This was based on many grounds amongst which the principle of effectiveness assumed a primary place.[4] This principle was phrased in the following terms: "It would indeed be incompatible with the generally accepted rules of interpretation to admit that a provision of this sort occurring in a special agreement should be devoid of purport or effect."[5] The statement was then substantiated by a reference to two pronouncements of the Permanent Court – its advisory opinion in the *Competence*

[1] *Id.* at 23. But see *id.* at 35–40 (Diss. Op. of Judge Ehrlich).

[2] See *Chorzow Factory Case* (Merits), *P.C.I.J.*, Ser. A, No. 17 at 61–2 (1928). Referring to the principle enunciated in the previous case the Court stated that "this principle would be quite unjustifiably extended if it were taken as meaning that the Court might have cognizance of any question whatever of international law even quite foreign to the Convention under consideration, for the sole reason that the manner in which such question is decided may have an influence on the effectiveness of the reparation asked for." As a result, the Court rejected the German contention that it was competent to decide on the exclusion of any potential set-off because it had the power to provide an effective reparation.

[3] *P.C.I.J.*, Ser. A, No. 22 at 13 (1929).

[4] The Court relied also on the history of the special agreement and the defendant's declaration that preceded it, the subsequent attitude of the parties, the logical interpretation of the text by reference to its context, and the necessity of bringing the dispute to an end. See [1949] *I.C.J. Rep.* 4, 24–6.

[5] *Id.* at 24.

of I.L.O. Case (1926) and its order in the *Free Zones Case* (1929). Strangely enough, no reference was made to the *Chorzów Factory Case* in which the principle was applied in a manner that would cover *a fortiori* the issue in the *Corfu Channel Case* (1949). Five judges, however, dissented from the conclusion reached by the present Court in this latter case. To them the extension of jurisdiction was not anticipated by the parties, and, at any rate, should have not been favored in case of doubt.[1]

The interpretation of jurisdictional instruments by "necessary implication," or by conferring on them their "full effect," is not without its risks, particularly in that it may easily lead the Court to impute to the parties an intention they did not share. In both the *Chorzów Factory Case* and the *Corfu Channel Case*,[2] the Court tried in the final analysis to justify resort to this method by explaining that unless jurisdiction was extended in that way, the decision would have left open the possiblity of further disputes instead of settling the dispute once and for all. This, however, does not dispense with the doubts encompassing this technique – doubts that were adequately expressed in Judge Ehrlich's dissent in the first of these cases and by the dissenting judges in the latter case.[3] One cannot avoid in this regard the impression that the Court has exerted much more caution in applying the principle of effectiveness in other areas of treaty interpretation, as Judge *ad hoc* Van Wyk tried to establish in his lengthy dissent in the *South-West Africa Cases*.[4] The mere application of the principle to jurisdictional instruments may be taken in itself as a clear indication of the rejection of any presumption of restrictive interpretation. But a *wide* application of what the Court asserts to be the full effect of the instrument or the implied intention of the parties could be taken as an evidence of something more: that is,

[1] See *id.* at 57 (Diss. Op. of Judge Winiarski); *id.* at 67 (Judge Badawi); *id.* at 73 (Judge Krylov), *id.* at 96–7 (Judge Azevedo) and at 128 (Judge *ad hoc* Ečer).

[2] See *P.C.I.J.*, Ser. A, No. 9 at 25 (1927); [1949] *I.C.J. Rep.* 4, 26.

[3] But see Chung, *Legal Problems Involved in the Corfu Channel Incident* 261 (1959) (defending the extension of jurisdiction in the *Corfu Channel Case* as in accordance with "an established principle." "If it is not a rule of customary international law, it is at least a *guiding* principle or *prérègle* as envisaged in Article 38, paragraph ((c), of the Statute ...") And see Rouyer-Hameroy, *supra*, p. 195, at 77. Compare, Lauterpacht, *The Development of International Law by the International Court* 246–7 (1958).

[4] [1962] *I.C.J. Rep.* 319, 582–90. The present Court refused a construction by implication when it was not necessary (*Reparation for Injuries in the Service of the U.N.* [1949] *I.C.J. Rep.* 174, 182, 198 (Adv. Op.)) or which would go beyond the scope of the declared purpose and object of the contract or would involve radical changes or additions (*Rights of U.S. Nationals in Morocco*, [1952] *I.C.J. Rep.* 176, 196–9) or which would do violence to the clear and unambiguous express provisions of the instrument (*Competence of Assembly regarding Admission to the U.N.*) [1950] *I.C.J. Rep.* 4, 8 (Adv. Op.).

an original tendency to adopt, in case of doubt, the interpretation favorable to the Court's jurisdiction *in matters incidental to the merits already within this jurisdiction*. Even if such an extension is conditioned by a criterion of necessity,[1] the Court can always find in the interpretation by necessary implication an easy device to implement this tendency.

f. Subsidiary devices

Besides the above-mentioned methods of interpretation, the Court has often resorted to some subsidiary devices to identify the intention of the parties regarding its jurisdiction. In the *Anglo-Iranian Oil Co. Case* (1952), for instance, a great emphasis in the present Court's negative decision on jurisdiction was based on the general policy of the declarant state at the time of drafting the declaration, particularly as expressed in the municipal law by which it approved the latter.[2] Rules of substantive law were also used at times to prove the validity or effectiveness of the jurisdictional instrument involved. A modern example of this is found in the *Temple of Preah Vihear Case* (1961) where the requirement of a "fundamental defect" as a reason for vitiating treaties was invoked to prove that the defect in the wording of the declaration of Thailand "did not cause the instrument to run counter to any mandatory requirement of law."[3]

Practical considerations supported in particular by the Court's relative freedom from formalistic limitations have finally enabled the Court to uphold its jurisdiction in many cases where a rigid outlook to its jurisdictional limitations could not have led to such a conclusion.[4] The concurrent use of many methods of interpretation in the same case has also served as a technique to support a conclusion that

[1] See *Mavrommatis Palestine Concessions Case, P.C.I.J.*, Ser. A, No. 2 at 28 (1924). And see Rouyer-Hameroy, *supra*, p. 195 at 72. Stating that the interpretation by implication requires an element of necessity he added, however, that "l'existence d'une nécessité est d'abord fonction du point de vue auquel se place l'observateur, et de sa mentalité. Il entre dans l'appréciation de la nécessité d'une chose par rapport à une autre, de nombreux éléments subjectifs."

[2] See [1952] *I.C.J. Rep.* 93, 106–7. The Court explained in justification of this attitude that the declaration is not a treaty text but a result of unilateral drafting. But see on the correctness of this justification *id.* at 142 (Diss. Op. of Judge Read); and Fitzmaurice, *supra*, p. 186, note 6 at 78–9.

[3] [1961] *I.C.J. Rep.* 17, 34. And see Chapter III, *supra*.

[4] See instances of this practice in the parts of this study related to the requirement of form, the requirement of prior negotiations and generally the establishment of jurisdiction on the basis of *forum prorogatum*.

could not adequately be justified by one method or the other if taken alone.[1]

Nothwithstanding this multitude of methods, throughout its interpretation of the jurisdictional instruments, the Court could not be said to have subjected itself to any double standard according to which one category of instruments should be treated more strictly or more liberally than the others. However, motivated as it seems by the coincidental rejection of jurisdiction more often in cases where jurisdiction was allegedly based on declarations of acceptance (see Appendix II), some writers noticed that a stricter attitude is followed by the Court in interpreting the declarations made under Article 36(2) of the Statute.[2] This study has found no evidence to support such a conclusion. The most that can be said in this respect is that cases brought before the Court by means of a unilateral application are quite often met by objections to jurisdiction except when the application is made subsequent to a special agreement. Once the objection is made and the Court assumes its function to determine its jurisdiction, the circumstances of every case, rather than the category of the instrument involved, influence the attitude adopted in the process of interpretation.

The opposite view was, however, slightly touched in the dissent of Judge Hudson in the *Lighthouses in Crete and Samos Case* (1937). In this case an important question presented itself. In interpreting the jurisdictional instrument should the Court be bound by the interpretation agreed upon by the parties as to the scope of the question submitted? This particular case was submitted by means of a special agreement which asked the Court to consider the question of whether a principle laid down by a previous judgment was applicable to certain territories not covered by that judgment. The principle involved was to the effect that a given contract was duly entered into and was operative as regards the defendant Government. The parties in the new case made it clear in their pleadings that the only question in dispute in that stage was the question of the applicability of this principle to the named territories and that the new case, as the Court

[1] This is particularly clear in the second phase of the *Corfu Channel Case*, [1949] *I.C.J. Rep.* 4, 24–6 and in the *Temple of Preah Vihear Case*, [1961] *I.C.J. Rep.* 17, 31–4.

[2] See *e.g.*, Simpson and Fox, *International Arbitration* 73–4 (1959). Compare, Lauterpacht, *supra*, p. 197, note 3 at 98–9. And see Judge Read's dissent in the *Anglo-Iranian Oil Co. Case*, (1952] *I.C.J. Rep.* 93, 142–4. Emphasizing that all jurisdictional clauses should be interpreted on the basis of the same principles, Judge Read criticized the Court's resort to extraneous evidence to reach what he considered a restrictive interpretation of the Iranian declaration.

put it, "in no way reopens the 'question of principle' which was decided in [the previous] judgment and which is now *res judicata*, namely that, in itself, the contract... was duly entered into."[1] Consequently, the Court confined itself to the former question only. Four judges, however, dissented on this point and went further to discuss the question of the validity of the making of the contract, as they found this second question to be equally covered by the special agreement. As to the declared intention of the parties to confine the adjudication to the question of applicability, Judge Hudson wrote the following:

> It is the task of the Court to interpret this special agreement. In the performance of this task, *the Court is not bound by the interpretation given to the instruments by the parties*, nor is it bound to confine itself to dealing with the instrument in the light of the arguments advanced by the parties. The questions to be decided are those contained in the special agreement as the Court itself construes that agreement; they may or may not be the same as those to which the parties have addressed themselves. *Whatever may be the position when obligatory jurisdiction is being exercised*, in answering a question placed before it by a special agreement, the Court must have full freedom to construe the terms of the agreement...[2]

Then, "viewing the special agreement as a whole" Judge Hudson, like the three other dissenting judges, found that "the parties intended to place before the Court" the question whether the contract was duly entered into as regards the territories not covered by the previous decision.

True as it may be that the Court is independent, in interpreting treaty texts, from the contentions of the parties,[3] the situation is not the same when it comes to jurisdictional instruments. Here jurisdiction is exercised only insofar as a clear mutual intention is directed to confer it on the Court. To say that the special agreement should be interpreted regardless of the common intention of the parties expressed before the Court, and to do this as an ascertainment of the real intention of the parties, would therefore seem to be a strange procedure. For even if the special agreement intended to confer on the Court a question wider in scope than what the parties confined themselves to before the Court, there is no doubt that the parties can, by their mutual agreement, limit the scope of the question originally submitted and even cause the whole case to discontinue. More unacceptable, however, is to suggest that this method is particularly appli-

[1] *P.C.I.J.*, Ser. A/B, No. 71 at 100 (1937).

[2] *Id.* at 120 (Diss. Op. of Judge Hudson) (Emphasis added).

[3] See *Free Zones Case*, *P.C.I.J.*, Ser. A/B, No. 46 at 138 (1932).

cable to special agreements. If the clear intention of the parties as manifested in their pleadings before the Court was to extend or limit the scope of the question submitted, the Court would ordinarily adhere to this agreed-upon modification, nothwithstanding the category of the instruments involved. The *Ambatielos Case* (1952), in which jurisdiction was based on a treaty, could be cited by way of an *a contrario* analogy as supporting this conclusion. The extension of jurisdiction by an agreement made through the pleadings of the parties was rejected in this latter case only on the basis that there was some doubt as to the existence of any unequivocal agreement upon this matter.[1] Other cases testifying more positively to the power of the parties to modify the case in the course of the proceedings and, hence, to the effectiveness of their common understanding of the scope of the question submitted to it, are found elsewhere in this study.[2] It is not, therefore, surprising that the majority of the Permanent Court disagreed with Judge Hudson on the point he raised in the *Lighthouses Case.*[3]

2. *The Court's Approach toward the Element of Form in the Acceptance of Its Jurisdiction*

Along with the use of the traditional methods of interpretation to reach the intention of the parties regarding its jurisdiction, the International Court has been able to establish or extend this jurisdiction in many cases merely by maintaining that once the intention is ascertained it need not be molded in any given form. As illustrated before, this approach, initiated in the second judgment of the Permanent Court and still honored in the recent pronouncements of the

[1] See [1952] *I.C.J. Rep.* 28, 39.

[2] See Chapter III, *supra*, and this Chapter, *infra*, at 265–266.

[3] The question of the extent to which an international tribunal is bound to respect the agreed upon interpretation given by the parties to the jurisdictional instruments prepared by them was particularly raised in the preparation of the draft on arbitral procedure by the International Law Commission. Commenting on what was Art. 19 of the first draft submitted by M. Scelle, Mr. El. Khouri (of Syria) expressed his fear that "the wording proposed [that the tribunal would have 'the widest powers in interpreting the compromis'] would give the arbitral tribunal powers to interpret the *compromis* even when the parties who had drawn it up agreed on its interpretation." This he opposed; for "[i]f the parties agreed on the interpretation of the *compromis* their interpretation should be accepted." [1952] *I.L.C. Yearbook* 55. A similar comment was given later by the Government of the Netherlands which suggested, as a result, the addition of the phrase "if the parties are at variance in this respect" to the text of the article (which became by that time Art. 11 of the draft). See Report of the I.L.C. Covering the Work of its Fifth Session, Annex I, U.N. Doc., *Gen. Ass. Off. Rec.*, 8th Sess., Supp. 9 (A/2456) at 34 (1953).

present Court,[1] goes far to account, *inter alia*, for the assumption of jurisdiction on the basis of *forum prorogatum* and for the permissive attitude toward the requirement of registration as applied to jurisdictional titles.

The little concern given the element of form was usually justified on the part of the Court by the fact that it is an international and not a domestic Court. International jurisdiction, the Court found, prescribes no particular form and leaves the parties "free to choose what form they please provided their intention results from it." Such rule is in conformity with international law in general "which places the principal emphasis on the intentions of the parties."[2]

This flexibility or rather "informality" in the attitude of the Court and its justification by the general informal character of international law is only to be commended. The Court's jurisdiction, it is true, is a jurisdiction carefully limited by the consent of states. But if the existence of such consent is proved beyond doubt, no additional limitation should be imposed merely for the sake of formalities, which the already limited scope of the Court's jurisdiction cannot, at any rate, easily afford.[3] On the other hand, the disregard of the requirement of form in this respect does not involve any undue expansion of jurisdiction. For in all cases where formality was neglected, the Court took pains to emphasize that the consent of the parties has been adequately ascertained. The Court's attitude toward the element of form could, therefore, be described as follows: The Court will not allow a party to withdraw the consent it has already given merely on the basis that such consent was not expressed in a given form, for no such form is required in the first place for the expression of the acceptance of the Court's jurisdiction.

3. The Use of Presumptions Related to the Consent of the Parties

The existence of a general presumption in favor of the freedom of states (including their freedom from international judicial action) has been frequently used as a subsidiary argument against the Court's

[1] See the clearest applications of this principle in *Mavrommatis Palestine Concessions Case*, *P.C.I.J.*, Ser. A, No. 2 at 34 (1924); *Minority Schools Case*, *P.C.I.J.*, Ser. A, No. 15 at 23–4 (1928); *Corfu Channel Case*, [1947–1948] *I.C.J. Rep.* 15, 27; *Temple of Preah Vihear Case*, [1961] *I.C.J. Rep.* 17, 31.

[2] *Temple of Preah Vihear Case*, *ibid.*

[3] Hence, there is no need to look for further theoretical justifications for the Court's flexible attitude in this regard. Compare, Rosenne, *The International Court of Justice* 266 (1957).

jurisdiction in cases of doubt.[1] On their part, writers are in disagreement as to the actual attitude of the Court in regard to this argument and generally toward the use of presumptions against or in favor of the Court's jurisdiction.[2] This is probably due to the fact that the Court has seldom clarified its stand on this issue and has left it to be concluded from its holdings in each case. Some individual judges have, however, pronounced directly on this question, either to assert the existence of a presumption against the Court's jurisdiction, or to prove that the Court's practice has not known such a presumption or has, on the contrary, established a presumption of jurisdiction in case of doubt.[3]

In ascertaining the Court's doctrine in this respect, one should make first a distinction between the advisory and the contentious types of jurisdiction. For the first type the present Court has indeed made it clear that it will not in principle refuse to answer the request for an advisory opinion, and that only compelling reasons can cause it to do so. This attitude, which is described in detail in Chapter IV of this study, leaves no room for doubting the establishment of a rebuttable presumption in favor of the Court's advisory jurisdiction. The existence of such a presumption, it should be submitted, was not certain under the Permanent Court, but the situation has changed since the present Court gave its opinion in the first phase of the *Peace Treaties Case* (1950).

As to the contentious jurisdiction, the question is subject to further refinements. The decisive factor, it seems, lies in the fact whether or not the Court's jurisdiction is objected to in the case at hand. For as

[1] See generally, Grossen, *Les Présomptions en Droit International Public* 119–21, 126–8 (1954).

[2] See *e.g.*, for the existence of a presumption of lack of jurisdiction in case of doubt, 1 Rousseau, *Principes Généraux du Droit International Public* 688–90 (1944); Grossen, *supra*, note 1 at 126–8 (giving the presumption a subsidiary character). For a denial of the existence of any presumption to this effect, see Lauterpacht, "Restrictive Interpretation and the Principle of Effectiveness in the Interpretation of Treaties," 26 *Brit. Yb. Int'l L.* 48, 65–7 (1949); Charles de Visscher, *Problèmes d'Interprétation Judiciaire en Droit International Public* 202 (1963). And see, for the existence of a "presumption of consent on the part of the litigating states," Rosenne, *supra*, p. 202, note 3 at 263.

[3] Compare, *Right of Passage Case*, [1957] *I.C.J. Rep.* 125, 180 (Diss. Op. of Judge *ad hoc* Chagla) assuming a presumption against jurisdiction), and *Mavrommatis Palestine Concessions Case, P.C.I.J.*, Ser. A, No. 2 at 60 (Diss. Op. of Judge Moore); *Ambatielos Case* (Merits), [1953] *I.C.J. Rep.* 10, 29 (Diss. Op. of Judges McNair, Basdevant, Klaestad and Read); *South-West Africa Cases* [1962] *I.C.J. Rep.* 319, 465 (Diss. Op. of Judges Spender and Fitzmaurice) (all denying a presumption of jurisdiction) with *Aerial Incident of July 27, 1955 Case*, [1959] *I.C.J. Rep.* 127, 195–6 (Diss. Op. of Judge *ad hoc* Goiten) (assuming a presumption of jurisdiction). Each of these separate opinions (with the exception of Judge Moore's) claimed that the view expressed in it was the doctrine previously followed by the Court!

proved above,[1] the Court has generally declined to raise *proprio motu* jurisdictional objections related to the parties' consent when both parties refrained from doing so. On the contrary, it did find in the direct dealing with the merits by a respondent Government a conclusive evidence of the acceptance of its jurisdiction. This could be interpreted as being the result of a presumption in favor of jurisdiction whenever the latter is not objected to by the defendant,[2] though the Court preferred to deal with it as a matter of inference of consent clearly manifested by the conduct of the parties.

Once, on the other hand, an objection is raised against the jurisdiction of the Court, its practice, as understood by this writer, negates the use of any presumption in favor of or against the conferment of jurisdiction. An objection to jurisdiction invokes the *compétence de la compétence,* and this is exercised without any *a priori* commitment on the part of the Court. As has been said in the very judgment which is sometimes cited – wrongly, it is submitted – as evidence of the existence of a presumption of jurisdiction, "the Court will, in the event of an objection or when it has automatically to consider the question [e.g., in the situation provided for in Article 53 of the Statute] only affirm its jurisdiction *provided that the force of the arguments militating in favor of it is preponderant.*"[3] If no such arguments exist, it will only be natural that the Court will reject jurisdiction as it did in scores of cases. But this latter conclusion does not, on the other hand, prove the existence, even in a subsidiary manner, of a presumption against jurisdiction.[4] It is but an evidence of the undisputed principle that the only basis of the Court's jurisdiction is to be found in its acceptance by the parties; if such acceptance is not proved to have been made, jurisdiction does not exist. No presumption is needed to justify this conclusion.

In this respect, one side remark may be made. The Court, as seen above, has definitely shown an inclination to favor the assumption of jurisdiction over matters *incidental to the merits of a dispute already within its competence,* provided that no clear intention has been ex-

[1] Chapter II, *supra.* at 56–68.

[2] See Salvioli, "La Jurisprudence de la Cour Permanente de Justice Internationale," 12 *Recueil des Cours* 1, 19 (1926–II).

[3] *Chorzów Factory Case, P.C.I.J.*, Ser. A, No. 9 at 32 (1927) (Emphasis added). And see this judgment relied upon as evidence of a presumption of jurisdiction in Bruns, "La Cour Permanente de Justice Internationale, son Organisation et sa Compétence," 62 *Recueil des Cours* 551, 625 (1937–IV).

[4] But see, Grossen, *supra*, p. 203, note 1 at 128.

pressed by the parties for the exclusion of such matters from the Court's jurisdiction.

4. The Reality of the Consent Required as the Basis of Jurisdiction

The International Court founds its jurisdiction solely on the consent of the parties. But by its interpretation of the instruments and conduct expressing such consent (particularly the interpretation by indirect inference) and by applying, in certain circumstances, presumptions favorable to the "extension" of jurisdiction, the Court has given the impression of being less dependent in its action on the consent of the parties than what appears from its general pronouncements to be the case.[1] And if one is to follow the dissenting judges, particularly in such controversial cases as the *Minority Schools Case* (1928), the *Anglo-Iranian Oil Co. Case* (1952), *The Ambatielos Case* (1952), the *Aerial Incident between Israel and Bulgaria Case* (1959) and the *South-West Africa Cases* (1962), the Court had on the whole less concern with the consent of the parties than it is usually asserted. This, if true, could not of course be imparted to any preestablished view according to which the Court is committed to enlarge or restrict its jurisdiction regardless of the consent of the parties. Any notion of this sort could easily be dismissed by the mere fact that the decisions cited above were not all to the same effect – jurisdiction was rejected in the *Anglo-Iranian Oil Co. Case* and the *Aerial Incident Case* and was upheld in the rest. The difference, if any, between a hypothetical "real consent" and the consent that the Court may find in a given case is only a consequence, indeed an inevitable consequence, of the very process of searching for the "intention" of the parties. In this respect, not only the International Court, but, in fact, all courts can only try to "read the mind of the parties" by applying the techniques of interpretation and evidence most suited to their function and to the legal system in which they work. Such techniques may not enable them to reach in every single case the exact intention of the parties. Nor is this a surprising fact, insofar as such intention could be judged only by its external manifestations. The techniques employed by the International Court in the interpretation of jurisdictional instruments, and generally in the ascertainment of the will of each party before it, have,

[1] See generally, Smith, *The Relation between Proceedings and Premises* 11–2 (1962), Fitzmaurice, "The Law and Procedure of the International Court of Justice ....," 34 *Brit. Yb. Int'l L.* 1, 90–7 (1958); Rosenne, *supra*, p. 202, note 3 at 8, 263. Compare, Lauterpacht, *supra*, p. 197, note 3 at 342–3.

therefore, one goal – to enable the Court to identify the intention of the parties. However, the choice of such techniques may be influenced in the mind of each judge by such factors as those elaborated above. Normally the choice preferred by the majority leads to a decision for or against jurisdiction, according to the finding on the question of consent. It is, therefore, this consent as found by the Court, and not any other hypothetical consent, that serves as the basis of jurisdiction.

Yet, the ascertainment of the consent of the parties does not always bring the question of jurisdiction to an end. In many cases, other techniques are used either to allow the Court to avoid dealing with the merits despite the agreement of the parties to confer jurisdiction on it, or else to enable it to extend the detailed limits of its jurisdiction even beyond such an agreement.

B. TECHNIQUES DERIVED FROM THE INHERENT QUALITIES OF THE COURT, AS A COURT OF INTERNATIONAL JUSTICE AND THE PRINCIPAL JUDICIAL ORGAN OF THE UNITED NATIONS

The fact that the International Court is a "judicial body" concerned with "international justice" was frequently emphasized by the Court in the process of determining its jurisdiction. It proved to be a helpful element that enabled the Court both to extend and to restrict, according to the case, the limits of its judicial action, though its invocation was mainly made as a justification for *declining* jurisdiction.[1] The details of this technique will be revealed through the study of its manifestations in the practice of the Court.

1. Requirements Based on the Fact that the Court is a Judicial Organ

a. Limits which characterize judicial action

The first general conclusion to be drawn from the judicial character of the Court is that *it will normally exercise its competence only within the limits which characterize judicial action.* In the contentious procedure this doctrine has its clearest expression in two cases: the *Free Zones Case* (1932) before the Permanent Court, and the *Haya de la Torre Case* (1951) before the present Court. In both cases, it should

[1] See *e.g., Eastern Carelia Case, P.C.I.J.*, Ser. B, No. 5 at 29 (1923) (Adv. Op.); *Free Zones Case, P.C.I.J.*, Ser. A, No. 22 at 12 (1929); *Free Zones Case, P.C.I.J.*, Ser. A/B, No. 46 at 161–2 (1932); *Haya de la Torre Case* [1951] *I.C.J. Rep.* 71, 79; *Constitution of the Maritime Safety Committee of I.M.C.O. Case*, [1960] *I.C.J. Rep.* 150, 153 (Adv. Op.). And see *infra*.

be particularly noted, there was no disagreement between the parties as to the submission to the Court of the question involved.

After it had announced in an order in the *Free Zones Case* that its Statute did not allow it to communicate "unofficially" to the parties the result of the deliberations upon a question submitted to it for decision,[1] the Permanent Court further relied on its judicial character to decline, in a later phase of the case, entertaining a request submitted to it by the parties. This request amounted to asking the Court to regulate in part the customs regime between the two parties subject to their subsequent approval. The answer given to the parties was that:

> ... The Court maintains its opinion that it would be incompatible with the Statute, and with its position as a Court of Justice, to give a judgment which would be dependent for its validity on the subsequent approval of the parties.[2]

Again noting that the settlement of tariff exemptions is "a matter depending on the interplay of economic interests in which no Government can afford to be controlled by an outside organ," it concluded that the questions involved were "outside the sphere in which a Court of Justice, concerned with the application of rules of law, can help in the solution of disputes between two states."[3]

In the *Haya de la Torre Case* (1951) the parties formulated their submissions so as to ask the present Court to make a choice amongst the various courses by which the asylum accorded Mr. de la Torre might be terminated. Finding that these courses were conditioned by facts and by possibilities which to a very large extent could be appreciated only by the parties, the Court held that:

> A choice among them could not be based on legal considerations, but only on considerations of practicability or of political expedience; it is not part of the Court's judicial function to make such a choice.[4]

This attitude of the Court, which could also be traced in its advisory function,[5] may be viewed as a manifestation of the doctrine generally

[1] See *P.C.I.J.*, Ser. A, No. 22 at 12 (order of August 19, 1929).

[2] *P.C.I.J.*, Ser. A/B, No. 46 at 161 (1932).

[3] *Id.* at 162. And see *id.* at 188 (Diss. Op. of Judge Negulesco).

[4] [1951] *I.C.J. Rep.* 71, 79. The Court reiterated this doctrine later in the same judgment by saying that it was unable "to give any practical advice as to the various courses which might be followed with a view to terminating the asylum, since, by doing so, it would depart from its judicial function." *Id.* at 83.

[5] See *e.g.*, *Constitution of the Maritime Safety Committee of I.M.C.O. Case* [1960] I.C.J. Rep. 150, 153. And *cf.*, *Interpretation of Peace Treaties Case* (*Second Phase*), [1950] *I.C.J. Rep.* 221, 229; *International Status of South-West Africa Case*, *id.* at 128, 140. Compare, Rosenne, *supra*, p. 202, note 3 at 458–9.

adopted by judicial organs to the effect that questions submitted to them should, in order that jurisdiction may properly be exercised, be of a legal or justiciable character. As such, it proves that the Court has not completely associated itself with the view that the mere submission of, or agreement to refer a dispute to a tribunal for settlement takes the controversy out of the class of nonjusticiable questions, and allows the tribunal to adjudicate on it.[1]

b. Requirement of a dispute and of a legal interest in contentious cases

Besides the general requirement discussed above, the Court has derived further prerequisites from its nature as a judicial entity. First among these is *the requirement that in contentious cases there should be a "dispute" between the parties,* as the Court is a tribunal and not a legal advisor to individual states. Yet, the Court was always far from being rigid or restrictive in ascertaining this requirement. As early as 1924 the Permanent Court gave its first definition of the term "dispute" as "a disagreement on a point of law or fact, a conflict of legal views or interest between two persons."[2] Such a definition, it is clear, does not require that the disagreement relates necessarily to the "legal rights" of the respective parties. In the *German Interests in Polish Upper Silesia Case* (1925), the Permanent Court went further to say that ' a difference of opinion does exist as soon as one of the Governments concerned points out that the attitude adopted by the other conflicts with its own views."[3] Maintaining the same flexible attitude in defining the term "dispute" when it related to the meaning and scope of two previous judgments in the *Chorzow Factory Case,* the same Court added, however, that it would be "desirable" that "a state should not proceed to take as serious a step as summoning another state to appear before the Court without having previously, within reasonable limits, endeavored to make it quite clear that a difference

[1] This view, which seems to base the classification of disputes into justiciable and non-justiciable upon the policy adopted by the state in seeking a solution for them rather than on their intrinsic nature, has not, however, been outrightly denied by the Court. On the contrary some statements of the Permanent Court especially, may support it. See, *e.g., Minority Schools Case, P.C.I.J.*, Ser. A, No. 15 at 22 (1928); *Chorzow Factory Case, P.C.I.J.*, Ser. A, No. 17 at 37 (1928). It could therefore be argued that the declining of jurisdiction in the cases mentioned above was due to practical considerations of propriety rather than to any commitment on the question of justiciability of disputes.

[2] *Mavrommatis Palestine Concessions Case, P.C.I.J.*, Ser. A, No. 2 at 11 (1924).

[3] *P.C.I.J.*, Ser. A., No. 6 at 14 (1925).

of views is in question which has not been capable of being otherwise overcome."[1]

The question of the definition of a dispute on the meaning or scope of a prior judgment came also before the present Court in one phase of the *Asylum Case* when a request for the "interpretation" of a judgment was made on the very day of its delivery. Here, the present Court proved to maintain the same understanding adopted by its predecessor. "Obviously – the Court wrote – one cannot treat as a dispute, in the sense of [Article 60 of the Statute] the mere fact that one Party finds the [previous] judgment obscure when the other considers it to be perfectly clear. A dispute requires a divergence of views between the parties on definite points."[2]

However, the greatest controversy in the history of the Court as to the existence of a dispute as a prerequisite for the Court's exercise of its jurisdiction was presented in the recent *South-West Africa Cases* (1962). In these cases Ethiopia and Liberia, suing the Republic of South Africa, asked the Court to declare that the latter was still subject to the obligationse mbodied in the Mandate on South-West Africa and that it had failed to respect such obligations. The issue had never been discussed before on a bilateral basis between Ethiopia or Liberia, on the one hand, and the Republic of South Africa on the other, though it was clear that both parties held different views both as to the legal obligations involved and as to the facts alleged by the applicants to have taken place. Objecting to the Court's jurisdiction in the case, South Africa invoked, *inter alia*, the nature and content of "the alleged disagreement" between the parties, pointing out that it did not constitute a dispute as required by the compromissory clause in the Mandate "more particularly, in that no material interests of the Government of Ethiopia and/or Liberia, or of their nationals, are involved in or affected thereby." This latter fact, not contested by the applicants, made of this case a unique one and was responsible in part for the meagre majority (8 to 7) by which the Court became able to establish its jurisdiction. The Court, after citing the *Mavrommatis Palestine Concessions Case* (1924), said:

[1] *Interpretation of Judgments No. 7 and 8 (the Chorzów Factory Case), P.C.I.J.*, Ser. A, No. 13 at 10–1 (1927). In that case, however, the Court refused to consider diplomatic negotiations a necessary condition for the existence of a dispute. See details on this point *infra* at 239–43. And see the question of the existence of a dispute joined to the merits after being raised in the *Administration of the Prince Von Pless Case, P.C.I.J.*, Ser. A/B, No. 52 at 13–4 (1933).

[2] [1950] *I.C.J. Rep.* 395, 403.

> ... it is not sufficient for one party to a contentious case to assert that a dispute exists with the other party. A mere assertion is not sufficient to prove the existence of a dispute any more than a mere denial of the existence of the dispute proves its nonexistence. Nor is it adequate to show that the interests of the two parties to such a case are in conflict. It must be shown that the claim of one party is positively opposed by the other. Tested by this criterion, there can be no doubt about the existence of a dispute between the Parties before the Court, since it is clearly constituted by their opposing attitudes relating to the performance of the obligations of the Mandate by the Respondent as Mandatory.[1]

This reasoning was further supported by Judge Jessup in his lengthy separate opinion. To him a "dispute" fulfulling the requirement has always been "narrowly" defined as "one which can be settled by the application of principles of law." That the dispute should rest on a legal right is "a question for the merits and not a question to be settled on a plea to the jurisdiction."[2] Excluding, therefore, this question, Judge Jessup concluded that the opposing views were ripe enough to constitution a dispute. The concurring Judge Bustamante traced the expression of this dispute in the documents of the League of Nations and the United Nations, which showed that "for several years the two applicant states, in their capacity as members of certain organs and committees of the United Nations have maintained points of view fundamentally opposed to those of the Mandatory with regard to the interpretation of various provisions of the Mandate and with regard to the application of the Mandate by the Mandatory in a series of concrete cases."[3] On the other hand, the dissenting Judge Basdevant agreed that the required dispute "found its precise expression in the submissions presented by the Parties."[4]

All such conclusions accepted by the majority were, however, strongly objected to – and for good reasons – by a number of the dissenting judges. Judges Spender and Fitzmaurice jointly argued that the case "finds its whole *fons et origo* in, and springs directly from the activities of the United Nations"; that the applicants were, in fact, appearing in a "representational capacity" to bring proceedings which the General Assembly of the United Nations could not bring

[1] [1962] *I.C.J. Rep.* 319, 328.

[2] *Id.* at 423. See also *id.* at 381 (Sep. Op. of Judge Bustamente); *id.* at 447 (Sep. Op. of Judge *ad hoc* Mbanefo). There may be involved in this argument a confusion between the legal right for the protection of which the suit is brought (which is a question for the merits) and the legal interest that the applicant should possess as a condition for the admissibility of the claim (see *infra*). The latter is normally manifested in a practical benefit, protected by law, that would be enjoyed by the applicant in case of a favorable decision on the merits.

[3] *Id.* at 381.

[4] *Id.* at 459.

for itself; and that the political conflict of views which took place in the Assembly was not "a dispute properly so called."[1] Similarly, Judge Morelli concluded, after an elaborate discussion of the requirement of a dispute, that "a manifestation of the will, at least of one of the parties, consisting in the making of a claim or of a protest, is a necessary element for a dispute to be regarded as existing."[2] Then, applying this to the present case, he found that it was not possible "to regard the attitude taken by Ethiopia and Liberia in United Nations organs as one of the elements for a dispute to be considered as existing between those States on the one hand and South Africa on the other."[3] This was further elucidated in the dissent of the South African national Judge Van Wyk who emphasized that even if the difference between the views of the parties was established, it was not enough to fulfill the requirement, for a dispute allowing the exercise of the Court's jurisdiction should relate to the "legal rights" of the parties.[4]

It was clear, therefore, in both the pleadings of South Africa and the separate opinions of the dissenting judges that the question of the existence of a dispute was closely linked with the nature of the rights involved. This brings us to what, if accepted, may be classified theoretically as another requirement derived from the judicial character of the Court, i.e., that the applicant (or the intervening party in case of intervention) should have a legal interest in the case. In the *South-West Africa Cases*, it was clear that the applicants did not have any material rights affected by the alleged actions of the respondent. This, South Africa contended, was a particular reason why the controversy did not constitute a dispute in the sense of Article 7 of the Mandate. The Court, itself satisfied that the views of the parties were "positively opposed" and that all that was required under the compromissory clause in the Mandate was "any dispute whatever," did not seem to be hampered by the lack of material interests on the part of the applicants. Its judgment affirming jurisdiction referred briefly to the clearly broad language of the compromissory clause to conclude that:

> ... the manifest scope and purport of the provisions of [Article 7 of the Mandate] indicate that the Members of the League were understood to have a legal right or interest in the observance by the Mandatory of its obligations both toward

[1] *Id.* at 547–9. Compare Judge Spender's separate opinion in the *Interhandel Case* [1959] *I.C.J. Rep.* 6, 60 where he gave a detailed description of the broad construction given by the Court to the requirement of the existence of a dispute.

[2] *Id.* at 567.

[3] *Id.* at 572.

[4] *Id.* at 658–9.

the inhabitants of the Mandated Territory, and toward the League of Nations and its Members.[1]

Thus, without pronouncing on the general requirement of a legal interest, the Court established that the applicants had, in the present case, a legal interest and implied that such interest need not be material.

The question was treated in greater detail by individual judges. Judge Jessup, for instance, though affirming that the existence of a legal right was a question for the merits, found it important to emphasize that "states may have legal interests in matters which do not affect their financial, economic, or other material, or say 'physical' interests,"[2] and illustrated this contention by instances in the disputes related to the minorities treaties, the labor conventions and those based on Mandates. Then, and despite his contention that the general interest in the proper operation of the Mandate was a legal interest, he argued that it was not certain that a legal interest like the one required for intervention under Article 62 of the Statute was a general requirement for the original submission.[3] The grounds of Judge Jessup's argument could, therefore, be summed up in this statement from the Separate Opinion of the national Judge Mbanefo:

> After finding no substance in the requirement of a material interest here, I am of the view that, even if any such interest is required to sustain an action under Article 7, absence of such interest may be a ground for refusing a claim but not for denying jurisdiction and, in any event, the applicants... have such interest in ensuring that the Mandatory carry out its international obligations under the Mandate.[4]

Three of the dissenting judges have particularly disagreed with the above separation of the question of the existence of a legal interest from that of the existence of a dispute.[5] To them, a dispute should relate to a certain conflict of legal interests. This view was elaborated in particular in the dissent of Judge Winiarski. Apart from the grounds

[1] *Id.* at 343. And see the *Northern Cameroons Case* [1963] *I.C.J. Rep.* 15, 36 where the Court spoke of the "procedural right", alleged by the applicant to belong to every member of the U.N., to invoke the judicial protection provided for in the trusteeship agreement.

[2] [1962] *I.C.J. Rep.* 319, 425.

[3] *Id.* at 432–3.

[4] *Id.* at 448.

[5] These are Judges Winiarski, Morelli and Van Wyk. See also the joint dissenting opinion of Judges Spender and Fitzmaurice, *id.* particularly at 558–9, where they confined their statement to the requirement of a dispute required under Art. 7 of the Mandate and found that this dispute must be related to the interests of the applicants.

related to the peculiarities of the case at hand, he based his conclusion on the following general reasons:[1]

First: The applicant state must, under the general rules, have "the capacity to institute the proceedings" (or rather the *qualité*),[2] and this he defined as "a subjective right, a real and existing individual interest which is legally protected."

Second: It is a general rule of both municipal and international law that no action can be instituted in the absence of an interest to be gained by the applicant (*Pas d'intérêt, pas d'action*). This rule, he added, was applied in both the first and second judgments of the Permanent Court.

Third: The Statute of the Court sanctions the rule above mentioned, as Article 62 thereof states that a request to intervene must be made by a state that has "an interest of a legal nature which may be affected by the decision in the case." As this was meant to exclude "political intervention," the same reasons behind it must be thought to hold good for the exclusion of a "political action."

Apart from the case of intervention under Article 62 of the statute where the requirement of a legal interest is explicitly provided for, the problem has never before presented itself in a pressing form in the work of the Court. In all cases, it seemed to have been clear that the applicant has instituted the proceedings to protect an interest of its own or of its own nationals with the exception of some of the Minorities cases between Germany and Poland where Germany was, however, enabled *by express provisions* to sue Poland for the respect of treaties relating to the German minority in Poland, even though the members of this minority were not German citizens.[3]

The *Wimbledon Case* (1923) has been often cited as a clear evidence of the requirement of a legal interest. Yet, its value is far from being

[1] See *id.* at 455–8. See also *id.* at 658–9 (Diss. Op. of Judge *ad hoc* Van Wyk) for the additional reason that: "If the word 'dispute' is given the meaning of 'disagreement embracing any difference of opinion' it leads to absurd results" allowing states to bring academic differences of opinion to the Court.

[2] The original French text of Judge Winiarski's opinion uses the word *qualité* which appears in the English translation as "capacity to institute the proceedings" *id.* at 455. Similar confusion between the two terms prevails in the work of the Court (see an early example in *P.C.I.J.*, Ser. A, No. 20/21 at 17 (1929)) and even in the official version of the Statute (Art. 34). The term "*qualité*" is normally used in the context of French law as a manifestation of the legal interest of the applicant, whereas the capacity to institute the proceedings is expressed by the term "*capacité*." Under this terminology a private corporation may have the *qualité* (i.e. the interest) to institute proceedings before the Court but it certainly does not have the capacity to do so, for such capacity is confined to states.

[3] See a discussion of the requirement of legal interest in these cases in Feinberg, *La Juridiction de la Cour Permanente de Justice dans le Système de la Protection Internationale des Minorités* 57–61 (1931).

conclusive. In that case the respondent left to the appreciation of the Court the question of whether proceedings could be instituted by the applicants and the Court answered by saying that: "It will suffice to observe for the purposes of this case that each of the four Applicant Powers has a clear interest in the execution of the provisions relating to the Kiel canal..."[1] But, one should not lose sight of two facts involved in that case. First, that the compromissory clause conferring jurisdiction on the Court had expressly restricted the resort to the Court to "any *interested* Power." Second, that in an interlocutory judgment in the same case concerning the request of Poland to intervene, after noting that Poland had abandoned basing its request on Article 62 of the Statute and claimed a right under Article 63 as a party to the treaty whose interpretation formed the merits of the case,[2] the Court said:

> The attitude thus adopted renders it unnecessary for the Court to consider and satisfy itself whether Poland's intervention in the suit before it is justified by an interest of a legal nature, within the meaning of Article 62 of the Statute.[3]

This could be taken as evidence that in the understanding of the Court, the requirement of a legal interest provided for in Article 62 was confined, at least in the sphere of intervention, to the limited scope of this very article, though it could admittedly be said, on the other hand, that this attitude of the Permanent Court was justified by the fact that its statute "presumed" the existence of a legal interest in the intervention made under Article 63.

A fair summary of the practice of the Court, particularly as revealed in the arguments in the *South-West Africa Cases,* could, therefore, be along the following lines. The existence of a dispute is required for the admissibility of the claim. This dispute, understood in a broad sense, should, in principle, relate to the legal interests of the applicant, at least in the sense that the latter should expect some benefit, protected by law, from a favorable decision on the merits. However, such benefit need not be material and will be assumed to exist in case the jurisdictional instruments clearly enable the applicant to bring the case before the Court even in the absence of any apparent and direct interest (as in the case of the protection of minorities who are

[1] *P.C.I.J.*, Ser. A, No. 1 at 20 (1923).

[2] Art. 62 speaks of the intervention by a state that has "*an interest of a legal nature* which may be affected by the decision in the case ..." Whereas Art. 63 speaks of the right of states parties to a convention the construction of which is before the Court to intervene in the case, without mentioning the requirement of a legal interest.

[3] *P.C.I.J.*, Ser. A, No. 1 at 13 (Interlocutory Judgment of June 18, 1923).

not nationals of the applicant state, and also, according to the majority view in the *South-West Africa Cases*, in the situation where a Mandatory is sued for its alleged violation of the Mandate by another (former) member of the League whose own rights have not been touched). This permissive outlook explains perhaps why, in all its history, the Court has not, with the partial exception of one case,[1] declined jurisdiction on the basis of the absence of a dispute or of a legal interest in instituting the proceedings.

The requirement of the existence of a dispute has been further used in two spheres affecting the Court's jurisdiction: one relating to the determination of the date in which the dispute arises, and one relating to the Court's jurisdiction to give declaratory judgments:

(i) The Determination of the Date of a Dispute

The jurisdictional instruments may confine the Court's jurisdiction to such disputes as would arise after a given time, or merely to "future disputes," and may further condition these to be arising out of subsequent facts and situations – exclusions that are particularly familiar in the declarations accepting the Court's continued jurisdiction.[2] In such situations, the Court becomes able, through the interpretation it gives to both the temporal reservation and the facts of the dispute, to determine whether or not the latter escapes the exclusion clause and falls within its jurisdiction. This method, elaborately discussed by Rosenne,[3] was particularly followed in such cases as the *Phosphates in Morocco Case* (1938), the *Electricity Company of Sofia and Bulgaria Case* (1939), the *Interhandel Case* (1959) and the *Right of Passage Case* (1960). In all these cases the determination of the date of the dispute was a decisive factor in the issue of jurisdiction to such a degree that the dissenting judges were able to reach different conclusions on the Court's jurisdiction, mainly by interpreting the facts of the dispute in a different manner than the one followed by the Court.[4]

[1] See *Electricity Company of Sofia and Bulgaria Case, P.C.I.J.*, Ser. A/B, No. 77 at 83, 84 (1939). And see further details *infra*.

[2] See Appendix VII, No. 4.

[3] See Rosenne, *The Time Factor* 40–9 (1960). And see Perrin, "L'Affaire de L'Interhandel – Phase des exceptions préliminaires," 16 *Annuaire Suisse de Droit International* 73, 139–151 (1959).

[4] See *e.g.*, *Phosphates in Morocco Case, P.C.I.J.*, Ser. A/B, No. 74 at 34–5 (Diss. Op. of Judge Van Eysinga) and at 36–7 O (Diss. Op. of Judge Cheng); *Electricity Company of Sofia and Bulgaria Case, P.C.I.J.*, Ser. A/B, No. 77 at 142–4 (Sep. Op. of Judge Erich). And see, the *Interhandel Case* where a more illustrative example is provided. The majority were of the opinion that the dispute arose after the date of the American declaration of 1945 but before the date of the Swiss declaration of 1948. See [1959] *I.C.J. Rep.* 6, 21–3. Judges Basdevant and Kojevnikov found that the dispute, as differentiated from the claim, arose

The interpretation of the elements of the dispute, by tracing the chronological development of events and the causal relationship between them and the conflict of views expressed in the controversy, along with the ascertainment of the link between the rise of such a conflict and the exclusion date, serves, therefore, as a major technique in determining jurisdictional issues. Such interpretation was commonly made free from any rigid criteria and was considered from the outset as a question "to be decided in regard to each specific case."[1] As Rosenne put it, this is a point "at which the subjective judicial appreciation of the case *as a whole*, what is sometimes called 'judicial discretion' or 'judicial propriety' takes control."[2]

(ii) The Jurisdiction to Give a Declaratory Judgment in a Contentious Procedure

The requirement of a "dispute" has never resulted, however, in depriving the Court from answering a question submitted to it by the parties in an abstract form. In fact, in many cases, particularly those submitted by means of a special agreement, the parties tend to formulate submissions as a question of what the situation at law is without reference to the consequences that may follow from that situation. All judgments given in such cases are, therefore, in a sense declaratory.[2] The argument arose, however, before the Permanent Court when Poland objected to the Court's jurisdiction in the *German Interests in Upper Silesia Case* (1926), partly on the basis that the first submission of Germany (being a request to declare a certain Polish law as not in conformity with the Treaty of Versailles) was an abstract question which the Court ought not to answer. The Court found "no reason why states should not be able to ask the Court to give an abstract interpretation of a treaty; rather would it appear – added the Court – that this is one of the most important functions which it can fulfil."[3] This view, it should be noted, was given by an almost unanimous Court (only the Polish national judge dissented

after the date of the Swiss declaration. *Id.* at 30, 31. And Judges Hackworth, Cordova, Koo and Spender argued that it arose before the date of the American declaration. *Id.* at 35, 43, 50, 60–73. See also, *Right of Passage Case* [1960] *I.C.J. Rep.* 6, 33–4 compared with *id.* at 74 (Diss. Op. of Judges Winiarski and Badawi), and at 116–8 (Diss. Op. of Judge *ad hoc* Chagla).

[1] See *Phosphates in Morocco Case, P.C.I.J.*, Ser. A/B, No. 74 at 24 (1938).

[2] Rosenne, *supra*, p. 215, note 3 at 48 (footnotes omitted). Compare, Briggs, "Reservations to the Acceptance of Compulsory Jurisdiction of the International Court of Justice," 93 *Recueil des Cours* 229, 294 (1958–I); Perrin, *supra*, p. 215, note 3 at 143–44.

[3] *Accord*, Hudson, *International Tribunals* 120 (1944).

[4] *P.C.I.J.*, Ser. A, No. 7 at 18–9 (1926).

for other reasons), including Judge Anzilotti who later proved more restrictive on this issue, as will be shown. Also to be recalled is the fact that the abstract formulation of the first German submission was never alleged to mean the absence of a dispute on the issue involved. In fact, when the Court was asked in another submission in the case (Submission 2 (b)) to state what attitude should have been adopted by the defendant in order to be in conformity with a certain treaty without any further claim being based on this, the Court, though it had established its jurisdiction to deal with that question in a previous judgment, found that it was "not in a position to give judgment on this submission, for though it can construe the submissions of the parties, it cannot substitute itself for them and formulate new submissions simply on the basis of arguments and facts advanced."[1]

The declaratory nature of the judgment on the first submission in the above case was further emphasized in a later case concerned, *inter alia*, with its interpretation. Such a nature did not prevent the Court from explaining that the judgment had its legal effects:

> The Court's judgment, No. 7, is in the nature of a declaratory judgment, the intention of which is to insure recognition of a situation at law, once and for all, and with binding force as between the parties, so that the legal position thus established cannot again be called in question insofar as the legal effects ensuing therefrom are concerned.[2]

When, a few years later, another case was submitted to the Court with some submissions formulated *in abstracto* by the applicants, the Permanent Court discussed and answered the said submissions, referring only to "the inconvenience resulting from the fact that [such submissions] are formulated as questions purely *in abstracto*, without any reference to the facts of the dispute which has arisen"[3] – a statement that establishes that, despite the abstract formulation, there was a relevant existing dispute. Judge Anzilotti dissented, however, on this point, Although no objection was made by the respondent as to the formulation of the applicant's submissions, Anzilotti wrote that:

> In its judicial capacity, the Court cannot answer questions: it must pass upon claims: ... A properly constituted action at law is only possible if a claim is presented in this form, for an action is hardly conceivable unless there is a person who makes against some other person a claim upon which it is for the judge to pass according to law.

[1] *Id.* at 34–5. And see this point as dealt with in Chapter II, *supra* at 74–5.

[2] *Interpretation of Judgments Nos. 7 and 8 (the Chorzow Factory Case), P.C.I.J.*, Ser. A, No. 13 at 20 (1927). And see the *Diversion of Waters from the Meuse Case, P.C.I.J.*, Ser. A/B, No. 70 at 79 (1937) (Indiv. Op. of Judge Hudson).

[3] *Interpretation of the Statute of the Memel Territory Case, P.C.I.J.*, Ser. A/B, No. 49 at 311 (1932).

The foregoing leads to the following conclusion: The Court could not answer the questions put in the application, because by so doing, it would be giving an advisory opinion for which the applicant Powers were not entitled to ask and which the Court was not entitled to give.[1]

This latter view may seemingly correspond to the attitude of the Permanent Court related to Submission 2 (b) in Judgment No. 7 when, as seen before, it refused to answer a point in its "purely interrogative form" not followed by properly set out claims. But the fact that the same Court followed a different attitude in the case at hand could be explained only by taking account of the relevance of the abstractly formulated question to the dispute on which the case is based. Whereas this question as presented in the *German Interests Case* (1926) was in itself of little relevance to the settlement of the dispute (being related to what the respondent should have done to avoid a violation which it already did), the questions involved in the *Memel Territory Case* (1932) were, despite their abstract form, at the heart of the dispute involved.

One is, therefore, inclined to conclude that the Permanent Court has exercised its jurisdiction to give declaratory judgments only when the abstract questions submitted had some relevance to a standing dispute between the parties. As to the degree of this relevance, it is clear that a submission was not required to relate necessarily to a concrete claim for redress in respect of a particular act, but it was required to relate to some dispute between the parties.[2] Through this principle, the Court maintained the double purpose of securing the exercise of its jurisdiction without extending the limits of the contentious procedure to cover requests by states for advisory opinions.

The present Court has shown no sign to depart from this tradition. Although no occasion has so far arisen where the doctrine was challenged, the Court has not hesitated to answer the questions submitted by the parties even when these were formulated as mere requests for the (disputed) proper law applicable in a given situation, and has recently stated in specific terms: "That the Court may in an appropriate case, make a declaratory judgment is indisputable."[3]

Simultaneously, some individual judges have characterized certain points in contentious cases as including requests for declaratory

[1] *Id.* at 350.

[2] See generally, Lauterpacht, *The Development of International Law by the International Court* 250–2 (1958).

[3] *Northern Cameroon Case*, [1963] *I.C.J. Rep.* 15, 37.

judgments – a process which enabled them to reach different conclusions on the Court's jurisdiction.[1]

c. Application of universal judicial maxims

In addition to the above-mentioned methods based on the judicial character of the Court, the Court has sought the *application of universal judicial maxims*, such as the rules of *non ultra petita* and *jura novit curia*. These two rules in particular have had a significant role in the Court's determination of the issues confronting it, both jurisdictional and substantive. They are examined here only as techniques used by the Court to support the conclusion that a certain issue is within or without its jurisdiction.

(i) The *Non Ultra Petita* Rule

The *non ultra petita* rule means simply that a tribunal will not exceed the limits of the demands of the parties by deciding points not submitted to it, or by awarding more than it is asked to award. This rule becomes particularly relevant in international adjudication where the parties' consent is the primary test for the assumption of jurisdiction.[2] In this respect, the rule becomes a derivative of the principle of consent, not in that it confers or detracts jurisdiction but as a limitation on the Court's power in deciding the case.[3] The scope of such a limitation differs of course according to the interpretation given by the Court to the points submitted to it, subject in principle to the Permanent Court's remark that though it "may construe the submissions of the parties, it cannot substitute itself for them and formulate new submissions simply on the basis of arguments and facts advanced."[4]

In the work of the present Court, the rule has been invoked to support the Court's conclusion not to award the applicant a compen-

[1] See *e.g., Monetary Gold Case,* [1954] *I.C.J. Rep.* 19, 43–4 (Diss. Op. of Judge Levi Carneiro); *Right of Passage Case* (Merits), [1960] *I.C.J. Rep.* 6, 74 (Diss. Op. of Judges Winiarski and Badawi).

[2] Compare the tendency of some arbitral tribunals to urge the respondent Government to take certain measures as acts of grace. *E.g. Representative of Elizabeth Cadenhead (Great Britain)* v. *U.S.A.*, 6 *U.N. Rep. Int'l Arb. Awards,* 40–41 (1914); *Home Frontier and Foreign Missionary Society of the United Brethren in Christ* (*U.S.A.*) v. *Great Britain, id.* at 42 (1920); *Adolph Studer* (*U.S.A.*) *v. Great Britain, id.* at 149 (1925).

[3] *Accord,* Fitzmaurice, *supra,* p. 205. note 1 at 98; Rosenne, *The International Court of Justice* 272 (1957).

[4] *German Interests in Polish Upper Silesia Case, P.C.I.J.*, Ser. A, No. 7 at 35 (1926). See also *Right of Passage Case,* [1960] *I.C.J. Rep.* 6, 77 (Sep. Op. of Judge Armand-Ugon).

sation greater than the one it asked for,[1] and to limit the judgment to the type of remedy suggested in the parties' agreement.[2] Yet, the most significant application of the rule has been in the field of the interpretation of previous judgments. On the only occasion where a judgment of the present Court was submitted to it for interpretation, it invoked the rule of *non ultra petita* to conclude that interpretation can in no way go beyond the limits of the judgment interpreted.[3]

Although all the above cases were based on special agreements, the rule is of general applicability. In fact, it applies as well to the advisory jurisdiction of the Court. In the *Customs Regime between Germany and Austria Case* (1931), Judge Anzilotti argued for broad application of this rule, not only to prevent the Court's answering a question other than that which has been put to it, but also to preclude it from confining itself to answering only a part of that question.[4] This latter conclusion could hardly be accepted in the sphere of advisory jurisdiction. It may, however, be invoked in relation to contentious cases if it is made clear that the parties' consent to adjudicate the dispute would not have been given had the case been confined to the part of the question that the Court found to be the only issue within its jurisdiction.[5]

The above examples notwithstanding, it has been noticed that "in respect of objections to the tribunal's jurisdiction in relation to the dispute as such, the rule [*non ultra petita*] can hardly have any application at all."[6] This remark is obviously based on the assumption that the Court is always free to raise on its own initiative objections to jurisdiction even if none of the parties does so. The validity of this general assumption has been questioned before. Yet, it is true, as will shortly be shown, that the Court might, in the determination of its jurisdiction, raise issues not argued by the parties, particularly by invoking the rule of *jura novit curia*. This does not necessarily mean that the *non ultra petita* rule has no place in this respect, though it affirms that in practical terms this rule finds its normal application

[1] See *Corfu Channel Case* (Assessment), [1949] *I.C.J. Rep.* 244, 249. The mere assessment of the amount of compensation was itself found by some individual judges in an earlier stage of the case to be *ultra petit.* See [1949] *I.C.J. Rep.* 4, 67 (Diss. Op. of Judge Badawi), at 96 (Diss. Op. of Judge Azevedo) and at 128 (Diss. Op. of Judge *ad hoc* Ečer).

[2] See *Minquiers and Ecrehos Case,* [1953] *I.C.J. Rep.* 47, 52–3.

[3] [1950] *I.C.J. Rep.* 395, 402–3.

[4] See *P.C.I.J.*, Ser. A/B, No. 41 at 69 (Adv. Op.) (Diss. Op. of Judge Anzilotti).

[5] But see, *Free Zones Case, P.C.I.J.*, Ser. A/B, No. 46 at 163 (1932) where the above argument, advanced in the case by France, was refused by the Court. The dissenting Judges Negulesco and Dreyfus accepted it, however. *Id.* at 199, 200.

[6] Fitzmaurice, *supra*, p. 205, note 1 at 104.

in the situation where the Court has already established its jurisdiction in the strict sense. In such a situation, the application of the rule results in confining the Court to the submissions of the parties as interpreted by the Court – the latter reservation being made to emphasize the discretionary aspect of the application of the rule.

(ii) The *Jura Novit Curia* Rule

The application of the *non ultra petita* rule has no effect on the power of the court to deal with issues duly submitted to it within the limits asked for by the parties. As to such issues, the Court maintains in principle full judicial freedom to decide them either on the bases discussed by the parties or on completely new bases. For the Court, being a judicial tribunal, knows and applies the law regardless of the arguments of the parties. *Jura Novit curia.* This has been manifested in more than one aspect of the work of the Court.

The first question to be raised in this regard is this: Can the Court take account of points other than the legal and factual bases of the suit elected by the parties? Must it, in the words of Carsten Smith, think (and not only speak) within the same confined area as the parties do?[1]

Limiting the question to jurisdictional issues, there is no doubt that the International Court has, more than once, discussed grounds of objections against its jurisdiction which were not mentioned in the proceedings. This phenomenon of what was called "surprising premises"[2] could be clearly traced in the few cases discussed above where the Court raised objections to its jurisdiction other than those introduced by the defendant.[3] Besides such cases, the present Court has based some of its judgments on grounds that the parties have not argued at all or have not argued fully.

In the *Monetary Gold Case* (1954), the Court made a finding on the question of whether the application of Italy was in conformity with the offer to accept jurisdiction made by the respondent Governments.[4] This question, though once raised on behalf of one of the respondents,[5]

[1] Smith, *The Relation between Proceedings and Premises* 20 (1962).
[2] *Id.* at 15.
[3] See Chapter II, *supra* at 61–66. Compare, *Norwegian Loans Case,* (1957) *I.C.J. Rep.* 9, 25.
[4] See [1954] *I.C.J. Rep.* 19, 28–29.
[5] See *id* at 28–9, and see *Case of the Monetary Gold Removed from Rome in 1943,* Pleadings, Oral Arguments and Documents 80–2 (Observations of the British Government) (*I.C.J.* 1954).

was not fully argued by the parties.[1] In the second phase of the *Nottebohm Case* (1955), the point became much clearer as the Court based its judgment of the nonadmissibility of the claim, solely on a ground that was not raised by the respondent nor argued between the parties.[2] Then in the *Norwegian Loans Case* (1957), some separate opinions discussed in detail the question of the validity of the declaration of the applicant [3] – though this issue was not referred to in the proceedings. And again in the *Aerial Incident Case* (*Israel v. Bulgaria*) (1959), both the Court and some individual judges based their conclusions on grounds that were almost alien to the proceedings.[4] As expounded above, the limitation of the effect of article 36(5) of the Statute to the original members of the United Nations (a ground that the Court clearly upheld) was not invoked by Bulgaria except in a passing reference during the oral argument, and the limitation of such effect to declarations made for a certain time (as argued by Judges Badawi and Armand-Ugon) was never raised or argued by the parties. With regard to this latter point, Judge Armand-Ugon was particularly conscious of the issue:

"This argument – he wrote – was not discussed in the oral proceedings; there is, however, nothing to prevent the argument being upheld, in accordance with the well-known principle applied by international courts in procedural matters, that the Court may *proprio motu* seek and select the legal basis for its decision on the final submissions of the parties – *jura novit curia.*"[5]

Despite the above practice, the present Court had, in the first phase of the *Ambatielos Case* (1952) refused to pronounce at that stage, on the seventh preliminary objection presented by the United Kingdom, because "it has not yet been fully argued by the Parties."[6] Strangely enough this latter fact did not cause the Court to join the objection to the merits or to examine it regardless of the insufficient proceedings

[1] This was one of the grounds of Judge Read's dissent in the case. See [1954] *I.C.J. Rep.* 19, 37.

[2] See [1955] *I.C.J. Rep.* 4, 24–6. Compare Judge Read's dissenting opinion in *id.* at 38–9.

[3] See [1957] *I.C.J. Rep.* 9, 43–8 (Diss. Op. Judge Lauterpacht), and at 68 (Diss. Op. of Judge Guerrero). And see details of this issue in Chapter VI, *infra.*

[4] See [1959] *I.C.J. Rep.* 127, 146 (that the effect of Art. 36 (5) of the Statute applies only to original members of the U.N.). See also *id.* at 148 (Diss. Op. of Judge Badawi) and at 154–5 (Diss. Op. of Judge Armand-Ugon) (that Art. 36(5) applies only to declarations made for a definite period of time).

[5] *Id.* at 155. See also *Minority Schools Case, P.C.I.J.*, Ser. A, No. 15 at 53–4 (1928) (Diss. Op. of Judge Huber); *Electricity Company of Sofia and Bulgaria; P.C.I.J.* Ser. A/B, No. 77 at 102–3 (Diss. Op. of Judge Urrutia).

[6] [1952] *I.C.J. Rep.* 28, 45. and see *Temple of Preah Vihear Case*, [1961] *I.C.J. Rep.* 17, 38 (Declaration by Judges Fitzmaurice and Tanaka).

(as it did in previous cases). Instead the Court established directly its jurisdiction over the case regardless of this point which was however discussed in a later stage as an argument concerning the merits. This attitude which gives the impression that the Court will rely only on the best argued group of the arguments advanced by the parties,[1] and which was repeatedly insisted upon by Judge Read in his dissenting opinions in later cases,[2] could not, however, be taken as typical of the Court's practice. On the contrary, a clearly identified tendency in the Court's determination of its jurisdiction has been to the effect that it is free to ascertain the validity of objections against its jurisdiction on the grounds it sees fit whether or not such grounds were fully argued by the parties. But because this ascertainment will normally relate to the consent of the parties, the Court can hardly depart from the materials expressing such consent to prove that its jurisdiction was or was not accepted. Thus, we reach again the conclusion upheld with regard to the invocation of objections to jurisdiction *proprio-motu*. No such objections will be raised by the Court to negate the consent of the parties when the latter is established by their express or tacit acceptance. But the Court maintains full judicial freedom, both to raise objections *besides* the objections raised by the parties and, in the absence of objections from the latter, to raise and decide objections that do not relate to the consent of the parties. Therefore, the Court may discuss, for instance, whether there is a dispute and whether the parties to the case are states even when such questions are completely absent from the pleadings. For, again, these questions are part of the law of the Court's jurisdiction (not of the parties' consent) and, being a court of justice, the Court knows and applies this law according to the maxim *jura novit curia*. But this is not to say that the Court will necessarily follow such a course. In point of fact, it tends to avoid any detailed treatment of its jurisdiction when all parties agree that it is established.

The *jura novit curia* rule may also – though no example could be cited for this in the work of the Court – enable the Court to decline entertaining the case in the situation where the parties condition their acceptance of jurisdiction on the application to the merits of certain

[1] See Smith, *supra*, p. 221, note 1 at 53.

[2] See *supra*, p. 222, notes 1, 2. And see *Customs Regime between Germany and Austria Case*, *P.C.I.J.*, Ser. A/B, No. 41 at 74, 76 (Adv. Op.) (Diss. Op. of Judges Adatci, Kellogg, Rolin-Jaequemyns, Hurst, Schücking, Van Eysinga and Wang).

rules that the Court finds to be in conflict with the basic principles of international law as it applies it.[1]

d. Judicial propriety (reference)

Finally, the judicial character of the Court has been used as a justification of the Court's reluctance to deal with certain issues even when they are duly submitted to it, merely on the ground that it is improper for the Court to decide them. This technique will, due to its importance, be dealt with separately under the title of "considerations of propriety and judicial discretion."

2. *Requirement Based on the Fact that the Court is an International Court*

a. International character of the dispute

Article 34 of the Statute of the Court provides that states *only* can be parties in cases before the Court, and Article 38 refers to the function of the Court as deciding "in accordance with international law" such disputes as are submitted to it. These provisions, along with the text of Article 14 of the Covenant of the League of Nations which had envisaged the jurisdiction of the Permanent Court as covering "any dispute of international character," substantiated a strong argument according to which only international disputes governed by international law could be properly decided by the Court. However, on the first occasion where this argument was tested, the Permanent Court adopted a much more permissive view. According to this view, the international character of the dispute is fulfilled by the simple fact that the dispute is between states, regardless of its contents as long as both parties agree on submitting it to the Court. This conclusion was reached in the *Serbian Loans* and *Brazilian Loans* cases (1929). First, the Court established that the disputes submitted to it *by special agreements* concluded by the parties in these cases were disputes between Governments distinct from the disputes between the individual creditors and the defendant Governments. Then it argued "from a general point of view" that "the true function of the Court is to decide disputes between States... on the basis of international law." But this, the Court found, was not an exclusive description of its function as "it would be scarcely accurate to say that only questions

[1] *Accord*, Smith, *supra*, p. 221, note 1 at 93.

of international law may form the subject of a decision of the Court."[1] To prove this point, the Court referred to sub-paragraph (c) of Article 36 of the Statute under which a declaration could be made for the acceptance of jurisdiction over a dispute concerning "the existence of any fact which, if established, would constitute a breach of an international obligation." Similarly, the Court argued, "when the two States have agreed to have recourse to the Court, the latter's *duty* to exercise its jurisdiction cannot be affected, in the absence of a clause in the statute on the subject, by the circumstance that the dispute relates to a question of municipal law rather than to a pure matter of fact."[2] As a result, the Court exercised its jurisdiction in the two cases despite the fact that their merits were, according to the Court itself, exclusively governed by municipal law.

This attitude, encouraged perhaps by the absence of objections from the respondent against the assumption of jurisdiction in these two cases, was met with a wide disagreement in the doctrinal writings that followed it.[3] But, in the actual cases only the Brazilian and the Serbian judges (i.e., the judges who possessed the nationality of the respondent Governments) dissented on this point. They referred in their dissents to several judgments of the Permanent Court in which the latter, it was asserted, had consistently followed the view that the subject matter of the dispute submitted to it should be governed by international law.[4] It is, however, to be noted that none of the previous judgments nor, for that matter, the subsequent judgments, had spelled out this latter view. On the contrary, despite the fact that all the disputes covered by these judgments were governed by international law, the emphasis of the Court, in deciding the jurisdictional issue, was on the necessity of an "interstate relation."[5] Therefore, the unrevised doctrine of the Permanent Court was to the effect that the "interstate"

[1] *Serbian Loans Case, P.C.I.J.*, Ser. A, No. 20/21 at 19 (1929).

[2] *Ibid.* (Emphasis added). And see the *Brazilian Loans Case, id.* at 101 where the Court simply referred to its judgment in the *Serbian Loans Case* given in the same day.

[3] See *e.g.*, Scerni, "La Procédure de la Cour Permanente de Justice Internationale," 65 *Recueil des Cours* 565, 613 (1938–III); Bruns, "La Cour Permanente de Justice Internationale, son organisation et sa compétence," 62 *id.* 551, 634 (1937–IV).

[4] See *Serbian Loans Case, supra*, note 1 at 62 (Diss. Op. of Judge Pessôa) and at 77 (Diss. Op. of Judge Novocovitch).

[5] See *e.g.*, *Mavrommatis Palestine Concessions Case, P.C.I.J.*, Ser. A, No. 2 at 12 (1924); *Chorzów Factory Case, P.C.I.J.*, Ser. A, No. 17 at 27 (1928). And see case concerning the *Consistency of Certain Decrees with the Constitution of the Free City, P.C.I.J.*, Ser. A/B, No. 65 at 61 (Adv. Op.) (Indiv. Op. of Judge Anzilotti) where he stated that the Court should not answer a request dealing with a question which related to the municipal law of a particular country "apart from any question of international law *or* of an international dispute." (Emphasis added).

character of the dispute was all that was required to satisfy the requirement that disputes submitted to it ought to be of international character.

The present Court has managed to avoid taking sides on this issue on the only occasion it was presented to it. This was the *Norwegian Loans Case* (1957). France, espousing the claims of French holders of bond certificates of Norwegian loans, sued Norway before the Court over what it termed "a legal dispute of an international character between the two states." The jurisdiction of the Court, France claimed, was based on the mutual acceptance made by France and Norway by means of their respective declarations. Norway, in response, submitted three preliminary objections to the jurisdiction of the Court, the first being that:

> ... the subject of the dispute, as defined in the Application, is within the domain of municipal law and not of international law, whereas the compulsory jurisdiction of the Court in relation to the parties involved is restricted, by their Declarations of November 16th, 1946 and March 1st. 1949, to disputes concerning international law.[1]

This objection was also supported by another subsidiary ground. Noting that the French declaration included a "self-judging reservation" for "matters which are essentially within the national jurisdiction as understood by the Government of the French Republic," Norway invoked the same reservation against France by force of reciprocity. This latter ground was relied upon by the Court as the only basis of its decision declining jurisdiction in the case, thus sparing it the burden of pronouncing on the first ground.

Although the decision in the *Norwegian Loans Case* (1957) was delivered by a majority of twelve votes to three, five judges – three dissenting and two concurring – found it important to pronounce on the issue of the international character of the dispute. Judges Lauterpacht, Basdevant, and Read were of the opinion that the issues involved were not exclusively related to the Norwegian municipal law but related also to international law, in that the municipal law in dispute was alleged to be in violation of international law, both on its face and in its application.[2] On the other hand, Judges Moreno Quintana and Badawi thought that the lack of jurisdiction ought to

[1] [1957] *I.C.J. Rep.* 9, 16. And see the detailed bases of this objection as discussed in the Norwegian Preliminary Objections, in 1 *Case of Certain Norwegian Loans*, Pleadings, Oral Arguments and Documents 119, 121–9 (*I.C.J.* 1957).

[2] See [1957] *I.C.J. Rep.* 9, 37 (Diss. Op. Judge Lauterpacht at 78 (Diss. Op. of Judge Basdevant) and at 80 (Diss. Op. of Judge Read).

have been based on the fact that the dispute was governed by municipal law,[1] thus raising anew the controversy involved in the old *Loans Cases* before the Permanent Court. Judge Badawi, in particular, devoted his separate opinion to what amounted to be a refutal of the doctrine and reasoning of the Permanent Court. In the very case at hand he refused to share the view of Judges Lauterpacht and Read that the dispute was of a mixed character for, as he saw it, it related exclusively to the interpretation of the loan contracts. The issues of international law which they said were involved have been raised only through Norway's denial of the international character of the dispute, and "it would be very strange, and even paradoxical, to consider that the denial of the international character of a question of a municipal law and the discussion entered into in that connection confer on that very question an international character."[2] As to sub-paragraph (c) of Article 36 of the statute on which both the Permanent Court (in the *Loans Cases* of 1929) and France (in the present case) have relied to justify the jurisdiction of the Court over issues not governed by international law, Judge Badawi provided this interpretation:

> Sub-paragraph (c) of Article 36 of the Statute relates to the special case where the Parties are in agreement as to the rule of international law or, more precisely, as to the international obligation, but are in disagreement as to the facts constituting a breach thereof.[3]

This interpretation clearly assumes that even on exercising jurisdiction under Article 36 (c), the original dispute should be governed by international law.

Because of this revival of the controversy, and particularly because of the total absence in both the judgment and the individual opinions in the *Norwegian Loans Case* (1957) of any reliance on the doctrine expressed by the Permanent Court in the Loans Cases of 1929, one can only state that the question of whether an interstate dispute exclusively governed by municipal law could properly be decided by the Court is still an open question insofar as the present Court is concerned. As the provisions of the Statute are admittedly capable of more than one interpretation in relation to this issue, the Court may be expected to adopt the interpretation enabling it to exercise its jurisdiction, provided that the consent of the parties is established. The Permanent Court, it is to be noted, though seeing itself as "the

[1] See *id.* at 28 and at 31–2.
[2] *Id.* at 33.
[3] *Id.* at 32.

organ of international law" and characterizing municipal laws as "merely facts,"[1] did not hesitate to follow this course when the parties submitted the question by a clear agreement.

The requirement that the dispute should be "interstate" may also involve the question of determining whether the parties are states.[2] This inquiry will not, however, normally arise if the parties to the case are parties to the statute except when the reality of the *legitima persona* is at issue.[3]

b. Matters of domestic jurisdiction

The exclusion of matters exclusively governed by municipal law could also be argued on the basis that such matters are within the domestic jurisdiction of the respondent state and therefore no international organ, the Court included, can interfere in them. This aspect of the problem was present in many cases, though the exclusion was explicitly provided for in the jurisdictional instruments in the cases where the Court pronounced on the issue. The details of this aspect will soon be discussed in the context of the quality of the Court as an organ of the United Nations.

c. Exhaustion of diplomatic and local remedies

Along with the above requirements and also based on the international character of the Court are the important requirements of the exhaustion of diplomatic negotiations and local remedies, both of which are dealt with in Section C of this Chapter.

3. Requirements Based on the Fact that the Court is the Principal Judicial Organ of the United Nations

a. The advisory procedure

Because the present Court is, by virtue of Article 92 of the Charter and Article 1 of its Statute, the principal judicial organ of the United

[1] See *German Interests in Polish Upper Silesia case*, *P.C.I.J.*, ser. A, No. 7 at 19 (1926).

[2] The Permanent Court had, in advisory proceedings, considered Danzig as a "state," see *Treatment of Polish Nationals in the Danzig Territory*, *P.C.I.J.*, ser. A/B, No. 44 at 23–5 (1932), and the European Commission of the Danube as "not a state," see *Jurisdiction of the European Commission of the Danube*, *P.C.I.J.*, ser. B, No. 14, at 64 (1927). When the same court was approached on the conditions according to which the "Confederacy of Six Nations of the Grand River" might submit to the Court certain differences with the U.S.A. and Great Britain, the Registrar simply referred, in reply, to Arts. 34, 35 of the statutes – an attitude which was later approved by the Court. See *P.C.I.J. Ann. Rep.*, ser. E, No. 8 at 158 (1931–32).

[3] *E.g.* in the *Serbian Loans Case* (1929) and *Brazilian Loans Case* (1929) before the Permanent Court and the *Anglo-Iranian Oil Co. Case* (1952) before the present Court.

Nations, it has, as seen above in detail, looked to its advisory function as a "duty" that it had to perform except for compelling reasons against such performance. The effect of this attitude on the scope of the advisory jurisdiction of this Court, as compared to its predecessor's, has been materialized in a presumption favorable to the exercise of the advisory function. As the Court has clearly put it:

The Court's Opinion is given not to the States, but to the organ which is entitled to request it; the reply of the Court, itself an organ of the United Nations, represents its participation in the activities of the organization and, in principle, should not be refused.[1]

b. The contentious procedure

As to the contentious procedure, the quality of the present Court as an organ of the United Nations has its impact in many articles of the Charter and the Statute. All members of the United Nations are *ipso facto* parties to the Statute (Article 93(1) of the Charter) and the conditions according to which non-members can become parties and non-parties can have access to the Court are to be made by other organs of the United Nations (Articles 93(2) of the Charter and 35(2), (3) of the Statute). But the clearest impact of the said quality on the Court's jurisdiction could be derived particularly from three provisions in the Charter: Articles 2(7), 36(3) and 102. The latter article which requires registration as a condition of the invocation of any treaty or international agreement before "any organ of the United Nations" has proved, however, to be of little significance as far as jurisdictional instruments were concerned.[2]

Similarly, the effect of Article 36(3) as a source of an *ad hoc* jurisdiction of the Court resulting from a recommendation made to the parties by the Security Council was found, on the detailed examination made above, to be doubtful.[3] As to Article 2(7), it provides that:

Nothing contained in the present Charter shall authorize the United Nations to intervene in matters which are essentially within the domestic jurisdiction of any state or shall require the Members to submit such matters to settlement under the present Charter; but this principle shall not prejudice the application of enforcement measures under Chapter VII.

Does this provision apply to the Court, as an organ of the United Nations, regardless of whether a similar exclusion is made by the parties?

[1] The *Peace Treaties Case* (First Phase), [1950] *I.C.J. Rep.* 65, 71. And see the details of this attitude in Chapter IV, *supra* at 118–25.

[2] See Chapter III, *supra* at 97–100.

[3] See Chapter IV, *supra* at 135–39.

The question seems to be easier to answer in the realm of advisory jurisdiction. For, if the organ making the request is not authorized to intervene in matters essentially within the domestic jurisdiction, no such matter will normally be submitted by it to the Court. If, however, an organ of the United Nations overlooking Article 2(7) of the Charter should request the Court's Opinion in a matter which the Court found to be "essentially within the domestic jurisdiction of any state," the Court could, and in theory must, find in this a compelling reason to decline an answer.[1] The argument was indeed made before the present Court in the *Peace Treaties Case* (1950), but was disposed of when the Court found that the question before it was a matter of treaty interpretation that could not be considered, at any rate, as a question of domestic jurisdiction.[2]

As to the contentious procedure, the question will not of course arise if the respondent Government proves to have excluded from its acceptance of the Court's jurisdiction all questions of domestic jurisdiction. In this case, the Court will need not invoke Article 2(7) of the Charter. Such an exclusion may be explicit in the jurisdictional instrument, and may also be implied. An instance of the latter is presented in the contentions of Bulgaria in the *Electricity Company of Sofia Case* (1939). In this case, jurisdiction was allegedly based on two grounds: a particular treaty of arbitration covering disputes with regard to the parties' respective rights which "include in particular those mentioned in Article 36 of the Statute," as well as the acceptance of the Optional Clause System. The respondent Government (Bulgaria) argued, therefore, that a reservation of domestic jurisdiction was implied in the limitation of the Court's jurisdiction to the four classes of legal disputes mentioned in Article 36(2), all of which involve international law or international obligations. This plea, which was found by the Court to be a defense on the merits and not a preliminary objection,[3] was not decided in the first stage of the case, and as the case was later

[1] See generally, Rosenne, *The International Court of Justice* 460–3 (1957).

[2] See [1950] *I.C.J. Rep.* 63, 70–1.

[3] See *P.C.I.J.*, ser. A/B, No. 77 at 77–8, 82–3 (1939). And see for support of the argument of the argument of an implied reservation of matters of domestic jurisdiction in every declaration of acceptance made in accordance with Art. 36(2) of the Statute, Briggs, *supra*, p. 216, note 1 at 310–1; 2 Oppenheim, *International Law* (7th ed. Lauterpacht 1952); Hambro, "Jurisdiction of the International Court of Justice," 76 *Recueil des Cours* 125, 187 (1950–I); Hudson, *The Permanent Court of International Justice* 471 (2d ed. 1943); Memorandum on the Signature by His Majesty's Government in the United Kingdom of the Optional Clause of the Statute of the Permanent Court of International Justice, Great Britain, *Parliamentary Papers*, Misc. No. 12 (1929), Cmd. 3452 at 12.

discontinued before the final hearing, the chance of a judicial pronouncement on the validity of the plea was lost.

Beyond the situation where matters of domestic jurisdiction are excluded by a special provision, the question of the application of Article 2(7) of the Charter to the competence of the present Court remains undecided. The provision was first invoked by Iran as one ground for its objection to the Court's jurisdiction in the *Anglo-Iranian Oil Co. Case* (1952).[1] The interest in invoking it, despite the fact that a reservation of domestic jurisdiction was inserted in both the British and Iranian declarations, is explained by the wording of these very reservations that excluded only matters "exclusively" rather than "essentially" (as in Article 2(7)) within the domestic jurisdiction.[2] The invocation was, however, met by opposition on the part of the United Kingdom, whose agent strongly opposed the application of Article 2(7) to the Court, mainly on the following grounds:[3]

(i) The prohibition in the Charter was addressed only to the organs whose authority is derived from the Charter, whereas the Court's jurisdiction is based only on the consent of the parties.

(ii) Article 2(7) speaks of the "intervention" in matters of domestic jurisdiction while the Court's judgment could never be the equivalent of an intervention in the customarily accepted sense of the word.

(iii) The application of Article 2(7) to the Court's competence is, at any rate, meaningless, as all matters of domestic jurisdiction are by definition beyond the scope of international law. The matters enumerated in Article 36(2) of the Statute fall, in particular, outside the scope of domestic jurisdiction.

These arguments, which the Court has never found a chance to pronounce upon (as it declined jurisdiction on another basis), were later revived by Waldock.[4]

First he argued that the word "Charter" as mentioned in Article 2(7) denotes only the articles of the Charter itself. Secondly, he rightly pointed out that: "There is nothing in the words of Article 2(7) to

[1] See *Anglo-Iranian Oil Co. Case*, Pleadings, Oral Argument and Documents 292, 466, 621 (*I.C.J.* 1952).

[2] Iran, however, argued also that the word "exclusively" in its declaration of 1932 [Appendix VI, No. 69] should be interpreted under the present Court to mean "essentially" so that it may correspond to the evolution of the wording of Art. 15(8) of the Covenant of the League as it was transferred to Art. 2(7) of the Charter of the U.N. See *id.* at 623 (Replique du Professeur Rolin).

[3] See *id.* at 572 (Argument by Sir Eric Beckett). And see *id.* at 162 (Annex to U.K. Memorial) and at 657 (Rejoinder by Sir Eric Beckett).

[4] See Waldock, "The Plea of Domestic Jurisdiction before International Legal Tribunals," 31 *Brit. Yb. Int'l L.* 96, 122–4 (1954).

preclude the Court, or any other Organ of the United Nations, from intervening in matters essentially within domestic jurisdiction if it has been authorized to do so by the states concerned in an instrument dehors the Charter."[1] Thirdly, and most importantly, he pointed out the fact that the jurisdiction of the Court is based solely on the consent of the parties without which the Court is not in principle authorized to interfere in any question, domestic or not. Therefore, the application of Article 2(7) which would have been justified were the Court clothed with a general compulsory jurisdiction, serves no purpose in the actual situation of the Court's jurisdiction limited as it is by its consensual basis.

In fact, Article 2(7) of the Charter does not, despite an argument to the contrary,[2] clearly seem to be relevant to the work of the Court. If the Court reaches the conclusion that the parties have accepted its jurisdiction to adjudicate the case, it will not be precluded from exercising jurisdiction merely because of the provision of Article 2(7). And, if the Court is convinced that no such acceptance was made, it will not need to resort to Article 2(7) in order to justify its lack of jurisdiction. The article may, however, serve as a *subsidiary* ground for declining jurisdiction in such cases where the consent is not beyond doubt and the issue is not clearly of an international character, for then the Court could declare that as an organ of the United Nations it is not authorized to deal with issues within the domestic jurisdiction of states which they have not clearly submitted to it.

Aside from this conclusion, Judge Lauterpacht expounded in his separate opinion in the *Interhandel Case* (1959) the thesis that:

> States are in any case fully protected from any interference whatsoever by the Court in matters which are according to international law essentially within their jurisdiction. They are so protected, not by virtue of any reservation, but in consequence of the fact that if a matter is exclusively within the domestic jurisdiction of a State, not circumscribed by any obligation stemming from a source of international law as formulated in Article 38 of its Statute, *the Court must inevitably reject the claim as being without foundation in international law*.[3]

[1] *Id.* at 123.

[2] See *e.g.*, Dubisson, *La Cour Internationale de Justice* 87 (1964); Maus, *Les Réserves dans les Déclarations d'Acceptation de la Juridiction de la Cour Internationale de Justice* 43 (1959); Rolin, "The International Court of Justice and Domestic Jurisdiction," 8 *Int'l Org.* 36, 39–40 (1954); Kelsen, *The Law of the United Nations* 784 (1950); Kelsen, *The Law of the United Nations* 784 (1950). And see Sohn, "The Jurisdiction of the International Court of Justice," 35 *A.B.A.J.* 924, 925 (1949); Hudson, "Compulsory Jurisdiction of the International Court of Justice," 40 *Proc. Am. Soc. Int'l L.* 12, 19 (1946).

[3] [1959] *I.C.J. Rep.* 6, 122 (Sep. Op. of Judge Lauterpacht) (Emphasis added). This argument leads to the following distinction: when matters of domestic jurisdiction are explicitly reserved, the Court will declare itself "without jurisdiction," and when no such reservation exists the Court will reject the claim on the merits if its domestic character is

This thesis conceives, therefore, of the plea of domestic jurisdiction as a substantive plea, a defense on the merits, and results in applying the content of Article 2(7) of the Charter to the merits of all cases before the Court. It should, however, be made clear that, with the possible exception of the *Electricity Company of Sofia Case* (1939), the International Court has always agreed with the parties' characterization of this plea as a preliminary objection; though it had, quite often, to join it to the merits before pronouncing on its validity.

4. *Judicial Discretion and the Considerations of Propriety*

Even when all the objective requirements for the exercise of its jurisdiction are satisfied, the Court, being a "judicial" organ dealing with "sovereign" states, may still prefer not to act on the case submitted to it. This may be due to considerations related to the proper administration of justice and may be motivated by what could be termed the "judicial policy" of the Court.

a. The contentious procedure

In the contentious procedure, a few cases have presented the Court with the issue of the subjective aspect of the propriety of its acting when the acceptance of its jurisdiction was beyond doubt. Such cases as the *Serbian Loans Case* (1929), the *Brazilian Loans Case* (1929), the *Free Zones Case* (1929), (1932) the *Société Commerciale de Belgique Case* (1939) before the Permanent Court, and the *Haya de la Torre Case* (1951), the *Monetary Gold Case* (1954), and the *North Cameroons Case* (1963) before the present Court, provide perhaps clear instances of this practice. The attitude of the Court toward the propriety of answering questions submitted to it in these cases was discussed elsewhere with the exception of the practice followed in the last two cases. Both of these cases present, however, the clearest examples of the Court's refusal to adjudicate on a matter within its jurisdiction merely for considerations of propriety.

The relevant facts of the first case (the *Monetary Gold Case* (1954)) are as follows. The Governments of the United States, the United Kingdom and France accepted as defendants the jurisdiction of the

established. *Accord*, Maus, *supra*, p. 232, note 2 at 111–2; Waldock, *supra*, p. 231, note 4 at 124. See also, for the thesis that in principle every preliminary objection based on the domestic character of the dispute should be joined to the merits; Perrin, "L'Affaire de L'Interhandel – Phase des exceptions préliminaires," 16 *Annuaire Suisse de Droit International* 73, 160–1 (1959).

Present Court for the purpose of the determination of (i) whether it was proper that a certain amount of gold (originally owned by Albania but found by the Allied Forces in Germany) should be delivered to the United Kingdom in partial satisfaction of the *Corfu Channel* judgment and (ii) whether the gold should be delivered to Italy on the ground of the priority of its claim to the gold over that of the United Kingdom. This acceptance of jurisdiction was made to meet any application covering these two questions or either of them made "by Italy or by Albania or by both." As a result, Italy instituted the proceedings, asking the Court to determine the two questions, each being drafted as a separate submission. Yet, in the course of preparing its memorial, this Government, noting the absence of any consent by Albania, which was virtually a party to the dispute at least as presented in the first question, submitted what it termed a "Preliminary Question." In this, it requested the Court:

> ... to adjudicate on the Preliminary Question of its jurisdiction to deal with the merits of the claim set forth under No. 1 of the Submissions of the Application...[1]

Dealing with this question, the only preliminary objection in the history of the International Court to be submitted by the applicant, the Court decided first by a unanimous vote that in the absence of the consent of Albania, it was not authorized to adjudicate upon the first Italian Submission.[2] Then it moved to consider "whether it can adjudicate upon the second claim in the Italian Application," i.e., the question of priority between the claims of the United Kingdom and Italy over the gold, which was not mentioned in the "Preliminary Question." Here, the Court established, despite the apparent fact that this question concerned only the two parties to the case, that it was in reality dependent on the first claim. Therefore, the Court concluded that "inasmuch as it cannot adjudicate on the first Italian claim, it must refrain from examining the question of priority between the claim of Italy and that of the United Kingdom."[3] Only one judge dissented on this point, calling for a declaratory judgment on the issue of priority without prejudging the question of the validity of the first Italian claim.[4]

[1] [1954] *I.C.J. Rep.* 19, 22.

[2] *Id.* at 33. Judges McNair and Read found that there was a "fundamental defect" in the application due to the absence of Albania *as a respondent* in the case. *Id.* at 35–8.

[3] *Id.* at 34.

[4] *Id.* at 43–4 (Diss. Op. of Judge Levi Carneiro). The Counsel of Italy in this case stated that his Government would not object to the examination of the question of priority "in a hypothetical form independently of the examination of the first Italian claim," but the

It is interesting to observe that on declining to deal with the two submissions in the Italian application, the Court has cautiously avoided the use of the term "jurisdiction" and was content to declare that it was not authorized to, or could not adjudicate upon these submissions. Such was certainly a careful choice of the words, at least in relation to the second submission where the consideration that kept the Court from adjudicating upon it was the Court's own concept of the proper administration of justice rather than any defect in the consent of the parties.

In the second case (the *Northern Cameroons Case* (1963)), the Court was asked by the Cameroon Republic to declare that the United Kingdom has breached its obligation as a trustee over the territory of Northern Cameroon. This territory was already integrated with the Federation of Nigeria as a result of a plebiscite arranged for by the United Kingdom in its capacity as a trustee. The jurisdiction of the Court was based on the trusteeship agreement that was in force at the time of seizing the Court but was terminated only two days thereafter. Though this termination was an extrinsic fact that should not normally influence the Court's jurisdiction as explained in Chapter III *supra*, the Court declined the exercise of its jurisdiction in the case. Affirming that "even if, when seised of an application, the Court finds that it has jurisdiction, it is not obliged to exercise it in all cases," the Court clearly stated that:

> If the Court is satisfied, whatever the nature of the relief claimed, that to adjudicate on the merits of an application would be inconsistent with its judicial function, it should refuse to do so.[1]

Then noticing that the termination of trusteeship over the territory and its integration with a third state has rendered adjudication "devoid of purpose," the Court considered that further proceedings in the case would not be "a proper discharge of its duties." As a result, the Court reached by ten votes to five the following carefully worded conclusion:

> . . . the Court has not felt called upon to pass expressly upon the several submissions of the Respondent, in the form in which they have been cast. The Court finds that the proper limits of its judicial function do not permit it to entertain the claims submitted to it in the Application of which it has been seised, with a view to a decision having the authority of *res judicata* between the Republic of Cameroon and the United Kingdom. Any judgment which the Court might pronounce would be without object.[2]

Court refused to consider this a formal request from the applicant Government adding that "it would, in any event, constitute a new proposition which is not based on the Washington Statement and to which the respondent States have not expressed agreement." *Id.* at 34.

[1] [1963] *I.C.J. Rep.* 15, 37.

[2] *Id.* at 38.

The conclusion to be derived from the review of these cases is that judicial discretion and considerations of propriety can overrule the technical principles of jurisdiction. For jurisdiction may be established over an issue that the Court will not, nonetheless, adjudicate upon. The independence of the issue of propriety from that of jurisdiction was not, however, as clear in most of the previously mentioned cases where judicial discretion was used along with the rules of jurisdiction to support the conclusion that the Court was with, or without, jurisdiction.

b. The advisory procedure

In the advisory function, considerations of propriety assume a greater part as the Court becomes more conscious of its position as an organ of the United Nations and is, in practice, faced in this field with many political considerations not normally present in the contentious procedure. Even the Permanent Court, which was not an organ of the League of Nations, had always to tackle the problem of reconciling this advisory function with its character as a court. As Judge Winiarski explained in his separate opinion in the *Judgments of the Administrative Tribunal of the I.L.O. Case* (1956), the Permanent Court was faced primarily with two dangers: the danger threatening its prestige as a Court of justice, and the danger of turning the advisory jurisdiction into a compulsory jurisdiction over existing disputes.[1] For this reason it maintained the power not to answer the request for an advisory opinion and made the exercise of its advisory function subject to judicial forms and safeguards – an attitude that resulted, as seen before, in declining jurisdiction in the *Eastern Carelia Case* (1923).

It also insisted whenever the question was raised that its advisory function was confined to legal disputes. The present Court, which has never openly discarded the doctrine of its predecessor in this respect has, however, developed, particularly in the *Peace Treaties Case* (1950), the *Reservations Case* (1951), the *Judgments of the Administrative, Tribunal Case* (1956), and the *Certain Expenses of the United Nations Case* (1962), a simple presumption according to which no request for an advisory opinion will, in principle, be refused. Yet this does not mean, as a matter of principle, that the Court has surrendered in the advisory field the judicial freedom it enjoys as a court of justice. On the contrary, the Court has emphasized in its latest Opinion that its advisory power is "of a discretionary character." Noting that it can

[1] See [1956] *I.C.J. Rep.* 77, 104 (Sep. Op. of Judge Winiarski).

answer only a request on a legal question, it emphatically added:

But even if the question is a legal one, which the Court is undoubtedly competent to answer, it may nonetheless decline to do so. As this Court said in its Opinion of 30 March 1950, the permissive character of Article 65 gives the Court the power to examine whether the circumstances of the case are of such a character as should lead it to decline to answer the Request (*Interpretation of Peace Treaties with Bulgaria, Hungary and Roumania* (First Phase) *I.C.J. Rep.* 1950, 72).[1]

The Court, however, followed this by repeating its previous pronouncements to the effect that "only compelling reasons should lead it to refuse to give a requested advisory opinion." Then referring to the argument that the determination of whether certain expenses of the United Nations in the Middle East and the Congo constituted "expenses of the Organization" as provided for in Article 17(2) of the Charter was a matter intertwined with political questions, it said:

It is true that most interpretations of the Charter of the United Nations have political significance, great or small. In the nature of things it could not be otherwise. The Court, however, cannot attribute a political character to a request which invites it to undertake an essentially judicial task, namely the interpretation of a treaty provision.[2]

Although the last part of this statement represents another application of the technique referred to before[3] according to which the Court tends to characterize requests for advisory opinions as abstract questions of treaty interpretation, the premises adopted in the first part of it amount to something more. The fact that the question submitted has a political significance is not "a compelling reason" for declining to answer the request. Presumably the statement requires a stricter standard for defining political questions, a standard which will hardly be satisfied as long as the question submitted could be characterized as a matter of treaty interpretation and, therefore, a legal question.

By first laying the presumption favoring the exercise of its advisory jurisdiction and then by ignoring the political significance of the question submitted as long as the latter could be qualified as a legal question, the Court has certainly used its judicial discretion to maintain the most effective, if not the widest, performance of its advisory function. It has, nonetheless, kept its hands untied, at least in theory, to decline the exercise of such a function when this is justified by "the

[1] *Certain Expenses of the United Nations Case*, [1962] *I.C.J. Rep.* 151, 155.

[2] *Ibid.* But see *id.* at 254 (Diss. Op. of Judge Koretsky).

[3] See Chapter IV, *supra* at 124–25.

circumstances of the case." As the Court did in the *Constitution of the Maritime Safety Committee of IMCO Case* (1960),[1] it will normally invoke its "judicial character" whenever this is needed to enable it to avoid answering questions of political nature.

5. *The Court as a* juge d'exception

The fact that the International Court is a court of limited jurisdiction (*juridiction d'attribution*) and not of general jurisdiction (*juridiction de droit commun*) has not been used by the Court as frequently as by other international tribunals to justify a restrictive approach toward jurisdiction.[2] True, the Permanent Court referred early in its second judgment and on many later occasions to the relevance of the fact that "its jurisdiction is limited,"[3] but nothing in the practice of the Court can be taken as an evidence that this fact has resulted in a particularly restrictive outlook in the exercise of the *compétence de la compétence,* even in cases where the consent of the parties was in doubt. The Court has, on the contrary, extended on several occasions its jurisdiction to areas not categorically provided for by the Statute (as when it affirmed its jurisdiction to render declaratory judgments) and to matters not specifically referred to it by the parties (as when it extended its jurisdiction to deal with issues incident to those submitted to it). It will not be accurate, however, to assume that the fact that the Court's jurisdiction is limited has no effect whatsoever on the manner according to which this jurisdiction is determined in specific cases. This fact, it should be noticed, has precluded the Court from devising a general presumption in favor of jurisdiction in contentious cases. It has, consequently, kept the maxim *boni judicis est ampliare jurisdictionem* without relevance to the *compétence de la compétence* as exercised in such cases, at least insofar as it may conflict

[1] See [1960] *I.C.J. Rep.* 150, 153: "The statements submitted to the Court have shown that linked with the question put to it there are others of a political nature. The Court as a judicial body is however bound in the exercise of its advisory function, to remain faithful to the requirements of its judicial character." And *cf., Interpretation of Peace Treaties Case (Second Phase),* [1950] *I.C.J. Rep.* 221, 229 (It is the duty of the Court to interpret the treaties, not to revise them); *International Status of South-West Africa Case,* [1950] *I.C.J. Rep.* 128, 140 (It is not for the Court to decide on the political or moral duties of the mandatory power).

[2] See instances of the invocation of the exceptional character of the tribunal as a ground for restrictive interpretation of the jurisdictional instrument in *Wapa (État serbe-croate-slovène) c. Républic d'Autriche,* 3 *Rec. des déc. des trib. arb. mixtes* 720, 727–8 (1923); *Von Tiedmann (Allemagne) c. État Polonais,* 6 *id.* 997, 1001 (1926); *Sorropoulos (Grèce) c. État Bulgare,* 7 *id.* at 47, 52–3 (1927); compare *Judgments of the Administrative Tribunal of the I.L.O. Case,* [1956] *I.C.J. Rep.* 77, 97 (Adv. Op.) And see Bos, *Les Conditions du Procès en Droit International Public* 103–4 (1957).

[3] See *Mavrommatis Palestine Concessions Case, P.C.I.J.,* ser. A, No. 2 at 16 (1924).

with the rule of consent.[1] This, of course, does not apply to the Court's advisory function. The latter does not, technically, cover a "limited jurisdiction" and has been considered by the present Court at least, a duty that should in principle be performed.

C. TECHNIQUES BASED ON THE ASCERTAINMENT OF JURISDICTIONAL FACTS

1. The Ascertainment of the Exhaustion of Diplomatic Negotiations

The condition that the resort to the Court should be made only after the failure to solve the dispute through the diplomatic channel is usually mentioned as a requirement in the admissibility of claims before the Court. If it is not specifically provided for in the jurisdictional instruments, it is invoked as a necessary manifestation of the requirement of the existence of a dispute.[2] However, the attitude of the Court has been generally to the effect that prior negotiations are not necessary if they are not explicitly provided for and that when they are required, they will be understood in the most permissive and practical terms.

This attitude was made clear in the early works of the Permanent Court. In the second case submitted to that Court, Greece was suing Great Britain for the alleged violations of the rights of a Greek citizen. The jurisdictional instrument provided that only disputes that "cannot be settled by negotiations" could be submitted to the Court. There was evidence that the individual Greek citizen had had lengthy discussions with the British Government over his case but the subsequent communications between the two Governments were characterized, as the Court acknowledged, by their "very small number and brevity." Great Britain consequently based its objection to the Court's jurisdiction partly on the ground that the dispute had not been proved to be incapable of settlement by negotiations between the two Govern-

[1] See *Right of Passage Case*, [1957] *I.C.J. Rep.* 125, 180 (Diss. Op. of Judge *ad hoc* Chagla). See also, Lauterpacht, *The Development of International Law by the International Court* 205 (1958).

[2] At one stage of the work of the Advisory Committee of Jurists which made the first draft of the Statute of the Permanent Court, a provision was suggested providing explicitly that a case might be brought before the Court only when "it has been found impossible to settle it by diplomatic means." This provision, the contents of which were taken for granted as valid, was dropped, however, and has not appeared in the Statute of the Permanent Court or of its successor's. See, *Procès Verbaux of the Proceedings of the Advisory Committee of Jurists* 263, 725–6 (1920).

ments. The Court, noting that "the question of the importance and chances of success of diplomatic negotiations is essentially a relative one," and that the prior negotiations between the private person and the British Government have, in fact, exhausted the matter, concluded that:

> When negotiations between the private person and the authorities have already – as in the present case – defined all the points at issue between the two Governments, it would be incompatible with the flexibility which should characterize international relations to require the two Governments to reopen a discussion which has in fact already taken place and on which they rely.[1]

Along with this permissive outlook, when the jurisdictional instrument spoke of the submission of "differences of opinion" to the Court without mentioning prior negotiations, the Permanent Court found in its Judgment No. 6 that:

> ... the absence of diplomatic negotiations proving the existence of the difference of opinion which is required under Article 23 of the Convention [i.e., the compromissory clause] cannot prevent the bringing of an action in the present case. Moreover, such absence would be of no practical importance, for even if the application were on this ground declared premature, The German Government would be free to renew it immediately afterwards.[2]

This attitude was again carried on in one phase of the *Chorzow Factory Case.* The Court, asked to interpret two prior judgments in the case, observed that "according to the tenor of Article 60 of the Statute, the manifestation of the existence of the dispute in a specific manner, as for instance by diplomatic negotiations, is not required."[3]

This, along with the permissive outlook toward the concept of "dispute" itself, were however slightly shaken by the Court's judgment on the preliminary objection in the *Electricity Company of Sofia Case* (1939). A certain point in the first Submission of the Applicant Government (Belgium) had never been subject to any diplomatic negotiations prior to the filing of the application. The respondent (Bulgaria) consequently objected to the admissibility of this point on the ground of the absence of a dispute over it. The Court, establishing its jurisdiction over the rest of the case on the basis of the parties'

[1] *Mavrommatis Palestine Concessions Case, supra,* p. 238, note 3 at 15. Yet, the Court reached the above conclusion only after affirming in principle that "before a dispute can be made the subject of an action at law, its subject matter should have been clearly defined by means of diplomatic negotiations." *Ibid.* Compare, *id.* at 61, 74 (Diss. Op. of Judge Moore).

[2] *German Interests in Polish Upper Silesia, P.C.I.J.*, Ser. A, No. 6 at 22 (1925). But see, *id.* at 36–7 (Diss. Op. of Count Rostworowski).

[3] *Interpretation of Judgments Nos. 7 and 8, P.C.I.J.*, ser. A, No. 13 at 10 (1927).

declarations, excepted the above-mentioned point where it held, without any reference to prior negotiations, that:

> ... the Belgian Government has not established the existence of such a dispute and accordingly... the Belgian application cannot be entertained insofar as concerns that part of the claim...[1]

As this holding bases the inadmissibility of the claim exclusively on the lack of a dispute, without imparting this to the lack of prior negotiations, it cannot be taken as a clear departure from the earlier attitude of the Permanent Court,[2] or as imposing a new requirement for the exercise of jurisdiction.

Nothing in the attitude of the present Court seems to contradict the earlier attitude of the Permanent Court either. In many judgments, it is true, the present Court has referred to the fact that negotiations were tried but failed,[3] but nowhere did the Court express in definite terms the view that the exhaustion of negotiations was a necessary requirement for the definition of the dispute. When the question was raised in an acute form in the *Right of Passage Case* (1957), in which no explicit requirement of negotiations was mentioned in the instruments, the Court discussed the problem but found no need to settle it. For it appeared to the Court from the circumstances of the case that even:

> ... assuming that there is substance in the contention that Article 36 (2) of the Statute by referring to legal disputes establishes as a condition of the jurisdiction of the Court a requisite definition of the dispute through negotiations, the condition was complied with to the extent permitted by the circumstances of the case.[4]

It is interesting to observe, in addition, that the national judge of the respondent state in this case came outright against his Government's assertion that resort to negotiations is necessary before invoking the Court's "compulsory" jurisdiction. Describing such a resort as only "desirable," he added that: "It is clear on the authorities that what the Court has insisted upon is the mere existence of a dispute, and a

[1] *P.C.I.J.*, ser. A/B, No. 77 at 83 (1939).

[2] Compare, Hudson, *The Permanent Court of International Justice* 416 (2d ed. 1943).

[3] See *e.g.*, *Asylum Case*, [1950] *I.C.J. Rep.* 266, 273; *Haya de la Torre Case*, [1951] *I.C.J. Rep.* 71, 77–8; *Norwegian Fisheries Case*, [1951] *I.C.J. Rep.* 116, 124. Moreover, in the *Asylum Case* (*Interpretation*) as the request for the interpretation of a judgment was made on the same day of its delivery, the Court declined jurisdiction on the basis of the lack of dispute "on definite points." [1950] *I.C.J. Rep.* 395, 403.

[3] [1957] *I.C.J. Rep.* 125, 149.

dispute has been defined as a divergence of opinions or views between two states."[1]

The permissive outlook towards the requirement of diplomatic negotiations even when this is explicitly provided for in the jurisdictional title has recently found a clear manifestation in the *South-West Africa Cases* (1962). Like the *Mavrommatis* cases before the Permanent Court, these recent cases are based on a Mandate that required the dispute submitted to the Court to be one which "cannot be settled by negotiations." As no such negotiations took place between the specific parties to the *South-West Africa Cases*, the respondent Government relied on this fact as one basis for its objection to the Court's jurisdiction. However, the Court was not impressed by this argument. First it noticed that "behind the present dispute there is another and similar disagreement on points of law and fact – a similar conflict of legal views and interests – between the Respondent on the one hand, and the other Members of the United Nations holding identical views with the applicants, on the other hand." As this similar disagreement reached an impasse before the time of filing the application, and as both the written pleadings and oral arguments of the parties confirmed the continuance of this deadlock, the Court reached the conclusion that "no reasonable probability exists that further negotiations would lead to a settlement."[2] Then in a language not dissimilar from that of its predecessor in its judgment in the first *Mavrommatis* case, it affirmed that "in this respect, it is not so much the form of negotiation that matters as the attitude and views of the Parties on the substantive issues of the question involved."[3] Moreover the Court, referring to the general debate in the United Nations organs over the subject matter of the dispute, added a new point inspired by the recent developments in international relations:

> ... diplomacy by conference or parliamentary diplomacy has come to be recognized in the past four of five decades as one of the established modes of international negotiation. In cases where the disputed questions are of common interest to a group of States on one side or the other in an organized body, parliamentary or conference diplomacy has often been found to be the most practical form of negotiation.[4]

[1] *Id.* at 173 (Diss. Op. of Judge *ad hoc* Chagla). See also, *Panevezys-Saldutiskis Railway Case*, *P.C.I.J.*, ser. A/B, No. 76 at 39 (1939) (Diss. Op. of Judge Van Eysinga).

[2] [1962] *I.C.J. Rep.* 319, 345.

[3] *Id.* at 346.

[4] *Ibid.* And see *id.* at 384 (Sep. op. of Judge Bustamante) and at 433–4, 436 (Sep. Op. of Judge Jessup).

Even the individual opinions that dissented on this point did not seem to press the argument for the necessity of the exhaustion of diplomatic means (despite the provision in the Mandate). Judges Spender and Fitzmaurice, for example, though stressing that this requirement is meant to protect the parties from unnecessary and premature litigations, wrote that they "would not wish to exaggerate the extent of negotiation that may be required to establish that there has been the minimum necessary in the circumstances to make it clear that the parties cannot settle their dispute." All that was required, they thought, was only that "*some* negotiation must... in fact have taken place between the actual Parties to the proceedings before the Court, in their capacity as individual States."[1]

2. The Ascertainment of the Exhaustion of Local Remedies

The rule according to which local remedies available in the respondent state should be exhausted before a valid resort to the International Court has been observed, on the whole, with more vigilance than that shown in the observance of the exhaustion of diplomatic means. Notwithstanding the controversy over the nature of the above-mentioned rule (i.e., whether it is related to the merits of the case, to the admissibility of the claim, or to the jurisdiction of the Court *ratone temporis*),[2] it could be viewed in this respect as a rule of conflict between the jurisdiction of the International Court and that of local courts.[3] According to this rule the Court will be able to exercise its jurisdiction only after it becomes certain that the local courts have already exercised theirs without according justice to the claimant. As such, the rule is not of general applicability. It is generally agreed that it does not apply to cases instituted by the applicant Government in its own behalf for a direct injury caused to it (rather than for an

[1] *Id.* at 561–2. *Cf.*, Perrin, "L'Affaire de L'Interhandel – Phase des exceptions préliminaires," 16 *Annuaire Suisse de Droit International* 73, 146–49 (1959).

[2] See a characterization of the rule as a substantive requirement conditioning a state's successful espousal of private claims before international tribunals in Lauterpacht, *The Development of International Law by the International Court* 350 (1958); Hudson, *International Court* 350 (1958); Hudson, *International Tribunals* 84 (1944) (and his dissent in the *Panevezys-Saldutiskis Railway Case, P.C.I.J.*, ser. A/B, No. 76 at 47 (1939). And see the requirement regarded as "a dilatory objection *ratione temporis*" in Rosenne, *The Time Factor* 71 (1960), and as a question of jurisdiction only when it is provided for in the jurisdictional title but otherwise a question of admissibility, in Waldock, *supra*, p. 231, note 4 at 115. Most other writers characterize the rule as relating to the admissibility of the claim. See generally, Law, *The Local Remedies Rule in International Law* 39–44 (1961); Perrin, *supra*, note 1 at 180–83.

[3] See this characterization as discussed in Fawcett, "The Exhaustion of Local Remedies: Substance or Procedure," 31 *Brit. Yb. Int'l L.* 452, 454 (1959).

injury caused to one of its nationals by the act or omission of the respondent). It has also been argued before the present Court that the rule has no application even in the latter case (indirect injury) if there was no previously established link of residence, contract, or otherwise between the injured individual and the respondent state. Also, the rule was said to be inapplicable when the injury results from a breach of international law and not of local law. In verifying such arguments and others to the same effect (a process which usually requires the joinder of the objections based on the non-exhaustion of local remedies to the merits of the case), the Court has shaped its attitude toward this highly controversial problem. Such an attitude, it should immediately be added, is still in many of its aspects far from being clearly defined.

For the Permanent Court, the question was first involved, though it was not raised, in the case concerning *Certain German Interests in Polish Upper Silesia* (1925). Germany sued Poland before the Court for injuries done by the latter to some German private interests. A part of the same dispute was, at the time of instituting the proceedings, pending before the German-Polish Mixed Arbitral Tribunal and, as related to the Factory at Chorzów, the dispute was also before a Polish civil court. Poland, therefore, after submitting that the Court had no jurisdiction because the dispute was, as it alleged, not covered by the treaty text invoked by Germany as the basis of jurisdiction, added, in the alternative, that the claims involved could not be entertained until the mixed arbitral tribunal had given judgment. No reliance was made on the fact that one aspect of the dispute was also before a local court. The Permanent Court, on its part, found first that it had jurisdiction under the treaty invoked; then, turning to the alternative objection, it dealt exclusively with the question of the pendency of the dispute before the arbitral tribunal. This, it noticed, was not a question of *litispendence* for both the subject matter and the parties to the dispute before the tribunal were different from those before the Court. As to the fact that an aspect of the dispute was before a local court in Poland, the Court simply made no reference to its effect, though it mentioned in the part of the judgment related to the facts that:

This action is still before that Court [the Civil Court of Kattowitz] which, however, decided on December 7, 1923, that there was no pendency, as notice of the action had not yet been served on the *Procurature générale* at Warsaw.[1]

[1] *P.C.I.J.*, ser. A, No. 6 at 10 (1925).

This attitude was explained in a later phase of the dispute. For after obtaining a decision on the merits of this case in Judgment No. 7, the parties disagreed as to its execution, and Germany brought a new case confined to a claim for indemnity related to the Chorzoẃ Factory. Poland objected again to the Court's jurisdiction on the ground that the compromissory clause did not contemplate differences in regard to reparations and, in the second place, because there were available other "special jurisdictions for claims which private persons might assert in the event of the suppression or diminution of their rights." Speaking of these special jurisdictions, Poland referred only to arbitral tribunals provided for by treaties in force. As a result the Court began its dealing with this second objection by the following remark:

It must first of all be observed that any jurisdiction which the Polish Courts may have does not enter into account. For the act on the part of the Polish Government, which the Court has held not to be in conformity with the Geneva Convention, consisted in the application of Articles 2 and 5 of the Polish law of July 14th, 1920, introduced into Polish Upper Silesia by the law of June 16th, 1922, which application, in the opinion of the Court (Judgment No. 7), is in itself a measure contrary to Article 6 and the following articles of the Convention. The Court of Huta Królewska (Königshütte) effected this application by ordering the entry in the land register of the Polish Treasury as owner of the factory in place of the Oberschlesische [the German company]. Accordingly, Poland has not argued that the Polish Courts have jurisdiction in regard to separation.[1]

This statement clearly establishes the first limitation on the rule of exhaustion of local remedies as understood by the Court. The Court will not look for such exhaustion if it is clear that the resort to local courts will not result in any satisfaction (e.g., because local courts have no jurisdiction over the case). The latter fact was not contested by the respondent state and, therefore, there was no difficulty as to who was to decide whether or not local courts had jurisdiction – a question that was to arise later in the *Panevezys-Saldutiskis Railway Case* (1939).

Another case between Germany and Poland, the *Administration of the Prince Von Pless Case*, revealed another aspect of the attitude of the Permanent Court toward this issue. After Germany had instituted the proceedings in which it espoused certain claims of Prince Von Pless (a Polish citizen of German origin) against Poland, the latter filed a preliminary objection against the admissibility of the case based, *inter alia*, on the non-exhaustion of remedies available in Polish law.[2]

[1] *Chorzoẃ Factory Case*, *P.C.I.J.*, ser. A, No. 9 at 26 (1927).
[2] See the Polish Preliminary Objection in *P.C.I.J.*, ser. C, No. 70 at 130, 133–8.

The Court noted in relation to this latter argument that Prince Von Pless first appealed to the competent Polish Commission against the amount of tax for which he had been assessed and then appealed against this Commission's decisions to the Supreme Polish Administrative Tribunal, whose decision was not yet given. Then referring to the German opposition to the application in this case of the local remedies rule, the Court added that:

> [It] does not consider it necessary to pass upon the question of the applicability of the principle as to the exhaustion of internal means of redress in the present Order since, in any event, it will certainly be an advantage to the Court as regards the points which have to be established in the case, to be acquainted with the final decision of the Supreme Polish Administrative Tribunal upon the appeals brought by the Prince Von Pless and now pending before that Tribunal...[1]

As a result, the Court followed this pragmatic approach by deciding that it would give an extension of the time-limits for the filing of the documents of the written proceedings on the merits if the Polish Agent so requested on the ground that the Polish Tribunal had not yet pronounced its judgment. This was made subject to the condition that the German Agent would not establish that there had been an unwarrantable delay in the delivery of the local judgment calculated to prejudice the proper operation of the treaty under which the case was brought.[2] Such an extension was, accordingly, given on the request of Poland, no objection being made by the German Agent.[3] Although the case was later discontinued before any judgment on the preliminary objection, the Court, by allowing the extension of the time-limits to a date when the local tribunal was expected to have given its final judgment, proved to have looked at the requirement of the exhaustion of local remedies (not as yet established in the case) in the most liberal manner. If the exhaustion of local remedies was required – the Court seemed to argue – then it needed not to be fulfilled at the moment of the filing of the application as long as it was possible to allow its fulfillment in the course of the proceedings.

The objection to the admissibility of the claim on the same basis was then invoked in the *Losinger Co. Case* (1936) where it was regarded "as a part of the defense on the merits, or at any rate as being founded on arguments which might be employed for the purposes of that defense."[4] The objection was therefore joined to the merits, but the

[1] *P.C.I.J.*, ser. A/B, No. 52 at 16 (Order of February 4, 1933).
[2] *Id.* at 17.
[3] See *P.C.I.J.*, ser. A/B, No. 57 at 169 (Order of July 4, 1933).
[4] See *P.C.I.J.*, ser. A/B, No. 67 at 23 (Order of June 27, 1936).

case was later discontinued before any further developments took place. Similarly, the non-exhaustion of local remedies was raised by Spain in the *Borchgrave Case* (1937) along with an objection to the Court's jurisdiction. After dismissing the latter, the Court noticed that the Advocate for the Spanish Government had withdrawn the plea of the non-exhaustion of local remedies as a preliminary objection but maintained it as a part of his defense in order that it might be joined to the merits. The Court, however, refused to undertake such a joinder. For, as it correctly put it, "it is possible to join to the merits only objections which are before the Court. The withdrawal of the preliminary objection leaves nothing of it as such to be joined to the merits."[1]

The first occasion on which the Permanent Court found an objection based on the local remedies rule to be well founded is the *Panevezys-Saldutiskis Case* (1939). After the objection was joined to the merits in this case,[2] which, as all the previously mentioned cases, was a case of "indirect injury" to the applicant state, the Court devoted a great part of its judgment to a discussion of the rule. There was no disagreement between the parties (Lithuania and Estonia) as to the existence and validity of the rule of local remedies. However, the Estonian Agent maintained that the rule was not applicable in that case for two reasons which might seem somewhat contradictory: First, because the courts in Lithuania could not entertain a suit in the same case and, second, because on one essential point in the dispute the highest court in Lithuania had already given a decision adverse to the Estonian company's claim. The Court agreed first of all that in principle:

> There can be no need to resort to the municipal courts if those courts have no jurisdiction to afford relief; nor is it necessary again to resort to those courts if the result must be a repetition of a decision already given.[3]

Then, alluding to the fact that what was involved in the case was property rights and contractual rights of individuals, the Court dealt first with the contention that Lithuanian courts had no jurisdiction:

> The question whether or not the Lithuanian courts have jurisdiction to entertain a particular suit depends on Lithuanian law and is one on which the Lithuanian courts alone can pronounce a final decision. It is not for this Court to consider the arguments which have been addressed to it for the purpose either of establishing the jurisdiction of the Lithuanian tribunals by adducing particular

[1] *P.C.I.J.*, ser. A/B, No. 72 at 169 (1937).
[2] See *P.C.I.J.*, ser. A/B, No. 75 at 56 (1938).
[3] *P.C.I.J.*, ser. A/B, No. 76 at 18 (1939).

provisions of the law in force in Lithuania, or of denying the jurisdiction of those tribunals by attributing a particular character (seizure *jure imperii*) to the act of the Lithuanian Government. Until it has been clearly shown that the Lithuanian courts have no jurisdiction to entertain [the] suit..., the Court cannot accept the contention of the Estonian Agent that the rule as to the exhaustion of local remedies does not apply in this case because Lithuanian law affords no means of redress.[1]

As to the second ground of the objection, the Court simply decided that the domestic decision cited by the respondent had no relevance to the issue before the Court and that another opinion of the Lithuanian *Conseil d'Etat*, which was also cited, was not a judicial decision in the proper sense.

As a result, the Court declared, for the first time, that "the objection regarding the non-exhaustion of the remedies afforded by municipal law is well founded," and concluded as a result that "the claim presented by the Estonian Government cannot be entertained (*est irrecevable*)."[2] It is interesting to notice that the Court did not simply prolong the proceedings till the applicant exhausted the local remedies; nor did it suspend the case till such measures were taken.[3] It found the case completely inadmissible, thus dis-seizing itself of it – a step to be repeated only in the *Interhandel Case* (1959) before the present Court.

The last occasion for the invocation of the local remedies rule before the Permanent Court was the *Electricity Company of Sofia Case* (1939). As explained before, Belgium brought this case before the Court on two different bases – a treaty between the parties, and their mutual declarations made under Article 36(2) of the Statute. Only the treaty provided explicitly for the exhaustion of local remedies as a condition for the valid submission of disputes brought under it before the Court. The latter, considering that it had power to decide the claim under both instruments as concurrent bases of jurisdiction, had to deal with an objection to its jurisdiction, based in part on the non-exhaustion of local remedies. In fact, the claim had already been brought before

[1] *Id.* at 19. Compare, *Forests in Central Rhodopia Case* (Greece *v.* Bulgaria) 3 *U.N. Rep Int'l Arb. Awards* 1406, 1420 (1933); 28 *Am. J. Int'l L.* 760, 789 (1934).

[2] *P.C.I.J.*, ser. A/B, No. 76 at 22 (1939). But see, *id.* at 35–7 (Diss. Op. of Judge Van Eysinga: The rule has no application when jurisdiction is unreservedly accepted by declarations made under Art. 36(2) of the Statute); *id.* at 47 (Diss. Op. of Judge Hudson: Objection based on the rule relates to the merits); *id.* at 51–5 (Diss. Op. of Judge Erich: Circumstances of the case justified departure from the rule).

[3] See a discussion of this suspensive effect of the rule in the *Electricity Company of Sofia and Bulgaria Case, P.C.I.J.*, ser. A/B, No. 77 at 98 (Diss. Op. of Judge Anzilotti) where he found it inappropriate in the circumstances of that case. See also, Rosenne, *supra* p. 243, note 2 at 71 n. 4; Law, *supra*, p. 243, note 2 at 52.

municipal courts prior to the institution of proceedings. However, this institution of proceedings took place only after the delivery of a decision from the court of appeal in the respondent state – a decision which according to the law of that state was still subject to further "appeal" to the court of cassation. Resort to this latter court was, it is true, already made, but its decision was given only during the proceedings before the Permanent Court. Discussing its jurisdiction first under the treaty, the Permanent Court found that: "The local remedies rule contemplated by the Treaty... implies the exhaustion of all appeals, including appeals to the court of cassation, a decision by which alone renders the judgment final either by annulling the judgment of the Court of Appeal and sending the case back to a re-trial, or by rejecting the appeal."[1] Accordingly, the Belgian application was found to be missing one of the conditions that the treaty required for invoking jurisdiction under its provisions. The treaty was, therefore, excluded as a basis of jurisdiction. Yet, in discussing its jurisdiction on the other ground (the declarations) the Court made no reference to the local remedies rule. It should be recalled in this respect that although such remedies were not completely exhausted at the time of instituting the proceedings, they became so before the judgment on the preliminary objection. It is, therefore, on this ground, and not because the requirement was altogether dispensed with under the declarations, that the Court's attitude should be understood. Consequently, it could be concluded that the Court's apparent strictness in viewing the requirement under the treaty was mitigated by the Court's flexibility in considering its jurisdiction under the declarations. One may, indeed, question whether the Court would not have found in the fact that local remedies were actually exhausted in the course of the proceedings an adequate basis for dismissing the objection were its jurisdiction in this case based solely on the treaty.[2]

The plea of the non-exhaustion of local remedies was raised before the present Court in at least five cases, but only once has this Court found it necessary to pronounce on it. This was in the *Interhandel Case* (1959). The plea was invoked by the United States among other bases

[1] *P.C.I.J.*, ser. A/B, No. 77 at 79 (1939).

[2] Some of the individual judges who found in the treaty the sole basis of jurisdiction were of the opinion that the objection should be dismissed. See *id.* at 114 (Diss. Op. of Judge Van Eysinga), at 139 (Sep. Op. of Judge de Visscher) and at 144 (Sep. Op. of Judge Erich). Typical of their argument is this statement from Judge Van Eysinga's dissent: "... it seems that it would be a pure formality to uphold the objection based on the local remedies rule, at a moment when these remedies have long been exhausted, and on the ground that an at earlier moment they had not yet been exhausted." *Id.* at 139.

of its objection to the Court's jurisdiction. The Court, without joining the objection to the merits, characterized this plea as "directed against the admissibility of the application" and discussed ahead of it the other objections related to "jurisdiction." Yet, as shown before, without reaching a definite conclusion on the objection based on the invocation of the "self-judging" reservation in the American declaration, the Court held the application inadmissible after the United States Supreme Court reopened the local remedies which were exhausted at the time of seisin. The local remedies rule was described in this judgment as "a well-established rule of customary international law," that applies *a fortiori* when domestic proceedings are still pending.[1] This is, however, the only case where an objection based on the rule was upheld by the present Court. As in the *Panevezys-Saldutiskis Case* (1939), the jurisdiction in this case was alleged to be based on declarations of acceptance. This fact would firmly overrule any contention to the effect that the rule has no application under the Optional Clause system, for, ironically, it was only in this framework that the rule was ever applied by the International Court to the effect of rendering the case inadmissible. Also, the judgment in the *Interhandel Case* did not have a suspensive effect but rather resulted in dis-seizing the Court completely of the case. However, the *Interhandel Case* differs in its application of the local remedies rule from the *Panevezys-Saldutiskis Case* in at least two aspects. In the latter case, there was no objection to the Permanent Court's proper "jurisdiction," *and* the judgment on the admissibility of the claim was given after a careful examination of the merits; whereas, the decision in the *Interhandel Case* was delivered – to the disappointment of many – regardless of an undecided objection to the Court's jurisdiction and before any detailed study of the merits.

In other cases before the present Court, the question was raised and even discussed in detail though no decision on it was found necessary. In the *Ambatielos Case* (1953), the Court was determining only whether the United Kingdom was under an obligation to arbitrate a certain claim with Greece according to a treaty between them. As a result, it refused to pronounce on whether Mr. Ambatielos had exhausted the local remedies in British courts. This question, the Court observed, presented "arguments in defence directed to the admissibility of the

[1] See [1959] *I.C.J. Rep.* 6, 27. The reopening of local remedies after the seisin of the Court is thus a change in a jurisdictional fact which influences the Court's attitude. However, it may be reasonable to expect the Court to keep the effect of this change within limits so that it may not cutail the admissibility of the claim for an indefinite period.

Ambatielos claim and are not in any way related to the question whether the claim is based on the Treaty of 1886."[1] The plea of the non-exhaustion of local remedies was also raised in the second phase of the *Nottebohm Case* (1955), but the Court found no occasion to pronounce on it as it held the claim inadmissible on another ground related to the nationality of the individual in question. The *Norwegian Loans Case* (1957), also decided on a completely different ground, presented nevertheless important questions related to the local remedies rule. Among these is the question of whether the application of the rule is conditioned by the existence of a link between the injured individual and the *respondent* state. France argued in this case that the rule can be applicable only to cases in which the injured alien has voluntarily entered and established his residence in the territory of the respondent state.[2] This contention was strongly objected to by Norway which referred to the arbitral awards in the *Finnish Shipowners Case* (1934) and the *Ambatielos Arbitration* (1956), along with many writings on international law, as evidence of a practice to the contrary.[3] The question, left unsettled in the *Norwegian Loans Case* (1957) [4] was raised again in the *Aerial Incident of 27 July 1955 Case* (Israel v. Bulgaria) (1959). It is to be recalled that Israel brought this case before the Court in its own behalf and in behalf of injured individuals. By stressing the direct injury done to its own interests and the breach of international law involved (as revealed in its first submission), Israel argued that the local remedies rule had no application whatsoever in that case.[5] It also argued that the rule was not applicable in relation to the claims of the injured individuals because there was "no link of any kind between any of the victims and any of the individual claimants and the Bulgarian State."[6] The Court again did not find it necessary to pronounce on the question [7] as it found itself without

[1] [1953] *I.C.J. Rep.* 10, 23. The same plea was later presented to the arbitration commission which upheld it as one basis for the invalidity of the claim of Greece. See [Foreign Office] *Award of Commission of Arbitration – The Ambatielos Claim* 27–32 (1956); 12 *U.N. Rep. Int'l Arb. Awards* 91, 118–123 (1956).

[2] See *Case of Certain Norwegian Loans*, Pleadings, Oral Arguments and Documents 408–9 (*I.C.J.* 1957).

[3] See *id.* at 451–5. And see the *Finnish Shipowners Case*, 3 *U.N. Rep. Int'l Arb. Awards* 1481 (1934), and the *Ambatielos Claim*, 12 *id.* at 91, 118–23. In both these arbitral cases the injured individuals had not resided in the respondent state, though they had contractual links with it.

[4] Compare [1957] *I.C.J. Rep.* 9, 97 (Diss. Op. of Judge Read).

[5] See *Aerial Incident of 27 July 1955*, Pleadings, Oral Arguments and Documents 526–7, 530–1 (*I.C.J.* 1959).

[6] *Id.* at 532.

[7] See [1959] *I.C.J. Rep.* 127, 146.

jurisdiction over the case. The requirement of a ' link" between the injured alien and the wrong-doing state as a prerequisite for the applicability of the local remedies rule is still, therefore, an open question. This is not so as to the non-applicability of the rule in cases of exclusive direct injury to the applicant state. No contention was ever made before the Court against this limitation. For, in fact, in all cases where the rule was invoked, it was raised against a Government instituting proceedings at least partly in behalf of injured individuals.[1]

On the whole, the International Court has not had enough occasions to establish a clearly defined doctrine on the question of the exhaustion of local remedies. It has made clear, however, that the fact of the non-exhaustion of such remedies will affect the admissibility of the claim only in certain types of cases and provided that it is proved beyond doubt.

3. *The Ascertainment of the Nationality of The Claim*

Like the exhaustion of local remedies, the nationality of the claim is a relevant jurisdictional fact in cases where the applicant Government is taking up a private claim against the respondent Government before the Court. For the established rule is, as stated by the Permanent Court, to the effect that "in the absence of a special agreement, it is the bond of nationality between the State and the individual which alone confers upon the State the right of diplomatic protection, and it is as part of the function of diplomatic protection that the right to take up a claim and to ensure respect for the rules of international law must be envisaged."[2]

The ascertainment of the nationality of the claim as a requirement for the valid exercise of jurisdiction has been commonplace in the work of arbitral tribunals. Inspired by the facts and, consequently, the equity of each case, these tribunals applied different standards in accepting evidence concerning the fact of nationality to the extent

[1] Attempts to exclude the application of the rule by contending that the dispute is primarily related to the applicant's own interests and resulted from a breach of international law is therefore commonplace. The argument was unsuccessfully made by Switzerland in the *Interhandel Case*, [1959] *I.C.J. Rep.* 6, 27, 28–9, and was raised, as seen above, by Israel in its dispute with Bulgaria. See generally, Meron, "The Incidence of the Rule of Exhaustion of Local Remedies," 35 *Brit. Yb. Int'l L.* 83, 84–94 (1959).

[2] *Panevezys-Saldutiskis Railway Case*, *P.C.I.J.*, ser. A/B. No. 76 at 16 (1939). And see *Reparations for Injuries suffered in the Service of the United Nations Case*, [1949] *I.C.J. Rep.* 174, 181 (Adv. Op.).

that what was accepted in some cases as conclusive evidence was refused in others as inadequate for establishing this fact.[1] Some arbitral awards tended, however, to adopt a presumption of nationality based on the fact that in the normal circumstances, Governments espouse only the claims of their nationals.[2] In such a situation, the claim is presumed to have the nationality of the applicant state unless the *respondent* proves the contrary.

So established was the requirement of the nationality of the claim before the Permanent Court that this Court raised it on its own initiative in the *Prince Von Pless Case* (1933). As seen above, Germany presented this case on behalf of the Prince, who was not a German citizen but was in fact a citizen of the respondent state. However, Germany founded the institution of the proceedings on a treaty text by which the respondent state (Poland) agreed to accept the jurisdiction of the Court over "any difference of opinion," as to questions arising out of that treaty, "between the Polish Government and any one of the Principal Allied and Associated Powers, or any other Power, a Member of the Council of the League of Nations." Poland, though objecting to the admissibility of the claim on other grounds, did not seem to have found that the nationality of the individual on whose behalf the claim was brought was of any relevance to the Court's jurisdiction. However, the Court, dealing with the objections submitted by Poland, found that:

> ... the claim thus made raises a question regarding the Court's jurisdiction and as this question is connected with another, namely, whether, on the basis of Article 72, Paragraph 3, of the Geneva Convention, a State in its capacity as a Member of the Council, may claim that an indemnity be awarded to a

[1] Compare *e.g.*, *Flutie Cases* (*U.S.A.*) v. *Venezuela*, 9 *U.N. Rep. Int'l Arb. Awards* 148, 151–5 (1903) (certified copies of certificates of naturalization not considered adequate proof of the fact of citizenship), with *William A. Parker* (*U.S.A.*) v. *Mexico*, 4 *id.* 35, 37–8 (1926) (affidavit of claimant, his brother and his friend considered adequate evidence). This clear discrepancy could only be justified by the facts of the first cases where the claimants' link with the respondent state outweighed greatly any nominal relationship they had with the U.S.A. See also the fact of nationality as proved in *Edgar A. Hatton* (*U.S.A.*) v. *Mexico* 4 *id.* 329, 331 (1928) (Affidavits); *Lillian Greenlaw* (*U.S.A.*) v. *Mexico*, *id.* at 626 (1930) (voting certificate); *Robert John Lynch* (*Great Britain*) *v. Mexico*, 5 *id.* at 17, 18–9 (1929) (consular certificate and a baptismal certificate). But see the latter certificates considered not adequate as a proof in *Carlos Klemp* (*Germany*) v. *Mexico*, *id.* at 579, 582 (1927), and the same as to a U.S. passport in *Jacob Margulies* (*U.S.A.*) v. *Austria and Hungary*, 6 *id.* at 279, 281 (1929).

[2] See generally, *Administrative Decision No. V* (United States-German Mixed Claims Commission) (Op. of the American Commissioner, Mr. Anderson) 7 *U.N. Rep. Int'l Arb. Awards* 119, 121–6. But see *id.* at 131 (Opinion of the German Commissioner). And see the presumption of nationality upheld after the presentation of a *prima facie* evidence in, *e.g.*, *Robert John Lynch Case*, 5 *id.* at 17, 19 (1929); *Martha Ann Austin Case* (U.S.A. v. Mexico), 4 *id.* at 623, 624 (1930).

national of the respondent State, which is a member of a minority; and as the latter question – which the Court feels called upon to raise *proprio motu* – concerns the merits, the Court cannot pass upon the question of jurisdiction until the case has been argued upon the merits.[1]

The case was, however, discontinued before any judgment was given. A few years later the issue of nationality was raised squarely in a preliminary objection made by Lithuania in the *Panevezys-Saldutiskis Case* (1939). The Court, which had joined this objection to the merits, began its treatment of it by affirming two general principles: States can espouse only the claims of their nationals; and an objection disputing the national character of a claim is of a preliminary character.[2] The latter principle was, however, found to be inapplicable in the case. For to decide that the company in whose behalf Estonia brought the claim was of Estonian nationality would have risked directly a decision on whether this company was the successor of a Russian Company that used to own the property in dispute. As this would have decided questions which formed an important part of the substantive dispute, the Court was not able to regard the objection "as one which in the particular circumstances of the case can be decided without passing on the merits."[3] Consequently, the objection was not admitted as a preliminary objection, nor was it considered later with the merits as the claim was found inadmissiable because of the non-exhaustion of local remedies.

One can, therefore, conclude that the requirement of the nationality of the claim, though raised by the Permanent Court, discussed before it, and affirmed by it as, in principle, required in cases of espousal of individual claims before the Court, did not present an occasion for a detailed treatment in any given case. Such an occasion was to come first before the present Court in the *Nottebohm Case* (1955).

After overruling the preliminary objections to its jurisdiction in the first phase of the *Nottebohm Case* (1953), the Court was faced with three objections to the admissibility of the claim related to the three jurisdictional facts dealt with in this section (i.e., the exhaustion of diplomatic means; the exhaustion of local remedies; and the nationality of the claim). Although the three questions were discussed before the Court, only the question of nationality was treated in the judgment. The Court showed a meticulous care in ascertaining first the validity

[1] *P.C.I.J.*, ser. A/B, No. 52 at 15 (1933).

[2] See *P.C.I.J.*, ser. A/B, No. 76 at 16–7 (1939).

[3] *Id.* at 17. Compare *id.* at 28 (Sep. Op. of Judges de Visscher and Rostworowski); *id.* at 30–5 (Diss. Op. of Judge Van Eysinga).

of the acquisition by Mr. Nottebohm of the nationality of the applicant state. It then discussed whether such nationality, if validly acquired, was effective as regards the respondent state, raising thereby an argument that was not discussed by the parties, and concluded that regardless of the validity of the naturalization for the purposes of the domestic law of the applicant, it could not be invoked against the respondent. As a result the Court found the claim inadmissible without any further investigation of the other pleas against admissibility.[1] This attitude of the Court reveals first that the question of nationality is to be considered ahead of the other objections to admissibility. Such is a logical order of dealing with pleas in bar, for if the requirement of nationality is proved to be lacking, none of the other requirements will be relevant. Also, the Nottebohm judgment shows the high degree of caution and indeed strictness with which the Court ascertains the jurisdictional facts once these are considered relevant.[2]

The nationality of the claim was also relevant in the *Interhandel Case* (1959) though it was involved there as a part of the merits and therefore was not dealt with by the only judgment given in the case which was restricted to preliminary objections. The question presented itself, however, in a preliminary objection submitted in another case decided in the same year: *The Aerial Incident Case* (*Israel* v. *Bulgaria*) (1959). In this case Bulgaria, after objecting to the jurisdiction of the Court, submitted the following objection against the *qualité* of the applicant in presenting the individual claims:

> Whereas the Government of Israel can act in defence of its nationals only; whereas it does not dispute that all or part of the damage in respect of which it seeks compensation was covered by insurance; whereas it provides no evidence of the Israel nationality of the insurers.
> For these reasons.
> To adjudge and declare that the Government of Israel has no capacity [Fr. *qualité*] to submit to the Court claims to a right to be indemnified which has been the subject of assignment or subrogation in favour of insurance companies not of Israel nationality.[3]

This objection, described by the Memorial of Israel as having "no basis either in law or in morals,"[4] presents nonetheless some of the

[1] See [1955] *I.C.J. Rep.* 4, 26.

[2] Three judges were, however, of the opinion that parts of the plea were prematurely adjudicated. See individual opinions of Judges Klaestad, Read and Guggenheim in *id.* at 30–3; 38–45; 65.

[3] [1959] *I.C.J. Rep.* 127, 133. The objection quoted above was presented with other objections to admissibility in a separate document other than the one including the objections to jurisdiction which was submitted on an earlier date. See *Aerial Incident of 27 July 1955*. Pleadings, Oral Arguments and Documents 132, 273 (*I.C.J.* 1959).

[4] Pleadings, *supra* at 105.

acute aspects of the requirement of nationality. First there is the question of insurance which, due to the spread of this system at present in foreign investments, may very well be encountered in future cases. Can a state take up the claim of its national before an international court if this national was fully compensated by an insurance company not itself a national of the same state? Israel argued that the insurance was based exclusively on contractual provisions to which neither of the Governments before the Court was a party and with which neither of these Governments was concerned.[1] It also argued that the Bulgarian objection was based on an "utterly unreasonable" and "strange theory" according to which the wrong-doing state could always escape any liability if the injured individual was covered by foreign insurance, for neither the state of which the individual is a national nor the state of the insurance company (which cannot be said, in the legal sense, to have suffered an "injury") would be able to espouse the claim.[2] Such arguments would, admittedly, make it difficult for the Court to uphold a plea following the lines of the Bulgarian objection mentioned above. However, this latter objection also has its persuasive grounds. If it is strange that the wrong-doing state should escape liability, it is also strange to be held financially liable against the insured party which suffered no financial loss, unless the insurance contract obliges this party to sue the wrongdoer and transfer the compensation to the insurer. Nor is it reasonable, as the advocate of Bulgaria argued, that Israel should be suing for the purpose of reimbursing insurers that are not of Israel nationality,[3] particularly as it is by no means certain that the state of the insurer will not be able to bring the latter's claim against the wrong-doing state. At any event, it is only unfortunate, from the viewpoint of the science of international law, that the Court, withholding jurisdiction in the case, found that it was not called upon to decide this issue.

The requirement of nationality was also involved in another aspect of the *Israel v. Bulgaria Case*. For Israel did not confine the individual claims it espoused to those of its nationals. Along with such claims it contended that:

> The Government of Israel considers that it is justified in this case in putting forward claims in respect of losses incurred by persons who are stateless.[1]

[1] *Ibid.*
[2] See *id.* at 533 (Statement of Mr. Rosenne, Agent of the Government of Israel.)
[3] *Id.* at 438–45 (Statement of M. Cot).
[4] *Id.* at 106, (Memorial of the Government of Israel).

This contention, recognized by Israel itself as in conflict with the "traditional rule," was based in this case on the fact that all injured individuals were flying in a commercial airliner under the Israel flag, and also on the alleged fact that Bulgaria had requested Israel to represent all individual claimants. Although the contention was not considered by the Court, its validity seems to rely on whether the latter fact (of the Bulgarian request) was proved. For the above contention amounts to a denial of the requirement of nationality which, it is submitted, could be ignored only with the consent of the respondent state. Israel might have had, however, a stronger case in presenting the claims of the stateless persons involved, were it possible for it to prove that such persons had their domicile or habitual residence within its territory.[1]

From the above analysis, it may be concluded that the International Court has tended to limit the number of the requirements that could be characterized as jurisdictional facts (as these are described in Chapter III). But once the Court recognizes a fact as relevant to its jurisdiction, it ascertains it with the greatest care. Such an ascertainment will in many cases, though not in all, require a joinder of the question of jurisdiction, or admissibility, to the merits. Regardless of such a joinder, the fact of the nationality of the claim, if invoked, will normally be dealt with first. Only after this is established will the Court consider other pleas in bar based on the nonperformance of a measure which should be taken before the Court can exercise its jurisdiction. In this respect, the parties are as free in the production of the evidence as the Court is in its evaluation.

D. OCCASIONAL TECHNIQUES

1. Ignoring the Effect of the Conflict of Jurisdiction with Other Judicial or Non-Judicial Bodies

The existence of other international organs entitled to hear and determine the same dispute as is covered by the Court's "continued

[1] See generally for the treatment of a stateless person as a national of the state within the territory of which he is habitually resident, particularly for the purpose of the espousal of his claims against other states [Harvard University Law School, Louis B. Sohn and R. R. Baxter, Reporters] *Convention on the International Responsibility of States for Injuries to Aliens* (*Draft No. 12 with Explanatory Notes*) Art. 21(3) (c) at 177, 180 (1961); Report of the International Law Commission covering the work of its Sixth Session, *U.N. Gen. Ass. Off. Rec.* 9th Sess., Supp. No. 9, at 8 (U.N. Doc. A/2693) (1954); Convention relating to the Status of Stateless Persons, Art. 16, signed at New York, Sept. 28, 1954, U.N. Doc., E/CONF. 17/5/Rev. 1). It is doubtful, however, whether the rule permitting the espousal of claims of this nature is already established in the field of international adjudication.

jurisdiction" may serve as a persuasive argument for the imcompetence of the Court. In practice this has not, however, been the case.

a. Conflict with judicial bodies

When it was argued before the Permanent Court that the dispute of which it was seized was pending before, or fell within the jurisdiction of, another international tribunal, the Court did not hesitate to determine by itself the effect of this fact on its own jurisdiction, thus assuming the role of a *tribunal des conflits*.[1] This role covers, in fact, not only the determination of the Court's jurisdiction but also, at least on a *prima facie* basis, that of the jurisdiction of the other tribunal or tribunals involved. It was first invoked in the *German Interests in Polish Upper Silesia Case* (1925) where the respondent state contended that some of the claims presented by the applicant were pending before a mixed arbitral tribunal. The Court, after raising the question of whether the doctrine of *litispendence* applied before it, managed to escape an answer by denying that the claims before it and those before the arbitral tribunal were identical.[2] This technique, however, was not possible to utilize in a later phase of the dispute (the *Chorzoẃ Factory Case* (1927)). In that phase, the claim was not pending before another international tribunal but there were two arbitral tribunals before which the same claim could have been brought. Obviously, the question of *litispendence* had to be faced. The Court expressed its doctrine to the effect that "when it has to define its jurisdiction in relation to that of another tribunal, [it] cannot allow its own competency to give way unless confronted with a clause which it considers sufficiently clear to prevent the possibility of a negative conflict of jurisdiction involving the danger of a denial of justice."[3] This doctrine, inspired by the lack of a *juge de droit commun* on the international plane, proved helpful in preserving the Court's jurisdiction. Applying it in the case, the Court tried, hesitantly, to establish that the other arbitral tribunals were not competent to deal with all aspects of the claim or to give the parties the kind of satisfaction they could get from the Court.[4] Yet, the line of argument presented by the Court seems to have clearly been motivated by the latter's concern to exercise its jurisdiction over the case – a concern that was perhaps

[1] See A. Hammarskjöld, "The Permanent Court of International Justice and its Place in International Relations," in his *Juridiction Internationale*, 227, 238 (1938).

[2] See *P.C.I.J.*, ser. A, No. 6 at 19–21 (1925).

[3] *P.C.I.J.*, ser. A, No. 9 at 30 (1927).

[4] See *id.* at 27–31.

justified by the Court's fear that the arbitral tribunals might not be able to exercise their jurisdiction or to accord the claimants an adequate remedy. The case stands, therefore, as evidence that the Court tended to maintain its pre-established jurisdiction even when it was reminded that the case fell also within the jurisdiction of other international tribunals.

The issue has hardly come before the present Court, but there is a hint in the *Ambatielos Case* (First phase) (1952) to the effect that the attitude of its predecessor is still maintained. As seen before, the applicant state in this latter case wanted the Court to go beyond the question of the arbitrability of the dispute and to adjudicate directly on its merits – a jurisdiction which was, according to the prior arrangement, to be exercised by an arbitration commission. The answer of the respondent state on this point, though in the affirmative, was not clear enough, so much so that the Court declined this proposed jurisdiction. However, it did not justify this refusal by the existence of the other international tribunal (the commission) which the Court itself found to be open to the parties. On the contrary, the Court's only justification was that the consent of the respondent was not very clear.[1] This could mean that were the consent of the parties on adjudicating the merits of the Ambatielos claim satisfactorily clear, the Court would have dealt with such merits, the jurisdiction of the commission notwithstanding.

Obviously, the Court will not prefer to exercise its jurisdiction to the exclusion of that of another tribunal if there is a clear provision in the relevant jurisdictional instruments limiting the resort to the Court to cases where no "other means of judicial settlement" are provided. In the absence of such a provision the problem of interpreting the instruments conferring jurisdiction on both the Court and the other tribunal is an open question on which many views have been expressed.[2] On the whole these views have called for the application to the conflicting jurisdictional instruments of the general rules of interpretation (*e.g.*, the rules *lex posterior, lex specialis*, etc.), as guide-

[1] See [1952] *I.C.J. Rep.* 28, 39.

[2] See *e.g.*, Delbez, *Les Principes Généraux du Contentieux International* 42 (1962); Maus, *Les Réserves dans les Déclarations d'Acceptation de la Juridiction* 119–20 (1959); Simpson and Fox, *International Arbitration* 75 (1959); 2 Guggenheim, *Traité de Droit International Public* 188 (1954); Hambro, "Some Observations on the Compulsory Jurisdiction of the International Court of Justice," 25 *Brit. Yb. Int'l L.* 133, 146–7 (1948); Ténékides, "Les Actes Compromissoires Concurrents," 17 *Rev. Dr. Int'l & Lég. Comp.* 719, 721–35 (1936). Most of these writers tended to confuse, however, the problem stated above with that of the concurrent bases of jurisdiction conferring it on the *same* court. The latter problem is discussed in Chapter III, *supra* at 102–4.

lines for the Court in determining the issue. It seems, however, that in cases of conflict of jurisdiction where no provision designates the tribunal which has the priority, the Court will tend to keep the case within its jurisdiction. This tendency is particularly certain whenever a doubt persists as to the power of the other tribunal to exercise jurisdiction over the case.

b. Conflict with non-judicial bodies

The priority given to the Court's own jurisdiction is even clearer when the organ alleged to share jurisdiction over the case is not a judicial body. Indeed, the Permanent Court has expressed the view that in such a situation its jurisdiction will not be affected except "in those exceptional cases in which the dispute which states might desire to refer to the Court would fall within the *exclusive* jurisdiction reserved to some other authority."[1]

Therefore, it does not affect the Court's jurisdiction that the same dispute could be considered by other organs of the United Nations or could be submitted by these to the Court for an advisory opinion. The situation is not the same, of course, when there is an agreement between the parties to resort first to one of these organs, or, as it is stipulated in many treaties accepting the Court's jurisdiction, when it is agreed that parties should seek first to solve the dispute through reconciliation. In such cases the exhaustion of the agreed-upon process is a pre-condition for the proper exercise of jurisdiction. The problem may, however, arise when the jurisdictional instruments limit the acceptance of the Court's continued jurisdiction to cases where the parties have *not* agreed to resort to "another method of *peaceful* (and not only 'judicial') settlement."[2] Would this mean that bringing the dispute to the attention of the Security Council or the General Assembly of the United Nations blocks the Court from exercising its jurisdiction when this is invoked under such instruments? Evidently

[1] *Minority Schools Case, P.C.I.J.*, ser. A, No. 15 at 23 (1928) (Emphasis added).

[2] See the declarations of acceptance containing this reservation in Appendix VII, No. 8. Obviously the problem will be easy to dispose of when the other organ is specifically designated. In the *Anglo-Iranian Oil Co. Case* (1952), however, a reservation in the declaration of Iran as to disputes before the Council of the League was interpreted by that Government to cover disputes before the Security Council of the U.N. which was not in existence when the declaration was made. See *Anglo-Iranian Oil Co. Case*, Pleadings, Oral Arguments and Documents 282, 474 (*I.C.J.* 1952). A reservation of the right to suspend judicial proceedings in respect of disputes considered by the Security Council exists only in the declaration of Australia [6]. Under the Permanent Court a larger number of declarations (17) reserved the same right as to disputes considered by the Council of the League [Appendix VII, No. 12]. The declaration of Canada [20] is the only one among these declarations which is still in force.

this question could be answered both in the negative and in the affirmative according to the interpretation given by the Court to the terms of the reservation. In such process of interpretation, the Court will normally take into consideration the intention of the parties. It will also have to consider whether the resort to such political organs as the Security Council was in the particular incident involved "agreed upon" by the parties, and whether it was, in their understanding, "a method of peaceful settlement."

In this respect, it was suggested that resort to the Security Council under Chapter VI of the Charter would not affect the Court's jurisdiction, whereas the Council's consideration of a question under Chapter VII of the Charter will exclude this question from the Court's jurisdiction, all the more so when the latter is limited by a reservation of "other methods of peaceful settlement."[1] It has also been proposed that, regardless of any reservation, the Security Council – unlike the Council of the League – can dis-seize the Court from a case pending before it and exercise itself jurisdiction over the case.[2] These are, however, mere suggestions. There is nothing in the Court's Statute, nor in its practice, to indicate that the parties cannot refer a case to the Court simply because it could be referred or has been referred to another organ of the United Nations. However, as a matter of *propriety* (and propriety is an element beyond jurisdiction), the Court is expected to follow the most cautious attitude in case the dispute invokes its relationship with such other organs. If a question submitted to it is brought before the Security Council or the General Assembly, the Court will most likely either continue adjudicating on the issue after differentiating it from that before the other organ, or merely adjourn the case until an action is taken by that organ.

2. *The Use of the Rules of Procedure*

The Rules of procedure have been invoked by the Court in the process of determining its jurisdiction. This has particularly been done in relation to the different patterns of incidental jurisdiction and has often resulted in extending the scope of the Court's powers over the case. Such an attitude may be observed in the Court's determination of the indication of interim measures of protection and the admission of counter-claims.

[1] See Maus, *supra*, p. 259, note 2 at 127–8.

[2] See Delbez, *supra*, p. 259, note 2 at 43. But *cf.*, Carlston, *The Process of International Arbitration* 173 (1946).

a. In the indication of interim measures

It has already been shown in the preceding chapter that in determining whether or not to indicate interim measures in the *Interhandel Case* (1959), the Court has excluded the consideration of the American preliminary objection against jurisdiction. This the Court justified, in part, by the fact that it was examining a question that falls under the procedure provided for in Article 61 of the Rules and was not, therefore, to be confused with the preliminary objection submitted in conformity with Article 62 of the Rules.[1] Such a separation between the two questions based on the fact that each of them is treated in a different Article of the Rules of procedure presents a clear example of the use of these Rules in the process of determining the Court's incidental jurisdiction.

b. In the admission of counter-claims

Similarly, the admission of counter-claims (which is a procedure provided for only in the Rules)[2] may very well be used as an indirect method of enlarging the scope of the Court's jurisdiction.[3] The first Rules of the Permanent Court allowed the respondent to present counter-claims in its counter-case under the sole condition that they be equally covered by the Court's jurisdiction (Article 40(2) of the 1922 and 1931 Rules of procedure). Under this provision the Court examined in the *Chorzow Factory Case* (1927) a submission made in the counter-case of the Polish Government which was characterized by both the Applicant Government and the Court as a counter-claim. No problem was raised as to the admissibility of such a submission which the Court found "juridically connected with the principal claim," but dismissed it on the merits.[4] In the same judgment, the Court also refused to consider a submission introduced by the applicant to prevent a set-off asked for by the respondent along with potential set-offs.[5]

After the amendment of the Rules of the Permanent Court in 1936, the provision relating to counter-claims introduced more restrictions,

[1] See Chapter IV, *supra* at 177–80.

[2] Because no reference is made in the statute to counter-claims, some judges of the Permanent Court argued that the presentation of a counterclaim in any form other than a separate application would be inconsistent with the Statute. See, *P.C.I.J.*, ser. D, No. 2 (4th Add.) 261–3 (1936).

[3] See Rosenne, *The International Court of Justice* 337 (1957); Hambro, *supra*, p. 259, note 2 at 155.

[4] See *P.C.I.J.*, ser. A, No. 17 at 37–8 (1928).

[5] *Id.* at 60–63, 64. And see a discussion of the differences between the set-off (*demande de compensation*) and the counter-claim (*demande reconventionnelle*) before international arbitral tribunal in Simpson and Fox, *supra*, p. 259, note 2 at 178.

which are still maintained in the text of the Rules of the present Court (Article 63). According to this provision, the counter-claim may be presented when (i) proceedings have been instituted by means of an application, and (ii) the counter-claim is submitted in the counter-memorial. Besides these two conditions for "seizing" the Court of a counter-claim, the latter will be entertained only "provided that such counter-claim is directly connected with the subject matter of the application and that it comes within the jurisdiction of the Court." The opportunity for applying this new provision arose twice before the Permanent Court. In the *Diversion of Water from the Meuse Case* (1937), the respondent state made a counter-claim the admission of which was not contested by the applicant. As in the *Chorzow Factory Case,* the Court noticed that the counter-claim was "directly connected with the principal claim" and rejected it only on the merits.[1] In the *Panevezys-Saldutiskis Case* (1939) a counter-claim was presented only as alternative to a preliminary objection, but as the latter was upheld, the counter-claim was not examined. On the whole it could, therefore, be said that the Permanent Court never had the occasion for a detailed examination of the admissibility of a counter-claim. In the two cases where counter-claims were examined, no objection was made to their admissibility and the Court was content to notice that they were directly connected with the merits.

By contrast, the question received a detailed treatment before the present Court in the *Asylum Case* (1950).[2] This case, brought before the Court by an application based on a special agreement, involved an original counter-claim made in the counter-memorial and an addition to this counter-claim made in the final submissions in the oral proceedings. The applicant objected to the admissibility of the counter-claim in its original form (because it raised new problems and thus tended to shift the grounds of the dispute) and also objected to both the Court's jurisdiction over, and the admissibility of, the addition to the counter-claim. Dealing first with the counter-claim in its original formulation, the Court established that a direct connection existed between this counter-claim and the second submission of the applicant. "The direct connection being thus clearly established – the Court

[1] See *P.C.I.J.*, ser. A/B, No. 70 at 28–32 (1937).

[2] Earlier in the second phase of the *Corfu Channel Case* the British Government argued that the part of the special agreement asking the Court to adjudicate on the responsibility of the U.K. toward Albania constituted a counter-claim due to the fact that the suit was brought by the U.K. See 3 *Corfu Channel Case*, Pleadings, Oral Arguments and Documents 264 (*I.C.J.* 1950). The Court, however, considering the special agreement as a whole to be the basis of its jurisdiction refused to follow the counter-claim procedure in that case.

concluded – the sole objection to the admissibility of the counter-claim in its original form is therefore removed."[1] On the merits the Court sustained this counter-claim in part. As a result, it became able to avoid a consideration of the addition to the counter-claim and the objections thereto:

> This part of the submission [i.e., the addition]... was intended as a substitution for the counter-claim in its original form if the latter were rejected: it disappears with the allowance of this counter-claim. Hence, it will not be necessary for the Court to consider either the objection on the ground of lack of jurisdiction or the objections on the grounds of inadmissibility... or to consider the merits of the claim thus submitted...[2]

Since that judgment in the *Asylum Case* (1950), the admissibility of counter-claims has not been subject to examination by the Court. The possibility of raising a counter-claim was, it is true, reserved in the *Norwegian Fisheries Case* (1951), and a counter-claim was submitted in the *U.S. Nationals in Morocco Case* (1952). Yet, no actual counter-claim was presented in the former case as the issue was later withdrawn,[3] and no objection to the admissibility of the counter-claim was made in the second case. In fact, the Court, when dealing with that counter-claim, did not even follow the attitude of its predecessor in emphasizing the connection between the principal claim and the counter-claim. The general attitude of the present Court seems, therefore, to be towards a liberal application of Article 63 of its Rules. It admitted the counter-claim, without discussion, when the applicant did not object to its admissibility, and when it did it investigated the connection between this claim and the principal claim even though the former was amended during the oral proceedings. The provision of Article 63 limits the presentation of counter-claims to cases where the proceedings have been instituted by means of application. This was taken by some writers to mean that counter-claims will not be admitted in cases based on special agreements.[4] However, the judgment in the *Asylum Case* (1950), itself based on a special agreement, testifies that if the proceedings are instituted by an application, it will not matter, for the purposes of the admissibility of counter-claims, whether this application relies or not on a special agreement.

[1] [1950] *I.C.J. Rep.* 266, 280.
[2] *Id.* at 288. But see, *id.* at 331 (Diss. Op. of Judge Read).
[3] See 1 *Norwegian Fisheries Case*, Pleadings, Oral Arguments and Documents 567 (*I.C.J.* 1951); 4 *id.* at 692.
[4] See *e.g.*, Hambro, *supra*, p. 259, note 2 at 155.

c. In the admission of the modification of the case

Along with the modification in a case caused by the admission of a counter-claim, modifications were regularly made before the International Court by means of amendments introduced by the parties to their respective submissions.

The conditions under which such modifications have taken place are neatly summarized in the following portion from Judge Read's dissenting opinion in the *Norwegian Loans Case* (1957):

> It is true that it has been the established practice of this Court, and of the Permanent Court, to permit the Parties to modify their submissions up to the end of the Oral Pleadings... But the right is subject to two limitations. The first limitation is that, when there is an appreciable change, the other Party must have a fair opportunity to comment on the amended submissions... The second condition is that the amendment must be an amendment. It must not consist of an attempt by the Applicant Government to bring a new and different dispute before the Court. If so, the amended submissions are not admissible, unless the new elements have been incorporated in the dispute either by the Respondent Government or by the two Governments in the course of the written, and Oral Proceedings.[1]

The practice of amending the submissions before the end of the oral pleadings was indeed followed in several cases [2] to the extent that it became the custom of the Court to ask the parties, at the end of the oral hearings, to state what their "final submissions" are. The problem arises, however, when an amendment introduced to the "original" submissions is found by the Court to cover a new claim. The Court will then have to ascertain whether the parties have consented to submit this new claim to it and whether it can, at any event, exercise jurisdiction over such claim in the circumstances of the case. The first question is particularly relevant when the Court's jurisdiction over

[1] [1957] *I.C.J. Rep.* 9, 80–1. Objections against the amendment of submissions were made before the Permanent Court. See *e.g., German Interests in Polish Upper Silesia Case, P.C.I.J.*, ser. C. No. 11 at 970 (1925) (Polish Rejoinder); *Chorzów Factory Case, P.C.I.J.*, ser. C, No. 13–I at 98 (1927) (statement of the Agent of Poland). The Court, however, accepted amendments made in the memorial as of right, and other amendments if taken by leave of Court. See generally, Feller, "Conclusions of the Parties in the Procedure of the Permanent Court of International Justice," 25 *Am. J. Int'l L.* 490, 502 (1931).

[2] See *e.g.*, the *S.S. Wimbledon Case, P.C.I.J.*, ser. A, No. 1 at 17 (1923); *German Interests in Polish Upper Silesia Case, P.C.I.J.*, ser. A, No. 7 at 45 (1926); *Readaptation of Mavrommatis Jerusalem Concessions Case, P.C.I.J.*, ser. A, No. 11 at 11 (1927); *Chorzow Factory Case, P.C.I.J.*, ser. A, No. 9 at 18 (1927); *Chorzow Factory Case (Merits), P.C.I.J.*, ser. A, No. 17 at 7 (1928); *Free Zones Case, P.C.I.J.*, ser. A/B, No. 46 at 155–6 (1932); *Peter Pazmany University Case, P.C.I.J.*, ser. A/B, No. 61 at 211 (1933); *Anglo-Iranian Oil Co. Case*, [1952] *I.C.J. Rep.* 93, 97–101, *Monetary Gold Case* [1954] *I.C.J. Rep.* 19, 28; *Norwegian Loans Case*, [1957] *I.C.J. Rep.* 9, 17, etc. And see for modification of claims before arbitral tribunals, Simpson and Fox, *supra*, p. 259, note 2 at 179–83.

the original claim is accepted on an *ad hoc* basis,[1] or is made to cover a period which expires before the submission of the new claim.[2] The exercise of jurisdiction over a new claim introduced in the course of the pleadings raises also problems of procedural character. This has been particularly made clear in the *Société Commerciale de Belgique Case* (1939) before the Permanent Court. After pointing out in this case that the Liberty of the parties to amend their submissions up to the end of the oral proceedings ought to be construed "reasonably and without infringing the terms of Article 40 of the Statute and Article 32 Paragraph 2 of the Rules which provide that the Application must indicate the subject of the dispute," the Court added that:

> ... it is clear that the Court cannot, in principle, allow a dispute brought before it by application to be transformed by amendments in the submissions into another dispute which is different in character. A practice of this kind will be calculated to prejudice the interests of third States to which, under Article 40, Paragraph 2, of the Statute, all applications must be communicated in order that they may be in a position to avail themselves of the right of intervention provided for in Article 62 and 63 of the Statute.[3]

The Court followed by clearly conceding that a complete change in the basis of the case might also affect its jurisdiction. Yet, it admitted the new change in the case before it as regular, basing this on the special circumstances of the case and "more especially the absence of any objection on the part of the Agent for the [respondent] Government."[4]

This flexible attitude is the most likely to be adopted by the present Court if the issue arises before it in similar circumstances. In fact, the problem has been invoked before this Court more than once, but in all such cases it declined jurisdiction without finding it necessary to pronounce on this issue.[5] Yet, it is possible to say that the procedural objection related to the rights of third parties would not, in itself, be considered a serious obstacle against the exercise of jurisdiction in such cases. The Court can always suspend the proceedings temporarily to permit notification to the interested states.[6]

[1] See the Permanent Court's dictum in the *Minority Schools Case, P.C.I.J.*, ser. A, No. 15 at 25 (1928).

[2] See *e.g., Anglo-Iranian Oil Co. Case* [1952] *I.C.J. Rep.* 93, 98, 101 where Iran contended that an addition to the submissions of the U.K. was made after Iran's denunciation of its declaration and was therefore outside the Court's jurisdiction.

[3] *P.C.I.J.*, ser. A/B, No. 78 at 173 (1939).

[4] *Ibid.*

[5] See *Anglo-Iranian Oil Co. Case,* [1952] *I.C.J. Rep.* 93, 97; *Monetary Gold Case,* [1954] *I.C.J. Rep.* 19, 28; *Norwegian Loans Case,* [1957] *I.C.J. Rep.* 9, 27. And see *id.* at 80–1 (Diss. Op. of Judge Read).

[6] See Rosenne, *The International Court of Justice* 298 (1957).

3. *Reformulation of Questions Submitted to the Court*

Along with the modifications made by the parties, the Court may itself restate the submissions presented to it in other terms so as to make them more readily adaptable to its jurisdiction. This technique has been followed in both the contentious and the advisory procedures, though it had its clearest applications in the reformulation by the Court of requests for advisory opinions.

a. The contentious procedure

It has already been shown that the Permanent Court did not object to exercising contentious jurisdiction over submissions formulated *in abstracto*, even though it found such a formulation at times to be undesirable.[1] This Court has also acknowledged, as seen before, that "though it can construe the submissions of the parties, it cannot substitute itself for them and formulate new submissions simply on the basis of arguments and facts advanced."[2] Yet, when the occasion arose in the *Chorzów Factory Case* (*Interpretation*) (1927), the Court did not hesitate to state that:

> ... *for the purpose of the interpretation of a judgment*, it cannot be bound by formulae chosen by the Parties concerned, but must be able to take an unhampered decision.[3]

Such an "unhampered decision" the Court was in fact able to take only after it had itself reformulated the "submissions" of the applicant Government, relying, for this purpose, on the Rules of procedure requiring the indication of the points in dispute, and on the rule that it "may within reasonable limits disregard the defects of form of documents placed before it."[4]

The same technique is not altogether alien to the work of the present Court. Through defining what the final submissions in the case were, this Court has practically reformulated the limits of the issues before it in more than one case. Examples of this attitude could be found in particular in the *Norwegian Fisheries Case* (1951) and the *Minquiers and Ecrehos Case* (1953). In the first of these cases, the Court excluded as many as nine submissions of the "final submissions" of the United

[1] See this Chapter, *supra* at 216–9.
[2] *German Interests in Polish Upper Silesia Case, P.C.I.J.*, ser. A, No. 7 at 34–5 (1926).
[3] *P.C.I.J.*, ser. A, No. 13 at 15–6. (Emphasis added). Compare *id.* at 23 (Diss. Op. of Judge Anzilotti).
[4] *Id.* at 16.

Kingdom on the basis that they appeared to be "a set of propositions which... purport to justify certain contentions and do not constitute a precise and direct statement of a claim."[1] On the same basis the Court understood the "submissions" of the parties in the *Minquiers Case* to cover only the first paragraph of the French conclusions.[2]

b. The advisory procedure

As to advisory jurisdiction, the Permanent Court did in its third opinion restate a vague question submitted to it and answered it only after limiting its scope.[3] Then it dealt directly with its power to reformulate the request for an advisory opinion in the *Interpretation of the Greco-Turkish Agreement Case* (1928). The request in that case did not include a statement of the question on which the opinion was sought and referred instead to a certain letter which, the Court found, did not exactly state the question. As a result, the Court declared that:

> ... it is essential that it should determined what this question is and formulate an exact statement of it, in order more particularly to avoid dealing with points of law upon which it was not the intention of the Council or the Commission to obtain its opinion.[4]

Nevertheless, the Court did not fail to point out the peculiar nature of this attitude. "In the present case – said the Court – it is possible for the Court to do this, owing to the relatively simple nature of the case. This, however, may not always be so." Yet, the Court felt free in other advisory cases to amplify the scope of the question covered by the request. Asked in the *Jaworzina Case* (1923) to express its view in relation to a given frontier region (the territory of Spisz), it covered in its opinion other frontier regions "insofar as the delimitation of the frontier in those regions and in the territory of Spisz may be interdependent."[5] Also, in the *Danzig and the I.L.O. Case* (1930), the Court restated the question of whether the Free City could become a member of the organization "to include the question whether the Free City, if admitted, could participate in the activities of the Labour Organization and fulfill the duties incumbent upon its members."[6]

The attitude of the Permanent Court in this respect was adequately summarized in the following statement in the Report by the Registrar

[1] *Norwegian Fisheries Case*, [1951] *I.C.J. Rep.* 26.
[2] See *Minquiers and Ecrehos Case*, (1953] *I.C.J. Rep.* 47, 52.
[3] See *Competence of the I.L.O. with respect to Agricultural Production Case*, *P.C.I.J.*, ser. B, No. 3 at 59 (1922).
[4] *P.C.I.J.*, ser. B, No. 16 at 13 (1928).
[5] *P.C.I.J.*, ser. B, No. 8 at 50 (1923).
[6] *P.C.I.J.*, ser. B, No. 18 at 9 (1930).

of that Court made in 1933 in relation to a proposed revision of the Rules:

> In several cases the Court has had to point out that the request has not contained a sufficiently exact statement of the question at issue, or even that any such statement has been lacking; the Court has done this either in the body of its advisory opinion or by letter from the Registrar. In no case, however, has the Court refused to give an advisory opinion for which it has been asked, merely owing to considerations of this kind. But it has allowed it to be understood that it might feel constrained in future to modify this conciliatory attitude.[1]

No occasion for the alteration of such an attitude occurred in the subsequent work of the Permanent Court (only two advisory cases were brought before that Court after 1933). Nor could it be said that the attitude has been modified in the work of the present Court. True, this latter Court has stated in the first *Admission to the U.N. Case* (1948), that it was its duty "to envisage the question submitted to it only in the abstract form which has been given to it,"[2] but this was rather an answer to the objection made before the Court that the question submitted to it was, in the particular circumstances of the case, a political question. Apart from this, the present Court had on occasion restated the submitted question in a more exact formula [3] and tended, in general, to answer the requests for opinions as if they were made only as questions for the proper interpretation of disputed legal texts.[4]

4. Passing over the Question of Jurisdiction and Disposing of the Case on Other Grounds

This technique is of an old standing in the history of international tribunals. It proved to be particularly helpful in cases where the jurisdictional question was too problematic to be directly tackled with in the decision. The first and the best known arbitral case treated in this manner is the *Alabama Arbitration* (1872). As explained in the first chapter of this study, the arbitral commission disposed of the difficult issue of whether it was competent to deal with the indirect losses incurred in that case by stating that there was no room in

[1] Report by the Registrar of the Court, June, 1933, *P.C.I.J.*, ser. D, No. 2 (3rd Add.) 803, 838 (1933).

[2] [1947–1948] *I.C.J. Rep.* 57, 61.

[3] See *e.g.*, *Interpretation of Peace Treaties Case* (First Phase), [1950] *I.C.J. Rep.* 65, 76, *Admissibility of Hearings of Petitioners by the Committee on South-West Africa Case*, [1956] *I.C.J. Rep.* 23, 25.

[4] See Chapter IV, *supra*.

applicable international law for compensating such losses "even if there were no disagreement between the two Governments to the competency of the tribunal to decide them."[1] The same technique was then followed by later arbitral tribunals which, finding it impossible to determine the jurisdictional issue, were content to state that no such determination was needed as the case ought, at any event, to be rejected on the merits.[2]

The Permanent Court, as it seems, did not need to resort to such a technique and was able to determine the question of jurisdiction whenever that was disputed before it. As to the present Court, it has made use of this technique only in one case, not by passing directly to a rejection of the claim on the merits, but by declaring the claim inadmissible before definitely deciding the question of jurisdiction in the *Interhandel Case* (1959).

Such a technique may be criticized as an escapist approach that for extra judicial reasons pays no regard to the order normally followed by tribunals in deciding cases [3] (i.e., determining first the question of jurisdiction, then, if this is established, considering the admissibility of the claim and pronouncing on the merits only after the claim is found admissible). Yet, it is clear that this technique presents an exceptional procedure that has been followed only when the respect for the above order confronted the tribunal with what it considered an unsurmountable difficulty. This difficulty as presented in the *Interhandel Case* related to the determination of the validity of the reservation by which the respondent Government has, in fact, arrogated to itself the very power of determining the Court's jurisdiction. The Court avoided the determination of this issue by saying that the objection based on it was "without object" in the case, and that the claim was, at any event, inadmissible. The validity of this type of reservation is, therefore, still an open question. Because of its importance in relation to the future work of the Court, it is dealt with exclusively in the following Chapter.

[1] Declaration of June 19, 1872, 1 Moore, *Arbitrations* 646. And see details of this case in Chapter I, *supra* at 17–9.

[2] See *e.g.*, *Successors of William Webster* (*United States*) *v. Great Britain*, 6 *U.N. Rep. Int'l Arb. Awards* 166, 167–8 (1925).

[3] See *e.g.*, Verzijl, "The International Court of Justice in 1959-Part I," 6 *Nederlands Tijdschrift voor Internationaal Recht* 362, 368–70, 376 (1959); Perrin, "L'Affaire de L'Interhandel – Phase des exceptions préliminaires," 16 *Annuaire Suisse de Droit International* 73, 176 (1959).

CHAPTER VI

THE COURT'S ATTITUDE TOWARD THE CHALLENGE TO ITS POWER TO DETERMINE ITS JURISDICTION

A. THE PROBLEM AS PRESENTED IN PRACTICE

1. *In the Jurisdictional Instruments*

The foregoing analysis of the characteristics and operation of the *compétence de la compétence* of the International Court, points beyond doubt to the fact that this is the most serious single power conferred on the Court. Attempts to deprive the Court of this power by the agreement of the parties or by a reservation in the acceptance of one of them has been referred to in previous parts of this study. Such attempts are reminiscent of reservations made, or suggested, in the course of international arbitration [1] where the practice of leaving for the parties the power to determine the nature of the controversy was not considered an intolerable transgression on the judicial nature of the arbitral tribunal.[2]

Under the Permanent Court some treaties contained provisions empowering the parties, or a third organ, to determine whether the dispute falls within the jurisdiction of the Court,[3] but no declaration of acceptance was made subject to such a reservation.[1] The writers

[1] See Chapter I, *supra* at 27. See also the proposals presented to the Second Peace Conference at the Hague (1907) by the Swedish, the Brazilian, the Portuguese, the American and the British Delegations for the amendment and additions to the Convention for the Pacific Settlement of International Disputes of July 29, 1899, in 2 [Ministère des Affaires Etrangères] *Actes et Documents de la Deuxième Conférence de la Paix* 885 (Annexe 22, Arts. 16, 17); 886 (Annexe 23, Arts. 1, 4); 895 (Annexe 34, Arts. 16, 16a); 899 (Annexe 37, Arts. 1, 2); 904 (Annexe 39, Art. 16). English translation in 2 [Scott] *The Proceedings of the Hague Peace Conferences. Translation of Official Texts. Conference of 1907* at 878, 879, 888, 892, 899.

[2] No precedent could be found where a reservation of the type mentioned above was held invalid. Some arbitral tribunals found, however, other types of reservations to be incompatible with their "dignity," with the principle of *res judicata*, or with the "purpose of the *compromis*" and as a result refused to give effect thereto. See *e.g.*, "Arbitrage au Sujet de la Détermination des Limites entre l'Autriche ou plutôt la Galicie et la Hongrie près du Lac dit 'L'Oeil de la Mer'" (1902), 8 *Rev. Dr. Int'l & Lég. Comp.* 196, 198, 212 (2 me sér. 1906).

[3] See Chapter II, *supra* at 48.

[4] Compare the reservations attached to the ratification of the Protocol of Signature deposited by El Salvador on August 29, 1930 [Appendix VI, No. 35]. The acceptance of this state excluded "disputes or differences concerning points or questions which cannot be

who envisaged the possibility of a declaration of this kind did not hesitate to declare it contrary to the very nature of the Optional Clause and as such invalid.[1] The Court itself had no chance to pronounce on the issue.

The problem presented itself with the acceptance by the United States of the continued jurisdiction of the present Court in 1946. This acceptance was made in a declaration excluding, *inter alia*, disputes with regard to matters which are "essentially within the domestic jurisdiction of the United States of America *as determined by the United States of America*."[2] Such a reservation has since been copied in eight other declarations,[3] three of which used, however, other terms than the word "determined." The declaration of France [49] excluded matters "which are essentially within the national jurisdiction as *understood* by the Government of the French Republic," the declaration of Liberia excluded disputes which Liberia "considers essentially within its domestic jurisdiction," and the declaration of Mexico excluded matters that "in the opinion of the Government of Mexico" fall essentially within its domestic jurisdiction. The French reservation was later dropped as was the reservation in the Indian and Pakistani declarations, thus leaving five declarations in force with this reservation in them. Besides these five declarations where the reservation applied only to matters determined to be of domestic jurisdiction, two reservations in declarations made by the United Kingdom presented also a challenge to the Court's *compétence de la compétence*. In its declaration of April 18, 1957 [142], the United Kingdom excluded from the acceptance disputes relating to any question "which, in the opinion of the Government of the United Kingdom, affects the national security of the United Kingdom or of any of its dependent territories." This reservation was confined in the following declaration of November 26, 1958 [143], to disputes which "had they been the subject of proceedings brought before the International Court of Justice previous to that date, would have been excluded from the Court's com-

submitted to arbitration in accordance with the political Constitution of this Republic" as well as "pecuniary claims made against the nation." Although the declaration did not reserve to the declarant state the power to decide whether a dispute was within the excluded categories, the terms of the reservations were perhaps broad enough to give room for a contention to that effect. See Hudson, *The Permanent Court of International Justice* 397 n. 49 (1934).

[1] See Lauterpacht, "The British Reservations to the Optional Clause," 10 *Economica* 137, 154, 169 (1930). See also Hudson, *supra*, at 397.

[2] See Appendix VI, No. 145.

[3] *I.e.*, declarations of France [49], India [67], Liberia [80], Mexico [88], Pakistan [103, 104], Sudan [117] and South Africa [137]. Declarations with underlined numbers are in force.

pulsory jurisdiction" under the above reservation. Finally, the reservation was dropped altogether in the last declaration of the United Kingdom dated November 27, 1963 [144]. This British reservation was described as "more unfortunate, if possible, than the United States reservation", on account of the lack of rules of international law to determine whether a question affects the "national security" of a state.[1] Consequently, the criticism directed against the American reservation was extended to this British one; "for not only is the category of 'national security' potentially incomprehensive, but it is not a category capable of any kind of judicial assessment."[2] Having been dropped, and because it was not copied in any other reservation, the discussion of the effect of this reservation has lost its practical value. Yet, the United Kingdom has another reservation which, under one interpretation, can still present a challenge to the Court's power to determine its jurisdiction. This is the reservation introduced first in the British declaration of June 2, 1955 [140], and repeated in all British declarations made since, as well as in the declaration of Cambodia [19] which copied it.[3] This reservation excludes from the acceptance of jurisdiction:

disputes relating to any matter excluded from compulsory jurisdiction or arbitration under any treaty, convention or other international agreement or instrument to which the United Kingdom is a party.

Of course this reservation could be interpreted strictly as a restatement of exclusions inserted in treaties which are, at any rate, applicable whenever these treaties are invoked; or it may have been merely an attempt to deprive the Court of the pattern of jurisdiction it exercised in the *Ambatielos Case* in disagreement with the United Kingdom. But the reservation is also susceptible of another interpretation wider in scope which would allow the declarant state to contend the exclusion from its acceptance of all matters excluded from compulsory jurisdiction or arbitration by any treaty, including matters which it considers as affecting its "vital interests, national honor, and interests of third states," as these were excluded in many old treaties to which the United Kingdom is a party. Such would be, in the words of Professor Briggs, "a throwback to the period before the League of Nations,"[2]

[1] See Briggs, "Reservations to the Acceptance of Compulsory Jurisdiction of the International Court of Justice," 93 *Recueil des Cours* 229, 302 (1958–I).
[2] Jennings, "Recent Cases on 'Automatic' Reservations to the Optional Clause," 7 *Int'l & Comp. L. Q.* 349, 362 (1958).
[3] See Appendix VII, No. 10(A).
[4] Briggs, *supra*, note 1 at 300.

and will invoke similar difficulties to the ones raised in relation to the American reservation.

Finally, the first declaration of Israel [72] seemed for a while to suggest that it was made with a reservation to the *compétence de la compétence*. Nothing in the wording of the declaration itself carried this meaning. The confusion was, however, introduced by the wording of the instrument of ratification. It first interpreted reservation (c) in the declaration, excluding "any dispute between the State of Israel and another State which refuses to establish or maintain normal relations with it," to apply to cases "where the absence of relations precedes the dispute which has arisen and exists independently of this dispute."[1] Then it went further to say that differences of opinion which might arise in a given case as to this issue will be subject to a decision by the Court in accordance with article 36(6). But referring to this latter Article, the instrument added:

> Having regard to this provision... the Government of Israel can bind neither itself nor its successors to comply strictly with this interpretation in the event of a dispute arising as to the jurisdiction of the Court in accordance with this declaration, and in the event of such a dispute arising, full freedom of action is reserved as to the manner in which the jurisdiction of the Court may be invoked.[2]

Obviously, if the words "this interpretation" in the above text refers to the statement that disputes over jurisdiction will be decided by the Court, then it should be said that the instrument of ratification flies in the face of the Court's independent power to determine its jurisdiction. Such a reading was, however, found by the Legal Advisor to the Israel Ministry of Foreign Affairs to be "a regrettable misunderstanding." For the intention in using the words "this interpretation" – he explained – was to refer to the interpretation contained in the instrument of ratification as a whole, "i.e., that the interpretation contained in the instrument of ratification was not to prejudge how the question of jurisdiction would be pleaded in a concrete case."[3] True as this may be, the question lost its practical relevancy after Israel had replaced the above declaration in 1956 with a new declaration [73] under which this difficulty does not arise.

In the actual situation the challenge to the Court's *compétence de la compétence* is, therefore, confined to such cases as may arise under a

[1] [1950–1951] *I.C.Y.B.* 193 (Original French text in [1950–1951] *Annuaire de la Cour Internationale de Justice* 191).

[2] *Id.* at 194.

[3] Rosenne, *The International Court of Justice* 342 n. 2 (1957).

treaty containing a *clause contraire* or under the declarations of Liberia, Mexico, the Sudan, South Africa, and the United States (and also under declarations reserving all matters excluded in treaties, if this is to be interpreted in the manner explained above). The problem has never arisen in practice in a case brought on the basis of a treaty. The arguments for and against the *Clause contraire* inserted in a compromissory provision in a treaty have however been exposed before.[1] It remains here to point out that a clause of this nature presents far less problems than a reservation in a declaration of acceptance. For, whereas the treaty clause raises only the question of its compatibility with article 36(6) and with the judicial nature of the Court, a reservation in a declaration raises, in addition, the serious question of its compatibility with Article 36(2), i.e., with the acceptance of a real obligatory jurisdiction, and, in one view, with Article 36(3) as well. The arguments for the validity of the latter reservation will consequently cover *a fortiori* the validity of the *clause contraire* in a treaty. But the arguments for the invalidity of the reservation do not necessarily extend to the treaty clause.

2. *In the Cases*

a. *The U.S. Nationals in Morocco Case*

The first case brought under instruments containing a reservation to the *compétence de la compétence* is the *U.S. Nationals in Morocco Case* (1952). At the time of instituting the proceedings in this case, both the declarations invoked as basis of jurisdiction (declarations of France [49] and of the United States [145] excluded matters of domestic jurisdiction as understood (in the first), or as determined (in the second), by the declarant State. At no time in the proceedings was this reservation invoked, however. The United States, as a respondent, objected first to the Court's jurisdiction on procedural grounds related to the identification of the applicant, adding at the end of its objection that it reserved "all rights it now possesses, including the right to file further preliminary objections."[2] Instead of exercising such a right, the United States later withdrew its preliminary objection.[3] Yet, in its counter-memorial this Government found it necessary to write that:

[1] See Chapter II, *supra* at.

[2] 1 *Case Concerning Rights of Nationals of the United States of America in Morocco*, Pleadings, Oral Arguments and Documents 238 (*I.C.J.*, 1952).

[3] See 2 *id.* at 434.

The United States Government does not raise any jurisdictional issue in the proceeding, even though it does not concur in the allegations with respect to the compulsory jurisdiction of the Court which have been presented by the French Government, it being its understanding that its abstaining from raising the issue does not affect its legal right to rely in any future case on its reservations contained in its acceptance of the compulsory jurisdiction of the Court.[1]

The Court, on its part, paid no attention to the fact that the parties' declarations were subject to the reservation. It could be argued that this was a tacit acceptance by the Court of the validity of the declarations despite the reservations as the Court would not have exercised a jurisdiction based on void instruments. Such an argument may, however, be countered by saying that regardless of the declarations, the Court was able to assume jurisdiction over the case since the moment of the withdrawal of the preliminary objection, simply on the basis of the principle of *forum prorogatum*.[2] This last contention is supported by the practice of the Court, analyzed before in detail, according to which it will not question the acceptance of its jurisdiction by the parties if none of them raises the issue.

b. Certain Norwegian Loans Case

The second relevant case is that concerning *Certain Norwegian Loans* (1957). France instituted the proceedings against Norway by an application relying on the declarations of the parties made under Article 36(2) of the Statute. The declaration of Norway [101] contained, besides a time-limit. the sole condition of reciprocity, whereas the declaration of the applicant [49] reserved, *inter alia*, "differences relating to matters which are essentially within the national jurisdiction as understood by the Government of the French Republic." Norway at first entered four preliminary objections against the Court's jurisdiction and the admissibility of the claim. The objections were later joined to the merits on the request of France and with the consent of Norway. Then in its counter-memorial, Norway withdrew its second objection thus confining the plea against jurisdiction to three grounds which it maintained "in their entirety" in its Final Submissions.[3] The only objection of interest here is the objection in which Norway argued first, and in detail, that the question could not fall within the sphere of the Optional Clause system because it was exclusively governed by

[1] 1 *id.* at 257, 262.

[2] *Accord*, Lauterpacht's Separate Opinion in the *Norwegian Loans Case*, [1957] *I.C.J. Rep.* 9, 60.

[3] See [1957] *I.C.J. Rep.* 9, 18.

municipal law.[1] In the second part of that objection Norway invoked, "if any doubt remained" as to the first point, the French reservation by force of reciprocity, thus declaring the dispute a matter of the national jurisdiction of Norway as understood by Norway.[2] Two remarks present themselves in relation to this use of the reservation. First, Norway made it clear that it relied on it only as a subsidiary ground, and in fact took pains to discuss with it other detailed grounds against jurisdiction and admissibility. Secondly, on invoking it Norway explained that it understood its terms to the effect that "such a reservation must be interpreted in good faith and should a Government seek to rely upon it with a view to denying the jurisdiction of the Court in a case which manifestly did not involve a matter which is essentially within the national jurisdiction it would be committing an *abus de droit* which would not prevent the Court from acting."[3] Following these objections, the French Government, aware of the serious "boomerang" effect of its reservation, referred in its Observations and Submissions to the Franco-Norwegian Arbitration of 1904 and to the first General Act of Geneva of 1928 to demonstrate that the two Governments have agreed to submit their disputes to arbitration or judicial settlement in certain circumstances including the present case.[4]

As to this latter point, the Court refused to deal with either of these treaties as a concurrent basis of jurisdiction, on the ground that if the French Government had intended to proceed upon that basis it would expressly have so stated.[5] And as to the subsidiary nature of the invocation of the reservation, the Court refused to look at it "in the sense that Norway would invoke the French reservation only in the event of the first ground of its Objection being held to be legally unfounded" and affirmed its freedom "to base its decision on the ground which in its judgment is more direct and conclusive."[6] This, the Court argued, was supported by the fact that the invocation of the reservation was maintained throughout the proceedings; and be-

[1] See "Exceptions Préliminaires Présentées par le Gouvernement du Royaume de Norvège," in 1 *Case of Certain Norwegian Loans*, Pleadings, Oral Arguments and Documents 119, 121–9 (*I.C.J.*, 1957).

[2] See *id.* at 129–32.

[3] *Id.* at 131 (English translation quoted from [1957] *I.C.J. Rep.* 9, 73 (Diss. Op. of Judge Basdevant)).

[4] See *id.* at 163, 173.

[5] [1957] *I.C.J. Rep.* 9, 25. (The question is discussed in detail in Chapter III, *supra*).

[6] *Ibid.*

cause abandonment cannot be presumed.[1] Finally, the Court refused to consider the general question of the validity of the reservation on the simple ground that such validity "has not been questioned by the parties" and the Court was not, therefore, called upon to examine it "in the light of considerations which are not presented by the issues in the proceedings."[2] As a result, the Court declined jurisdiction on the sole basis of the invocation of the reservation.

Along with the other considerations expressed in the individual opinions which will be exposed later, the Court's approach in the *Norwegian Loans Case* is subject to the following observations: (i) The court has ordered the joinder of the objections to the merits and has heard arguments related to the admissibility of the claim and its very merits, before declining jurisdiction on a basis that could have been relied upon in a judgment given *in limine litis*. (ii) The Court had more than one opportunity to avoid declining its jurisdiction on the basis above mentioned: (a) It could have discussed, as did Judge Basdevant,[3] whether Norway was justified in invoking the reservation. Norway itself seemed to have invited such a discussion by insisting that the invocation should be made in good faith. And the wording of the reservation itself may, as Judge Read noticed,[4] have helped in this respect. (b) It could, on the other hand, have considered its jurisdiction in the light of the first part of the first objection only, as Judges Moreno Quintana and Badawi have done,[5] supported in this by the subsidiary and hesitant manner in which Norway invoked the reservation. (c) Thirdly, the Court could have ignored the declarations of acceptance altogether and considered, instead, basing its jurisdiction on the treaties referred to by the applicant in the course of the proceedings, or directly declining the admissibility of the claim, on the basis of the third preliminary objection – the non-exhaustion of local remedies. (iii) The Court preferred, however, to base its decision directly on the invocation of the reservation, giving an "automatic" effect to it as it stood and as it was exercised in the case, while simultaneously insisting that its judgment does not prejudge the question of the validity of the reservation. This approach, supported by a wide majority of the Court, amounts in fact to saying that "the case came

[1] *Id.* at 25–6. But see, *id.* at 93 (Diss. Op. of Judge Read).

[2] *Id.* at 27. But see, *id.* at 34, 61 (Sep. Op. of Judge Lauterpacht), and at 68 (Diss. Op. of Judge Guerrero).

[3] See *id.* at 76.

[4] See *id.* at 94.

[5] See *id.* at 28, 29–33.

within the scope of the reservation *if it be valid*."[1] As such, it could not have been followed but for the absence from the proceedings of any challenge to the validity of the reservation and the declaration to which it was attached. However, as this challenge presented itself in subsequent cases, the apporach had to differ accordingly.

c. The Interhandel Case

The *Interhandel Case* (1959) brought against the United States by the application of Switzerland relying on the mutual declarations of acceptance of the parties, afforded two occasions for the consideration of the issue.

The first occasion was the phase of the case in which the Court considered the indication of interim measures of protection, on the request of Switzerland. As seen above,[2] the United States met this request by objecting to the Court's jurisdiction over the merits of the case on four grounds two of which were based on the lack of jurisdiction *ratione temporis*, one on the non-exhaustion of local remedies, and one on the fact that part of the dispute was a matter of domestic jurisdiction as determined by the United States itself and another part was a matter of domestic jurisdiction according to international law.[3] The developments which subsequently took place and the attitude of the Court in regard thereto are exposed at the last section of Chapter IV above. It has been shown there that the Court refused to consider the American objections to jurisdiction in the context of the procedure on the interim measures. It, therefore, found that it had jurisdiction to indicate such measures, but declined to do so for the lack of urgency. The clear implication of this attitude is that, regardless of its validity for the purposes of substantive jurisdiction, a declaration to which the "automatic" reservation is attached, may be relied upon as a basis of a valid seisin, and consequently, for the conferment of the incidental jurisdiction to indicate interim measures.[4]

In the subsequent proceedings on the preliminary objections, Switzerland argued that the reservation according to which the United States "determined" that some aspect of the dispute was within its domestic jurisdiction, was invalid. Relying on the opinion of judges Lauterpacht and Guerrero in the *Norwegian Loans Case* (1957), the

[1] Jennings, *supra*, p. 273, note 2 at 361.

[2] Chapter IV at 177–180.

[3] See Preliminary Objections of the Government of the United States of America, *Interhandel Case*, Pleadings, Oral Arguments and Documents 303–26 (*I.C.J.*, 1959).

[4] See generally, Briggs, *supra*, p. 273, note 1 at 355–9, and Chapter IV, *supra*.

Swiss Observations based such invalidity on the incompatibility of the reservation with both paragraphs 2 and 6 of Article 36 of the Statute. However, they avoided the question of the effect of the invalidity of the reservation on the whole declaration of the United States, on the ground that the latter invoked the reservation only as to a part of the dispute suggesting that it had accepted jurisdiction over the other parts, and in such a situation it would not matter whether the acceptance was based on the declaration or on the principle of *forum prorogatum*.[1] Finally, the observations went to argue that even if the reservation was valid its invocation in the case at hand was not, due to the clear international character of the question to which it was applied.[2] On the other hand, the United States which had declared in the earlier phase of the case that after the reservation was invoked "the subject matter of the determination is not justiciable,"[3] reiterated more strongly that such invocation was conclusive and not subject to review.[4] Simultaneously, the United States exposed, merely for "the information of the Court," the details of the facts to which the reservation was applied, on the understanding that "their submission does not in any way modify the conclusion that the determination of the United States is not subject to review or approval by this Court."[5] This unequivocal stand, which was clearly disputed by Switzerland, was later found by the United States' Agent to have "lost immediate practical significance"[6] and to have become "somewhat moot,"[7] though it was never withdrawn. This loss of practical significance was due to an event in the domestic litigation of the dispute in the United States which prevented that Government from taking the actions which it determined in the objection to be within its domestic jurisdiction (the sale and disposition of the stock in dispute). Accordingly, the Court, which had discussed and refused the first and second preliminary objections along with part (b) of the fourth objection, and had temporarily postponed the consideration of the question of exhaustion of local remedies till it considered the fourth objection as a whole, found that:

Although the Agent for the United States maintained the objection throughout the oral arguments, it appears to the Court that, thus presented – part (a) of

[1] Pleadings, *supra*, p. 279, note 3 at 411.
[2] *Id.* at 410.
[3] *Id.* at 320, 452.
[4] See *id.* at 466, 610.
[5] *Id.* at 320. And see Reply of the U.S. Agent in *id.* at 601, 610.
[6] *Id.* at 475.
[7] *Id.* at 507.

the Fourth Objection [invoking the reservation] only applies to the claim of the Swiss Government regarding the restitution of the assets of Interhandel which have been vested on the United States. Having regard to the decision of the Court set out below in respect of the Third Preliminary Objection of the United States [i.e., the decision accepting the contention that local remedies were not yet exhausted], it appears to the Court that part (a) of the Fourth Preliminary Objection is without object at the present stage of the proceedings.[1]

For these reasons the Court, by 10 votes to 5, found that it was not necessary to adjudicate on the validity of the American reservation or of its invocation in the case.

Compared with its attitude in the *Norwegian Loans Case* (1957), the Court's approach in the *Interhandel Case* (1959) invites the following remarks:

By considering the fourth preliminary objection in the latter case before the third objection, on the ground that the former related to its jurisdiction whereas the third objection related to the admissibility of the claim, the Court gave the impression that it cannot consistently adjudicate on the issue of admissibility except after it establishes its jurisdiction. Yet, it ended up by declaring the claim inadmissible without finally disposing of the question of whether its jurisdiction covered the issue to which the United States invoked its reservation. This occurred despite the fact that the respondent had continued to maintain the invocation of the reservation – a fact that was found particularly important in the *Norwegian Loans Case*.

In fact in the *Interhandel Case* the Court has examined first all the grounds on which it might have been possible to decline jurisdiction without adjudicating on the reservation problem. Hence, it dealt with part (b) of the Fourth Objection before part (a) for no other apparent reason. Failing, however, to find in these other objections an adequate ground for declining jurisdiction, the only escape route to avoid adjudicating on the reservation problem was to pass directly to the issue of admissibility. Had it not been possible for the Court to find the claim inadmissible, it would not have found part (b) of the fourth objection "without object" in the case.

In summation, by the Order in the first phase of the *Interhandel Case* the Court found in the invocation of the United States' domestic jurisdiction reservation no bar to the exercise of the incidental jurisdiction to indicate interim measures. Similarly it seemed to have

[1] [1959] *I.C.J. Rep.* 4, 26.

refused, in its decision given in the second phase of the case, to see in such an invocation a bar to proceed to the issue of admissibility.[1]

d. The Aerial Incident of July 27th, 1955 Case (*U.S.A.* v. *Bulgaria*)

The issue of the value of the reliance on the reservation of matters within domestic jurisdiction as drafted in the United States declaration presented itself in a more acute form in the *Aerial Incident of July 27th, 1955 Case* (*U.S.A. v. Bulgaria*). In filing its application in this case, the United States referred to the unconditional Bulgarian declaration made under the Permanent Court [18], but not to its own declaration. It simply stated for itself that it "submits to the Court's jurisdiction for the purpose of this case."[2] Bulgaria objected to the jurisdiction of the Court on several grounds, the second among which invoked the United States' domestic jurisdiction reservation. Thus finding that no room was left for the application of the principle of *forum prorogatum*, the United States had to base its argument on the mutual effect of the declarations of the parties. Consequently, it advanced – to the surprise of many, and inconsistently with its allegations in the *Interhandel Case* – the following argument:

> The United States maintains that the reservation in question does not permit the Government of the United States, or any other Government seeking to rely on this reservation reciprocally, arbitrarily to characterize the subject matter of a suit as essentially within the domestic jurisdiction. Where a subject matter is quite evidently one of international concern, and has so been treated by the parties to the suit, it is not open to either of them to determine that the matter lies essentially within domestic jurisdiction.[3]

The argument which went directly to say that the "United States reservation (b) does not permit the United States or any other state to make an arbitrary determination, in bad faith,"[4] meant, as Leo Gross put it, that the reservation was "neither automatic nor peremptory nor self-judging but subject to the judgment of the Court."[5] This would have been particularly surprising to the late Judge Lauterpacht

[1] *Accord*, Briggs, "Interhandel: The Court's Judgment of March 21, 1959, on the Preliminary Objections of the United States," 53 *Am. J. Int'l L.* 547, 558 (1959).

[2] Application Instituting Proceedings on behalf of the Government of the United States of America, *Aerial Incident of 27 July 1955*, Pleadings, Oral Arguments and Documents 22, 23 (*I.C.J.*, 1959).

[3] *Id.* at 301, 305 (Observations and Submissions of the U.S.A.). See also this argument as maintained in the Preliminary Objections of Norway in 1 *Case of Certain Norwegian Loans*, Pleadings, *supra*, p. 277, note 1 at 131, and by Switzerland in the Oral Hearings in the *Interhandel Case*, Pleadings, *supra*, p. 279, note 3 at 579.

[4] Pleadings, *supra*, note 2 at 308.

[5] Gross, "Bulgaria Invokes the Conally Amendment," 57 *Am. J. Int'l L.* 357, 368 (1962).

who took pains to emphasize in his separate opinion in the *Interhandel Case* (1959) that an interpretation of this sort runs directly counter to the intention of the United States, and would put the Court in the invidious position of having to make pronouncements that are odious and offensive.[1]

After maintaining this argument for a while, the United States, aware of the weakness of its position in the case since the Court has found in the *Israel v. Bulgaria Case* that the Bulgarian declaration discontinued with the dissolution of the Permanent Court, reevaluated the wisdom of running the risk of committing itself to such a view. It therefore reversed its position in a letter sent by its Agent to the Registrar requesting the discontinuance of the proceedings and explicitely withdrawing the argument advanced in the observations submitted less than three months earlier:

> The necessary premise of the argument was that the Court must have jurisdiction for the limited purpose of deciding whether a determination under reservation (b) is arbitrary and without foundation. On the basis of further study and consideration of the history and background of reservation (b) and the position heretofore taken by the United States with respect to reservation (b) in litigation before the Court, it has been concluded that the premise of the argument is not valid and that the argument must therefore be withdrawn.[2]

Then, referring to its position in the *Interhandel Case,* the United States reiterated its understanding that: "A determination under reservation (b) that a matter is essentially domestic constitutes an absolute bar to jurisdiction irrespective of the propriety or arbitrariness of the determination," and agreed that "Bulgaria is accorded the same rights and powers with respect to reservation (b) as the United States."[3]

It is clear that this letter was not made for the sole purpose of the discontinuation of the case. The United States has meant it also to represent, for the future, its understanding of the legal scope of its reservation as "an absolute bar to jurisdiction."[4]

e. *The Aerial Incident of July 27th, 1955 Case* (*United Kingdom* v. *Bulgaria*)

One should not fail in this respect to recall that in the case raised against Bulgaria by the United Kingdom for the compensation of

[1] See [1959] *I.C.J. Rep.* 4, 111–5. And see further details of this opinion *infra.*

[2] Pleadings, *op. cit., supra*, p. 282, note 2 at 676, 677.

[3] *Ibid.*

[4] *Accord,* Gross, "The Jurisprudence of the World Court: Thirty-Eighth Year," 57 *Am. J. Int'l L.* 751, 771 (1963).

losses incurred in the same aerial incident, the latter state referred in its application to two bases of jurisdiction. One was the effect of the declaration of Bulgaria along with the applicant's own declaration of April 18, 1957 [142] which contained a reservation as to matters that "in the opinion of the Government of the United Kingdom" affect national security. And the second alternate basis was the United Kingdom's specific and unconditional *ad hoc* submission to the jurisdiction of the Court "for all the purposes of the present dispute" suggested to meet the unconditional acceptance in the Bulgarian declaration.[1] The invocation of this latter basis of jurisdiction was certainly meant to cope with the potentiality of Bulgaria's use of the "boomerang" effect of the British reservation. Yet, the decision in the *Israel v. Bulgaria Case* (declaring the expiry of the Bulgarian declaration) caused the British Government to request that proceedings be discontinued, before Bulgaria had the chance to submit any objections to jurisdiction. This latter case, the *United Kingdom v. Bulgaria,* has not, therefore, provided any of the arguments that were potentially possible to be raised in regard to the British reservation and which were soon to arise as shown above in the *United States v. Bulgaria* case.

B. POSSIBLE APPROACHES TO THE PROBLEM – THE ARGUMENT IN THEORY

Since it was first envisaged, the type of reservation involved in the instruments and cases above mentioned has been subject to a doctrinal controversy that presented itself adequately in the individual opinions rendered in the *Norwegian Loans* and the *Interhandel* cases. In this respect, at least four different approaches can be discerned:

1. Invalidity of the Reservation and the Instrument to which it is Attached – The Lauterpacht Approach

This first approach, to which the name of Judge Lauterpacht is attached both for the fact that he was first to adopt it, and because he vehemently upheld it on all occasions where the question arose before the Court, is based on the understanding that the reservation in question has an "automatic" effect. By this it is meant that after

[1] See Application Instituting Proceedings on behalf of the Government of the United Kingdom, Pleadings, *supra*, p. 282, note 2 at 34, 36.

the invocation of the reservation "the part of the Court is limited to the automatic function of registering the fact that the reservation has been invoked and that the Court is bound to hold, without examining its merits, that it is without jurisdiction."[1] On this assumption, the argument proceeds to maintain a two-fold conclusion; not only is this type of reservation null and invalid but it is also inseparable from the instrument containing it and consequently nullifies this instrument as a whole.

a. The Invalidity of the Reservation

As to the invalidity of the self-judging reservation, this is not simply due to the fact that this type of reservations is not provided for in Article 36(3) of the Statute. In the whole history of the International Court only one judge thought that this provision "specifies the only conditions which States may impose, viz, that of reciprocity on the part of one or more states, and of a limitation in time."[2] Otherwise, it is generally recognized that reservations are allowed if they are not incompatible with the Statute. However, a self-judging reservation falls, in this argument, within this latter limitation. It is inconsistent with the Statute. Such inconsistency exists regardless of the type of instrument containing the reservation, but becomes much more apparent if this instrument is a declaration made under Article 36(2) of the Statute. The argument is based in particular on the following grounds:

(i) An instrument accepting the Court's jurisdiction under the condition that its signatory can exclude by its unilateral decision any question from such jurisdiction, is, by virtue of this reservation, not a legal instrument upon which a state can rely as a *matter of right* for the purpose of invoking the jurisdiction of the Court. This follows simply from the lack of the element of legal obligation in an instrument of this type.[3]

(ii) This instrument cannot, at any rate, form a declaration in the sense meant in Article 36(2) of the Statute, as the provision speaks of the acceptance of the "obligation" of "compulsory jurisdiction." Certainly there is no obligation of this sort in an instrument allowing

[1] *Interhandel Case*, [1959] *I.C.J. Rep.* 6, 103 (Diss. Op. of Judge Lauterpacht). *Accord*, his Separate Opinion in the *Norwegian Loans Case*, [1957] *I.C.J. Rep.* 9, 34.

[2] Dissenting Opinion of Judge Levi Carneiro in the *Anglo-Iranian Oil Co. Case*, [1952] *I.C.J. Rep.* 93, 154. And see other non-judicial authorities to the same effect cited in Chapter IV, *supra*, p. 153, note 5.

[3] See this argument discussed in detail in Lauterpacht's Separate Opinion in the *Norwegian Loans Case* [1957] *I.C.J. Rep.* 9, 48–50.

the declarant to deprive the Court automatically of the exercise of jurisdiction.

(iii) Regardless of the type of instrument involved, an acceptance of jurisdiction under this reservation runs counter to Article 36(6) and is, therefore, incompatible with the Statute. According to this Article, it is the Court and the Court alone that is to decide its jurisdiction.[1] It will be of little avail in this respect to contend that by registering the statement by the respondent Government excluding the case from its jurisdiction, the Court will be exercising its power under Article 36(6).

(iv) The reservation is contrary to a fundamental principle of judicial organization and presents an attempt to deprive the Court of one of its "inherent" and most important powers, or indeed of its "duty," as a court of justice, to ascertain its jurisdiction.[2]

As a result, it should become impossible for the Court according to this argument to sustain the self-judging reservation without violating the injunction in the first Article of its Statute as well as in Article 92 of the Charter according to which the Court shall function in accordance with the provisions of the Statute.

b. The Invalidity of the Instrument as a Whole

Some earlier writers have suggested that "under no circumstances could it be maintained that whilst a reservation was invalid the acceptance to which it was attached stood..."[3] This sweeping generalization emanated from a strict approach to the consensual basis of the Court's jurisdiction, and was perhaps inspired by the old theory of the law of treaties according to which every single provision of a treaty is indissolubly linked with the fate of the entire instrument. This is not, however, the basis of the modern argument for the invalidity of the whole instrument to which a self-judging reservation is attached. This argument recognizes that "it is legitimate – and perhaps obligatory – to sever an invalid condition from the rest of the instrument and to treat the latter as valid provided that having regard to the intention of the parties and the nature of the instrument the condition in question does not constitute an essential part of the instrument. *Utile non debet per inutile vitiari.*"[4] Yet, because the self-

[1] See details in Chapters I, II *supra* at 32–8, 48–51.

[2] See Lauterpacht's Separate Opinion, *supra*, p. 285, note 3 at 44–6.

[3] Fachiri, *The Permanent Court of International Justice* 100 (2d ed. 1932).

[4] Lauterpacht, *supra*, p. 285, note 3 at 56–7. *Accord*, Maus, *Les Réserves dans les Déclarations d'Acceptations de la Juridiction de la Cour Internationale de Justice* 91–2 (1959).

judging reservation has proved to be – at least in the instruments upon which actual cases were brought before the Court – an essential and deliberate condition of the acceptance of jurisdiction, the instrument and the reservation cannot be separated. The latter being invalid, it follows necessarily, if any respect is to be given to the will of the accepting state, that the whole acceptance of the Court's jurisdiction under this reservation is invalid too.

In this respect, there is no place for the argument that by allowing the whole instrument to fall the Court is permitting a state to benefit from its own wrong. As noticed by Judge Lauterpacht, there is no element of illegality involved in making an instrument accepting jurisdiction under a self-judging reservation.[1] Such an instrument is simply non-existent from a legal point of view. This is not necessarily a sanction against the party introducing the reservation for it operates equally in relation to it and to its actual or potential opponents.[2]

Although the argument above expounded is of general scope and was generally meant to apply to declarations as well as to other types of instruments,[3] it was given only in regard to the self-judging reservation in the declarations of France [49] and the United States [145]. In the work of the Court, it was fully upheld only by two judges: Lauterpacht and Spender.[4] Yet, it seems to present a popular theme in doctrinal writings.[5]

The result of this approach is obviously that an instrument including a self-judging reservation is incapable of conferring any jurisdiction on the Court (not even in Lauterpacht's view the incidental jurisdiction to indicate interim measures). This important sequence is to follow in all cases where such an instrument is involved regardless of whether the reservation is invoked or not and whether, if invoked, its use was justified by the circumstances of the case. Such a clear-cut position

[1] *Interhandel Case*, [1959] *I.C.J. Rep.* 6, 118.

[2] *Id.* at 118–9.

[3] See *e.g.*, Lauterpacht, *supra*, p. 285, note 3 at 62 where he discussed the invalidity of argreements accepting jurisdiction subject to reservations identical to the one embodied in the French declaration of 1949 [49].

[4] See Judge Lauterpacht's individual opinions in the *Norwegian Loans Case*, [1957] *I.C.J. Rep.* 9, 34–66; the *Interhandel Case* (Indication of Interim Measures) [1957] *I.C.J. Rep.* 105, 117–20; the *Interhandel Case* (Prel. Obj.), [1959] *I.C.J. Rep.* 6, 95–122. And see Judge Spender's separate opinion in the latter case, *id.* at 54–74.

[5] See *e.g.*, Dubisson, *La Cour Internationale de Justice* 186, 189 (1964); 2 Cavaré, *Droit International Public Positif* 319 (1962); Maus, *supra*, p. 286, note 4 at 160; Jennings, *supra*, p. 273, note 2 at 362, Waldock, "The Decline of the Optional Clause," 32 *Brit. Yb. Int'l L.* 244, 272–3 (1956) (also his, "The Plea of Domestic Jurisdiction before International Legal Tribunals," 31 *id.* at 96, 136 (1954)). And see Berlia, "La Jurisprudence des Tribunaux Internationaux en ce qui concerne leur Compétence," 88 *Recueil des Cours* 109, 115–8 (1955).

differentiates this approach from all the others, despite the incidental similarity between some of the practical consequences ensuing from it and those resulting from approach "4" below.

2. *Invalidity of the Reservation and Validity of the Acceptance*

The second approach to the problem agrees with the first in invalidating the self-judging reservation for its incompatibility with the Statute and with the general rules of judicial organization. It contends, however, that such invalidity does not extend to the whole instrument by which the Court's jurisdiction is accepted. Expounding this argument as applied to the United States declaration [145], Judge Armand-Ugon stated in the *Interhandel Case* (1959) that:

> This Declaration consists of two parts, acceptance of the Court's jurisdiction and reservations to that acceptance. Those two elements of a single judical act are separable. Nothing justifies us, when reading the text, in considering them as an indivisible whole.[1]

Two methods have been employed in justification of this argument. There is *first* the approach adopted in particular by Judge Guerrero in the *Norwegian Loans Case,* i.e., to argue for the invalidity of the reservation assuming that such invalidity cannot lead to depriving the Court of jurisdiction conferred by the instrument to which the reservation is attached, no regard being made to whether the state making the reservation would have accepted jurisdiction in the absence of this reservation.[2] This has been based on a doctrine pronounced by the Court in the *Right of Passage Case* (1957), according to which "a text emanating from a Government must, in principle, be interpreted as producing and as intended to procedure effects in accordance with

[1] [1959] *I.C.J. Rep.* 6, 91. See also, *id.* at 76 (Diss. Op. of Judge Klaestad). Judge *ad hoc* Carry agreed also with this conclusion. *Id.* at 32.

[2] See [1957] *I.C.J. Rep.* 9, 67–70 (Diss. Op. of Judge Guerrero). In this opinion Judge Guerrero did not explicitly state that the Court had jurisdiction over the case. He reached a seemingly self-contradicting conclusion by describing the whole French declaration as "null and void" while declaring that he "cannot agree that the Court is without jurisdiction." *Id.* at 70. Compare Guerrero, "La Qualification Unilatérale de la Compétence Nationale," in [Constantopoulos et al.] *Grundprobleme des Internationalen Rechts, Festschrift für Jean Spiropoulos* 207, 212 (1957), where he seemed to be subscribing to approach "1," above. (The Article was apparently written before the judgment in the *Norwegian Loans Case*). See also for the invalidity of the reservation and the validity of the acceptance in the rest of the declaration, Perrin, "L'Affaire de L'Interhandel-Phase des exceptions préliminaires," 16 *Annuaire Suisse de Droit International* 73, 167–68 (1959); Verzijl, "La Cour Internationale de Justice – Affaire Relative à Certains Emprunts Norvégiens," 4 *Nederlands Tijdschrift voor Internationaal Recht* 373, 399–400 (1957) and his, "The International Court of Justice in 1959," Part I, 6 *id.* 362, 377–8 (1959).

existing law and not in violation of it."[1] It has also been supported by the weak argument that the invocation of the reservation in a given case will run counter to "the *Nottebohm* rule that a unilateral attempt to withdraw jurisdiction in a case already pending before the Court cannot deprive the Court of jurisdiction already established."[2]

Aware of the basic weakness of this view, presented in disregard of the intention of the parties, the *second* method attempted to establish that in the actual cases where the problem arose jurisdiction was truly and effectively accepted despite the reservation.[3] Thus it implies that if the evidence is to the effect that the state making the reservation could not have accepted the Court's jurisdiction without this reservation being attached, it will then be inevitable to agree that the invalidity of the reservation entails the fall of the whole instrument.[4]

By maintaining that an instrument containing a self-judging reservation presents a valid acceptance of the court's jurisdiction, the reservation being of no effect on the rest of the instrument, this approach leads to a situation opposite to that reached in approach "1" – the conferment of jurisdiction on the Court. Yet in this approach, the jurisdiction conferred should be subject to the exclusion of matters which are *by international law* essentially within domestic jurisdiction, for it is clear that the instrument including the reservation carries no intention to confer on the Court jurisdiction over such matters.

3. *Validity of the Reservation to be Judged by its Use in Each Case*

In all the cases where the self-judging reservation was invoked, an argument was made, as seen above, to the effect that the reservation should be interpreted "in good faith," and that a state would commit an "abuse of right" if its invocation of it was "unreasonable" in the circumstances of the case. To be sure, this argument assumes that the

[1] [1957] *I.C.J. Rep.* 125, 142. Cited in this context by Briggs, *supra*, p. 273, note 1 at 360.

[2] Briggs, *id.* at 362. However, the bearing of the above *Nottebohm* rule is apparently doubtful. The self-judging reservation is "an intrinsic fact, built into and forms an integral part of the declaration," while the "unilateral attempt" referred to in the *Nottebohm* text was the extrinsic fact of the termination of the declaration after the seisin. See Gross, *supra*, p. 282, note 5 at 378.

[3] See [1959] *I.C.J. Rep.* 6, 71 (Diss. Op. of Judge Klaestad).

[4] See a discussion of this distinction in the *Norwegian Loans Case* [1957] *I.C.J. Rep.* 9, 56–7 (Sep. Op. of Judge Lauterpacht). See also, Iaccarino, "Della c.d. Competenza sulla Competenza dei Tribunali Internazionali," 14 *Diritto Internazionale* 357, 404 (1960); Perrin, *upra*, p. 288, note 2 at 165–72.

reservation is valid on its face. It understands its terms, however, to mean that the determination of the reserving state of whether a matter falls within the Court's jurisdiction is not final but is still subject to the Court's review.

There could be two criteria at least for interpreting the requirement of good faith in this respect. The first is an objective criterion according to which the invocation of the reservation will be in good faith only if the Court finds that the question involved falls *by international law* within the domestic jurisdiction of the reserving party. The second criterion is more subjective in character and is based on the prior practice of the state concerned. If it proves that the question has been *traditionally considered by it* as a matter within its domestic jurisdiction, its invocation of the reservation in regard to this question should in this view be accepted by the Court as made in good faith.[1] In standard writings, however, it is the first criterion which is usually referred to as the test for the good faith of the reserving party.

The argument for this approach relies, in particular, on the established general principle that all legal instruments, including those containing the reservation, are presumed to be made in good faith, and should be interpreted on this basis. It is also based on the theory of "abuse of right" which has been gaining ground in both municipal and international law. Besides, the Court's review of the determination made by a reserving party may be inspired by the wording of the reservation itself. Thus, noting that the French declaration [49] reserved matters of national jurisdiction "as *understood*, by the French Republic," a dissenting judge in the *Norwegian Loans Case* (1957) found that:

> The words actually used "as understood", if given their natural and ordinary meaning, connote a real understanding, and not a fictitious understanding unrelated to the facts.[2]

[1] See a proposal for redrafting the self-judging reservation in the U.S. declaration so as to exclude "matters which have been traditionally considered" by the U.S. as matters within its domestic jurisdiction in Sohn, "International Tribunals: Past, and Future," 46 *A.B.A.J.* 23, 26 (1960). A clear example of questions traditionally considered by the U.S. Government as within its domestic jurisdiction though they may not necessarily be so under the general criteria of international law can be found in the disputes relating to the Panama Canal. See further examples in [American Bar Association – Section of International and Comparative Law] *Report on the Self-judging Aspect of the United States' Domestic Jurisdiction Reservation with Respect to the International Court of Justice* 43–4 (1959).

[2] [1957] *I.C.J. Rep.* 9, 95 (Diss. Op. of Judge Read). However, Judge Read wrote that he was "disinclined to bring notions of 'good faith' and '*abus de droit*' into the question." *Id.* at 94.

This latter argument which supports especially the subjective concept of good faith was, however, said to be inapplicable to the reservations using the words "as determined" instead of "as understood,"[1] which cover almost all reservations of this type now in force.[2]

This approach was critized on several grounds, particularly by the supporters of approaches "1" and "2" above. First, it is argued that it disregards the very terms of the reservation, and the intention of its drafters to leave for the reserving party the exclusive power of determining the issue. Its bases are also found to be of doubtful validity: It is inconceivable in fact, and at any rate extremely undesirable, to challenge the good faith or judgment of the state making the determination.[3] On the other hand, the theory of "abuse of right" is, as Judge Anzilotti found in the *Electricity Company of Sofia and Bulgaria Case* (1939), "an extremely delicate one" to the extent that a judge should "hesitate long before applying it to such a question as the compulsory jurisdiction of the Court."[4]

Along with the above considerations one may add that in practical terms this approach may lead to the same position reached according to approach "2." When the good faith of the state invoking the reservation is judged by applying the standards of international law to its determination of the issue, a "self-judging" reservation covering matters of domestic jurisdiction will be confined in fact to the exclusion of matters which are by international law within the domestic jurisdiction of the state invoking it. As such matters are excluded even when the self-judging reservation is found null, the practical consequence of this approach will not be different from that of approach "2." Yet, unlike approach "2," this third approach is gaining grounds in doctrinal writings, apparently for its moderate overtones.[3]

[1] See *Interhandel Case*, [1959] *I.C.J. Rep.* 6, 58 (Sep. Op. of Judge Spender).

[2] See Appendix VII, No. 6 (B). Declaration of Liberia [80] uses the word "consider" and declaration of Mexico [88] uses the words "in the opinion of."

[3] See generally *Norwegian Loans Case*, [1957] *I.C.J. Rep.* 9, 50–2 (Sep. Op. of Judge Lauterpacht); *Interhandel Case*, [1959] *I.C.J. Rep.* 6, 57–9 (Sep. Op. of Judge Spender); *id.* at 111–5 (Diss. Op. of Judge Lauterpacht). And see, Briggs, "Reservations to the Acceptance of Compulsory Jurisdiction of the International Court of Justice," 93 *Recueil des Cours* 229, 303 (1958–I); Maus, *supra*, p. 286, note 4 at 158–61.

[4] *P.C.I.J.*, ser. A/B, No. 77 at 98 (1939).

[5] See *e.g.*, Perrin, *supra*, p. 288, note 2 at 172–74; Gross, *supra*, p. 282, note 5 at 376–8. The latter imputes this doctrine to Guggenheim, Bourquin and, inaccurately, to Briggs. Gross himself though commending this approach concludes in favor of declaring the reservation incompatible with Art. 36(6) the integrity of which is safeguarded, at least for the members of the U.N. by Art. 103 of the Charter. *Id.* at 380–1. And see *supra*, p. 282, note 3 for the instances in which this approach was defended in practice.

4. *Validity of the Reservation in All Cases*

Finally, there is the view which upholds that the invocation of the self-judging reservation removes, in all cases, the dispute from the Court's jurisdiction, not because the reservation invalidates the acceptance of jurisdiction, but simply because this acceptance was made subject to the reservation. According to this view the reservation, though not in conformity with Article 36(6) of the Statute, does not violate it. In the words of Hudson:

> ... a state may make exceptions to the jurisdiction which it recognizes, and while the [Connally] amendment is not in the spirit of Para. 6 of Article 36, it seems difficult to maintain that it constitutes a violation of that provision.[1]

In this sense, a declaration containing this reservation is like a declaration accepting jurisdiction only in relation to some states and not, as Article 36(2) provides, "in relation to any other state accepting the same obligation." This is not in conformity with the Article, but still is not incompatible with it. Thus, all arguments basing the invalidity of the reservation on its violation of Article 36(6) will not be applicable.

As to the incompatibility of the reservation, when included in a declaration, with the Optional Clause system, the answer is made by reference to the very "optional" character of this system. The reservation can be viewed as rendering the acceptance subject to an additional fact without the realization of which the "option" is not yet made. This jurisdictional fact is the abstention from invoking the reservation. If the reservation is invoked, this means that jurisdiction was never accepted on the issue. When it is not, this means that jurisdiction was always accepted over the issue, unless it is excluded for other reasons. In neither case is the Court deprived of a jurisdiction inherent in its Statute. Admittedly, this is not a desirable state of affairs, but nevertheless, it does not, in this argument, constitute an invalid practice in the present stage of development of the law of international adjudication.

This approach, which accepts as valid on its face and in its application the reservation challenging the Court's power to determine its

[1] Hudson, "The World Court: America's Declaration Accepting Jurisdiction," 23 *A.B.A.J.* 832, 836 (1946) (Compare Hudson, *The Permanent Court of International Justice* 397 (1934)). See also, Kelsen, *The Law of the United Nations* 529 (1951); Wilcox, "The United States Accepts Compulsory Jurisdiction," 40 *Am. J. Int'l L.* 699, 718–9 (1946); Hyde, "The United States Accepts the Optional Clause," *id.* at 778, 780. And see for the validity of the self-judging reservation in general Brierly and Kaeckenbeeck in their responses to the questionnaire addressed by M. Rousseau in 43 *Annuaire* 28, 32 (1950–I).

jurisdiction, was followed by one judge of the present Court,[1] and is implicitly assumed in the works of many others.[2] Its practical consequence is that the Court should declare itself without jurisdiction whenever the reservation is invoked without discussing the manner in which such an invocation is made. But when neither party takes advantage of the reservation (e.g., in the *U.S. Nationals in Morocco Case* (1954)), there is nothing inherent in it to bar the Court from exercising jurisdiction.

The practical consequences of this approach may seem to be the same as those of Approach "1," above. According to that latter approach, the instrument containing the reservation is incapable of conferring jurisdiction, but, if no objection is made to the Court's jurisdiction this could always be exercised on the basis of *forum prorogatum*. In other words, the two theoretically opposed approaches seem to concur in the final practical result: there is no jurisdiction when the reservation is invoked, and there is jurisdiction when it is not.

This apparent similarity does not, however, hide many practical difference.

a. As to incidental jurisdiction. In the Lauterpacht theory the instrument containing the reservation does not serve even as a basis for the exercise of the incidental jurisdiction of indicating interim measures of protection, nor on the same grounds, for any other incidental jurisdiction. This result does not ensue in approach "4."

b. In the situation where the principle of forum prorogatum has no application. If the defendant state chooses not to invoke the reservation while objecting to jurisdiction in general on other grounds and the Court finds against it on all these grounds, under approach "4" the Court will then have jurisdiction. This can hardly be the case under approach "1" where jurisdiction may be exercised only on the basis of *forum prorogatum* which can not always be relied upon after the defendant has already denied its acceptance of jurisdiction over the case as a whole.[3]

[1] See *Interhandel Case* (interim Measures), [1957] *I.C.J. Rep.* 105, 113–4 (Diss. Op. of Judge Koo).

[2] It could even be said, despite the assurances given by the Court in both the *Norwegian Loans Case* and the *Interhandel Case* that the question of the validity of the reservation was not considered, that by acting upon the invocation of this reservation in the former case and by passing to the question of admissibility in the latter, the Court has in a sense implicitly considered the declaration containing the reservation as valid. An opposite conclusion is reached in Anand, *Compulsory Jurisdiction of the International Court of Justice* 212 (1961).

[3] *Accord*, Jennings, "Recent Cases on Automatic Reservations to the Optional Clause," 7 *Int'l & Comp. L.Q.* 349, 363 (1958). It could be argued, however, that even under approach

c. As to the equality of the parties. In approach "4" the subjective determination may lead to the same question being within the Court's jurisdiction in a case (when the reservation is not invoked) and outside this jurisdiction in another (when the reservation is invoked). Also, different parties are apt to differ in their characterization of a question as essentially of domestic jurisdiction. Such is a situation where, in Waldock's words, "the equality of obligation which is specifically provided for in the Optional clause is more apparent than real. Worse, the balance is in favour of the less scrupulous State."[1] Obviously, this situation does not arise in approach "1."

C. THE COURT'S ATTITUDE – PREDICTIONS FOR THE FUTURE

Among the above alternatives, what is the expected choice of the Court?

In answering this question, one has to take in consideration the previous trends presented in the cases where the problem arose, as well as the change in the composition of the Court which has taken place since the determination of these cases. Enough flexibility should also be allowed to meet the requirements that may be imposed by the peculiarties of each future case. In this respect, the following distinctions must be made:

1. Attitude in Relation to Incidental Jurisdiction

It has been made sufficiently clear that instruments containing the reservation provide, in the opinion of the Court, a valid basis of seisin, and that a valid seisin is all that is required for the Court's exercise of its preliminary incidental jurisdiction.[2] It follows that, as a rule, incidental jurisdiction could be exercised in cases based on such instruments. Obviously, this does not cover the incidental jurisdiction of the *compétence de la compétence* of which the reservation is meant to deprive the Court. Yet, the question is subject to further considerations. Because the reservation does not deprive the Court of its other

"1" above the Court may deduce from the non-invocation of the reservation an acquiescence in the international character of the dispute and therefore will be able after dismissing the other objections to assume jurisdiction on the basis of *forum prorogatum.*

[1] Waldock, "The Plea of Domestic Jurisdiction before International Legal Tribunals," 31 *Brit. Yb. Int'l L.* 96, 135 (1954).

[2] See Chapter IV, *supra* at 174–80.

incidental powers, the Court in fact exercises the *compétence de la compétence* over each of these patterns of jurisdiction, despite the reservation. Thus, the Court has discussed in the first phase of the *Interhandel Case* (1957) whether or not it had jurisdiction to indicate interim measures. Moreover, depriving the Court of the *compétence de la compétence* as related to substantive jurisdiction cannot be complete. In order to reach the conclusion that the reservation is valid or not, the Court necessarily exercises an aspect of this power which it cannot be deprived of.

2. *Attitude in Relation to Primary Jurisdicton*

As to the effect of the reservation on the Court's determination of whether it has jurisdiction on the merits, two situations should be distinguished:

a. In case both parties agree as to the validity of the reservation

This is normally the case when the reservation is contained in an agreement or a treaty between the parties. It is also the practical situation in most cases brought on the basis of mutual declarations where one or both declarations contain the reservation, unless the case is brought by a state whose declaration does not contain the reservation against one whose declaration does. For otherwise, there will be little wisdom in attacking the reservation. Thus, if both parties have the reservation in their declarations or if the reservation is attached to the applicant's declaration only, the defendant may find it easier to invoke the reservation being sure that the applicant cannot attack it as invalid.[1] In all such cases where no objection to the validity of the reservation is raised, the Court cannot declare it invalid without reversing its stand in the *Norwegian Loans Case* (1957), and, in fact, its general policy of not raising issues related to the parties'

[1] This was the situation in both the *Norwegian Loans Case* (1957) and the *Aerial Incident of July 27, 1955* (*U.S.A. v. Bulgaria*) *Case* (1960). Two questions should be considered in this respect. First, whether the reserving state can assail its own declaration, and second, whether it is always practically more advisable for the respondent to invoke the reservation in the applicant's declaration than to challenge its validity. As to the first question, it is doubtful that a state can assail its own declaration as invalid, especially if it is in the position of applicant. See Lauterpacht's Sep. Op. in the *Norwegian Loans Case, op. cit.* at 61; Maus, *supra*, p. 286, note 4 at 93. As to the second question, it is true that the respondent may find it more advisable not to invoke the reservation in regard to the issue in dispute lest this invocation should be quoted against it in future cases. In this situation, the defendant may prefer to base its objection against jurisdiction on the invalidity of the applicant's declaration if the reservation attached to that declaration is absent in its own.

consent *proprio motu.*[1] One can therefore safely state, that in the absence of a challenge to the validity of the reservation, the Court will be inclined to give it its full effect when reliance is made on it. This effect could, however, be influenced by the interpretation given by the reserving state to its own reservation. In a situation similar to that of the United States, before it reversed its position, in the *Aerial Incident Case* with Bulgaria, the Court may very well take the reservation to mean what its drafter contends to be its real meaning.

b. In case the validity of the reservation is questioned by one of the parties

This is most likely to occur in practice only in the situation where a suit is brought by a non-reserving state against a reserving state. If the reserving state chooses to invoke the reservation thus declaring the issue within its domestic jurisdiction, the applicant state may then attack the reservation as invalid, while necessarily maintaining that its invalidity does not entail the invalidity of the whole declaration (approach "2," *supra*). This was the situation in the *Interhandel Case* (1959). Judging by the previous attitude of the Court elaborated above, the Court will prefer in this situation to dispose of the jurisdictional issue on other grounds if this is possible. It may in this respect deal first with other objections made against its jurisdiction or even against the admissibility of the claim, regardless of whether these objections are put in the document of the party invoking them before or after the objection based on the reservation.

Yet, if the circumstances of the case are such that the Court has to face the issue (e.g., if there is only one objection to jurisdiction based on the reservation, or if the Court found all other objections to be unsound) a decision has to be made on the validity of the reservation. Nothing in the practice of the Court suggests that it will be inclined to follow the Lauterpacht theory. On the contrary, its position in both the *Norwegian Loans Case* and the *Interhandel Case* cannot be reconciled with this theory. In fact, with the exception of Judge Spender (now President of the Court) whose term ends in 1967 none of the present judges of the Court is clearly committed to this theory. The same holds true as to the second approach according to which the reservation is invalid but is separable from the rest of the declaration.

The Court will therefore be left with the third and fourth alternatives. The choice between them, it is submitted, will be decided mainly

[1] See Chapter II, *supra* at 66–68.

by the manner in which the reservation will be invoked. In practice it has always been alleged that the matter excluded by the invocation of the reservation is at any rate objectively within the domestic jurisdiction of the reserving state. Normally the Court will be inclined to uphold the party's determination made in accordance with the reservation if the merits of the case do not clearly contradict such an assertion. But if such a determination is so flagrant to the extent of being clearly unacceptable by objective standards, the Court may find it difficult to uphold it. It will then dismiss the objection relying, possibly, on the general theories of good faith and abuse of right. This is, however, a rare possibility. The question of domestic jurisdiction is elastic enough to allow a wide use of the reservation, which is not necessarily an abuse of it. Yet, it is not inconceivable that an abuse may take place. The invocation by Bulgaria of the reservation in its dispute with the United States over the Aerial Incident of July 27th, 1955, might be cited in this regard.

This conclusion assumes that the Court will have to decide, at least on a *prima facie* basis, whether the reservation was properly invoked. Such a decision can result only from the exercise of the *compétence de la compétence*, and therefore affirms anew that this power is partly exercised even in the situation where the parties provide for its exclusion.

At this point, it may be relevant to state that the above analysis is a prediction of the potential attitude of the Court on the issue, and not necessarily of the desired or the theoretically most correct attitude. It could not be said, on the other hand, to be particularly favorable or unfavorable to the enlargement of the scope of the Court's jurisdiction. It is, if any thing, favorable to the freedom of the parties to accept jurisdiction under their own terms, even if these are not in conformity with the Statute. This is only a reflection of the present stage of development in international adjudication. Its merits should therefore be judged against this background.

CONCLUSIONS

(1) Notwithstanding the controversy as to the scope of the power of international arbitral tribunals to determine their own jurisdiction, the power of the International Court covers in this respect both the interpretation of jurisdictional instruments *and* the determination of the nature of the controversy. This is how it was envisaged in the earliest proposals for a permanent international court and this is how it has since been conceived in practice. Therefore, in the absence of a clear self-judging reservation in the acceptance of the respondent, the contention that the dispute is political or domestic will not in itself take it out of the Court's jurisdiction. The Court will still have the power to study the case according to the Court's own standards and may, as a result, reach a conclusion different from the one advocated by the respondent party. This general principle applies regardless of the pattern of jurisdiction involved. The Court is competent to find out whether a dispute brought under declarations of acceptance falls within the categories enumerated in Article 36(2) of the Statute as much as it is competent to determine whether a dispute submitted under a treaty accepting its jurisdiction is covered by the terms of this treaty.

The power of the International Court to determine its jurisdiction has therefore two aspects: the interpretation of the jurisdictional instruments and the interpretation (and characterization) of the facts of the dispute itself. In fact, the jurisdiction of the Court can result only from the interaction of the elements involved in this process. If the alleged jurisdictional title does not convey the consent of the parties, or, if the facts of the dispute are such as to make it improper for the Court to exercise jurisdiction over them, a negative decision on jurisdiction is the natural result. An affirmative decision would, on the other hand, require the interaction of the right instruments with the right facts. In neither case can the decision be reached if the Court were deprived of the power to look at these two elements. To say that the instrument conferring continued jurisdiction enables the respondent to exclude *any* consideration by the Court of the acceptance contained in such an instrument is like saying that the facts of the dispute make it possible for the respondent to exclude the latter from the Court's jurisdiction by its unilateral characterization of the issue. Both arguments amount to denying the Court the power to reach a decision on its jurisdiction and constitute merely a request for the removal of the case from the list *in limine litis.*

Such an effect is defeated by the text of Article 36(6) of the Statute, and by the very nature of the Court as a judicial institution. This does not suggest that the attempts made in the instruments accepting jurisdiction to leave the determination of the nature of the controversy to the discretion of each party must be altogether ignored. The Court is not an isolated phenomenon without connections with the other facts of international life. For this reason it has been following in this respect the most cautious attitude. Avoiding any explicit statement on the validity of clauses reserving for the accepting party the power to determine whether or not the dispute is within its domestic jurisdiction, the Court has nevertheless found in these clauses no bar to the exercise of its preliminary incidental jurisdiction to indicate interim measures. It also suggested, when it refrained from questioning the validity of such clauses, that it did so because none of the parties has raised the question. And when the question was raised the Court managed to avoid the consideration of it only on the basis of its irrelevance to a decision in the case at hand. In doing this, the Court has not come outright for or against the clause, nor is it expected to do so in future cases of the same type as these presented before. Even when pressed by the circumstances of the case to face the issue, the Court, as it has already been suggested, will not consider the clause as invalid on its face and may only condemn its invocation when the abuse is *prima facie* obvious. But regardless of what the Court will eventually say, its conclusion can only be reached through the exercise of the power provided for in Article 36(6). This power is thus exercised in varied degrees in all cases, including the case where depriving the Court of it is the very issue involved.

(2) This aspect of the Court's power to determine its jurisdiction, developed and analyzed in Chapters I and VI above, is perhaps the most significant characteristic of this power. In addition to it, an

analysis of the approach and tendencies of the Court leads to the conclusion that the power at issue has acquired, through practice, certain characteristics which might not necessarily be shared by other courts of justice. As explained in detail in Chapter II, this power is quite general in scope; it covers all the patterns of jurisdiction outlined in Chapter IV. It therefore appears as an accessory power of the Court which becomes immediately involved whenever a jurisdictional question of any type is raised. Yet, as related to the parties' acceptance of jurisdiction, this power was exercised only when invoked by one of the parties. The failure of the respondent to object to jurisdiction is normally taken as an acquiescence in the validity of the alleged basis of jurisdiction, and is in itself sufficient to confer jurisdiction on the basis of *forum prorogatum*. However, in such circumstances the power can still be exercised in regard to questions beyond the issue of consent such as the ability to appear before the Court and the propriety of exercising the jurisdiction conferred. The power may also be exercised more than once in the same case. This is clear when it relates each time to a different issue on which no decision has previously been made. But even after the Court has affirmed its jurisdiction over a case it may find in a later decision that the claim is inadmissible. Furthermore, the possibility of finding itself without jurisdiction after an affirmative decision on jurisdiction has already been given should not be excluded, though the Court has never done so in practice. Finally, this power which is normally, but not necessarily, invoked and exercised in a preliminary stage of the proceedings, should not be excessively exercised so as to allow the Court to arrogate to itself jurisdiction where it does not possess it in fact. This is, however, a mere guideline which does not entail practical legal consequences. There is no organ competent to review the Court's exercise of this power, and it would involve too much strain on the present international judicial machinery if each party to a case before the Court were to be given the right to determine itself the extent to which the Court's determination of its jurisdiction has been proper.

(3) The operation of the Court's power to determine its own jurisdiction begins at the very moment in which the Court is seized of a given case. It is this moment which constitutes the critical date of the efficacy of the jurisdictional instruments and consequently of the Court's evaluation thereof. Later developments, it is true, may render it improper for the Court to exercise a jurisdiction conferred by instruments which were effective at the moment of seisin. Subsequent

changes in the jurisdictional facts may also have their direct effect on questions of jurisdiction and admissibility. But the general rule remains to the effect that the *compétence de la compétence* is determined with regard to the date of seisin. In such a determination it may be possible to dispose of the question of jurisdiction merely on account of the invalidity or inadequacy of the instruments invoked. There is usually no need to consider the merits of the case in the process of determining jurisdiction. But when the problem relates to the applicability of the jurisdictional instruments to the facts of the dispute, or else to the lack of an indispensable jurisdictional fact, a decision on jurisdiction may very well require a study of the merits of the case and hence a joinder of the two questions may become necessary. In practice, such a joinder took place only in a few cases as the Court has shown some reluctance to follow this procedure in the absence of an agreement between the parties.

(4) The Court's substantive jurisdiction which constitutes the subject matter or the merits of the *compétence de la compétence* is of two major types: contentious and advisory. The former covers primary jurisdiction and incidental jurisdiction. The primary jurisdiction of the Court is either *ad hoc* or continued. *Ad hoc* jurisdiction is conferred by a special agreement made before the filing of the application or by an agreement deduced from the acceptance by the respondent of the Court's jurisdiction after the application is filed. Continued jurisdiction is conferred either by a treaty between the parties to the case or by their mutual declarations made under the Optional Clause. In addition, there is a rather weak contention to the effect that the Statute of the present Court along with the Charter of the United Nations enable the Security Council to confer on the Court a compulsory contentious jurisdiction merely by calling upon the parties to refer the dispute to the Court. Incidental jurisdiction covers matters which may arise as incidents of the proceedings before the Court and is exercised in preliminary as well as consequential patterns. Obviously, the *compétence de la compétence* is itself a form of preliminary incidental jurisdiction distinguished, however, by its own characteristics which makes it relevant to all other patterns of jurisdiction including the advisory function.

The differences between the patterns outlined above may be determined by reference to the jurisdictional instruments involved in each of them. It is also manifested in the manner in which jurisdiction is determined. As each pattern has its own characteristics the jurisdictional problems which arise under one pattern may be irrelevant as far as others are concerned. The distinction is therefore important both in analyzing the previous practice of the Court and in predicting its future tendencies.

(5) This process of analysis and prediction cannot be complete without first ascertaining the techniques followed by the Court in each case allowing it to dispose of jurisdictional issues one way or the other. The discussion of such techniques, carried out in detail in Chapter V, revealed that there are behind the scene factors which influence the Court's decisions as to its jurisdiction. Major among these are the composition of the Court, the merits of the case, the justice of the claim and the prospects of compliance with a decision on the merits. Naturally, none of these factors is explicitly referred to in decisions on jurisdiction. On the contrary, some of them have been declared by the Court as irrelevent in this respect. Indeed reference has always been made in contentious cases to the consent of the parties as the decisive factor in matters of jurisdiction. This consent is, however, subject to different interpretations according to the method employed. Moreover, it may be disregarded, even after it is ascertained, by virtue of other techniques such as the invocation of the nature of the Court as a court of international justice or the reliance on the lack of a required jurisdictional fact. The result is that the consent which has a decisive effect on matters of jurisdiction is in fact the consent discovered or assumed by the Court and not any other hypothetical consent which a party may allege to have shared with another.

Some of the techniques used by the International Court are familiar in the work of all courts. Yet the Court has been particularly original in the choice of its techniques. It did not resort to the fact that it is a *juge d'exception* to build a presumption against its jurisdiction, as some other international tribunals have done. It has made a generous use of its Rules of Procedure in determining questions of jurisdiction. It exerted a relatively wide discretion in reformulating the issues before it and in ignoring the effect of the existence of other organs having a concurrent jurisdiction over the case. And, of course, it found in the fact that it is the principal judicial organ of the United Nations a distinguishing factor of particular influence, especially in regard to its advisory function. More than once the Court has shown that unless the case is brought by the right applicant and unless this applicant is particularly cautious in its formulation of the issues submitted, there may be involved a great hazard of losing the case on jurisdictional grounds.

(6) The tendencies of the Court in the matter of determining its jurisdiction and the extent to which each of these tendencies is now established have been discussed in the context of each special problem. It can be noted that there are a few conflicting tendencies, and that no feeling of inevitability should be attached even to the most established among them. Yet, it could be said that the Court has already made a law of jurisdiction rich enough to allow a rather accurate prediction of its stand in future cases. The details of this law have grown with the continuing exercise of the Court's *compétence de la compétence,* but its basic norm can still be traced to the Permanent Court's broad dictum that "there is no dispute which States entitled to appear before the Court cannot refer to it."

If it is recalled that technically the Court's primary jurisdiction is not compulsory and that its decisions are not backed by any particular sovereign, it will be realized how delicate a task it has been to exercise this power to the extent commensurate with its importance as the most significant single power possessed by a court of limited jurisdiction.

TABLE OF APPENDICES

APPENDIX I

THE WORK OF THE INTERNATIONAL COURT
1920–1965

The work of the

Court	Total Number of Cases [1]	Number of Advisory Opinions	Number of Contentious Cases	Number of Cont. Cases Discontinued	Number Judgmen
The Permanent Court of International Justice 1920–1946 [Active between 1922–1939]	71	27 Notes: 1) Of 28 advisory cases. Request was withdrawn in "*The question of the expulsion of the Acumenical Patriarch.*" Ser. E, No. 16 at 105 2) All opinions were requested by the Council of the League	43	11 Notes: 1) Plus the *Gerliczy Case.* Ser. E, No. 16 at 154–8 2) 2 cases were discontinued after a judgment on the prel. obj. (Ser. A/B, No. 73; Ser. E, No. 16 at 145)	31 Note: Besides the locutory jud accepting Po intervention *Wimbledon* ((Ser. A, No. 11–14)
The International Court of Justice 1945– [Period covered 1947 – January 1st 1965]	58	13 Notes: 1) 11 opinions requested by the General Assembly of the UN. 2) One requested by the Executive Board of UNESCO. 3) One requested by IMCO.	46 Note: Three cases are pending	14	28

[1] Preliminary objection proceedings are counted as new cases, except when the objection is joined to the merits and one judgment is given in the case.

[2] As contended in the application instituting the proceedings in the case.

International Court

. of Judgments ı Jurisdiction d Admissibility Only	Contentious Cases Based on Mutual Declarations [2]	Contentious Cases Based on Special Agreements	Contentious Cases Based on Treaties [2]	Contentious Cases Based on Unilateral Applications Invoking Jurisdiction (*forum prorogatum*)
8 : other cases ob- ons to juris- on were joined erits. these 6 cases later dis- inued	12 Notes: 1) In 2 cases (Ser. A/B, Nos. 68; 77) jurisdiction was allegedly based also on treaties. In the first case the Court took note that applicant no longer relied on declarations. 2) 5 cases were discontinued and one was left unsettled (the *Gerliczy Case*)	12 Notes: 1) 2 cases were discontinued 2) The *Borchgrave Case* is counted twice	21 Notes: 1) In 2 cases jurisdiction was also allegedly based on declarations and was upheld in one on the latter basis only. [Ser. A/B, No. 77] 2) In one case jurisdiction was upheld on implicit acceptance. Ser. A, No. 15 3) 4 cases were discontinued	— Note: But see Ser. A, No. 15 where jursidiction allegedly based on a treaty was upheld because it was not challenged in the right time.
15 s: he *Nottebohm* *ase* involves judgments.	16 Notes: 1) In one case jurisdiction was based primarily on a special agreement ([1960] Rep. 192) 2) 2 cases were discontinued	6 Notes: 1) Including 2 of the *Corfu Channel Cases* ([1949] Rep. 4; 244) 2) Mutual declarations were also invoked in one case ([1960] Rep. 192) and were in force in 2 cases ([1953] Rep. 47; [1959] Rep. 209)	15 Notes: 1) One case is counted twice. Discontinued in 1961 [Rep. 9] it was reinstituted in 1962. Now pending 2) 4 cases were discontinued	9 Notes: 1) In only one case application was found to have been met with acceptance [1948] Rep. 15 2) The other 8 cases were discontinued by administrative orders

APPENDIX II

PRELIMINARY OBJECTIONS RELATED TO JURISDICTION

A Survey of Cases Where Preliminary Objections Were Explicitly Invoked. [Operation of Article 36(6) of the Statute and Article 62 of the Rules of Court] *

* *Article 36(6) of the Statute* of the International Court of Justice:

"In the event of a dispute as to whether the Court has jurisdiction the matter shall be settled by the decision of the Court."

Article 62 of the Rules of Court of the International Court of Justice:

1. A preliminary objection must be filed by a party at the latest before the expiry of the time-limit fixed for the delivery of its first pleadings.
2. The preliminary objection shall set out the facts and the law on which the objection is based, the submissions and a list of the documents in support; these documents shall be attached; it shall mention any evidence which the party may desire to produce.
3. Upon receipt of the Registrar of a preliminary objection filed, by a party, the proceedings on the merits shall be suspended and the Court, or the President if the Court is not sitting, shall fix the time-limit within which the other party may present a written statement of its observations and submissions; documents in support shall be attached and evidence which it is proposed to produce shall be mentioned.
4. Unless otherwise decided by the Court, the future proceedings shall be oral.
5. After hearing the parties the Court shall give its decision on the objection to the merits. If the Court overrules the objection or joins it to the merits, it shall once more fix time-limits for the further proceedings.

A. Under the Permanent Court of International Justice *

No.	Case	Parties	Reference	Alleged Basis of Jurisdiction	Decision on Jurisdiction [1]
1	Mavrommatis Palestine Concessions	Greece/ Great Britain	Ser. A, No. 2 (1924)	Mandate for Palestine (Art. 26)	Affirmative (in part)
2	German Interests in Polish Upper Silesia	Germany/Poland	Ser. A, No. 6 (1925)	Geneva Convention concerning Upper Silesia (Art. 23)	Affirmative
3	Claim for Indemnity of the Factory of Chorzow	Germany/Poland	Ser. A, No. 9 (1927)	As in No. 2	Affirmative
4	Readaptation of the Mavrommatis Jerusalem Concessions	Greece/ Great Britain	Ser. A, No. 11 (1927)	As in No. 1	Negative
** 5	Interpretation of the Statute of Memel	France, Great Britain, Italy, Japan, Lithuania	Ser. A/B, No. 47 (1932)	Convention Concerning Memel (Art. 17)	Affirmative
6	Prince Von Pless Administration	Germany/Poland	Ser. A/B, No. 52 (1933)	As in No. 2	Preliminary objections joined to the merits. Case later discontinued (Ser. A/B, No. 59)
7	Appeal against the Judgments Delivered on Dec. 21st, 1931 by the Hungaro-Czechoslovak Mixed Arbitral Tribunal	Czechoslovakia/ Hungary	Ser. A/B, No. 56 (1933)	Agreement No. II of Paris (28.4.1930) (Art. 10)	Objections in the two cases joined together. Applications later withdrawn and cases discontinued (Ser. A/B, No. 56)
8	Appeal against a Judgment Delivered on April 13, 1932 by the Hungaro-Czechoslovak Mixed Arbitral Tribunal	Czechoslovakia/ Hungary	Ser. A/B, No. 56 (1933)	As in No. 7	
9	Pajzs, Csáky, Esterházy	Hungary/ Yugoslavia	Ser. A/B, Nos. 66, 68 (1936)	Agreements Nos. II and III of Paris (28.4.1930); and	Objections joined to the merits (Ser. A/B, No. 66).

				alternatively, the mutual declarations of acceptance	The Court noticed the expiry of the respondent's declaration before the date of the application and took note that applicant no longer relied on it. First submission in the case could not be entertained (*n'est pas recevable*) but second was adjudicated on the merits. (Ser. A/B, No. 68).
10	Losinger Co.	Switzerland/ Yugoslavia	Ser. A/B, Nos. 67, 69	Declarations	Objection joined to the merits (No. 67). Case later withdrawn (No. 69)
11	The Borchgrave	Belgium/Spain	Ser. A/B, No. 72 (1937)	Special Agreement (other basis were also involved)	Affirmative. Case later discontinued (Ser. A/B, No. 73)
12	Phosphates in Morocco	Italy/France	Ser. A/B, No. 74 (1938)	Declarations	Negative
13	Panevezys-Saldutiskis Railway	Estonia/ Lithuania	Ser. A/B, No. 75 (1938); No. 76 (1939)	Declarations	Objections joined to the merits (No. 75). Negative (No. 76)
14	Electricity Company of Sofia and Bulgaria	Belgium/ Bulgaria	Ser. A/B, No. 77 (1939)	Treaty of Conciliation, Arbitration and Judicial Settlement of 23.6.1931 *and* the mutual declarations (concurrent bases)	Affirmative (in part)
***					

* Though these are the only cases where preliminary objections related to jurisdiction were invoked, jurisdictional questions were also raised in all other cases under the Permanent Court except those published in: Ser. A, Nos. 3, 10, 23 and Ser. A/B, Nos. 53, 63, 70, 71.

** In the *Minority Schools in Upper Silesia Case* [Ser. A, No. 15]Poland objected to the Court's jurisdiction only in its Rejoinder, after having filed the counter-case without any objection or reservation related to jurisdiction. The Court found that by the time of advancing this belated objection Poland had already accepted the Court's jurisdiction over the case.

*** In the *Gerliczy Case* (1939), the last to be submitted to the Permanent Court, the applicant, not party to the stature, alleged that the jurisdiction of the court was based on mutual declarations of acceptance. The defendant expressed its intention to file a preliminary objection, but the case did not proceed any further. See Ser. E, No. 16 at 154–158.

[1] Under this heading the word "affirmative" indicates that the objection was overruled and that the Court found it had jurisdiction, and the word "negative" means that the objection was upheld.

B. Under the International Court of Justice *

No.	Case	Parties	Reference	Alleged Basis of Jurisdiction	Decision on Jurisdiction
1	The Corfu Channel	United Kingdom/ Albania	[1948] I.C.J. Rep. 15	1. Recommendation of the Security Council 2. Voluntary acceptance of Albania	Affirmative (on the second basis only)
2	Rights of Nationals of the U.S.A. in Morocco	France/U.S.A.	[1952] Rep. 176	Declarations	Preliminary objection withdrawn
3	The Ambatielos	Greece/ United Kingdom	[1952] Rep. 28	Treaty of Commerce and Navigation of 16.7.1926 (Art. 29)	Affirmative (in part)
4	Anglo-Iranian Oil Company	United Kingdom/ Iran	[1952] Rep. 93	Declarations	Negative
5	The Nottebohm	Liechtenstein/ Guatemala	[1953] Rep. 111	Declarations	Affirmative. Case later found inadmissible ([1955] Rep. 4)
6	Monetary Gold Removed from Rome	Italy/United Kingdom, France, U.S.A.	[1954] Rep. 19	Treaty. (Statement accompanying the Washington Agreement of 25.4.1951) and the declaration of Italy	Negative
7	Certain Norwegian Loans	France/Norway	[1957] Rep. 9	Declarations	Negative (after the objections were joined to the merits)
8	Right of Passage over Indian Territory	Portugal/India	[1957] Rep. 125	Declarations	Affirmative. Two of the six objections were rejected after being joined to the merits ([1960] Rep. 6, 32–33)
9	The Interhandel	Switzerland/ U.S.A.	[1959] Rep. 6	Declarations	Claim held inadmissible because of the non-exhaustion of local remedies
10	Aerial Incident of 27 July 1955	Israel/Bulgaria	[1959] Rep. 127	Declarations	Negative
11	Aerial Incident of 27 July 1955	U.S.A./Bulgaria	[1960] Rep. 146	Declarations	Case withdrawn

12	Compagnie du Port des Quais et des Entrepots de Beyrouth and Société Radio-Orient	France/Lebanon	[1960] Rep. 186	Franco-Lebanese Agreement of 24.1.1948 (Art. 23)	Case withdrawn
13	Barcelona Traction, Light and Power, Co., Limited	Belgium/Spain	[1961] Rep. 9	Treaty of Conciliation, Judicial Settlement, and Arbitration of 19.7.1927	Case withdrawn. (New proceedings were instituted on 19.6.1962. See below No. 18)
14	Temple of Preah Vihear	Cambodia/ Thailand	[1961] Rep. 17	Declarations	Affirmative
15 & 16	South-West Africa Cases (2 cases)	Ethiopia/Union of South Africa, and Liberia/ Union of South Africa	[1962] Rep. 319	Mandate for South-West Africa	Affirmative (one Judgment)
17	Case Concerning the Northern Cameroons	Cameroon/ United Kingdom	[1963] Rep. 15	Trusteeship Agreement for the Territory of the Cameroons (13.12.1946) (Art. 19)	Negative (decision of 2.12.1963)
18	The Barcelona Traction, Light and Power Company (New application)	Belgium/Spain		As in No. 13	Affirmative. One objection joined to the merits.

* The Court has also discussed jurisdictional issues in cases where no preliminary objections were made. Only nine cases did not include discussions on jurisdiction largely because they formed later stages of cases where jurisdiction was discussed or because they were based on prior agreements. These nine cases are found in: [1949] *I.C.J. Rep.* 244; [1950] *id.* 266; [1950] *id.* 395; [1951] *id.* 116; [1953] *id.* 47; [1958] *id.* 55; [1959] *id.* 209; [1960] *id.* 192; and [1962] *id.* 6.

** A third case related to *the Aerial Incident of 27 July 1955* was instituted by the *United Kingdom against Bulgaria.* It was, however, discontinued before Bulgaria presented its Counter Memorial. [1959] *I.C.J. Rep.* 264. Normally Bulgaria would have filed a preliminary objection in that case as well.

APPENDIX III

AD HOC JURISDICTION BY MEANS OF A PRIOR SPECIAL AGREEMENT

A Survey of the Special Agreements That Conferred an *Ad Hoc* Jurisdiction on the International Court *

* *Article 36(1) of the Statute* of the International Court of Justice:

"The jurisdiction of the Court comprises all cases which the parties refer to it ..."

Article 40(1) of the Statute of the International Court of Justice:

"Cases are brought before the Court, as the case may be, either by the notification of the special agreement or by a written application addressed to the Registrar. In either case the subject of the dispute and the parties shall be indicated."

A. Under the Permanent Court of International Justice [1]

No.	Parties to the Special Agreement	Date	Reference	Case Related	Remarks
1	Bulgaria/Greece	18.3.1924	Ser. C, No. 6 at 9	Interpretation of Paragraph 4 of the Annex Following Article 179 of the Treaty of Neuilly (Ser. A, No. 3)	Agreement not registered in the Secretariat of the League
2	France/Switzerland	30.10.1924	Ser. C, No. 17–I (vol. 2) at 490	Free Zones of Upper Savoy and the District of Gex (Ser. A, No. 22)	Agreement not registered
3	France/Turkey	12.10.1926	Ser. C, No. 13–II at 25	The S.S. Lotus (Ser. A, No. 10)	Agreement not registered. Turkey, in addition, being a non party to the statute, filed a particular declaration accepting the jurisdiction of the Court. (See Ser. C, No. 13–II at 9, 28)
4	Brazil/France	17.8.1927	Ser. C, No. 16–IV at 145	Brazilian Federal Loans Issued in France (Ser. A, No. 20/21)	Agreement registered (75 L.N.T.S 91) Jurisdiction discussed *ex officio* and affirmed
5	France/ Serb-Croate-Slovene	19.4.1928	Ser. C, No. 16–III at 292	Serbian Loans Issued in France (Ser. A, No. 20/21)	Agreement not registered. Jurisdiction discussed *ex officio* and affirmed
6	Czechoslovakia, Denmark, France, Germany, Great Britain, Sweden and Poland	30.10.1928	Ser. C, No. 17–II at 244	Territorial jurisdiction of the International Commission of the River Oder (Ser. A, No. 23)	Agreement registered (87 L.N.T.S. 103) Agreement notified by one party (Great Britain)
7	Italy/Turkey	30.5.1929	Ser. C, No. 75 at 9	Territorial Waters between Castellorizo and Anatolia (Ser. A/B, No. 51)	Agreement not registered. Turkey, in addition, made a particular declaration (Ser. C, No. 61 at 9). Agreement notified by one party (Turkey). The case was later withdrawn
8	France/Greece	15.7.1931	Ser. C, No. 74 at 11	The Lighthouses Case between France and Greece (Ser. A/B, No. 62)	Agreement not registered

[illegible]	[illegible]	[illegible]	[illegible]	The Oscar Chinn Case (Ser. A/B, No. 63)	Agreement registered (154 L.N.T.S. 361)
10	France/Greece	28.8.1936	Ser. C, No. 82 at 10	Lighthouses in Crete and Samos (Ser. A/B, No. 71)	Agreement not registered. Agreement notified by one party (France)
11	Belgium/Spain	20.2.1937	Ser. C, No. 83 at 10	The Borchgrave Case (Prel. obj. Ser. A/B, No. 72; discontinuance Ser. A/B, No. 73)	Agreement not registered. ***Preliminary objection*** advanced by respondent: against jurisdiction and admissibility of claim. The Court unanimously overruled objections to jurisdiction and refused to join objection to admissibility to the merits after its withdrawal as a preliminary objection. Case later discontinued

[1] Besides the agreements enumerated above, an agreement to submit a specific issue in the *Mavrommatis Jerusalem Concessions Case* to the jurisdiction of the Court resulted from the written proceedings. See Ser. A, No. 5 at 27–28. The Permanent Court also found that the parties had concluded *implied agreements* to accept its jurisdiction in the *Minority Schools Case*, Ser. A, No. 15 at 22–26; and in the *Société Commerciale de Belgique Case*, Ser. A/B, No. 78 at 174.

B. Under the International Court of Justice

No.	Parties to the Special Agreement	Date	Reference	Case Related	Remarks
1	Albania/United Kingdom	25.3.1948	2 I.C.J. Pleadings, The *Corfu Channel Case* 28–29	2 Cases: The *Corfu Channel Case* (merits) [1949] Rep. 4; (assessment) *Id.* at 244	Case originally instituted by the United Kingdom application (not based on any prior agreement). The Special Agreement was signed on the date of judgment affirming jurisdiction and was considered by the Court as basis of further proceedings. See [1948] Rep. 55. Agreement not registered.
2	Colombia/Peru	31.8.1949	1 I.C.J. Pleadings, *Asylum Case* 170	The *Asylum Case* [1950] Rep. 266	Case submitted by application from Colombia mentioning also other treaty texts as basis of jurisdiction. Peru submitted a counter-claim that was found admissible in its original form. Agreement not registered
* 3	France/United Kingdom	29.12.1950	1 I.C.J. Pleadings, *Minquiers and Ecrehos Case* 18–19	*The Minquiers and Ecrehos Case* [1953] Rep. 47	Agreement registered during the proceedings, 118 *U.N.T.S.* 149. Both parties also had declarations in force. Agreement notified by one party (United Kingdom)
4	Belgium/Netherlands	7.3.1957	I.C.J. Pleadings, *Sovereignty over Certain Frontier Lands Case* 8	*Sovereignty over Certain Frontier Lands Case* [1959] Rep. 209	Agreement registered on 14.12.1957: 282 *U.N.T.S.* 241. Both parties also had declarations in force. Agreement notified by one party (the Netherlands)
5	Honduras/Nicaragua	21.7.1957	1 I.C.J. Pleadings, *Case Concerning the Arbitral Award made by the King of Spain* 27–28	*Case Concerning the Arbitral Award Made by the King of Spain on 23 Dec. 1906* [1960] Rep. 192	Agreement registered on 28.9.1957: 277 *U.N.T.S.* 184. Case submitted by the application of Honduras. Application relied also on the mutual declarations.

* In the *Haya de la Torre Case*, the court was asked by one party in the *Asylum Case* to indicate the manner for the execution of the judgment in the latter case. No clear basis of jurisdiction was elucidated in the application but the Court found that its jurisdiction was accepted by the

APPENDIX IV

CONTINUED JURISDICTION BY MEANS OF TREATIES *

A Survey of the Treaties that were Invoked as the Basis of the Jurisdiction of the International Court **

* *Article 36(1) of the Statute* of the International Court of Justice:

"The jurisdiction of the Court comprises ... all matters provided for ... in treaties and conventions in force."

Article 37 of the Statute of the International Court of Justice:

"Whenever a treaty or convention in force provides for reference of a matter to a tribunal to have been instituted by the League of Nations, or to the Permanent Court of International Justice, the matter shall as between the parties to the present Statute, be referred to the International Court of Justice."

** For a survey of *all* treaties that have conferred a continued jurisdiction on the Permanent Court, see *P.C.I.J.*, Ser. D, No. 6; and Ser. E, No. 16 at 404–443.

For the treaties that confer jurisdiction on the present Court, see [1962–63] *I.C.J.Y.B.* 260–271. And see *id.* at 233–236 for a survey of the instruments governing relationships of organs of the United Nations and International organizations with the present Court.

A. Under the Permanent Court of International Justice [1]

No.	Title of Treaty	Date of Signature	Case Related	Remarks
1	Treaty of Versailles (Art. 386)	28.6.1919	S. S. Wimbledon. Ser. A, No. 1	Intervention of Poland (a signatory of the treaty) was allowed. See text of treaty in Cmd. No. 393 (T.S. No. 4 of 1919)
2	Mandate for Palestine (Art. 26)	24.7.1922	Mavrommatis Concession Cases	3 cases: Ser. A, No. 2 (jurisdiction); No. 5 (merits); No. 11 (jurisdiction). Mandate not registered in *L.N.T.S.*, see text in League of Nations Off. J., 3rd Ass. 1012 (1922)
3a)	German-Polish Convention Concerning Upper Silesia (Art. 23)	15.5.1922	German Interests in Polish Upper Silesia	2 cases: Ser. A, No. 6 (jurisdiction); No. 7 (merits). Convention registered: 9 *L.N.T.S.* 466
b)	Same	15.5.1922	Chorzoẃ Factory	2 cases: Ser. A, No. 9 (jurisdiction); No. 17 (merits)
c)	Same (Art. 72)	15.5.1922	Rights of Minorities in Upper Silesia (Minority Schools Case). Ser. A, No. 15	Jurisdiction based in the Court's judgment on the implied acceptance of respondent
d)	Same (Art. 72)	15.5.1922	Prince Von Pless Administration. Ser. A/B, No. 52	Case later withdrawn. Ser. A/B, No. 59
4	Convention Concerning the Memel Territory (Art. 17)	8.5.1924	Interpretation of the Statute of Memel	2 cases: Ser. A/B, No. 47 (jurisdiction); No. 49 (merits). Convention registered; 29 *L.N.T.S.* 86
5	Minorities Treaty between and Poland (Art. 12)	29.6.1919	Polish Agrarian Reform	Case discontinued (Ser. A/B, No. 60). See text in Cmd. No. 223 (T.S. No. 8 of 1919)
6	Agreement No. II of the Agreements relating to the obligations resulting from the Treaty of Trianon (Agreement No. II of Paris) (Art. 10)	28.4.1930	Appeals against judgments of the Mixed Arbitral Tribunals	3 cases: the first two were discontinued (Ser. A/B, No. 56), the third was decided on the merits (Ser. A/B, No. 61). Agreement registered: 121 *L.N.T.S.* 81
7	Same as above, and Agreement No. III relating to the obligations resulting from the Treaty of Trianon (Art. 22)	28.4.1930	Pajzs, Csáky, Esterházy. Ser. A/B, No. 68	Agreement No. III is registered in 121 *L.N.T.S.* 90. Jurisdiction was based, alternatively, on mutual declarations but these were no longer relied upon as the respondent's declaration lapsed on date of appli-

				cation. Jurisdiction upheld under the agreements but first submission in the case could not be "entertained"
8	Convention of Conciliation, Arbitration and Judicial Settlement Concluded between Belgium and Greece	25.6.1929	Société Commerciale de Belgique. Ser. A/B, No. 78	Treaty registered 128 *L.N.T.S.* 117. The Court found jurisdiction to be partly based on the implied agreement between the parties. ***Id.*** at 174
9	Treaty of Conciliation, Arbitration and Judicial Settlement Concluded between Belgium and Bulgaria	23.6.1931	Electricity Company of Sofia and Bulgaria. Ser. A/B, Nos. 77, 79	Treaty registered: 137 *L.N.T.S.* 191. Jurisdiction was contended to have been ***concurrently*** based on declarations. The Court denied it under the treaty and upheld it on the other ground
10	Statute of the Permanent Court of International Justice	16.12.1920	Interpretation of Judgment No. 3; Interpretation of Judgments No. 7, 8	2 cases: Ser. A, No. 4; Ser. A, No. 13

[1] Ten treaties (including the Statute of the Court) were invoked in 21 cases.

B. Under the International Court of Justice [1]

No.	Title of Treaty	Date Signature	Cases Related	Remarks
1	Convention of Montreux between Egypt and Other Powers (Art. 13)	8.5.1937	Case Concerning the Protection of French Nationals and Protected Persons in Egypt. [1950] Rep. 59	Case discontinued. Convention registered: 182 *L.N.T.S.* 37
2	Protocol of Friendship and Co-operation between Columbia and Peru (Art. 7)	24.5.1934	Haya de la Torre. [1951] Rep. 71	The Protocol did not provide a clear basis of jurisdiction in the case. The Court founded jurisdiction on the clear conduct of the parties. [1951] Rep. 78. The Protocol was cited also in the application in the *Asylum* case. [1950] Rep. 266.
3	Treaty of Commerce and Navigation between Greece and Great Britain (Art. 29)	16.7.1926	Ambatielos	2 cases: [1952] Rep. 28 (Prel. Obj.); [1953] *Id.* 10 (Merits). Treaty Registered: 61 *L.N.T.S.* 15
4	The "Statement" accompanying the Washington Agreement between France, United Kingdom and U.S.A. (Para. 6)	25.4.1951	Monetary Gold Removed from Rome in 1943. [1954] Rep. 19	Agreement registered: 91 *U.N.T.S.* 21. Instrument referred to in the pleadings as a "special agreement." See Pleadings at 165. Italy (the applicant) made a declaration of acceptance in conformity with the Security Council Resolution of 15.10.1946
5	Franco-Lebanese Agreement Regarding the Settlement of Certain Financial Problems Relating to French Companies (Art. 23)	24.1.1948	Electricité de Beyrouth Company. [1954] Rep. 107	Case discontinued. Agreement registered during the proceedings, 173 *U.N.T.S.* 99
5(b)	Same as above	24.1.1948	Case concerning the Compagnie du Port, des Quais et des Entrepots de Beyrouth, and the Société Radio-Orient. [1960] Rep. 186	Case discontinued.
6	Treaty of Conciliation, Judicial Settlement and Arbitration between Belgium and Spain (Arts. 2, 7)	19.7.1927	Case concerning the Barcelona Traction, Light and Power Company Limited. [1964] Rep. 6	Case discontinued (then reinstituted in 1962. See No. 6(b) below) Treaty registered: 80 *L.N.T.S.* 17

6(b)	Same as in No. 6	19.7.1927	Case concerning the Barcelona Traction, Light and Power Company Limited (Belgium v. Spain) (New application 1962)	Treaty refers to jurisdiction of the Permanent Court: Belgium is an Original member of the U.N. but Spain became member only on 14.12.1955. *Case is pending*
7	Mandate for German South-West Africa (Art. 7)	17.12.1920	South-West Africa Cases: Ethiopia v. South Africa; Liberia v. South Africa [1962] Rep. 319	2 cases joined together. Jurisdiction affirmed. *The two cases are now pending* for a judgment on the merits. Mandate not published in *L.N.T.S.* See text in League of Nations Off. J., 2d Ass. 89 (1921)
8	Trusteeship Agreement for the Territory of the Cameroons (Art. 19)	13.12.1946	Case concerning the Northern Cameroons	Agreement registered: 8 *U.N.T.S.* 119. Jurisdiction denied in decision dated 2.12.1963. [1963] Rep. 15
9	Statute of the International Court of Justice	24.9.1945	Interpretation of the Judgment of Nov. 20, 1950 in the Asylum *Case.* [1950] Rep. 395	

1 Nine treaties (including the Statute of the Court) were invoked in 15 cases.

APPENDIX V

CONTINUED JURISDICTION BY MEANS OF DECLARATIONS "A" *

A Survey of the *Cases* in which Declarations of Acceptance were Invoked as the Basis of the Jurisdiction of the International Court

* *Article 36(2), (3), (4), (5) of the Statute* of the International Court of Justice:

(2) The States parties to the present Statute may at any time declare that they recognize as compulsory *ipso facto* and without special agreement, in relation to any other state accepting the same obligation the jurisdiction of the Court in all legal disputes concerning:

a. the interpretation of a treaty;
b. any question of international law;
c. the existence of any fact which if established, would constitute a breach of an international obligation;
d. the nature or extent of the reparation to be made for the breach of an international obligation;

(3) The declarations referred to above may be made unconditionally or on condition of reciprocity on the part of several or certain states, or for a certain time.

(4) Such declarations shall be deposited with the Secretary-General of the United Nations who shall transmit copies thereof to the parties of the Statute and to the Registrar of the Court.

(5) Declarations made under Article 36 of the Statute of the Permanent Court of International Justice and which are still in force shall be deemed, as between the parties to the present Statute, to be acceptances of the compulsory jurisdiction of the International Court of Justice for the period which they still have to run and in accordance with their terms.

A. Under the Permanent Court of International Justice

No.	Case	Reference	Parties	Declarations (by their number in appendix VI)	Remarks
1	Renunciation of the Treaty of Nov. 2, 1865 between China and Belgium	Ser. A, Nos. 18/19 (1929)	Belgium/China	10, 21	Case discontinued
2	Legal Status of Eastern Greenland	Ser. A/B, No. 53 (1933)	Denmark/Norway	28, 99	Jurisdiction not challenged
3 & 4	Legal Status of the South Eastern Territory of Greenland	Ser. A/B, No. 55 (1933)	Denmark/Norway	28, 99	2 cases-discontinued
5	The Pajzs, Csáky, Esterházy	Ser. A/B, No. 68 (1936)	Hungary/ Yugoslavia	62, 63 147	Jurisdiction was based in the first place on two treaties. As declaration of respondent lapsed before the date of application, declarations were later dropped as a basis of jurisdiction in the case
6	The Losinger Company	Ser. A/B, No. 69 (1936)	Switzerland/ Yugoslavia	124, 147	Case discontinued
7	The Division of water from the Meuse	Ser. A/B, No. 70 (1937)	Netherlands/ Belgium	91, 10	Jurisdiction not challenged
8	Phosphates in Morocco	Ser. A/B, No. 74 (1938)	Italy/France	74, 47	Jurisdiction challenged and denied *ratione temporis*
9	The Panevezys-Saldutiskis Railway	Ser. A/B, No. 76 (1939)	Estonia/ Lithuania	36, 37, 38 85	Application challenged as inadmissible. Objection upheld after being joined to the merits
10	The Electricity Company of Sofia & Bulgaria (Prel. Obj.)	Ser. A/B, No. 77 (1939)	Belgium/Bulgaria	10, 18	Jurisdiction was also based on a treaty. After being challenged the Court upheld it on the basis of the declarations
11	Same (merits)	Ser. E 16 at 145–146	Belgium/Bulgaria	As above	Case discontinued

12	Gerliczy	Ser. E16 at 154-158 (short summary)	Liechtenstein/ Hungary	81 62, 63	Declaration of applicant (not member of the League) was made under the Council's resolution of 17.5.1922. Defendant intended to object to the jurisdiction but the case did not proceed any further

B. Under the International Court of Justice

No.	Case	Reference	Parties	Declarations (by their number in Appendix VI)	Remarks
1	Fisheries Case	[1951] Rep. 116	United Kingdom/ Norway	139, 101	Jurisdiction not challenged
2	Anglo-Iranian Oil Co. Case (Prel. Obj.)	[1952] Rep. 93	United Kingdom/ Iran	139, 69	Jurisdiction challenged and denied
3	Case Concerning Rights of Nationals of the U.S.A. in Morocco	[1952] Rep. 176	France/U.S.A.	49, 145	A preliminary objection filed by the U.S.A. was withdrawn
4	Nottebohm Case (Prel. Obj.)	[1953] Rep. 111	Liechtenstein/ Guatemala	82, 57	Jurisdiction was challenged *ratione temporis*, but the objection was overruled. Case was later found inadmissible. See No. 6 below
5	Nottebohm Case (Second Phase)	[1955] Rep. 4	Liechtenstein/ Guatemala	82, 57	Objections to the admissibility of the claim upheld by the Court
6	Case of Certain Norwegian Loans (Prel. Obj.)	[1957] Rep. 9	France/Norway	49, 101	Jurisdiction challenged and denied
7	Case Concerning Right of Passage over Indian Territory (Prel. Obj.)	[1957] Rep. 125	Portugal/India	112, 66	Jurisdiction challenged on six bases, four of which were refused and two were joined to the merits and later refused. See No. 13 below
8	Case Concerning the Application of the Convention of 1902 Governing the Guardianship of Infants	[1958] Rep. 55	Netherlands/Sweden	94, 122	Jurisdiction not challenged
9	Interhandel Case (Prel. Obj.)	[1959] Rep. 6	Switzerland/U.S.A.	126, 145	Jurisdiction challenged on 4 grounds. The Court found the application inadmissible because of the non-exhaustion of local remedies
10	Case Concerning the Aerial Incident of July 27, 1955 (Prel. Obj.)	[1959] Rep. 127	Israel/Bulgaria	73, 18	Jurisdiction challenged and denied

11	Case Concerning the Aerial Incident of July 27, 1955	[1959] Rep. 26 (order)	United Kingdom/ Bulgaria	142, 18	Case discontinued before the filing of the counter-memorial
12	Case Concerning the Right of Passage over Indian Territory (Merits)	[1960] Rep. 6	Portugal/India	112, 66	Two objections to jurisdiction that were joined to the merits were overruled
13	Case Concerning the Aerial Incident of July 27, 1955	[1960] Rep. 146 (order)	U.S.A./Bulgaria	145, 18	Case discontinued after the filing of objections to jurisdiction and of the claimant's observations on them
14	The Arbitral Award Made by the King of Spain on 23 December 1906	[1960] Rep. 192	Honduras/ Nicaragua	61, 97	Jurisdiction was primarily based on a Special Agreement
15	Case Concerning the Temple of Preah Vihear (Prel. Obj.)	[1961] Rep. 17	Cambodia/ Thailand	19, 127, 128 129	Jurisdiction challenged. Objections rejected
16	Case Concerning the Temple of Preah Vihear (Merits)	[1962] Rep. 6	Cambodia/ Thailand	19, 127, 128 129	

APPENDIX VI

CONTINUED JURISDICTION BY MEANS OF DECLARATIONS "B"

A Survey of All the Declarations Accepting the Continued Jurisdiction in Accordance with Article 36(2) of the Statute.

No.	Country	Reference † Vol.	P.	Date of Signature	Date of Deposit Ratificat[ion]
1	Albania	D6	52	17.9.1930	17.9.1930
2	Albania	E12	335	7.11.1935	
3	Argentina	E12	335	28.12.1935	
4	Australia	D6	49	20.9.1929	18.8.193
5	Australia	E16	335	21.8.1940	

† Reference is made to the publications of the Permanent Court (the Series, its Number and the Page), and to the Yearbooks of the present Court (the year of publication and the number of the page).

* I.e., the acceptance applies only to ***future disputes*** arising out of ***subsequent facts or situations.***

Conditions	Remarks
tification ciprocity years (from the date of the deposit of ratification) uble exclusion * cepting the disputes: (a) relating to the territorial status of Albania; (b) with regard to questions which by international law fall exclusively within the jurisdiction of Albania; (c) relating directly or indirectly to the application of treaties providing for another method of pacific settlement. above (without the requirement of ratification) r 5 years as from 17.9.1935	
tification ciprocity years (from date of deposit of ratification) uble exclusion cepting: (a) cases where the parties have agreed or shall agree to have recourse to another method of pacific settlement; (b) questions already settled; (c) questions which by international law, fall within the local jurisdiction or the constitutional regime of each state.	Instrument never ratified.
tification ciprocity years and thereafter until notice of termination is given. uble exclusion cepting: (a) disputes in regard to which the parties have agreed or shall agree to have recourse to some other method of peaceful settlement; (b) disputes between Members of the League of Nations who are also Members of the British Commonwealth of Nations; (c) disputes with regard to questions which by international law fall exclusively within the jurisdiction of Australia. e right is reserved in respect of disputes considered by the Council of the League, to suspend judicial proceedings under certain conditions. servation added in 7.9.1939 (E16–334): disputes arising out of events occurring during present crisis (war exclusion).	A reservation was added on 7.9.1939. Denounced on 21.8.1940.
ciprocity years (as from August 21, 1940) uble exclusion (as from 18.8.1930) cepting the disputes mentioned in (a), (b), (c) above [No. 4] plus:	Received in the Secretariat of the League of Nations on 2.9.1940. Australia is an original member of the U.N. Denounced on 6.2.1954.

No.	Country	Reference Vol.	P.	Date of Signature	Date of Deposit Ratificat
6	Australia	Yb 53–54	210	6.2.1954	
7	Austria	D6	38	14.3.1922	
8	Austria	D6	41	12.1.1927	13.3.19
9	Austria	E13	278	22.3.1937	30.4.19
10	Belgium	D6	39	25.9.1925	10.3.19

* The declarations described as "in force" are those which appear in the last issue of the *I.C.J. Yearbook* (1962–63) or are made after its publication.

Conditions	Remarks
utes arising out of events occurring at a time when His ajesty's Government in the Commonwealth of Australia ere involved in hostilities (war exclusion). right is reserved in respect of disputes considered by the uncil of the League to suspend judicial proceedings under rtain conditions.	
procity n 6.2.1954 until notice of termination is given. ble exclusion (as from 18.8.1930) ı the exceptions in No. 5, and: utes arising out of or concerning jurisdiction or rights aimed or exercised by Australia:) in respect of the continental shelf of Australia and the territories under the authority of Australia, as that continental shelf is described or delimited in the Australian Proclamations of 10 Sept., 1953, or in or under the Australian Pearl Fisheries Acts; in respect of the natural resources of the sea bed and subsoil of that continental shelf, including the products of sedentary fisheries, or;) in respect of Australian waters, within the meaning of the Australian Pearl Fisheries Acts, being jurisdiction or rights claimed or exercised in respect of those waters by or under those acts, except a dispute in relation to which the parties have first agreed upon a *modus videndi* pending the final decision of the Court of the dispute.	The right to suspend judicial proceedings is reserved here also in respect of disputes considered by the *Security Council.* Declaration in force*
procity ars	The declaration was made (*sous condition de reciprocité*) and otherwise declared the acceptance of jurisdiction "*purement et simplement*" – See the same in Nos. 18, 42, 79, 84, 95, 108, 118, 146
fication procity years (from the date of the deposit of the instrument of tification)	
fication procity ars (as from March 13, 1937)	
fication procity ears ble exclusion ept in cases where the parties may have agreed or may ree to have recourse to some other method of pacific ttlement.	First Declaration to include a double exclusion. See: *Denunciation of Treaty of Nov. 2,1865 between Belgium and China Case*; *Water from the Meuse Case*; *Electricity Company of Sofia Case.*

No.	Country	Reference Vol.	P.	Date of Signature	Date Deposi Ratific
11	Belgium	Yb 58–59	130	10.5.1948	25.6.19
12	Belgium	Yb 58–59	207	3.4.1958	17.6.1
13	Bolivia	E13	276	7.7.1936	7.7.1
14	Bolivia	Yb 47–48	131	5.7.1948	
15	Brazil	D6	37	1.11.1921	1.11.1
16	Brazil	E13	277	26.1.1937	26.1.1
17	Brazil	Yb 47–48	130	12.2.1948	
18	Bulgaria	D6	36	(1921)	12.8.1

Conditions	Remarks
tification iprocity ears uble exclusion cept in cases of agreement to employ other means of peaceful ettlement.	Belgium is an original member of the United Nations.
tification iprocity ears and thereafter until terminated uble exclusion cept in cases of agreement to employ other means of peaceful ettlement.	Declaration in force
iprocity years	The phrase used is: "unconditionally in relation to any other Member or State accepting the same, that is to say, one the sole condition of reciprocity." Bolivia is an original member of the U.N.
iprocity ears	Received by the Secretary General of the U.N. on 16.7.1948.
iprocity ears en the jurisdiction will also be accepted by at least two f the Powers permanently represented in the Council of the eague of Nations.	The declaration was inserted in the instrument of ratification of the Protocol of Signature of the Statute. Entered into force on 5.2.1930.
iprocity years cept in questions which by international law fall exclusively ithin the jurisdiction of the Brazilian Courts of law or hich belong to the constitutional regime of each State.	
iprocity ears (as from 12.3.1948)	
iprocity	The acceptance is made "*purement et simplement*". No time limit. See the *Electricity Company of Sofia & Bulgarian Case.* In the *Aerial Incident of 27 July 1955 Case* the Court held that this declaration had lapsed with the dissolution of the Permanent Court on 18.4.1946. Bulgaria became a member of the U.N. on 14.12.1955.

No.	Country	Reference Vol.	P.	Date of Signature	Date of Deposit Ratificati
19	Cambodia	Yb 57–58	195	9.9.1957	
20	Canada	D6	50	20.9.1929	28.7.193
21	China	D6	38	13.5.1922	
22	China	Yb 46–47	218	26.10.1946	
23	Columbia	D6	54	6.1.1932	
24	Columbia	E14	275	30.10.1937	30.10.19
25	Costa Rica	D6	35	Before 28.1.1921	
26	Czechoslovakia	D6	47	19.9.1929	
27	Denmark	D6	34	28.1.1921	13.6.19

Conditions	Remarks
:iprocity years and thereafter until terminated :epting: a) disputes in regard to which there is an agreement to have recourse to some other method of peaceful settlement; b) disputes with regard to questions which by international law fall exclusively within the jurisdiction of the Kingdom of Cambodia; c) disputes relating to any matter excluded from judicial settlement or compulsory arbitration by virtue of any treaty, convention or other international agreement or instrument to which the Kingdom of Cambodia is a party.	Deposited on 19.9.1957. Declaration in force. See: *Temple of Preah Vihear Case.*
:ification :iprocity years and thereafter until notice of termination ıble exclusion ne reservations as in (4) above servation added 7.12.1939 (E16–336): isputes arising out of events occurring during the present var (war exclusion).	Canada is an original member of the U.N. Declaration in force.
iprocity ears	See *Denunciation of Treaty of 2.11.1865 between Belgium and China Case.*
iprocity ears and thereafter until denounced on 6 months' notice.	Declaration in force.
:iprocity a corrected version the acceptance was confined to future isputes (after Jan. 6, 1932) [Letter of the Secretary General f the League of Nations dated 27.8.1936 (E13–276)].	
:iprocity ture disputes (as from 6.1.1932)	Columbia is an original member of the U.N. Declaration in force.
iprocity	Protocol of signature not ratified.
tification :iprocity years (as from the date of deposit of the instrument of atification) uble exclusion :ept in case of agreement to have recourse to some other nethod of pacific settlement. ject to the right of either party to a dispute to submit it, efore any recourse to the Court, to the Council of the League f Nations.	Instrument never ratified.
tification :iprocity ears	

No.	Country	Reference Vol.	P.	Date of Signature	Date o Deposit Ratificat
28	Denmark	D6	39	11.12.1925	28.3.192
29	Denmark	E12	337	4.6.1936	
30	Denmark	Yb 46–47	219	10.12.1946	
31	Denmark	Yb 56–57	212	10.12.1956	
32	Dominican Republic	D6	38	30.9.1924	4.2.19
33	Egypt	E15	216	30.5.1939	
34	Egypt	Yb 56–57	212	18.7.1957	
35	El Salvador	D6	34	Before 28.1.1921 (date of first publication of the undated Declaration)	29.8.19
36	Esthonia	D6	38	2.5.1923	2.5.19

Conditions	Remarks
bove (renewed) 10 years.	See: *Eastern Greenland Case. South Eastern Greenland Case.*
bove (renewed) 10 years (as from June 13, 1936)	Denmark is an original member of the U.N.
procity ears (as from 10.12.1946)	
procity ars (as from 10.12.1956) and thereafter for further periods 5 years, if this declaration is not denounced by notice of t less than six months before the expiration of any five ars period.	Declaration deposited on 11.12.1956. Declaration in force.
fication procity	Dominican Republic is an original member of the U.N. Declaration in force.
fication procity ars (from date of deposit of instrument of ratification) ble exclusion pting: cases where the parties have agreed or shall agree to have recourse to another method of pacific settlement; disputes relating to the rights of sovereignty of Egypt or to questions which by international law fall exclusively within it jurisdiction.	Instrument not ratified.
procity in all legal disputes that may arise under paragraph 9(b) the Declaration of the Government of Egypt dated April 24, 57 on "the Suez Canal and the arrangements for its operion."	Article 9 paragraph (b) of the Declaration dated April 24, 1957 provides that: "Differences arising between the Parties to the said Convention [the Constantinople Convention of 1888] in respect of the interpretation or the applicability or the provisions, if not otherwise resolved, will be referred to the International Court of Justice." Declaration in force.
procity pting: disputes or differences concerning points or questions which cannot be submitted to arbitration in accordance with the political constitution of El Salvador; disputes arising before the date of ratification; pecuniary claims made against the nation.	Acceptance made in the Protocale of signature of the Statute. *Reservations were introduced in the deed of ratification.* [D6–52] Declaration in force.
procity ars future disputes, in regard to which the parties have not reed to have recourse to some other method of pacific ttlement.	See: *Panevezys-Saldutiskis Railway Case.*

No.	Country	Reference Vol.	P.	Date of Signature	Date Deposi Ratifica
37	Esthonia	D6	42	25.6.1928	
38	Esthonia	E14	275	6.5.1938	
39	Ethiopia	D6	40	12.7.1926	16.7.19
40	Ethiopia	E8	440	15.4.1932	
41	Ethiopia	E11	256	18.9.1934	
42	Finland	D6	35	(1921)	6.4.1
43	Finland	D6	41	3.3.1927	
44	Finland	E13	278	9.4.1937	
45	Finland	Yb 57–58	199	25.6.1958	
46	France	D6	45 n. 1	2.9.1924	
47	France	D6	45	19.9.1929	25.4.1
48	France	E12	336	7.4.1936	

Conditions	Remarks
above 10 years as from 2.5.1928	
above 10 years as from 2.5.1938	
iprocity ears ept in future disputes in regard to which the parties may ave agreed to have recourse to some other method of pacific ettlement.	
above 2 years (as from 16.7.1931)	
above 2 years (as from 18.9.1934) with retrospective effect to over the period from July 16, 1933 to Sept. 18, 1934.	
ification iprocity ears	
iprocity years (as from 6.4.1927)	
iprocity years (as from 6.4.1937)	
iprocity ears and thereafter for 5 years periods unless terminated on onths' notice. ure situations or facts (as from 25.6.1958).	Finland became a member of the U.N. on 14.12.1955. Declaration in force.
tification iprocity years (unless denounced in a given circumstance) ept when the dispute is under an attempt of conciliation efore the Council of the League.	Instrument never ratified
tification iprocity ears uble exclusion all disputes which cannot be settled by a procedure of onciliation or by the Council according to the terms of rticle 15(b) of the Covenant. ept in cases in which the parties have agreed or shall agree o have recourse to some other method of arbitral settlement.	See: *Phosphates in Morocco Case.*
above 5 years (as from 25.4.1936)	Renewal

No.	Country	Reference Vol.	P.	Date of Signature	Date of Deposit of Ratification
49	France	Yb 46–47	220	18.2.1947	1.3.194
50	France	Yb 58–59	212	10.7.1959	
51	Germany	D6	42	23.9.1927	29.2.192
52	Germany	E9	290	9.2.1933	5.7.193
53	Greece	D6	44	12.9.1929	

Conditions	Remarks
tification ciprocity ve years (as from 1.3.1949) and thereafter until denounced uble exclusion cepting: (a) disputes in which the parties have agreed or shall agree to have recourse to some other method of peaceful settlement; b) disputes relating to matters which are essentially within the national jurisdiction as understood by the Government of the French Republic.	See: *U.S. Nationals in Morocco Case*; *Norwegian Loans Case.* The instrument of ratification signed on 3.2.1949, and deposited on 1.3.1949, was denounced on 10.7.1949. Notice the reservation concerning domestic jurisdiction.
ciprocity years and thereafter until denounced igle exclusion (all disputes which may arise in respect of facts or situations subsequent to the declaration). cepting: (a) disputes with regard to which the parties may have agreed or may agree to have recourse to another method of peaceful settlement; (b) disputes relating to questions which by international law fall exclusively within the domestic jurisdiction; (c) disputes arising out of any war or international hostilities and *disputes arising out of a crisis affecting the national security* or out of any measure or action relating thereto; (d) disputes with any State which, at the date of occurrence of the facts or situations giving rise to the dispute has not accepted the compulsory jurisdiction of the I.C.J. for a period at least equal to that specified in this declaration.	Declaration in force.
tification ciprocity years uble exclusion cept in cases of agreement to have recourse to another method of pacific settlement.	
tification years (as from 1.3.1933) uble exclusion from 29.2.1928 servations as in No. 51	Renewal
ciprocity years cepting: (a) disputes relating to the territorial status of Greece including those concerning its rights of sovereignty over its ports and lines of communication; b) disputes relating directly or indirectly to the application of treaties or conventions accepted by Greece and providing for another procedure.	

No.	Country	Reference Vol.	P.	Date of Signature	Date o[f] Deposit Ratificat[ion]
54	Greece	E11	255	12.9.1934	19.7.193
55	Greece	E16	340	8.9.1939	20.2.194
56	Guatemala	D6	41	17.12.1926	
57	Guatemala	Yb 46–47	219	27.1.1947	
58	Haiti	D6	37	7.9.1921	
59	Honduras	Yb 47–48	129	2.2.1948	
60	Honduras	Yb 53–54	211	19.4.1954	
61	Honduras	Yb 60–61	241	20.2.1960	
62	Hungary	D6	42	14.9.1928	13.8.19
63	Hungary	E10	269	30.5.1934	9.8.19
64	Hungary	E16	340	12.7.1939	

Conditions	Remarks
fication procity ars (as from 12.9.1934) ı reservations as above in No. 53.	Renewal
fication procity ars (as from 12.9.1939) ı reservations as above in No. 53.	Renewal operative as from 8.9.1939
fication procity	Instrument never ratified
procity ars all legal disputes except the dispute between England and ıatemala concerning the restoration of the territory of lize which the Government of Guatemala would agree to bmit to the judgment of the Court if the case were decided *aequo et bono.*	See: *Nottebohm Case.*
	Deposited on 4.10.1921. Without conditions; reciprocity not mentioned. Haiti is an original member of the U.N. – Declaration in force.
procity ars (as from 10.2.1948)	Declaration deposited 10.2.1948
procity ars (as from 24.5.1954) automatically renewable in absence notice of termination.	Declaration deposited 24.5.1944 Renewal
procity	Deposited 10.3.1960. For an indefinite term, starting from the date on which it is deposited. Declaration in force. See: *Arbitral Award of 23.12.1906 Case.*
fication procity ırs from the date of deposit of the instrument of ratification.	
fication procity ırs (as from 13.8.1934)	Renewal See: *Pajzs, Csáky, Esterházy Case;* the *Gerlizcy Case.*
fication procity the period from 13.8.1939–10.4.1941	Instrument never ratified

No.	Country	Reference Vol.	P.	Date of Signature	Date Depos Ratific
65	India	D6	48	19.9.1929	5.2.19
66	India	E16	341	28.2.1940	
67	India	Yb 55–56	186	9.1.1956	
68	India	Yb 59–60	241	14.9.1959	

Conditions	Remarks
tification ciprocity years and thereafter until terminated uble exclusion th the reservations in No. 4 above. servation added in 27.9.1939: The acceptance will not be egarded as covering disputes arising out of events occurring luring the present hostilities (war exclusion).	Denounced 28.2.1940
ciprocity ears (as from 28.2.1940) and thereafter until terminated. uble exclusion from 5.2.1920 th all the reservations in the above declaration	Deposited on 7.3.1940. India is an original member of the U.N. Denounced on 9.1.1956. See: ***Right of Passage Case.***
ciprocity ective until denounced uble exclusion from 26.1.1950 cepting: a) disputes in regard to which the parties to the dispute have agreed or shall agree to have recourse to some other method of peaceful settlement; b) disputes with the Government of any country which on the date of this declaration is a member of the Commonwealth of Nations; c) disputes in regard to matters which are essentially within the domestic jurisdiction of India as determined by the Government of India; d) disputes arising out of or having reference to any hostilities, war, state of war or belligerent or military occupation in which the Government of India are or have been involved.	Denounced on 8.2.1957. Notice the reservation concerning domestic jurisdiction.
ciprocity til denounced uble exclusion from 26.1.1950. cepting: a) cases of agreement to have recourse to other methods of peaceful settlement; b) disputes with other members of the Commonwealth of Nations; c) disputes in regard to matters which are essentially within the jurisdiction of the Republic of India; d) disputes concerning any question relating to or arising out of belligerent or military occupation or the discharge of any function, pursuant to any recommendation or decision of an organ of the U.N., in accordance with which the Government of India have accepted obligations; e) disputes in respect of which any other party to a dispute has accepted the compulsory jurisdiction of the I.C.J. exclusively for or in relation to the purposes of such disputes; or where the acceptance of the Court's compulsory jurisdiction on behalf of a party to the dispute was deposited or ratified less than twelve months prior	Declaration in force. Notice the special reservation concerning the discharge of functions pursuant to recommendations or decisions of organs of the U.N.

No.	Country	Reference Vol.	P.	Date of Signature	Date o Deposit Ratificat
69	Iran	D6	53	2.10.1930	19.9.193
70	Iraq	E15	215	22.9.1938	
71	Ireland [Irish Free State]	D6	44	14.9.1929	11.7.19

Conditions	Remarks
to the filing of the application bringing the dispute before the Court; (f) disputes with the Government of any state with which, on the date of an application to bring a dispute before the Court, the Government of India has no diplomatic relations.	
tification ciprocity years and thereafter until terminated uble exclusion r all disputes relating directly or indirectly to the application of treaties accepted by Iran. cepting: (a) disputes relating to the territorial status of Iran, including those concerning the rights of sovereignty of Iran over its Islands and ports; (b) disputes in regard to which the parties have agreed or shall agree to have recourse to some other method of peaceful settlement; (c) disputes with regard to questions which, by international law, fall exclusively within the jurisdiction of Iran. bject to Iran's right to demand the suspension of proceedings before the Court in regard to any dispute referred to the Council of the League of Nations.	Denounced on 9.7.1951. See: *Anglo-Iranian Oil Co. Case.*
tification ciprocity years and thereafter until terminated. uble exclusion cepting: (a) disputes in regard to which the parties have agreed or shall agree to have recourse to some other method of peaceful settlement; (b) disputes with the Government of any other Arab State; (c) disputes with regard to questions which by international law fall exclusively within the jurisdiction of Iraq; (d) disputes affecting the territorial status of Iraq, including those concerning the right of sovereignty of Iraq over its waters and communications. bject to the right of Iraq to demand the suspension of proceedings before the Court in respect of any dispute submitted to and under consideration by the Council *or Assembly* of the League of Nations.	Instrument never ratified.
tification ciprocity years	Ireland became a member of the U.N. on 14.12.1955. Declaration presumably lapsed by the dissolution of the P.C.I.J. on 18.4.1946 [analogy with the declaration of Bulgaria as in the *Aerial incident of 27 July 1955 Case*]. The declaration did not exclude disputes with other members of the British Commonwealth.

No.	Country	Reference Vol.	P.	Date of Signature	Date of Deposit Ratificat
72	Israel	Yb 50–51	193	4.9.1950	25.10.195
73	Israel	Yb 56–57	214	17.10.1956	
74	Italy	D6	43	9.9.1929	7.9.19

Conditions	Remarks
ification iprocity ars (as from date of deposit of ratification) utes arising out of future situations or facts. epting:) disputes involving a legal title created or conferred by a Government or authority other than the Government of the State of Israel or an authority under the jurisdiction of that Government;) disputes in respect of which the parties have agreed or shall agree to have recourse to another means of peaceful settlement;) disputes relating to matters which are essentially within the domestic jurisdiction of the State of Israel;) disputes between the State of Israel and another State which refuses to establish or maintain normal relations with it.	The declaration was deposited on 11.10.1950. The instrument of ratification was signed on 28.6.1951.
iprocity m 25.10.1956 until terminated. all legal disputes concerning situations or facts which may ise subsequent to 25.10.1951. epting:) disputes involving a legal title created or conferred by a Government or authority other than the Government of Israel or an authority under the jurisdiction of that Government;) disputes in respect to which the parties have agreed or shall agree to have recourse to another means of peaceful settlement;) disputes between the State of Israel and any other State whether or not a Member of the U.N. which does not recognize Israel or which refuses to establish or maintain normal *diplomatic* relations with Israel when the absence or breach of normal relations precedes the dispute and exists independently of that dispute;) disputes relating to matters which are essentially within the domestic jurisdiction of the State of Israel;) disputes arising out of events occurring between 15.5.1948 and 20.7.1949;) without prejudice to the above, disputes arising out of or having reference to, any hostilities, war, state or war, breach of the peace, breach of armistice agreement or belligerent or military occupation (whether such war shall have been declared or not, and whether any state of belligerency shall have been recognized or not) in which the Government of Israel are or have been or may be involved at any time.	See: *Aerial Incident of 27 July 1955* case. Declaration in force. Notice the broadness of the war exclusion.
ification iprocity ars ure disputes ject to any other method of settlement provided by a special	See: *Phosphates in Morocco Case.* On 19.5.1953 Italy made a particular declaration (under the Security Council's resolution of Oct. 1946) which

No.	Country	Reference Vol.	P.	Date of Signature	Date Deposi Ratific
75	Japan	Yb 58–59	214	15.9.1958	
76	Latvia	D6	44 n. 1	11.9.1923	
77	Latvia	D6	43	10.9.1929	26.2.1
78	Latvia	E11	256	31.1.1935	26.2.1
79	Liberia	D6	36	(1921)	
80	Liberia	Yb 51–52	185	3.3.1952	17.4.1
81	Liechtenstein	E15	213	22.3.1939	

Conditions	Remarks
convention and in cases where a solution by means of diplomacy or by the action of the Council of the League of Nations s not attained.	was limited to specific disputes. On its basis Italy made its application in the *Monitary Gold Removed from Rome in 1943 Case.* See: Yb 53–54 at 37.
ciprocity ears and thereafter until terminated by a written notice uble exclusion r all disputes not settled by other means of peaceful settlement es not apply to disputes which the Parties thereto have agreed or shall agree to refer for final and binding decision to arbitration or judicial settlement.	Japan became a party to the Statute on 2.4.1954 and a member of the U.N. on 18.12. 1956. Declaration in force.
tification ciprocity ears ture disputes – in respect of which the parties did not agree to have recourse to another method of peaceful settlement.	Instrument never ratified.
tification ciprocity ears uble exclusion cept in cases where the Parties have agreed or shall agree to have recourse to some other method of peaceful settlement.	
tification ciprocity ears and thereafter until terminated uble exclusion as from 26.2.1930 cept in cases where the parties have agreed or shall agree to have recourse to some other method of peaceful settlement.	Renewal
tification ciprocity	Instrument never ratified.
tification ciprocity ears (as from date of deposit of ratification) and thereafter until terminated. ture disputes cepting: (a) disputes which the republic of Liberia considers essentially within its domestic jurisdiction; (b) disputes which the parties have agreed or may agree to bring before other tribunals as a result of agreements already existing or which may be made in the future.	Declaration deposited on 20.3.1952. The instrument of ratification signed on 30.3.1953. Notice the reservation concerning domestic jurisdiction. Declaration in force.
ears	Declaration received on 29.3.1939. It was made in accordance with Paragraph 4 of No. 2 in the Reso-

No.	Country	Reference Vol.	P.	Date of Signature	Date of Deposit of Ratificati
82	Liechtenstein	Yb 49–50	165	10.3.1950	
83	Lithuania	D6	37	5.10.1921	16.5.192
84	Lithuania	D6	51	14.1.1930	
85	Lithuania	E11	257	8.3.1935	
86	Luxemburg	D6	52 n. 1	1921	
87	Luxemburg	D6	52	15.9.1930	
88	Mexico	Yb 47–48	129	23.10.1947	
89	Monaco	E13	72	22.4.1937	

Conditions	Remarks
cept in cases where the Parties have agreed or shall agree to have recourse to another method of pacific settlement.	lution of the Council of the League dated 17.5.1922. Reciprocity not mentioned. See the *Gerliczy Case*. (Application made on June 17, 1939 – no written proceedings were filed.)
ciprocity til terminated take effect from the date on which Liechtenstein becomes a party to the Court's Statute [29.3.1950].	Declaration deposited on 29.3.1950. Declaration in force. See: *Nottebohm Case*. Liechtenstein is not a member of the U.N., but is a party to the Statute since 29.3.1950.
ears	Reciprocity not mentioned.
ears (as from 14.1.1930)	Renewal. Reciprocity not mentioned.
ciprocity ears (with effect from 14.1.1935)	Renewal Declaration received on 12.3.1935. See: *Panevezys-Saldutiskis Railway Case*.
tification ciprocity ears	Instrument never ratified.
ciprocity ears and thereafter for 5 years periods unless terminated on months' notice. uble exclusion cept in cases where the parties have agreed or shall agree to have recourse to another procedure or to another method of peaceful settlement.	Luxemburg is an original member of the U.N. Declaration in force.
ciprocity ears (as from 1.3.1947) and thereafter until terminated on months' notice. uble exclusion cepting disputes arising from matters that in the opinion of the Mexican Government are within the domestic jurisdiction of the United States of Mexico.	Declaration deposited on 28.10.1947. Declaration in force. Notice the reservation concerning domestic jurisdiction.
ciprocity ears uble exclusion cept in cases where the parties have agreed or shall agree to have recourse to another method of peaceful settlement.	General declaration made under the resolution of 17.5.1922 of the Council of the League. Monaco was not a member of the League of Nations and is not a member of the United Nations nor a party to the Statute.

No.	Country	Reference Vol.	P.	Date of Signature	Date o[f] Deposit Ratificat[ion]
90	Netherlands	D6	35	6.8.1921	
91	Netherlands	D6	40	2.9.1926	
92	Netherlands	E13	276	5.8.1936	
93	Netherlands	Yb 46–47	217	5.8.1946	
94	Netherlands	Yb 55–56	187	1.8.1956	
95	New Zealand	D6	47	19.9.1929	29.3.193[illegible]
96	New Zealand	E16	343	8.4.1940	
97	Nicaragua	D6	51	24.9.1929	
98	Norway	D6	36	6.9.1921	3.10.19[illegible]

Conditions	Remarks
iprocity ars ure disputes – in regard to which the parties have not agreed have recourse to some other method of pacific settlement.	
iprocity ears (as from 6.8.1926) ure disputes epting disputes in regard to which the parties may have greed, after the entry into force of the Court's Statute, to ave recourse to some other method of pacific settlement.	Renewal See: *Water from the Meuse Case.*
iprocity ears (as from 6.8.1936) ure disputes with the same exception as in above (No. 91).	Renewal
iprocity ears and thereafter until terminated ure disputes – with the same exception as in above (No. 91).	Renewal
iprocity ears (as from 6.8.1956) and thereafter for similar periods nless notice is given not less than 6 months before expiry any such period. utes arising after 5.8.1921 epting disputes in respect of which the parties, excluding e jurisdiction of the I.C.J., may have agreed to have recourse some other method of pacific settlement.	Declaration in force. See: *Application of Guardianship Convention of 1902 Case.*
ification procity ears and thereafter unless terminated ble exclusion other reservations as in No. 4 above ar exclusion added on 7.9.1939 [E16–342] for disputes which ay arise out of events occurring during the present hostilities.	Denounced on 30.3.1940.
procity ars (as from 1.4.1940) and thereafter until terminated ble exclusion from 29.3.1930 exclusion n all other reservations mentioned above.	New Zealand is an original member of the U.N. Declaration in force.
onditionally	Reciprocity not mentioned. Nicaragua is an original member of the U.N. Declaration in force. See: *Arbitral Award of 23.12.1906 Case.*
ification procity ars	

No.	Country	Reference Vol.	P.	Date of Signature	Date Deposi Ratific.
99	Norway	D6	41	22.9.1926	
100	Norway	E12	336	19.5.1936	
101	Norway	Yb 46–47	219	16.11.1946	
102	Norway	Yb 56–57	218	17.12.1956	
103	Pakistan	Yb 47–48	131	22.6.1948	
104	Pakistan	Yb 56–57	219	23.5.1957	
105	Pakistan	Yb 60–61	210	12.9.1960	

Conditions	Remarks
:iprocity : 10 years (as from 3.10.1926)	Renewal See: ***South Eastern Greenland Case***; ***Eastern Greenland Case.***
ciprocity years (as from 3.10.1936)	Renewal Declaration deposited on 29.5.1936 Norway is an original member of the U.N.
:iprocity years (as from 3.10.1946)	Renewal See: ***Fisheries Case, Norwegian Loans Case.***
:iprocity ears (as from 3.10.1956) and thereafter for additional periods f 5 years unless terminated on 6 months' notice.	Renewal Deposited on 19.12.1956 Declaration in force.
:iprocity ears and thereafter until the expiration of six months after .otice of abrogation. :ure disputes :epting: a) disputes the solution of which the parties shall entrust to other tribunals by virtue of agreements already in existence or which may be concluded in the future; b) disputes with regard to matters which are essentially within the domestic jurisdiction of the Government of Pakistan as determined by the Government of Pakistan; c) disputes arising under a multilateral treaty unless (1) all parties to the treaty affected by the decision are also parties to the case before the Court, or (2) the Government of Pakistan specially agree to jurisdiction.	Deposited on 9.7.1948 Denounced on 21.12.1956 Notice the reservation concerning domestic jurisdiction.
:iprocity force until terminated disputes arising after 24.6.1948 th same reservations in No. 103 above.	Denounced on 12.12.1960
:iprocity force until terminated. disputes arising after 24.6.1948. :epting: a) disputes the solution of which the parties shall entrust to other tribunals; b) disputes relating to questions which by international law fall exclusively within the domestic jurisdiction of Pakistan; c) disputes arising under a multilateral treaty unless (1) all parties to the treaty affected by the decision are also parties to the case before the Court. (2) The Government of Pakistan specially agree to jurisdiction.	Declaration in force.

No.	Country	Reference Vol.	P.	Date of Signature	Date of Deposit of Ratificati[on]
106	Panama	D6	37	25.10.1921	14.6.192[illegible]
107	Paraguay	E9	290	2.5.1933	
108	Peru			19.9.1929	29.3.193[illegible]
109	Philippines	Yb 47–48	128	12.7.1947	
110	Poland	D6	54	24.1.1931	
111	Portugal	D6	33	16.12.1920	8.10.19[illegible]
112	Portugal	Yb 55–56	185	19.12.1955	

Conditions	Remarks
ciprocity	Declaration in force.
conditionally	Reciprocity not mentioned. Denounced on 26.4.1938. See for observations made by Governments, regarding the withdrawal of Paraguay Ser. E14–57, n. 2 and E15–227, n. 2. Listed in the I.C.J. Y.B. as a declaration in force until 1960. Not mentioned in the Yearbook of 1960–61, nor since.
tification ciprocity years (as from date of ratification) ture situations or facts cept in cases where the parties may have agreed either to have recourse to some other method of settlement by arbitration or to submit the dispute previously to the Council of the League of Nations.	
ciprocity years (as from 4.7.1946) and thereafter until notification of abrogation.	Deposited 28.8.1947. Declaration in force.
tification ciprocity ears uble exclusion cepting: a) cases where the parties have agreed or shall agree to have recourse to some other method of peaceful settlement; b) disputes with regard to matters which by international law are solely within the domestic jurisdiction of States; (c) disputes arising between Poland and States which refuse to establish or maintain normal diplomatic relations with Poland; d) disputes connected directly or indirectly with the World War or with the Polono-Sovietic war; (e) Disputes resulting directly or indirectly from the provisions of the Treaty of Peace signed at Riga on 18.3.1921; (f) disputes relating to provisions of international law connected with the last two points.	Instrument never ratified.
ciprocity ear and thereafter until denounced r disputes arising out of events both prior and subsequent to the declaration of acceptance of the "optional clause" which Portugal made on 16.12.1920. served – the right to exclude from the scope of the declaration at any time during its validity any given category or categories of disputes, by notifying the Secretary General of the U.N. and with effect from the moment of such notification.	Reciprocity not mentioned though the acceptance is made "as provided for in ... paragraph 2 of Article 36 ..." Declaration in force. See: *Right of Passage Case.*

No.	Country	Reference Vol.	P.	Date of Signature	Date o[f] Deposit Ratificat[ion]
113	Roumania	D6	53	8.10.1930	9.6.193
114	Roumania	E12	337	4.6.1936	
115	Somalia	Yb 62–63	254	25.3.1963	
	South Africa (see Union of South Africa, Nos. 135–137)				
116	Spain	D6	43	21.9.1928	
117	Sudan	Yb 57–58	208	30.12.1957	

Conditions	Remarks
·fication procity espect of the Governments recognized by Roumania ars ıre situations or facts epting:) the matters for which a special procedure has been or may be established;) any question of substance or procedure which might directly or indirectly cause the existing territorial integrity of Roumania and of her sovereign rights including her rights over her ports and communications, to be brought into question;) disputes relating to questions which according to international law, fall under the domestic jurisdiction of Roumania. rved – the right of Roumania to submit the dispute to the uncil of the League of Nations before having recourse to e Court.	
5 years (as from 9.6.1936) ı the same conditions of the above (No. 113).	Renewal
procity l terminated on notice egal disputes, excepting) disputes in respect of which any other party to the dispute has accepted the compulsory jurisdiction of the International Court of Justice only in relation to or for the purpose of the dispute;) where the acceptance of the Court's compulsory jurisdiction on behalf of any other party to the dispute was deposited or ratified less than twelve months prior to the filing of the application bringing the dispute before the Court. reserved: the right at any time by means of a notification ldressed to the Secretary General of the U.N., and with fect as from the moment of such notification, either to add , amend, or withdraw any of the foregoing reservations or ıy that may hereafter be added.	Deposited on 11.4.1963. Declaration in force.
procity ears ble exclusion ept in cases where the parties may have agreed or may ree to have recourse to some other method of pacific settlement.	
procity l terminated ble exclusion (as from 1.1.1956)	Deposited on 2.1.1958. Declaration in force.

No.	Country	Reference Vol.	P.	Date of Signature	Date Deposi Ratifica
118	Sweden	D6	36	16.8.1921	
119	Sweden	D6	40	18.3.1926	
120	Sweden	E12	336	18.4.1936	
121	Sweden	Yb 46–47	220	5.4.1947	
122	Sweden	Yb 56–57	221	6.4.1957	
123	Switzerland	D6	34	Before 28.1.1921	25.6.1
124	Switzerland	D6	39	1.3.1926	24.7.1
125	Switzerland	E13	277	23.9.1936	17.4.1
126	Switzerland	Yb 47–48	127	6.7.1948	
127	Thailand [Siam]	D6	49	20.9.1929	7.5.1

Conditions	Remarks
cepting: a) disputes in regard to which the parties have agreed or shall agree to have recourse to some other method of peaceful settlement; b) disputes in regard to matters which are essentially within the domestic jurisdiction of the republic of the Sudan as determined by the Government of the Republic of the Sudan; (c) disputes arising out of events occurring during any period in which the Republic of the Sudan is engaged in hostilities as a belligerent.	Notice the reservation concerning domestic jurisdiction.
ciprocity ears	
ciprocity years (as from 16.8.1926)	Renewal
ciprocity years (as from 16.8.1936)	Renewal
ciprocity years uble exclusion	Sweden became a member of the U.N. on 19.11.1946.
ciprocity years (as from 6.4.1957) and thereafter for periods of the ame duration unless terminated on 6 months' notice uble exclusion (as from 6.4.47).	Declaration in force. See: ***Application of Guardianship Convention of 1902 Case.***
tification ciprocity ears	
tification ciprocity years (as from the deposit of the instrument of ratification)	Renewal See: *Losinger Case.*
tification ciprocity years (as from the deposit of the instrument of ratification)	Renewal
ciprocity force from the date on which Switzerland becomes a party o the Court's Statute [28.7.1948] until terminated on a year's notice.	Deposited on 28.7.1948. Declaration in force. See: the ***Interhandel Case.*** Switzerland is not a member of the U.N. but is a party to the Statute since 28.7.1948.
tification ciprocity years disputes as to which no other means of pacific settlement is agreed upon between the parties.	

No.	Country	Reference Vol.	P.	Date of Signature	Date of Deposit of Ratification
128	Thailand	E16	344	3.5.1940	
129	Thailand	Yb 49–50	165	20.5.1950	
130	Turkey	E12	335	12.3.1936	
131	Turkey	Yb 47–48	127	22.5.1947	
132	Turkey	Yb 53–54	211 n.	8.6.1954	
133	Turkey	Yb 58–59	224 n. 1	August 1958	
133a	Turkey	Yb 63–64		19.3.1964	
134	Uganda	Yb 63–64		3.10.1963	
135	Union of South Africa	D6	46	19.9.1929	7.4.193[illegible]
136	Union of South Africa	E16	334	7.4.1940	
137	Union of South Africa	Yb 55–56	184	12.9.1955	

Conditions	Remarks
years (as from 7.5.1940) ith the conditions in the first declaration (No. 127).	Renewal Deposited on 9.5.1940.
years (as from 3.5.1950) ith the conditions in the first declaration (No. 127).	Renewal See: *Temple of Preah Vihear Case.*
ciprocity ears ture disputes cept in disputes relating directly or indirectly to the application of treaties or conventions providing for some other method of peaceful settlement.	
ciprocity ears (as from 22.5.1947) uble exclusion cepting disputes for which it would be appropriate to apply, directly or indirectly, agreements and conventions concluded by Turkey providing for a different method of settling disputes.	Deposited on 6.6.1947. Notice the wording of the reservation concerning other methods of peaceful settlement.
ciprocity ears (as from 22.5.1952)	Renewal
ciprocity ears (as from 23.5.1957)	Renewal Deposited on 7.8.1958.
ciprocity ears (as from 23.5.1962)	Renewal Declaration in force.
ciprocity	Declaration in force.
tification ciprocity years and thereafter until terminated uble exclusion th all the reservations mentioned in No. 4 above servation added on 18.9.1939 [E16–332] regarding disputes arising out of events occurring during present hostilities.	Denounced on 7.4.1940. [Termination deposited on 20.4.1940]
ciprocity til notice of termination is given uble exclusion ar exclusion (disputes arising out of events occurring during any period in which the Union of South Africa is engaged in hostilities as a belligerent). th all other reservations mentioned in No. 4 above.	Deposited on 20.4.1940. Denounced on 12.9.1955. [Termination deposited on 13.9.1955]
ciprocity til terminated uble exclusion	Deposited on 13.9.1955. Declaration in force.

No.	Country	Reference Vol.	P.	Date of Signature	Date of Deposit Ratificat
	United Arab Republic [See Egypt, Nos. 33, 34]				
138	United Kingdom	D6	45	19.9.1929	5.2.193
139	United Kingdom	E16	339	7.3.1940	
140	United Kingdom	Yb 54–55	188	2.6.1955	

Conditions	Remarks
:epting: a) disputes in regard to which the parties have agreed or shall agree to have recourse to some other method of peaceful settlement; o) disputes with the Government of any other country which is a member of the Commonwealth of Nations; c) disputes with regard to matters which are essentially within the jurisdiction of the Government of the Union of South Africa as determined by the Government of the Union of South Africa; d) disputes arising out of events during any period in which the Union of South Africa is engaged in hostilities as a belligerent.	Notice the reservation concerning domestic jurisdiction.
tification :iprocity years and thereafter until terminated ıble exclusion th all the reservations mentioned in No. 4 above ervation added on 7.9.1939 [E16–337] regarding disputes rising out of events occurring during the present hostilities.	Denounced on 28.2.1940.
:iprocity ears (as from 28.2.1940) and thereafter until terminated ıble exclusion (as from 5.2.1930) r exclusion th all other reservations as in No. 4 above	Denounced on 1.6.1955. See: ***Fisheries Case***; ***Anglo-Iranian Oil Co. Case.***
:iprocity til terminated ıble exclusion (as from 5.2.1930) cepting: a) disputes in regard to which the parties have agreed or shall agree to have recourse to some other method of peaceful settlement; b) disputes with any other member of the British Commonwealth; c) disputes with regard to questions which by international law fall exclusively within the jurisdiction of the U.K.; d) disputes arising out of events occurring between 3.9.1939 and 2.9.1945; e) [without prejudice to the above reservations], disputes arising out of, or having reference to any hostilities, war, state of war, or belligerent or military occupation in which the Government of the U.K. are or have been involved; f) disputes relating to any matter excluded from compulsory adjudication or arbitration under any treaty, convention or other international agreement or instrument to which the U.K. is a party.	Denounced on 31.10.1955.

No.	Country	Reference Vol.	P.	Date of Signature	Date Deposi Ratifica
141	United Kingdom	Yb 55–56	185	31.10.1955	
142	United Kingdom	Yb 56–57	223	18.4.1957	
143	United Kingdom	Yb 58–59	225	26.11.1958	

Conditions	Remarks
; above [No. 140] 'ith a reservation added as to: disputes in respect of which arbitral or judicial proceedings are taking, or have taken place, with any state which, at the date of the commencement of the proceedings, had not itself accepted the compulsory jurisdiction of the International Court of Justice.	Denounced on 12.4.1957.
; above [No. 141] 'ith two more reservations as to: (a) disputes relating to any question which in the opinion of the Government of the U.K. affects the national security of the U.K. or of any of its dependent territories; (b) disputes in respect of which any other party to the dispute has accepted the compulsory jurisdiction of the I.C.J. only in relation to or for the purposes of the dispute; or where the acceptance of the Court's compulsory jurisdiction on behalf of any other party to the dispute was deposited or ratified less than twelve months prior to the filing of the application bringing the dispute before the Court.	Denounced on 26.11.1958. Notice the reservation concerning national security. See: ***Incident of 27 July 1955 Case*** (U.K. v. Bulgaria)
eciprocity ntil terminated ouble exclusion (as from 5.2.1930) xcepting: (a) disputes in regard to which the parties have agreed or shall agree to have recourse to some other method of peaceful settlement; (b) disputes with the Government of any other country which is a Member of the British Commonwealth of Nations; (c) disputes with regard to questions which by international law fall exclusively within the jurisdiction of the U.K.; (d) disputes arising out of events occurring between 3.9.1939 and 2.9.1945; (e) disputes arising out of, or having reference to, any hostilities, war, state of war, or belligerent or military occupation in which the Government of the U.K. are or have been involved; (f) disputes concerning any question relating to or arising out of events occurring before the date of the present declaration which had been subject of proceedings before the Court previous to that date and would have been excluded from the Court's compulsory jurisdiction under the reservation mentioned in para. (a) of the conditions of declaration No. 142 above (automatic reservation as related to matters of national security); (g) disputes relating to any matter excluded from compulsory adjudication or arbitration under any treaty, convention or other international agreement or instrument to which the U.K. is a party; (h) disputes in respect of which arbitral or judicial proceedings are taking, or have taken, place with any State which, at the date of the commencement of the proceed-	Declaration terminated on 27.11.1963

No.	Country	Reference Vol.	P.	Date of Signature	Date of Deposit of Ratification
144	United Kingdom	Yb 63–64		27.11.1963	
145	U.S.A.	Yb 46–47	217	14.8.1946	
146	Uruguay	D6	35	Before 28.1.1921 (date of first publication)	27.9.1921
147	Yugoslavia	D6	51	16.5.1930	24.11.1930

Conditions	Remarks
ings had not itself accepted the compulsory jurisdiction of the I.C.J.; (i) disputes in respect of which any other party of the dispute has accepted the compulsory jurisdiction of the I.C.J. only in relation to or for the purposes of the dispute, or where the acceptance of the Court's compulsory jurisdiction on behalf of any other party to the dispute was deposited or ratified less than twelve months prior to the filing of the application bringing the dispute before the Court. Reserved also is the right either to add to, amend or withdraw any of the foregoing reservations or any that may hereafter be added.	
As above (No. 143) without exception (f)	Declaration in force.
Reciprocity 5 years and thereafter until terminated on 6 months' notice Future disputes Excepting: (a) disputes the solution of which the parties shall entrust to other tribunals by virtue of agreements already in existence or which may be concluded in the future; (b) disputes with regard to matters which are essentially within the domestic jurisdiction of the U.S.A. as determined by the U.S.A.; (c) disputes arising under a multilateral treaty, unless (1) all parties to the treaty affected by the decision are also parties to the case before the Court or (2) the U.S.A. specially agree to jurisdiction.	Deposited 26.8.1946. Declaration in force. See: the *U.S. Nationals in Morocco Case*; *Interhandel Case*; *Aerial Incident of July 27, 1955* (U.S.A. v. Bulgaria). Notice the reservation concerning domestic jurisdiction.
Reciprocity	Uruguay is an original member of the U.N. Declaration in force.
Ratification In relation to any Government recognized by the Kingdom of Yugoslavia and on condition of reciprocity. 5 years (as from deposit of ratification) Future disputes Excepting: (a) disputes relating to questions which by international law, fall exclusively within the jurisdiction of the Kingdom of Yugoslavia; (b) cases where the parties have agreed or shall agree to have recourse to some other method of peaceful settlement.	See: *Pajzs, Czáky, Esterházy Case*; *Losinger Case*.

APPENDIX VII

CONTINUED JURISDICTION BY MEANS OF DECLARATIONS "C"

A Survey of the *Reservations* in the Declarations Accepting the Continued Jurisdiction of the International Court.

No.	The Reservation	Declarations Containing the Reservation *	No.	Remarks
1	Ratification	1, 3, 4, 8, 9, 10, 11, 12, *20*, 26, 27, *32*, 33, 42, 49, 51, 52, 54, 55, 56, 62, 63, 64, 65, 69, 70, 71, 72, 74, 77, 78, *80*, 95, *98*, 113, 122, 124, 125, 127, 135, 147.	41	Ratification was mostly required in old declarations (made under the P.C.I.J.) Some declarations were ratified though ratification was not a condition. See 83, *106*, 111, *146*.
2	Reciprocity †	*All* but: *58*, 81, 83, 84, *97*, 107, *112*.	140	Only declarations *58*, *97*, 107 were made without any conditions, the others (81, 83, 84, *112*) failed to mention the word "reciprocity." Neither wording would necessarily mean that the condition of reciprocity becomes dispensed with. (Chapter IV) Therefore, the use of the term "reciprocity" should not normally be considered as introducing a "reservation."
3	Duration A. Declarations made for a certain period without automatical renewal.	1, 2, 3, 5, 7, 8, 9, 10, 11, 13, 14, 15, 16, 17, 21, 26, 27, 28, 29, 30, 33, 36, 37, 38, 39, 40, 41, 42, 43, 44, 46, 47, 48, 51, 52, 53, 54, 55, 57, 59, 62, 63, 64, 71, 72, 74, 76, 77, 81, 83, 84, 85, 86, 89, 90, 91, 92, 98, 99, 100, 101, 108, 110, 113, 114, 115, 118, 119, 120, 121, 123, 124, 125, 127, 128, 129, 130, 131, 132, 133, *133a*, 147.	82	The longest period *specified* for the duration of a declaration is the one in the declaration of Ireland [71]: 20 years. Only declaration No. *133a* [of Turkey] is now in force.
	B. Declarations made for a certain period to be renewed automatically for similar periods.	*31*, *45*, *87*, *94*, *102*, 103, *122*.	7	In all these declarations the acceptance will continue unless the declaration is terminated on a 6 months' notice.
	C. Declarations made for a certain period and thereafter until terminated.	4, *12*, *19*, *20*, *22*, 49, *50*, 60, 65, 66, 69, 70, *75*, 78, *80*, *88*, 93, 95, *96*, *109*, *112*, 135, 138, 139, *145*.	25	Among these declarations only Nos. *22*, *88*, *145* condition the termination on 6 months' notice.
	D. Declarations made for an unlimited period [until denounced].	*6*, 67, *68*, *73*, *82*, 104, *105*, 111, *115*, *117*, *126*, 136, *137*, 140, 141, 142, 143, *144*.	18	Among these declarations only no. 126 conditions the termination on 1 year's notice.
	E. Declarations made for an unlimited period [without	18, 23, *24*, 25, *32*, *34*, *35*, 56, *58*, *61*, 79, *97*, *106*, 107, *134*, *146*.	16	Declaration no. 107 was nevertheless denounced. For observations made by Governments regarding

4	Exclusions Regarding Time:			
	A. Limitation to future disputes.	*24*, *35*, 36, 37, 38, 74, 76, *80*, 90, 91, 92, 93, *94*, 103, 104, *105*, 130, *145*, 147.	19	
	B. Limitation to disputes arising out of future facts or situations.	*45*, *50*, 72, *73*, 108, 113, 114.	7	It is noticed that there is no practical difference between Group B and Group C.
	C. Double exclusion: limitation to future disputes arising out of future facts or situations.	1, 2, 3, 4, 5, *6*, 10, 11, *12*, *20*, 25, 33, 47, 48, 49, 51, 52, 65, 66, 67, *68*, 69, 70, *75*, 77, 78, *87*, *88*, 89, 95, 96, 100, 116, *117*, 121, *122*, 131, 135, 136, *137*, 138, 139, 140, 141, 142, 143, *144*.	47	
	D. Exclusion of disputes arising in a given period.	*73*, 140, 141, 142, 143, *144*.	6	The periods excluded ***are in fact war periods.***
	E. War exclusions.	4, 5, *6*, *20*, *50*, 65, 66, 67, *68*, *73*, 95, *96*, 110, *117*, 135, 136, *137*, 138, 139, 140, 141, 142, 143, *144*.	24	In declarations 4, *20*, 65, 95, 135, 138, the war exclusion was added on the occasion of the second world war and was limited to "the present hostilities." Declaration *50* adds in the exclusion, disputes arising out of "*crisis* affecting national security." Declaration *68* added the disputes arising out of the discharge of functions pursuant to any recommendation or decision of an organ of the U.N. Declaration 110 limited the exclusion to the [first] world war and the Polano-Sovietic war.
5	Disputes concerning the Territorial Status (and Territorial Rights) of the Declaring State.	1, 2, *6*, 53, 54, 55, 69, 70, 113.	9	Declaration 6 [of Australia] excluded disputes related to the continental shelf of Australia and the Australian waters. Declarations 53, 54, 55 [of Greece] excluded disputes relating to the territorial status of Greece "including its rights of sovereignty over its ports and lines of communications." The same is found in declaration No. 69 [of Iran]: "... over its Islands and ports," in No. 70 [of Iraq]: "over its waters and communications," and in No. 113 [of Roumania]: "over her ports and communications."

* The reference is to the declarations by their numbers as in Appendix No. VI. Declarations in force are in italics.
† Compare with Reservation no. 20 below.

No.	The Reservation	Declarations Containing the Reservation	No.	Remarks
6	Disputes Arising out of Matters within the Domestic Jurisdiction of the Declaring State:			
	A. As determined by international law.	1, 2, 3, 4, 5, *6*, 16, 19, *20*, 33, *50*, 65, 66, *68*, 69, 70, 72, *73*, *80*, 95, 99, *105*, 113, 135, 136, 138, 139, 140, 141, 142, 143, *144*, 147.	33	All but declarations Nos. 3, 68, 72, 73, 80, 113 used the wording "fall *exclusively* under the domestic jurisdiction..." Declarations 68, 72, 73, 80 used the term "*essentially*" instead. Declarations 3, 113 did not use either term.
	B. As determined or understood by the declaring State.	49, 67, *80*, *88*, 103, 104, *117*, *137*, *145*.	9	Declaration 49 (of France) uses the words "as understood," and Declaration No. 88 (of Mexico) uses the words "in the opinion of." The reservation has been revoked in later declarations by France, India and Pakistan, and is still in force in the declarations of Liberia (80), Mexico (88), the Sudan (117), the Republic of South Africa (137) and the U.S.A. (145).
7	Disputes Affecting the National Security of the Declaring State.	*50*, 142, 143.	3	Declaration No. 50 [of France] excluded "disputes arising out of a *crisis* affecting the national security..." Declarations 142 [of the U.K.] *left it to the U.K. to decide that the dispute affects its national security.* It also extends to "the national security of its dependent territories." Declaration 143 [of the U.K.] limits this "automatic" reservation to disputes arising before its date, which would have been extended under declaration 142. The reservation is dropped in the new declaration of 1963 [144].
8	Disputes in regard to which the Parties Have Agreed or Shall Agree to Have Recourse to Another Method of Peaceful Settlement.	1, 2, 3, 4, 5, 10, 11, 12, 19, *20*, 26, 33, 37, 38, 39, 40, 47, 48, 49, *50*, 51, 52, 53, 54, 55, 65, 66, 67, *68*, 69, 70, 72, *73*, 74, *75*, 76, 77, 78, *80*, 81, *87*, 89, 90, 91, 92, 93, *94*, 95, *96*, 103, 104, *105*, 108, 110, 113, 116, *117*, 127, 130, 131, 132, 133, *133a*, 135, 136, 137, 138, 139, 140, 141, 142, 143, *144*, *145*.	74	Declarations 1, 2, 53, 54, 55 excluded disputes relating... to the application of treaties providing for another method of pacific settlement. Declarations 91, 92, 93 [of the Netherlands] limited the exclusion to the cases where the parties may have agreed "*after the entry into force of the Court's Statute*" to have recourse to other methods, and declaration *94* (of the same country) refers to the agreements between the parties "excluding the jurisdiction of the I.C.J."

				Declarations 131–*133a* [of Turkey] exclude disputes "for which ***it would be appropriate*** to apply agreements" providing for a different method.
9	Disputes Arising with a Member of a Particular Group of States:			
	A. With another member of the Commonwealth of Nations.	4, 5, *6*, *20*, 65, 66, *68*, 95, *96*, 135, 136, *137*, 138, 139, 140, 141, 142, 143, *144*.	19	Pakistan, though a member of the Commonwealth did not include this reservation in any of its declarations [see Nos. 103, 105, 104]. Nor did Ireland [71].
	B. With another Arab State.	70	1	Declaration of Iraq – never ratified.
10	Disputes Relating to Matters Excluded from Judicial Settlement.			
	A. By a treaty or another international instrument.	19, 140, 141, 142, 143, *144*.	6	Declarations of Cambodia [19] and the U.K.
	B. By the constitution of the declarant State.	*35*	1	Declaration of El Salvador. Reservation introduced in the instrument of ratification. Both Argentina [3] and Brazil [16] excluded questions which belong to the constitutional regime of each state.
11	Disputes with States that Do Not Have Normal Relations With the Declaring State:			
	A. No normal relations.	72	1	First declaration of Israel.
	B. No normal diplomatic relations.	*68*, *73*, 110.	3	Declarations 72, *73* [of Israel]; 110 [of Poland] refer to states which "***refuse to establish or maintain***" normal relations (72) or normal diplomatic relations (*73*, 110) with the declaring State.
	C. With States that do not recognize the declarant State.	*73*	1	
	D. With States not recognized by the declarant State.	113, 114, 147.	3	Declarations of Roumania (113, 114) and of Yugoslavia.
12	Disputes Considered by:			
	A. The Council of the League of Nations.	4, 5, *20*, 26, 46, 47, 48, 65, 66, 69, 70, 74, 108, 135, 136, 138, 139.	17	The reservation is generally made to maintain the right to "suspend" judicial proceedings under certain conditions.

No.	The Reservation	Declarations Containing the Reservation	No.	Remarks
				Declaration 26 [of Czechoslovakia] made the acceptance "subject to the right of either party to the dispute to submit it before any recourse to the Court to the Council of the League of Nations." Declaration 74 [of Italy] made the recourse to the Court possible only "in cases where a solution by means of diplomacy or by the action of the Council of the League of Nations is not attained." Declaration 108 [of Peru] limited this to the case where the parties "may have agreed... to submit the dispute... to the Council." Declaration 70 [of Iraq] extends the reservation to "disputes under consideration by the Council *or Assembly* of the League of Nations."
	B. By the Security Council.	*6*	1	Declaration of Australia.
13	Disputes With States that Have Not Accepted the Compulsory Jurisdiction:			
	A. At the date of the commencement of arbitral or judicial proceedings respecting the same dispute.	141, 142, 143, *144*.	4	Declarations of the U.K.
	B. For at least a period equal to that in the declaration.	*50*	1	Declaration of France.
	C. Before a given period (12 months) prior to the filing of the application to the Court.	*68*, *115*, 142, 143, *144*.	5	Declarations of India [68], Somalia [115] and the U.K.
	D. Except for the purposes of the dispute at hand.	*68*, *115*, 142, 143, *144*.	5	As above.
14	Disputes Involving a Legal Title Created or Conferred by Another Government	72, *73*	2	Declarations of Israel.

15	Disputes Arising Under a Multilateral Treaty.	103, 104, *105*, *144*.	4	Declarations of Pakistan and the U.S.A. The reservation is made under two exceptions.
16	Specific Disputes.	57, 110.	2	Declaration 57 [of Guatemala] excludes the dispute between England and Guatemala concerning the restoration of the territory of Belize, except if the case were decided *ex aequo et bono*. Declaration 110 [of Poland] excludes disputes resulting from the treaty of Peace signed at Riga on 18.3.1921.
17	Limitation to Specific Disputes with Specific Parties.	*34*, 69	2	Declaration [34] [of Egypt (U.A.R.)] is limited to disputes between the parties of the Suez Canal Convention [1888] as to its interpretation or the applicability of its provisions. Declaration 69 [of Iran] is limited to disputes arising with regard to situations or facts relating to the application of treaties or conventions accepted by Iran.
18	Pecuniary Claims Against the Declaring State.	*35*	1	Declaration of El Salvador.
19	Reserving the Right to Add, Amend or Withdraw Any Reservation.	*112*, *115*, 143, *144*.	4	Declaration of Portugal [*112*] reserves the right "to exclude from its scope at any time, any given category or categories of disputes, by notifying the Secretary General of the U.N. and with effect from the moment of such notification."
20	Conditioning the Entry into Force of the Declaration on the Acceptance of Some States of the Compulsory Jurisdiction.	15	1	Declaration of Brazil. This type of reservation explains what was historically meant by the term "on condition of reciprocity" in Article 36 (3) of the Statute.

BIBLIOGRAPHY OF WORKS CITED[1]

I. DOCUMENTARY SOURCES

A. Publications of the Court:

The International Court of Justice, Reports of Judgments, Advisory Opinions and Orders. 1947–1963.

—, Pleadings, Oral Arguments and Documents. 1948–1963.

—, Yearbooks. 1947–1964.

The Permanent Court of International Justice, Advisory Committee of Jurists, Documents Presented to the Committee Relating to Existing Plans for the Establishment of a Permanent Court of International Justice. 1920.

—, Procès Verbaux of the Proceedings of the Committee. June 16th–July 24th 1920 with Annexes. The Hague, Van Langenhuysen, 1920.

The Permanent Court of Justice, Series A. Judgments and Orders. Nos. 1 to 24 (1922–1930).

—, Series B. Advisory Opinions. Nos. 1 to 18 (1922–1930).

—, Series A/B. Judgments, Orders and Advisory Opinions. Nos. 40 to 80 (1931–1940).

—, Series C. Acts and Documents Relating to Judgments and Advisory Opinions. Nos. 1–19, 52–87 (1922–1939).

—, Series D. Acts and Documents Concerning the Organization of the Court. Nos. 1 to 6 (1922–1940).

—, Series E. Annual Reports. Nos. 1 to 16 (1925–1945).

B. Publications of the United Nations:

United Nations Administrative Tribunal, Statute and Rules. AT/11/Rev. (U.N. Pub. Sales No. 62.x.3)

United Nations Conference on International Organization. San Francisco 1945. Documents. 16 vols. London and New York 1945.

United Nations General Assembly Official Records.

United Nations Secretariat, Commentary on the Draft Convention on Arbitral Procedure Adopted by the International Law Commission in its Fifth Session, U.N. Doc. A/CN.4/92 (1955) (U.N. Pub. Sales No. 1955. v. 1).

—, Repertory of Practice of the United Nations Organs (U.N. Pub. Sales No. 1955 v. 2) (vol. I–V).

—, Reports of International Arbitral Awards (U.N. Rep. Int'l Arb. Awards). 12 vols. 1948–1963 (Prepared by the Registry of the I.C.J.)

[1] Comprehensive annual bibliographies of publications relating to the Court have been published since 1925 by the registry of the Court. See *P.C.I.J.*, Series E, and the Yearbooks of the present Court.

—, Systematic Survey of Treaties for the Pacific Settlement of International Disputes 1928–1948. Lake Success, N.Y. 1948. (U.N. Pub. Sales No. 1949. v. 3)
United Nations Security Council Official Records.
United Nations Treaty Series.
Yearbooks of the International Law Commission.

C. Publications of the League of Nations:

League of Nations, Documents Concerning the Action Taken by the Council of the League of Nations under Article 14 of the Covenant and the Adoption by the Assembly of the Statute of the Permanent Court of International Justice. Geneva, 1921.
—, Documents Concerning the Action Taken by the Assembly on the Statute of the Permanent Court of International Justice. Geneva, 1921.
League of Nations Documents, Records of the Assembly, Plenary Meetings.
League of Nations Documents, Records of the Assembly, Committees.
League of Nations Official Journal.
League of Nations Treaty Series.

D. Other Sources:

British Command Papers.
Darby, W. E., *International Tribunals. A Collection of the Various Schemes Which Have Been Propounded; and of Instances in the Nineteenth Century.* London, J. M. Dent & Co., 4th ed. 1904.
European Yearbook. vol. V, 1959.
Foreign Relations of the United States.
Hudson, Manley O., *International Legislation.* vol. I. Washington, Carnegie Endowment for International Peace, 1931.
[International American Conference] Reports of Committees and Discussions Thereon. Washington, U.S. Government Printing Office, 1890.
Journal Officiel de la Communauté du Charbon et de l'Acier.
Khalil, M., *The Arab States and the Arab League. A Documentary Record.* 2 vols. Beirut, Khayat, 1962.
Lapradelle A. de, et Politis, N., *Recueil des Arbitrages Internationaux.* 2 vols. Paris, A. Pedone, vol. I, 1905; vol. II, 1924.
[Malloy, William M.], *Treaties, Conventions, International Acts, Protocols and Agreements between the United States of America and Other Powers 1776–1909.* 2 vols. Washington, U.S. Government Printing Office, 1910.
Martens, Fr. de, *Nouveau Recueil de Traités.* Goettingen 1817–42.
—, *Nouveau Recueil Général de Traités* (3me série). Leipzig, 1909–43.
Miller, D. H., *The Drafting of the Covenant of the League of Nations.* 2 vols. New York, G. P. Putnam's Sons, 1928.
[Miller, Hunter] *Treaties and Other International Acts of the United States of America.* vol. I. Washington, U.S. Government Printing Office, 1931.
[Ministère des Affaires Etrangères], *Conférence Internationale de la Paix.* La Haye, Imprimerie Nationale, 1899.
—, *Deuxième Conférence de la Paix, Actes et Documents.* 2 vols. La Haye, Imprimerie Nationale, 1908.
Moore, John Bassett, *History and Digest of the International Arbitrations to Which the United States Has Been a Party.* 6 vols. Washington, U.S. Government Printing Office, 1898.
—, *A Digest of International Law.* 8 vols. Washington, U.S. Government Printing Office, 1906.

Recueil des Décisions des Tribunaux Arbitraux Mixtes. 10 vols. Paris, Librairie de la Société de Recueil Sirey, 1922–1930.

[Scott, James Brown] *The Hague Court Reports*. 2 vols. New York, Oxford University Press, 1916.

—, *The Proceedings of the Hague Peace Conferences*. The Conference of 1899. New York, Oxford University Press, 1920.

—, *The Proceedings of the Hague Peace Conferences*. The Conference of 1907. 4 vols. New York, Oxford University Press, 1920.

—, *The International Conferences of American States 1899–1928*. New York, Oxford University Press, 1931.

II. BOOKS, ARTICLES, MEMORANDA AND REPORTS

Acrement, Albert, *La Procédure dans les Arbitrages Internationaux*. Paris, Imprimerie Sueur-Charruey, 1905.

[Al-Farsy] Reports of Committee IV/1 to Commission IV of the San Francisco Conference, Doc. No. 913, IV/1/74(1), 13 *U.N. Conf. Int'l Org. Docs.* 381 (1945).

Alvarez, A., *et al.*, see *Réforme*.

[American Bar Association – Section of International and Comparative Law] Report on the Self-Judging Aspect of the United States Domestic Jurisdiction Reservation with respect to the International Court of Justice. August 1959.

Anand, R. P., *Compulsory Jurisdiction of the International Court of Justice*. Bombay, Asia Publishing House, 1961.

Audry, Léon, *La Revision de la Sentence Arbitrale*. Paris, E. Duchemin, 1914.

Balasko, A., *Causes de Nullité de la Sentence Arbitrale en Droit International Public*. Paris, Editions A. Pedone, 1938.

Barclay, Sir Thomas, *The New Method of Adjusting International Disputes and the Future*. Londin, Constable & Co. Ltd., 1917.

[Basdevant] Report of the Washington Committee of Jurists, April 25, 1945, Doc. No. Jurist 86, J/73, 14 *U.N. Conf. Int'l Org. Docs.* 821 (1945).

Bastid, S., "La Jurisprudence de la Cour Internationale de Justice," 78 *Recueil des Cours* 579 (1951–I).

Baxter, R. R., see Sohn.

Bebr, Gerhard, *Judicial Control of the European Communities*. London, Stevens, 1962.

Berlia, Georges, "La Jurisprudence des Tribunaux Internationaux en ce qui concerne leur Compétence," 88 *Recueil des Cours* 109 (1955)

Biscottini, *Contributo alla Teoria degli Atti Unilaterali nel Diritto Internazionale*. Milano, Giuffre, 1951

Bishop, C. M., *International Arbitral Procedure*. Washington, J. Byrne & Co., 1931.

Bluntschli, J. K., *Le Droit International Codifié* (trans. by Lardy). Paris, Guillaumin et cie, 2d ed. 1874.

Bonfils, H., *Manuel de Droit International Public*. Paris, A. Rousseau, 1st ed. 1894; 5th ed. 1908; 7th ed. 1914.

Borel, Eugene, "Les Voies de Recours contre les Sentences Arbitrales," 52 *Recueil des Cours* 1 (1935–II).

Bos, Maarten, *Les Conditions du Procès en Droit International Public*. Leyden, 1957. [19 Bibliotheca Visseriana].

Bosco, Giacinto, *Rapporti e Conflitti fra Giurisdizioni Internazionali*. Rome, A.R.E., 1932. [20 Publicazioni dell'Associazione Italiana per la Società delle Nazioni].

Boskey, Shirley, see Broches, A.

Brierly, J. L., "Vital Interests and the Law," 21 *Brit. Yb. Int'l L.* 51 (1944).
—, "Réponse," [au questionnaire adressé par M. Ch. Rousseau], 43 *Annuaire* 27 (1950–I).
—, *The Law of Nations*. Oxford, Clarendon Press, 6th ed. Waldock. 1963.
Briggs, Herbert, "Reservations to the Acceptance of Compulsory Jurisdiction of the International Court of Justice," 93 *Recueil des Cours* 229 (1958–I).
—, "Interhandel: The Court's Judgment of March 21, 1959, on the Preliminary Objections of the United States," 53 *Am. J. Int'l L.* 547 (1959).
—, "La Compétence Incidente de la Cour Internationale de Justice en tant que Compétence Obligatoire," 64 *Rev. Gén. Dr. Int'l Pub.* 217 (1960).
Broches, A. & Boskey, Shirley, "Theory and Practice of Treaty Registration – Part II," 4 *Nederlands Tijdschrift voor Internationaal Recht* 277 (1957).
Bruns, Viktar, "La Cour Permanente de Justice Internationale, son Organisation et sa Compétence, 62 *Recueil des Cours* 551 (1937–IV).
Bustamante, Antonio S. de, *The World Court* (Trans. by Read). New York, MacMillan, 1925.
Caflisch, Lucius C., "The Recent Judgment of the International Court of Justice: The Case Concerning the Aerial Incident of July 27, 1955," 54 *Am. J. Int'l L.* 855 (1960).
Calvo, Carlos, *Droit International Théorique et Pratique*. vol. III. Paris, A. Rousseau, 5th ed. 1896.
Card, see Rouard de Card.
Carlston, Kenneth S., *The Process of International Arbitration*. New York, Columbia University Press, 1946.
Castberg, Frede, "L'Excès de Pouvoir dans la Justice Internationale," 35 *Recueil des Cours* 357 (1931–I).
Cavaré, Louis, *Le Droit International Public Positif*. vol. II. Paris, Editions A. Pedone, 2d ed. 1962.
Cecchetto, R., "La Posizione dell'Italia rispetto all'Art. 37 dello Statuto della Corte Internazionale di Giustizia," 39 *Rivista di Diritto Internazionale* 339 (1956).
Cheng, Bin, *General Principles of Law as Applied by International Courts and Tribunals*. London, Stevens, 1953.
Chung, Il Yung, *Legal Problems Involved in the Corfu Channel Incident*. Genève, E. Droz, 1959.
Cocatre-Zilgien, A., "Les Mesures conservatoires en Droit International," 11 *Rev. Egyptienne Dr. Int'l* 73 (1955).
Conac, Gerard, "L'Affaire Relative à l'Incident Aérien du 27 Juillet 1955 entre Israel et la Bulgarie devant la Cour Internationale de Justice," 64 *Rev. Gén. Dr. Int'l Pub.* 711 (1960).
[Constantopoulos *et al.*] *Grundprobleme des Internationalen Rechts, Festschrift für Jean Spiropoulos*. Bonn, Schimmelbusch & Co. 1957.
Cory, Helen, *Compulsory Arbitration on International Disputes*. New York, Columbia University Press, 1932.
Creasy, Sir Edward S., *First Platform of International Law*. London, J. Van Voorst, 1876.
Deák, Francis, *The Hungarian Rumanian Land Dispute*. New York, Columbia University Press, 1928.
Delbez, Louis, *Les Principes Généraux du Contentieux International*. Paris, R. Richon et R. Durand-Auzias, 1962.
[Descamps, Chevalier] Report of the Third Committee to the Conference, July 25, 1899 in [Scott] The Proceedings of the Hague Peace Conferences. The Conference of 1899 at 106.

Desrioux, J., see Wittenberg.
Dubisson, M., *La Cour Internationale de Justice*. Paris, R. Richon et R. Durand-Auzias, 1964.
Dumbauld, Edward, *Interim Measures of Protection in International Controversies*. The Hague, M. Nijhoff, 1932.
Engel, Salo, "The Compulsory Jurisdiction of the International Court of Justice," 40 *Georgetown Law Journal* 41 (1951–1952).
Enrique, Giuliano, "L'Acceptation sans Réciprocité de la Juridiction de la Cour Permanente de Justice Internationale," 13 *Rev. Dr. Int'l & Leg. Comp.* 834 (3me sér. 1932).
Erskine, John, *An Institute of the Law of Scotland* (new edition, Macallan). Edinburgh, Bell & Bradfute, 1838.
Fachiri, Alexander P., *The Permanent Court of International Justice*. London, Oxford University Press, 2d ed. 1932.
—, "Repudiation of the Optional Clause," 20 *Brit. Yb. Int'l L.* 52 (1939).
Farmanfarma, Ali Naghi, *The Declared Jurisdiction of the International Court of Justice*. Montreux, Imprimerie Ganguin & Laubscher, 1952.
Fawcett, J. E. S., "The Exhaustion of Local Remedies: Substance or Procedure," 31 *Brit. Yb. Int'l L.* 452 (1954).
Feinberg, Nathan, *La Juridiction de la Cour Permanente de Justice dans le Système de la Protection Internationale des Minorités*. Paris, A. Rousseau, 1931.
Feller, A. H., "Conclusions of the Parties in the Procedure of the Permanent Court of International Justice," 25 *Am. J. Int'l L.* 490 (1931).
Finkelstein, Maurice, "Judicial Self-Limitation," 37 *Harv. L. Rev.* 338 (1923–1924).
Fiore, Pasquale, *Trattato di Diritto Internazionale Pubblico*. vol. II. Torino Unione Tipografico – Editrice, 3rd ed. 1888.
Fitzmaurice, Sir Gerald, "The Law and Procedure of the International Court of Justice, International Organizations and Tribunals," 29 *Brit. Yb. Int'l L.* 1 (1952).
[—], Texts of Articles of the Code of the Law of Treaties, [1956] *I.L.C. Yearbook* 104, U.N. Doc. No. A/CN. 4/101 (1956).
—, "The Law and Procedure of the International Court of Justice, 1951–54 Treaty Interpretation and Other Treaty Points," 33 *Brit. Yb. Int'l L.* 203 (1957).
—, "The Law and Procedure of the International Court of Justice, 1951–54: Questions of Jurisdiction, Competence and Procedure," 34 *Brit. Yb. Int'l L.* 1 (1958).
Foda, Ezzeldin, *The Projected Arab Court of Justice*. The Hague, M. Nijhoff, 1957.
Goldman, Berthold, "Human Rights Tribunals," in [Union International des Avocats] *International Courts* 72. Paris, Dalloz et Sirey, 1958.
Goldschmidt, "Projet de Règlement pour les Tribunaux Arbitraux Internationaux," 6 *Rev. Dr. Int'l & Leg. Comp.* 421 (1874).
Goyard, Claude, *La Compétence des Tribunaux Judiciaires en Matière Administrative*. Paris, Editions Montchrestien, 1962.
Gross, Leo, "Some Observations on the International Court of Justice," 56 *Am. J. Int'l L.* 33 (1962).
—, "Bulgaria Invokes the Connally Amendment," 56 *Am. J. Int'l L.* 357 (1962).
—, "The Jurisprudence of the World Court: Thirty Eighth Year (1959)," 57 *Am. J. Int'l L.* 751 (1963).
—, "Limitations Upon the Judicial Function," 58 *Am. J. Int'l L.* 415 (1964).
Grossen, J. M., *Les Présomptions en Droit International Public*. Neuchatel, Delachaux et Niestlé, 1954.

Guermanoff, Dimitri, *L'Excès de Pouvoir de l'Arbitre*. Paris, Université de Paris, 1929.

Guerrero, J. Gustave, "La Qualification Unilatérale de la Compétence Nationale," in [Constantopoulos *et al.*] *Grundprobleme des Internationalen Rechts* 207 (1957).

Guggenheim, Paul, "Les Mesures Conservatoires dans la Procédure Arbitrale et Judiciaire," 40 *Recueil des Cours* 649 (1932–II).

—, "L'Elaboration d'une Clause Modèle de Compétence Obligatoire de la Cour Internationale de Justice," 44 *Annuaire* 468 (1952–I).

—, *Traité de Droit International Public*. vol. II, Geneve, Georg, 1954.

Hall, William Edward, *A Treatise on International Law*. Oxford, The Clarendon Press, 8th ed., Higgins, 1924.

Hambro, Edward Isak, *L'Exécution des Sentences Internationales*. Paris, Sirey, 1936.

—, "Some Observations on the Compulsory Jurisdiction of the International Court of Justice," 25 *Brit. Yb. Int'l L.* 133 (1948).

—, "Observations" [au Questionnaire et au rapport provisoire de M. Ch. Rousseau], 44 *Annuaire* 165 (1952–I).

—, "Jurisdiction of the International Court of Justice," 76 *Recueil des Cours* 125 (1950–I).

Hammarskjöld, A., "The Permanent Court of International Justice and its Place in International Relations," in his *Juridiction Internationale* at 227. Leiden, Sijthoff, 1938.

—, "Quelques Aspects de la Question des Mesures Conservatoires en Droit International Positif," in *id.* at 299.

—, "Quelques Aspects de la Fonction Consultative de la Cour Permanente de Justice Internationale," in *id.* at 283.

Hardy, Jean, "The Interpretation of Plurilingual Treaties by International Courts and Tribunals," 37 *Brit. Yb. Int'l L.* 72 (1961).

[Harvard Research in International Law] Draft Convention on the Law of Treaties, 29 *Am. J. Int'l L.* (2 Supp.) (1935).

Heffter, August W., *Le Droit International de l'Europe* (Trans. by Bergson). Paris, A. Cotillon & cie., 1883.

Hogg, James, "The International Court: Rules of Treaty Interpretation," 43 *Minnesota Law Review* 369 (1958–59).

—, "The International Court: Rules of Treaty Interpretation II," 44 *id.* at 5 (1959–60).

Holtzendorf, Franz Von, *Elements de Droit International Public* (Trans. by Zographos). Paris, A. Rousseau, 1891.

Huber, Max, "Classification des Conflits Justiciables" (Commentaire), 29 *Annuaire* 241 (1922).

Hudson, Manley O., *The Permanent Court of International Justice*. New York, Macmillan 1934.

—, *The Permanent Court of International Justice*. New York, Macmillan, 2d ed. 1943.

—, *International Tribunals*. Washington, Carnegie Endowment for International Peace & Brookings Institution, 1944.

—, "The Twenty-Fourth Year of the World Court," 40 *Am. J. Int'l L.* 1 (1946).

—, "Compulsory Jurisdiction of the International Court of Justice," 40 *Proceedings of the American Society of International Law* 12 (1946).

—, "The World Court: America's Declaration Accepting Jurisdiction," 23 *A.B.A.J.* 832 (1946).

—, see Documentary Sources.

Hyde, Charles Cheney, "The United States Accepts the Optional Clause," 40 *Am. J. Int'l L.* 778 (1946).

Iaccarino, U. M., "Della c.d. Competenza sulla Competenza dei Tribunali Internazionali," 14 *Diritto Internazionale* 357 (1960).

[Institut de Droit International] "Projet de Règlement pour la Procédure Arbitrale Internationale," 1 *Annuaire* 126 (1877).

[Institut für ausländisches Öffentliches Recht und Völkerrecht] *Statut et Règlement de la Cour Permanente de Justice Internationale*. Berlin, Carl Heymanns Verlag, 1934.

[International Law Commission] Report of the I.L.C. Covering the Work of its Third Session, *U.N. Gen. Ass. Off. Rec.*, 6th Sess., Supp. No. 9 (U.N. Doc. No. A/1858) (1951).

—, Report of the I.L.C. Covering the Work of its Fourth Session, *U.N. Gen. Ass. Off. Rec.*, 7th Sess., Supp. No. 9 (U.N. Doc. No. A/2163) (1952).

—, Report of the I.L.C. Covering the Work of its Fifth Session, *U.N. Gen. Ass. Off. Rec.*, 8th sess., Supp. No. 9 (U.N. Doc. No. A/2456) (1953).

—, Report of the I.L.C. Covering the Work of its Sixth Session, *U.N. Gen. Ass. Off. Rec.*, 9th sess., Supp. No. 9 (U.N. Doc. No. A/2693) (1954).

—, Report of the I.L.C. Covering the Work of its Tenth Session, *U.N. Gen. Ass. Off. Rec.*, 13th Sess., Supp. No. 9 (U.N. Doc. No. A/3859) (1958).

Jauffret, see Parisot.

Jenks, C. Wilfred, "Compétence Obligatoire des Instances Judiciaires et Arbitrales Internationales," (rapport), 48 *Annuaire* 57 (1959–II).

—, *The Prospects of International Adjudication*. London, Stevens, 1964.

Jennings, R. Y., "Recent Cases on Automatic Reservations to the Optional Clause," 7 *Int'l & Comp. L.Q.* 349 (1958).

Jessup, Philip, "The International Court of Justice of the United Nations," 21 *Foreign Policy Reports* 154 (August 1945).

—, "The International Court of Justice and Legal Matters," 42 *Illinois Law Review* 273 (1948).

Johnson, D. H. N., "The Effect of Resolutions of the General Assembly of the United Nations," 32 *Brit. Yb. Int'l L.* 97 (1955–56).

Jones, Mervyn, "Corfu Channel Case – Jurisdiction," 35 *Transactions of the Grotius Society* 91 (1949).

Jully, L., "Le Premier Arrêt de la Cour Internationale de Justice," 48 *Friedens Warte* 144 (1948).

Kaeckenbeeck, Georges, "Réponse" [au questionnaire adressé par M. Ch. Rousseau], 43 *Annuaire* 29 (1950–I).

Kelsen, Hans, "Compulsory Adjudication of International Disputes," 37 *Am. J. Int'l L.* 397 (1934).

—, *The Law of the United Nations*. New York, Frederick A. Praeger Inc., 1951.

Lapradelle, Albert de, "L'Excès de Pouvoir de l'Arbitre," 2 *Rev. Dr. Int'l* 5 (Paris 1928).

—, *et al.*, see *Réforme*.

— et Politis, N., *Recueil des Arbitrages Internationaux*. 2 vols. Paris, A. Pedone, vol. I 1905; vol. II 1924.

Lauterpacht, Sir Hersch, "The Legal Remedy in Case of Excess of Jurisdiction," 9 *Brit. Yb. Int'l L.* 117 (1928).

—, "The British Reservations to the Optional Clause," 10 *Economica* 137 (1930).

—, *The Function of Law in the International Community*. Oxford, Clarendon Press, 1933.

—, *The Development of International Law by the Permanent Court of International Justice*. London, Longmans, Green & Co., 1934.

—, *The Development of International Law by the International Court.* London, Stevens, 1958.

[—], International Law Commission, Report on the Law of Treaties, U.N. Doc., A/CN 4/63 (1953).

Law, Castor H., *The Local Remedies Rule in International Law.* Geneva, E. Droz, 1961.

Lawson, Ruth C., "The Problem of the Compulsory Jurisdiction of the World Court," 46 *Am. J. Int'l L.* 219 (1952).

Magyary, Géza, *La Juridiction de la Cour Permanente de Justice Internationale,* Paris, Les Editions Internationales, 1931.

Maine, Sir Henry Sumner, *On Early Law and Custom.* London, J. Murray, New ed. 1890.

Malloy, William H., see Documentary Sources.

Martens, Fedor F., *Traité de Droit International* (Trans. by Leo). Paris, Chevalier-Marescq et cie, 1887.

Maus, Bertrand, *Les Réserves dans les Déclarations d'Acceptation de la Juridiction Obligatoire de la Cour Internationale de Justice.* Genève, E. Droz, 1959.

McNair, Arnold, "The Council's Request for an Advisory Opinion from the Permanent Court of International Justice," 7 *Brit. Yb. Int'l L.* 1 (1926).

Memorandum on the Signature by His Majesty's Government in the United Kingdom of the Optional Clause of the Statute of the Permanent Court of International Justice, Great Britain, *Parliamentary Papers Misc.* No. 12 (1929) Cmd. 3452.

Merignhac, A., *Traité Théorique et Pratique de L'Arbitrage International.* Paris, Larose, 1895.

Meron, Theodor, "The Incidence of the Rule of Exhaustion of Local Remedies," 35 *Brit. Yb. Int'l L.* 83 (1959).

Miller, D. H., *The Drafting of the Covenant of the League of Nations.* 2 vols. New York, G. P. Putnam's Sons, 1928.

Miller, Hunter, see Documentary Sources.

Montesqieu, *L'Esprit des Lois.* Edit. de Leyde 1749.

Moore, John Bassett, Memorandum on Advisory Opinions Submitted on February 18th, 1922, *P.C.I.J.*, ser. D., No. 2 at 383 (1922).

—, see Documentary Sources.

Morelli, G., "La Theorie Générale du Procès International," 61 *Recueil des Cours* 257 (1937–III).

Oppenheim, L., *International Law.* vol. II. London, Longmans, Green & Co., 7th ed. Lauterpacht 1952.

Parisot, D. et Jauffret, A., *Manuel de Procédure Civile et Voies d'Exécution.* Paris, R. Pichon et R. Durand-Auzias, 7th ed. 1962.

Perassi, T., "I Caratteri Formali della Clausola Facoltativa sulla Giurisdizione Obligatoria della Corte Permanente de Giustizia Internazionale," 24 *Rivista di Diritto Internazionale* 127 (1932).

Perrin, G., "L'Affaire de l'Interhandel-Phase des exceptions préliminaires," 16 *Annuaire Suisse de Droit International* 73 (1959).

Philipse, *Les Fonctions Consultatives de la Cour Permanente de Justice Internationale.* Lausanne, Librarie Payot & cie., 1928.

Piedelièvre, R., *Précis de Droit International Public.* Paris, R. Pichon, 1895.

Politis, N., *La Justice Internationale.* Paris, Hachette, 1924.

Pradier Fodéré, Paul L. E., *Traité de Droit International Public.* Paris, G. Pedone-Lauriel, 1894.

Ralston, J. H., *The Law and Procedure of International Tribunals.* Stanford University Press, rev. ed. 1926.

—, *Supplement to the Law and Procedure of International Tribunals.* Stanford University Press, 1936.

La Réforme Agraire en Roumanie et les Optants Hongrois de Transylvanie devant la Société des Nations. [Alvarez, A., *et al.*]. Paris, Imprimerie du Palais, 1927.

La Réforme Agraire Roumanie en Transylvanie devant la Justice Internationale et le Conseil de la Société des Nations – Quelques Opinions [Lapradelle et al.] Paris, Editions Internationales, 1928.

Reuter, Paul, *International Institutions* (Trans. by Chapman). London, G. Allen, 1958.

—, *Cours de Droit International Public, Les Modes de Solution des Conflits Internationaux.* Paris, Cours de Droit, 1958.

Revon, Michel, *L'Arbitrage International, son Passé, son Présent, son Avenir.* Paris, A. Rousseau, 1892.

Rivier, Alphonse P. O., *Principes du Droit des Gens.* vol. II. Paris, A. Rousseau, 1896.

Rolin, Henri, "The International Court of Justice and Domestic Jurisdiction," 8 *Int'l Org.* 36 (1954).

Rolin-Jaequemyns, G., "Quelques Mots sur la Phase Nouvelle du Differend Anglo-American," 4 *Rev. Dr. Int'l & Leg. Comp.* 127 (1872).

Rosenne, Shabtai, "Res Judicata: Some Recent Decisions of the International Court of Justice," 28 *Brit. Yb. Int'l* 365 (1951).

—, "The Advisory Competence of the International Court of Justice," 30 *Rev. Dr. Int'l* 10 (Geneva, 1952).

—, "The *Forum Prorogatum* in the International Court of Justice," 6 *Rev. Hellénique Dr. Int'l* 1 (1953).

—, *The International Court of Justice. An Essay in Political and Legal Theory.* Leyden, A. W. Sijthoff, 1957.

—, *The Time Factor in the Jurisdiction of the International Court of Justice.* Leyden, A. W. Sythoff, 1960.

—, *The World Court.* Leyden, A. W. Sythoff, 1962.

Rouard de Card, Edgard, *Droit International, L'Arbitrage International dans le Passé, le Présent, et l'Avenir.* Paris, A. Durand et Pedone-Lauriel, 1877.

Rousseau, Charles, "Le Conflit Italo-Ethiopien," 44 *Rev. Gén. Dr. Int'l Pub.* (1937).

—, *Principes Généraux du Droit International Public.* vol. I. Paris, A. Pedone, 1944.

—, "La Détermination des Affaires qui Relèvent Essentiellement de la Compétence Nationale des Etats," 44 *Annuaire* 137 (1952–II).

—, *Droit International Public.* Paris, Recueil Sirey, 1953.

Rouyer-Hameray, Bernard, *Les Compétences Implicites des Organisations Internationales.* Paris, R. Pichon et R. Durand-Auzias, 1962.

Rudstein, Simon, "La Cour Permanente de Justice Internationale comme Instance de Recours," 43 *Recueil des Cours* 1 (1933–I).

Salvioli, Gabriele, "La Corte Permanente di Giustizia Internazionale," 15 *Rivista di Diritto Internazionale* 11 (1923).

—, "La Jurisprudence de la Cour Permanente de Justice Internationale," 12 *Recueil des Cours* 1 (1926–II).

—, "Les Rapports entre le Jugement sur la Compétence et celui sur le Fond dans la Jurisprudence Internationale," 36 *Rev. Gén. Dr. Int'l Pub.* 108 (1929).

—, "Sul Potere dell'Arbitro a Pronunciarsi sulla sua Competenza," 13 *Diritto Internazionale* 119 (1959).

Scerni, Mario, "La Procédure de la Cour Permanente de Justice Internationale," 65 *Recueil des Cours* 565 (1938–III).

Schwarzenberger, Georg, "Trends in the Practice of the World Court," 4 *Current Legal Problems* 2 (London 1951).

Scott, James Brown, see Documentary Sources.

Shachor-Landau, C., "The Judgment of the International Court of Justice in the Aerial Incident Case between Israel and Bulgaria," 8 *Archiv des Völkerrechts* 277 (1960).

Simpson, J. L., Fox, H., *International Arbitration*. London, Stevens, 1959.

Siorat, Lucien, "L'Article 37 du Statut de la Cour Internationale de Justice," 8 *Annuaire Français de Droit International* 285 (1962).

Smith, Caarsten, *The Relation between Proceedings and Premises*. Oslo, Universitets-forlaget, 1962.

Sohn, Louis B., "Exclusion of Political Disputes from Judicial Settlement," 38 *Am. J. Int'l L.* 694 (1944).

—, "The Jurisdiction of the International Court of Justice," 35 *A.B.A.J.* 924 (1949).

—, "International Tribunals: Past, Present and Future," 46 *A.B.A.J.* 23 (1960).

[— and Baxter, R. R.] *Convention on the International Responsibility of States for Injuries to Aliens* (Draft No. 12 with Explanatory Notes). Cambridge, Harvard Law School, 1961.

Solus, Henry et Perrot, Roger, *Droit Judiciaire Privé*. Paris, Sirey, 1961.

Some Opinions, Articles and Reports Bearing upon the Treaty of Trianon and the Claims of the Hungarian Nationals with regard to their Lands in Transylvania. 2 vols. London, W. P. Griffith & Son, 1928.

Stuyt, A. M., *Survey of International Arbitrations 1794–1938*. The Hague, M. Nijhoff, 1939.

Taylor, Hannis, *A Treatise on International Public Law*. Chicago, Callaghan & Co., 1901.

Ténékides, C. G., "Les Actes Compromissoires Concurrents," 17 *Rev. Dr. Int'l & Leg. Comp.* 719 (3me sér. 1936).

Thévenaz, H., *La Nouvelle Cour Internationale de Justice*, 45 Friedens-Warte 406 (1945).

Tunc, André, *Cours de Procédure Civile*. Paris, Les Cours de Droit. 1961.

[Union International des Avocats] *Juridictions Internationales*. Paris, Dalloz et Sirey, 1958.

Van Kleffens, E. N., "Sovereignty in International Law," 82 *Recueil des Cours* 1 (1953–I).

[Vargas, M. A.] Report of the Rapporteur of Committee IV/2 of the San Francisco Conference, Doc. No. 933, IV/2/42(2), 13 *U.N. Conf. Int'l Org. Docs.* 703 (1945).

Verdross, A., "L'Excès de Pouvoir du Juge Arbitral dans le Droit International Public," 9 *Rev. Dr. Int'l & Leg. Comp.* 225 (3me sèr. 1928).

Verzijl, J. H. W., "Cour Internationale de Justice – Affaire Relative à Certains Emprunts Norwégiens," 4 *Nederlands Tijdschrift voor Internationaal Recht* 373 (1957).

—, "The International Court of Justice in 1959, Part I", 6 *id.* at 362 (1959).

—, "The International Court of Justice in 1959, Part II", 7 *id.* at 1 (1960).

Vineuil, Paul De, "La Cour Permanente de Justice Internationale en 1929," 11 *Rev. Dr. Int'l & Leg. Comp.* 749 (3me sèr. 1930).

de Visscher, Charles, *Theory and Reality in Public International Law* (Trans. by Corbett). Princeton University Press, 1957.

—, *Problèmes d'Interprétation Judiciaire en Droit International Public*. Paris, A. Pedone, 1963.

Vulcan, C., "La Clause Facultative," 18 *Acta Scandinavia Juris Gentium* 30 (1947–48).

Waldock, C. H. M., "*Forum Prorogatum* or Acceptance of a Unilateral Summons to Appear before the International Court," 2 *I.L.Q.* 377 (1948).

—, "The Plea of Domestic Jurisdiction before International Legal Tribunals," 31 *Brit. Yb. Int'l L.* 96 (1954).

—, "Decline of the Optional Clause," 32 *Brit. Yb. Int'l L.* 244 (1956).

Wehberg, Hans, "Réponse" [au questionnaire adressé par M. Ch. Rousseau], 43 *Annuaire* 39 (1950–I).

Wilcox, Francis, "The United States Accepts Compulsory Jurisdiction," 40 *Am. J. Int'l L.* 699 (1946).

Williams, Sir John Fischer, "The Optional Clause," 11 *Brit. Yb. Int'l L.* 63 (1930).

Wilson, Robert R., *International Agreements for Obligatory Arbitration* (Doctorate Thesis – Harvard University) Limited publication 1957.

—, "Reservation Clauses in Agreements for Obligatory Arbitration," 23 *Am. J. Int'l L.* 68 (1929).

Winiarski, B., "Quelques Réflexions sur le Sois-Disant *Forum Prorogatum* en Droit International," in [Constantopoulos *et al.*] *Grundprobleme des Internationalen Rechts* 445 (1957).

Wittenberg, J. C. et Desrioux, J., *L'Organisation Judiciaire. La Procédure et la Sentence Internationales*. Paris, A. Pedone, 1937.

INDEX